Mastering SFML Game Development

Create complex and visually stunning games using all the
advanced features available in SFML development

Raimondas Pupius

BIRMINGHAM - MUMBAI

Mastering SFML Game Development

First published: January 2017

Production reference: 1240117

Published by Packt Publishing Ltd.
Livery Place
35 Livery Street
Birmingham
B3 2PB, UK.
ISBN 978-1-78646-988-5

www.packtpub.com

Credits

Author

Raimondas Pupius

Reviewer

Maxime Barbier

Commissioning Editor

Amarabha Banerjee

Acquisition Editor

Reshma Raman

Content Development Editor

Amrita Noronha

Technical Editor

Sneha Hanchate

Copy Editor

Safis Editing

Project Coordinator

Kinjal Bari

Proofreader

Safis Editing

Indexer

Mariammal Chettiyar

Graphics

Kirk D'Penha

Production Coordinator

Arvindkumar Gupta

About the Author

Raimondas Pupius is a game development enthusiast from Lithuania, currently working towards getting a degree in software engineering, as well as a few projects of his own. Having started his unofficial education in this field at the age of 9 and being introduced to video games even prior to that has guided him to this particular career choice, which was only strengthened by the experience earned from his first book "SFML Game Development By Example". The ultimate dream is, of course, starting a company of his own and making professional games for a living. His other interests include web development, which was his primary interest before game development, music and linguistics.

First, I would like to express my deepest thanks to Prachi Bisht for offering me the opportunity to write another book and bringing me on board. In addition to that, I would like to thank Amrita Noronha, Mamata Walkar, and all of the reviewing staff for being so great to work with and handling the production duties.

Lastly, I would like to thank my mom, my grandmother and my beautiful wife, as well as her entire family for showing me endless love and support throughout this entire ordeal. I wouldn't be where I am today without your kindness, understanding, and patience during my late night binge-writing. This book is dedicated to you!

About the Reviewer

Barbier Maxime is a software engineer at Rennes in France. He loves programming crazy things or experiments, and shares them to the open source community on Github since 2010, and really like game programming. As his favorite technology is C++ he has become an expert with it. He has also developed severals libraries and games with this language. Game programming is a hobby for him, and he really likes the challenges involved by such project. He also loves sharing his knowledge with other people, that was the main reason of it's activity on the open source community.

He had wrote the book "SFML Blueprints" and has comments others such as "SFML Game Development" and "Getting Started with OUYA".

www.PacktPub.com

For support files and downloads related to your book, please visit www.PacktPub.com.

Did you know that Packt offers eBook versions of every book published, with PDF and ePub files available? You can upgrade to the eBook version at www.PacktPub.com and as a print book customer, you are entitled to a discount on the eBook copy. Get in touch with us at service@packtpub.com for more details.

At www.PacktPub.com, you can also read a collection of free technical articles, sign up for a range of free newsletters and receive exclusive discounts and offers on Packt books and eBooks.

https://www.packtpub.com/mapt

Get the most in-demand software skills with Mapt. Mapt gives you full access to all Packt books and video courses, as well as industry-leading tools to help you plan your personal development and advance your career.

Why subscribe?

- Fully searchable across every book published by Packt
- Copy and paste, print, and bookmark content
- On demand and accessible via a web browser

Customer Feedback

Thank you for purchasing this Packt book. We take our commitment to improving our content and products to meet your needs seriously--that's why your feedback is so valuable. Whatever your feelings about your purchase, please consider leaving a review on this book's Amazon page. Not only will this help us, more importantly it will also help others in the community to make an informed decision about the resources that they invest in to learn.

You can also review for us on a regular basis by joining our reviewers' club. **If you're interested in joining, or would like to learn more about the benefits we offer, please contact us**: customerreviews@packtpub.com.

Table of Contents

Preface

Designing a game from scratch can be one of the most difficult journeys to embark on. With the amount of work that goes into it, it's would not be farfetched to compare game development to building a car. It combines many different areas of expertise that would, otherwise, not be overlapping, meaning the mastermind behind it has to, often enough, also act as the *Jack of all trades*. Not many other types of projects can claim that they found a way to combine advanced lighting calculations, accurate physics simulations, and the inner-workings of a fully fledged, stable, and self-sustaining economy-model into something cohesive. These are just some of those *trades* one has to pick up, and in the fast-growing world of gaming, new ones are constantly popping into existence. Among all of the noise, some patterns slowly begin to emerge as time passes by. With several different generations having access to gaming now, and a couple of them not knowing the world without it, certain expectations begin to form within the zeitgeist. The breath-taking inventions and technical demos of yesterday have become the common-place features of today, and the beacons of light shining onto tomorrow. Keeping up with these features and not being left behind in the dark is what makes a good game developer today, and that's where we come in. Although it won't teach you everything, this book will do a solid job at giving you an edge by not only expanding your repertoire of techniques and ideas, but also setting a clear goal into the future, that's always going to keep progressing into something bigger and better.

As the first two chapters fly by, you will learn about setting up a basic, yet powerful RPG-style game, built on top of flexible architectures used in today's games. That same game will then be given extra graphical oomph, as we cover building an efficient particle system, capable of easy expansion and many different graphical options. Subsequently, you will be brought up to speed to the practicalities and benefits of creating custom tools, such as a map editor, for modifying and managing the assets of your game. Usage of SFML's shaders will also be touched on, right before we embark on a journey of cutting SFML out completely in Chapter 7, *One Step Forward, One Level Down – Integrating OpenGL*, by using raw OpenGL and rendering something on screen all by ourselves. This is followed by us exploring and implementing advanced lighting techniques, such as normal and specular maps, to really give the game scene a graphical kick with dynamic lights. Of course, there can be no light that doesn't cast a shadow, which is why Chapter 9, *The Speed of Dark – Lighting and Shadows*, covers and implements shadow-mapping in 3D, allowing us to have realistic, three-dimensional shadows. This is all topped off by making final optimizations to the game that will not only make it run as fast as possible, but also provide you with all of the tools and skills necessary to keep making improvements into the future.

While this book aims to inspire you to be the *Jack of all trades*, it will also make you a master of some by enabling your games to look and run as good as they possibly can. There is a long road ahead of us, so make sure you pack your ambition, and hopefully we shall see each other again at the finish line. Good luck!

What this book covers

Chapter 1, *Under the Hood – Setting up the Backend*, covers the usage of several underlying architectures that will power our game.

Chapter 2, *It's Game Time! – Designing the Project*, partakes in actually building and running the game project of the book, using the architectures set up in Chapter 1, *Under the Hood – Setting up the Backend*.

Chapter 3, *Make It Rain! – Building a Particle System*, deals with the complexities of implementing an efficient and expansive particle system.

Chapter 4, *Have Thy Gear Ready – Building Game Tools*, gets the ball rolling on building custom game tools by setting up their backend.

Chapter 5, *Filling the Tool Belt – A few More Gadgets*, finishes implementing the map editor that can be used to place, edit, and otherwise manipulate map tiles, entities, and particle emitters.

Chapter 6, *Adding Some Finishing Touches – Using Shaders*, explains and uses the newly re-architected renderer that allows for easy use of shaders, by implementing a day/night cycle in our game.

Chapter 7, *One Step Forward, One Level Down – OpenGL Basics*, descends into the depths of technicalities of using raw OpenGL, guiding us through rendering basic shapes, texturing them, and creating the means of movement around the world.

Chapter 8, *Let There Be Light – An Introduction to Advanced Lighting*, introduces and applies the concepts of lighting up our game world in three-dimensions, using normal maps to add the illusion of extra details, and adding specular highlights to create shining surfaces.

Chapter 9, *The Speed of Dark – Lighting and Shadows*, expands on the lighting engine by implementing dynamic, three-dimensional, point-light shadows being cast in all directions at once.

Chapter 10, *A Chapter You Shouldn't Skip – Final Optimizations*, wraps up the book by making our game run many times faster, and providing you with the tools of taking it even further.

What you need for this book

First and foremost, a compiler that supports new C++ standards is required. The actual SFML library is also needed, as it powers the game we're building. Chapters 7 and up require the newest versions of the GLEW and GLM libraries as well. Any other individual tools that may be used throughout the course of this book have been mentioned in the individual chapters they're used in.

Who this book is for

This book is for beginning game developers, who already have some basic knowledge of SFML, intermediate skills in modern C++, and have already built a game or two on their own, no matter how simple. Knowledge in modern OpenGL is not required, but may be a plus.

Conventions

In this book, you will find a number of styles of text that distinguish between different kinds of information. Here are some examples of these styles, and an explanation of their meaning.

Code words in text, database table names, folder names, filenames, file extensions, pathnames, dummy URLs, user input, and Twitter handles are shown as follows: "We can include other contexts through the use of the include directive. "

A block of code is set as follows:

```
class Observer{
public:
  virtual ~Observer(){}
  virtual void Notify(const Message& l_message) = 0;
};
```

When we wish to draw your attention to a particular part of a code block, the relevant lines or items are set in bold:

```
using Subscribtions =
  std::unordered_map<EntityMessage,Communicator>;
```

New terms and **important words** are shown in bold. Words that you see on the screen, in menus or dialog boxes for example, appear in the text like this: "clicking the **Next** button moves you to the next screen".

Warnings or important notes appear in a box like this.

Tips and tricks appear like this.

Reader feedback

Feedback from our readers is always welcome. Let us know what you think about this book-what you liked or disliked. Reader feedback is important for us as it helps us develop titles that you will really get the most out of. To send us general feedback, simply e-mail feedback@packtpub.com, and mention the book's title in the subject of your message. If there is a topic that you have expertise in and you are interested in either writing or contributing to a book, see our author guide at www.packtpub.com/authors.

Customer support

Now that you are the proud owner of a Packt book, we have a number of things to help you to get the most from your purchase.

Downloading the example code

You can download the example code files for this book from your account at http://www.packtpub.com. If you purchased this book elsewhere, you can visit http://www.packtpub.com/support and register to have the files e-mailed directly to you.

You can download the code files by following these steps:

1. Log in or register to our website using your e-mail address and password.
2. Hover the mouse pointer on the **SUPPORT** tab at the top.
3. Click on **Code Downloads & Errata**.
4. Enter the name of the book in the **Search** box.
5. Select the book for which you're looking to download the code files.
6. Choose from the drop-down menu where you purchased this book from.
7. Click on **Code Download**.

Once the file is downloaded, please make sure that you unzip or extract the folder using the latest version of:

- WinRAR / 7-Zip for Windows
- Zipeg / iZip / UnRarX for Mac
- 7-Zip / PeaZip for Linux

The code bundle for the book is also hosted on GitHub at `https://github.com/PacktPubl ishing/Mastering-SFML-Game-Development`. We also have other code bundles from our rich catalog of books and videos available at `https://github.com/PacktPublishing/`. Check them out!

Downloading the color images of this book

We also provide you with a PDF file that has color images of the screenshots/diagrams used in this book. The color images will help you better understand the changes in the output. You can download this file from `https://www.packtpub.com/sites/default/files/down loads/MasteringSFMLGameDevelopment_ColorImages.pdf`.

Errata

Although we have taken every care to ensure the accuracy of our content, mistakes do happen. If you find a mistake in one of our books-maybe a mistake in the text or the code-we would be grateful if you could report this to us. By doing so, you can save other readers from frustration and help us improve subsequent versions of this book. If you find any errata, please report them by visiting `http://www.packtpub.com/submit-errata`, selecting your book, clicking on the **Errata Submission Form** link, and entering the details of your errata. Once your errata are verified, your submission will be accepted and the errata will be uploaded to our website or added to any list of existing errata under the Errata section of that title.

To view the previously submitted errata, go to `https://www.packtpub.com/books/content/support` and enter the name of the book in the search field. The required information will appear under the **Errata** section.

Piracy

Piracy of copyrighted material on the Internet is an ongoing problem across all media. At Packt, we take the protection of our copyright and licenses very seriously. If you come across any illegal copies of our works in any form on the Internet, please provide us with the location address or website name immediately so that we can pursue a remedy.

Please contact us at `copyright@packtpub.com` with a link to the suspected pirated material.

We appreciate your help in protecting our authors and our ability to bring you valuable content.

Questions

If you have a problem with any aspect of this book, you can contact us at `questions@packtpub.com`, and we will do our best to address the problem.

1

Under the Hood - Setting up the Backend

Introduction

What is the heart of any given piece of software? The answer to this question becomes apparent gradually while building a full-scale project, which can be a daunting task to undertake, especially when starting from scratch. It's the design and capability of the back-end that either drives a game forward with full force by utilizing its power, or crashes it into obscurity through unrealized potential. Here, we're going to be talking about that very foundation that keeps any given project up and standing.

In this chapter, we're going to be covering the following topics:

- Utility functions and filesystem specifics for Windows and Linux operating systems
- The basics of the entity component system pattern
- Window, event, and resource management techniques
- Creating and maintaining application states
- Graphical user interface basics
- Essentials for the 2D RPG game project

There's a lot to cover, so let's not waste any time!

Pacing and source code examples

All of the systems we're going to be talking about here could have entire volumes dedicated to them. Since time, as well as paper, is limited, we're only going to be briefly reviewing their very basics, which is just enough to feel comfortable with the rest of the information presented here.

 Keep in mind that, although we won't be going into too much detail in this particular chapter, the code that accompanies this book is a great resource to look through and experiment with for more detail and familiarity. It's greatly recommended to review it while reading this chapter in order to get a full grasp of it.

Common utility functions

Let's start by taking a look at a common function, which is going to be used to determine the full absolute path to the directory our executable is in. Unfortunately, there is no unified way of doing this across all platforms, so we're going to have to implement a version of this utility function for each one, starting with Windows:

```
#ifdef RUNNING_WINDOWS
#define WIN32_LEAN_AND_MEAN
#include <windows.h>
#include <Shlwapi.h>
```

First, we check if the RUNNING_WINDOWS macro is defined. This is the basic technique that can be used to actually let the rest of the code base know which OS it's running on. Next, another definition is made, specifically for the Windows header files we're including. It greatly reduces the number of other headers that get included in the process.

With all of the necessary headers for the Windows OS included, let us take a look at how the actual function can be implemented:

```
inline std::string GetWorkingDirectory()
{
    HMODULE hModule = GetModuleHandle(nullptr);
    if (!hModule) { return ""; }
    char path[256];
    GetModuleFileName(hModule,path,sizeof(path));
    PathRemoveFileSpec(path);
    strcat_s(path,"");
    return std::string(path);
}
```

First, we obtain the handle to the process that was created by our executable file. After the temporary path buffer is constructed and filled with the path string, the name, and extension of our executable is removed. We top it off by adding a trailing slash to the end of the path and returning it as a `std::string`.

It will also come in handy to have a way of obtaining a list of files inside a specified directory:

```
inline std::vector<std::string> GetFileList(
    const std::string& l_directory,
    const std::string& l_search = "*.*")
{
    std::vector<std::string> files;
    if(l_search.empty()) { return files; }
    std::string path = l_directory + l_search;
    WIN32_FIND_DATA data;
    HANDLE found = FindFirstFile(path.c_str(), &data);
    if (found == INVALID_HANDLE_VALUE) { return files; }
    do{
        if (!(data.dwFileAttributes & FILE_ATTRIBUTE_DIRECTORY))
        {
            files.emplace_back(data.cFileName);
        }
    }while (FindNextFile(found, &data));
    FindClose(found);
    return files;
}
```

Just like the directory function, this is specific to the Windows OS. It returns a vector of strings that represent file names and extensions. Once one is constructed, a path string is cobbled together. The `l_search` argument is provided with a default value, in case one is not specified. All files are listed by default.

After creating a structure that will hold our search data, we pass it to another Windows specific function that will find the very first file inside a directory. The rest of the work is done inside a `do-while` loop, which checks if the located item isn't in fact a directory. The appropriate items are then pushed into a vector, which gets returned later on.

The Linux version

As mentioned previously, both of the preceding functions are only functional on Windows. In order to add support for systems running Linux-based OSes, we're going to need to implement them differently. Let's start by including proper header files:

```
#elif defined RUNNING_LINUX
#include <unistd.h>
#include <dirent.h>
```

As luck would have it, Linux does offer a single-call solution to finding exactly where our executable is located:

```
inline std::string GetWorkingDirectory()
{
    char cwd[1024];
    if(!getcwd(cwd, sizeof(cwd))){ return ""; }
    return std::string(cwd) + std::string("/");
}
```

Note that we're still adding a trailing slash to the end.

Obtaining a file list of a specific directory is slightly more complicated this time around:

```
inline std::vector<std::string> GetFileList(
    const std::string& l_directory,
    const std::string& l_search = "*.*")
{
    std::vector<std::string> files;
    DIR *dpdf;
    dpdf = opendir(l_directory.c_str());
    if (!dpdf) { return files; }
    if(l_search.empty()) { return files; }
    std::string search = l_search;
    if (search[0] == '*') { search.erase(search.begin()); }
    if (search[search.length() - 1] == '*') { search.pop_back(); }
    struct dirent *epdf;
    while (epdf = readdir(dpdf)) {
      std::string name = epdf->d_name;
      if (epdf->d_type == DT_DIR) { continue; }
      if (l_search != "*.*") {
        if (name.length() < search.length()) { continue; }
        if (search[0] == '.') {
          if (name.compare(name.length() - search.length(),
            search.length(), search) != 0)
          { continue; }
        } else if (name.find(search) == std::string::npos) {
          continue;
```

[10]

```
        }
    }
    files.emplace_back(name);
  }
  closedir(dpdf);
  return files;
}
```

We start off in the same fashion as before, by creating a vector of strings. A pointer to the directory stream is then obtained through the `opendir()` function. Provided it isn't `NULL`, we begin modifying the search string. Unlike the fancier Windows alternative, we can't just pass a search string into a function and let the OS do all of the matching. In this case, it falls more under the category of matching a specific search string inside a filename that gets returned, so star symbols that mean anything need to be trimmed out.

Next, we utilize the `readdir()` function inside a `while` loop that's going to return a pointer to directory entry structures one by one. We also want to exclude any directories from the file list, so the entry's type is checked for not being equal to `DT_DIR`.

Finally, the string matching begins. Presuming we're not just looking for any file with any extension (represented by `"*.*"`), the entry's name will be compared to the search string by length first. If the length of the string we're searching is longer than the filename itself, it's safe to assume we don't have a match. Otherwise, the search string is analyzed again to determine whether the filename is important for a positive match. Its first character being a period would denote that it isn't, so the file name's ending segment of the same length as the search string is compared to the search string itself. If, however, the name is important, we simply search the filename for the search string.

Once the procedure is complete, the directory is closed and the vector of strings representing files is returned.

Other miscellaneous helper functions

Sometimes, as text files are being read, it's nice to grab a string that includes spaces while still maintaining a whitespace delimiter. In cases like that, we can use quotes along with this special function that helps us read the entire quoted segment from a whitespace delimited file:

```
inline void ReadQuotedString(std::stringstream& l_stream,
  std::string& l_string)
{
  l_stream >> l_string;
  if (l_string.at(0) == '"'){
```

```
    while (l_string.at(l_string.length() - 1) != '"' ||
        !l_stream.eof())
    {
        std::string str;
        l_stream >> str;
        l_string.append(" " + str);
    }
}
l_string.erase(std::remove(
    l_string.begin(), l_string.end(), '"'), l_string.end());
}
```

The first segment of the stream is fed into the argument string. If it does indeed start with a double quote, a `while` loop is initiated to append to said string until it ends with another double quote, or until the stream reaches the end. Lastly, all double quotes from the string are erased, giving us the final result.

Interpolation is another useful tool in a programmer's belt. Imagine having two different values of something at two different points in time, and then wanting to predict what the value would be somewhere in between those two time frames. This simple calculation makes that possible:

```
template<class T>
inline T Interpolate(float tBegin, float tEnd,
    const T& begin_val, const T& end_val, float tX)
{
    return static_cast<T>((
        ((end_val - begin_val) / (tEnd - tBegin)) *
        (tX - tBegin)) + begin_val);
}
```

Next, let's take a look at a few functions that can help us center instances of `sf::Text` better:

```
inline float GetSFMLTextMaxHeight(const sf::Text& l_text) {
    auto charSize = l_text.getCharacterSize();
    auto font = l_text.getFont();
    auto string = l_text.getString().toAnsiString();
    bool bold = (l_text.getStyle() & sf::Text::Bold);
    float max = 0.f;
    for (size_t i = 0; i < string.length(); ++i) {
        sf::Uint32 character = string[i];
        auto glyph = font->getGlyph(character, charSize, bold);
        auto height = glyph.bounds.height;
        if (height <= max) { continue; }
        max = height;
    }
```

```
    return max;
  }

  inline void CenterSFMLText(sf::Text& l_text) {
    sf::FloatRect rect = l_text.getLocalBounds();
    auto maxHeight = Utils::GetSFMLTextMaxHeight(l_text);
    l_text.setOrigin(
      rect.left + (rect.width * 0.5f),
      rect.top + ((maxHeight >= rect.height ?
        maxHeight * 0.5f : rect.height * 0.5f)));
  }
```

Working with SFML text can be tricky sometimes, especially when centering it is of paramount importance. Some characters, depending on the font and other different attributes, can actually exceed the height of the bounding box that surrounds the sf::Text instance. To combat that, the first function iterates through every single character of a specific text instance and fetches the font glyph used to represent it. Its height is then checked and kept track of, so that the maximum height of the entire text can be determined and returned.

The second function can be used for setting the absolute center of a sf::Text instance as its origin, in order to achieve perfect results. After its local bounding box is obtained and the maximum height is calculated, this information is used to move the original point of our text to its center.

Generating random numbers

Most games out there rely on some level of randomness. While it may be tempting to simply use the classical approach of rand(), it can only take you so far. Generating random negative or floating point numbers isn't straightforward, to say the least, plus it has a very lousy range. Luckily, newer versions of C++ provide the answer in the form of uniform distributions and random number engines:

```
#include <random>
#include <SFML/System/Mutex.hpp>
#include <SFML/System/Lock.hpp>

class RandomGenerator {
public:
  RandomGenerator() : m_engine(m_device()){}
  ...
  float operator()(float l_min, float l_max) {
    return Generate(l_min, l_max);
  }
```

```
      int operator()(int l_min, int l_max) {
        return Generate(l_min, l_max);
      }
    private:
      std::random_device m_device;
      std::mt19937 m_engine;
      std::uniform_int_distribution<int> m_intDistribution;
      std::uniform_real_distribution<float> m_floatDistribution;
      sf::Mutex m_mutex;
    };
```

First, note the `include` statements. The `random` library provides us with everything we need as far as number generation goes. On top of that, we're also going to be using SFML's mutexes and locks, in order to prevent a huge mess in case our code is being accessed by several separate threads.

The `std::random_device` class is a random number generator that is used to seed the engine, which will be used for further generations. The engine itself is based on the *Marsenne Twister* algorithm, and produces high-quality random *unsigned integers* that can later be filtered through a **uniform distribution** object in order to obtain a number that falls within a specific range. Ideally, since it is quite expensive to keep constructing and destroying these objects, we're going to want to keep a single copy of this class around. For this very reason, we have integer and float distributions together in the same class.

For convenience, the parenthesis operators are overloaded to take in ranges of numbers of both *integer* and *floating point* types. They invoke the `Generate` method, which is also overloaded to handle both data types:

```
    int Generate(int l_min, int l_max) {
      sf::Lock lock(m_mutex);
      if (l_min > l_max) { std::swap(l_min, l_max); }
      if (l_min != m_intDistribution.min() ||
        l_max != m_intDistribution.max())
      {
        m_intDistribution =
          std::uniform_int_distribution<int>(l_min, l_max);
      }
      return m_intDistribution(m_engine);
    }

    float Generate(float l_min, float l_max) {
      sf::Lock lock(m_mutex);
      if (l_min > l_max) { std::swap(l_min, l_max); }
      if (l_min != m_floatDistribution.min() ||
        l_max != m_floatDistribution.max())
      {
```

```
        m_floatDistribution =
            std::uniform_real_distribution<float>(l_min, l_max);
    }
    return m_floatDistribution(m_engine);
}
```

Before generation can begin, we must establish a lock in order to be thread-safe. Because the order of l_min and l_max values matters, we must check if the provided values aren't in reverse, and swap them if they are. Also, the uniform distribution object has to be reconstructed if a different range needs to be used, so a check for that is in place as well. Finally, after all of that trouble, we're ready to return the random number by utilizing the parenthesis operator of a distribution, to which the engine instance is fed in.

Service locator pattern

Often, one or more of our classes will need access to another part of our code base. Usually, it's not a major issue. All you would have to do is pass a pointer or two around, or maybe store them once as data members of the class in need. However, as the amount of code grows, relationships between classes get more and more complex. Dependencies can increase to a point, where a specific class will have more arguments/setters than actual methods. For convenience's sake, sometimes it's better to pass around a single pointer/reference instead of ten. This is where the **service locator** pattern comes in:

```
class Window;
class EventManager;
class TextureManager;
class FontManager;
...
struct SharedContext{
  SharedContext():
    m_wind(nullptr),
    m_eventManager(nullptr),
    m_textureManager(nullptr),
    m_fontManager(nullptr),
    ...
  {}

  Window* m_wind;
  EventManager* m_eventManager;
  TextureManager* m_textureManager;
  FontManager* m_fontManager;
  ...
};
```

As you can see, it's just a `struct` with multiple pointers to the core classes of our project. All of those classes are forward-declared in order to avoid unnecessary `include` statements, and thus a bloated compilation process.

Entity component system core

Let's get to the essence of how our game entities are going to be represented. In order to achieve highest maintainability and code compartmentalization, it's best to use composition. The entity component system allows just that. For the sake of keeping this short and sweet, we're not going to be delving too deep into the implementation. This is simply a quick overview for the sake of being familiar with the code that will be used down the line.

The ECS pattern consists of three cornerstones that make it possible: entities, components, and systems. An entity, ideally, is simply an identifier, as basic as an integer. Components are containers of data that have next to no logic inside them. There would be multiple types of components, such as position, movable, drawable, and so on, that don't really mean much by themselves, but when composed, will form complex entities. Such composition would make it incredibly easy to save the state of any entity at any given time.

There are many ways to implement components. One of them is simply having a base component class, and inheriting from it:

```
class C_Base{
public:
  C_Base(const Component& l_type): m_type(l_type){}
  virtual ~C_Base(){}

  Component GetType() const { return m_type; }

  friend std::stringstream& operator >>(
    std::stringstream& l_stream, C_Base& b)
    {
      b.ReadIn(l_stream);
      return l_stream;
    }

  virtual void ReadIn(std::stringstream& l_stream) = 0;
protected:
  Component m_type;
};
```

The `Component` type is simply an *enum class* that lists different types of components we can have in a project. In addition to that, this base class also offers a means of filling in component data from a string stream, in order to load them more easily when files are being read.

In order to properly manage sets of components that belong to entities, we would need some sort of manager class:

```
class EntityManager{
public:
  EntityManager(SystemManager* l_sysMgr,
    TextureManager* l_textureMgr);
  ~EntityManager();

  int AddEntity(const Bitmask& l_mask);
  int AddEntity(const std::string& l_entityFile);
  bool RemoveEntity(const EntityId& l_id);

  bool AddComponent(const EntityId& l_entity,
    const Component& l_component);

  template<class T>
  void AddComponentType(const Component& l_id) { ... }

  template<class T>
  T* GetComponent(const EntityId& l_entity,
    const Component& l_component){ ... }

  bool RemoveComponent(const EntityId& l_entity,
    const Component& l_component);
  bool HasComponent(const EntityId& l_entity,
    const Component& l_component) const;
  void Purge();
private:
  ...
};
```

As you can see, this is a fairly basic approach at managing these sets of data we call entities. The `EntityId` data type is simply a type definition for an **unsigned integer**. Creation of components happens by utilizing a factory pattern, lambdas and templates. This class is also responsible for loading entities from files that may look a little like this:

```
Name Player
Attributes 255
|Component|ID|Individual attributes|
Component 0 0 0 1
Component 1 Player
```

```
Component 2 0
Component 3 128.0 1024.0 1024.0 1
Component 4
Component 5 20.0 20.0 0.0 0.0 2
Component 6 footstep:1,4
Component 7
```

The `Attributes` field is a bit mask, the value of which is used to figure out which component types an entity has. The actual component data is stored in this file as well, and later loaded through the `ReadIn` method of our component base class.

The last piece of the puzzle in ECS design is systems. This is where all of the logic happens. Just like components, there can be many types of systems responsible for collisions, rendering, movement, and so on. Each system must inherit from the system's base class and implement all of the pure virtual methods:

```
class S_Base : public Observer{
public:
    S_Base(const System& l_id, SystemManager* l_systemMgr);
    virtual ~S_Base();

    bool AddEntity(const EntityId& l_entity);
    bool HasEntity(const EntityId& l_entity) const;
    bool RemoveEntity(const EntityId& l_entity);

    System GetId() const;

    bool FitsRequirements(const Bitmask& l_bits) const;
    void Purge();

    virtual void Update(float l_dT) = 0;
    virtual void HandleEvent(const EntityId& l_entity,
        const EntityEvent& l_event) = 0;
protected:
    ...
};
```

Systems have signatures of components they use, as well as a list of entities that meet the requirements of said signatures. When an entity is being modified by the addition or removal of a component, every system runs a check on it in order to add it to or remove it from itself. Note the inheritance from the `Observer` class. This is another pattern that aids in communication between entities and systems.

An `Observer` class by itself is simply an interface with one purely virtual method that must be implemented by all derivatives:

```
class Observer{
public:
  virtual ~Observer(){}
  virtual void Notify(const Message& l_message) = 0;
};
```

It utilizes messages that get sent to all observers of a specific target. How the derivative of this class reacts to the message is completely dependent on what it is.

Systems, which come in all shapes and sizes, need to be managed just as entities do. For that, we have another manager class:

```
class SystemManager{
public:
  ...
  template<class T>
  void AddSystem(const System& l_system) { ... }

  template<class T>
  T* GetSystem(const System& l_system){ ... }
  void AddEvent(const EntityId& l_entity, const EventID& l_event);

  void Update(float l_dT);
  void HandleEvents();
  void Draw(Window* l_wind, unsigned int l_elevation);

  void EntityModified(const EntityId& l_entity,
    const Bitmask& l_bits);
  void RemoveEntity(const EntityId& l_entity);
  void PurgeEntities();
  void PurgeSystems();
private:
  ...
  MessageHandler m_messages;
};
```

This too utilizes the factory pattern, in that types of different classes are *registered* by using templates and lambdas, so that they can be constructed later, simply by using a `System` data type, which is an `enum class`. Starting to see the pattern?

The system manager owns a data member of type `MessageHandler`. This is another part of the observer pattern. Let us take a look at what it does:

```
class MessageHandler{
public:
  bool Subscribe(const EntityMessage& l_type,
    Observer* l_observer){ ... }
  bool Unsubscribe(const EntityMessage& l_type,
    Observer* l_observer){ ... }
  void Dispatch(const Message& l_msg){ ... }
private:
  Subscribtions m_communicators;
};
```

Message handlers are simply collections of `Communicator` objects, as shown here:

```
using Subscribtions =
  std::unordered_map<EntityMessage, Communicator>;
```

Each possible type of `EntityMessage`, which is just another *enum class*, is tied to a communicator that is responsible for sending out a message to all of its observers. Observers can subscribe to or unsubscribe from a specific message type. If they are subscribed to said type, they will receive the message when the `Dispatch` method is invoked.

The `Communicator` class itself is fairly simple:

```
class Communicator{
public:
  virtual ~Communicator(){ m_observers.clear(); }
  bool AddObserver(Observer* l_observer){ ... }
  bool RemoveObserver(Observer* l_observer){ ... }
  bool HasObserver(const Observer* l_observer) const { ... }
  void Broadcast(const Message& l_msg){ ... }
private:
  ObserverContainer m_observers;
};
```

As you can gather, it supports the addition and removal of observers, and offers a way to broadcast a message to all of them. The actual container of observers is simply a vector of pointers:

```
// Not memory-owning pointers.
using ObserverContainer = std::vector<Observer*>;
```

Resource management

Another vital part of larger projects is an efficient way of managing resources. Since we're going to have several types of resources, such as textures, fonts, and sounds, it would make sense to have separate managers for all of them. It's time for a base class:

```
template<typename Derived, typename T>
class ResourceManager{
public:
  ResourceManager(const std::string& l_pathsFile){
    LoadPaths(l_pathsFile);
  }
  virtual ~ResourceManager(){ ... }
  T* GetResource(const std::string& l_id){ ... }
  std::string GetPath(const std::string& l_id){ ... }
  bool RequireResource(const std::string& l_id){ ... }
  bool ReleaseResource(const std::string& l_id){ ... }
  void PurgeResources(){ ... }
protected:
  bool Load(T* l_resource, const std::string& l_path) {
    return static_cast<Derived*>(this)->Load(l_resource, l_path);
  }
private:
  ...
};
```

The idea behind this particular resource management system is certain segments of code *requiring* and later *releasing* a certain resource identifier. The first time a resource is required it will be loaded into memory and kept there. Every time it's required after that will simply increment an integer that gets stored with it. The integer represents how many instances of code rely on this resource being loaded. Once they are done using the resource, it begins being released, which brings the counter down each time. When it reaches zero, the resource is removed from memory.

It's fair to point out that our resource manager base class utilizes the **Curiously Recurring Template Pattern** for setting up the resource instances after they're created. As manager classes don't really need to be stored together in the same container anywhere, static polymorphism makes a lot more sense than using virtual methods. Since textures, fonts, and sounds may be loaded in different ways, each subsequent manager must implement their own version of the Load method, like so:

```
class TextureManager : public ResourceManager<TextureManager,
  sf::Texture>
{
public:
```

```
    TextureManager() : ResourceManager("textures.cfg"){}

    bool Load(sf::Texture* l_resource, const std::string& l_path){
      return l_resource->loadFromFile(
        Utils::GetWorkingDirectory() + l_path);
    }
};
```

Each single manager also has its own file, listing the relationships between names of resources and their paths. For textures, it can look something like this:

```
Intro media/Textures/intro.png
PlayerSprite media/Textures/PlayerSheet.png
...
```

It simply avoids the need to pass around paths and filenames, by instead relating a name to each resource.

Windows system

There's a lot that goes on behind the scenes when it comes to dealing with open windows. Everything from window dimensions and titles to keeping track of and dealing with special events is centralized within a designated window class:

```
class Window{
public:
  Window(const std::string& l_title = "Window",
    const sf::Vector2u& l_size = {640,480},
    bool l_useShaders = true);
  ~Window();

  void BeginDraw();
  void EndDraw();

  void Update();

  bool IsDone() const;
  bool IsFullscreen() const;
  bool IsFocused() const;

  void ToggleFullscreen(EventDetails* l_details);
  void Close(EventDetails* l_details = nullptr);

  sf::RenderWindow* GetRenderWindow();
  Renderer* GetRenderer();
  EventManager* GetEventManager();
```

```
    sf::Vector2u GetWindowSize();
    sf::FloatRect GetViewSpace();
  private:
    ...
  };
```

Note the two highlighted methods. They will be used as call-backs in the event manager we'll discuss in the near future. Also note the return method for an object type `Renderer`. It's a utility class that simply invokes the `.draw` call on a `RenderWindow`, thus localizing it and making it much easier to use shaders. More information on that will be revealed in `Chapter 6`, *Adding Some Finishing Touches – Using Shaders.*

Application states

Another important aspect of a more complex application is keeping track of and managing its states. Whether the player is in the thick of the game, or simply browsing through the main menu, we want it to be handled seamlessly, and more importantly, be self-contained. We can start this by first defining different types of states we'll be dealing with:

```
enum class StateType { Intro = 1, MainMenu, Game, Loading };
```

For seamless integration, we want each state to behave in a predictable manner. This means that a state has to adhere to an interface we provide:

```
class BaseState{
friend class StateManager;
public:
  BaseState(StateManager* l_stateManager)
    :m_stateMgr(l_stateManager), m_transparent(false),
    m_transcendent(false){}
  virtual ~BaseState(){}

  virtual void OnCreate() = 0;
  virtual void OnDestroy() = 0;

  virtual void Activate() = 0;
  virtual void Deactivate() = 0;

  virtual void Update(const sf::Time& l_time) = 0;
  virtual void Draw() = 0;
  ...
  sf::View& GetView(){ return m_view; }
  StateManager* GetStateManager(){ return m_stateMgr; }
protected:
```

```
    StateManager* m_stateMgr;
    bool m_transparent;
    bool m_transcendent;
    sf::View m_view;
};
```

Every state in the game will have its own view that it can alter. In addition to that, it is given the hooks to implement logic for various different scenarios, such as the state's creation, destruction, activation, deactivation, updating, and rendering. Lastly, it enables the possibility of being blended with other states during updating and rendering, by providing the m_transparent and m_transcendent flags.

Managing these states is pretty straightforward:

```
class StateManager{
public:
    StateManager(SharedContext* l_shared);
    ~StateManager();
    void Update(const sf::Time& l_time);
    void Draw();
    void ProcessRequests();
    SharedContext* GetContext();
    bool HasState(const StateType& l_type) const;
    StateType GetNextToLast() const;
    void SwitchTo(const StateType& l_type);
    void Remove(const StateType& l_type);
    template<class T>
    T* GetState(const StateType& l_type){ ... }
    template<class T>
    void RegisterState(const StateType& l_type) { ... }
    void AddDependent(StateDependent* l_dependent);
    void RemoveDependent(StateDependent* l_dependent);
private:
    ...
    State_Loading* m_loading;
    StateDependents m_dependents;
};
```

The StateManager class is one of the few classes in the project that utilizes the shared context, since the states themselves may need access to any part of the code base. It also uses the factory pattern to dynamically create any state that is bound to a state type during runtime.

In order to keep things simple, we're going to be treating the loading state as a special case, and only allow one instance of it to be alive at all times. Loading might happen during the transition of any state, so it only makes sense.

One final thing that's worth noting about the state manager is it's keeping a list of state dependants. It's simply an STL container of classes that inherit from this interface:

```
class StateDependent {
public:
  StateDependent() : m_currentState((StateType)0){}
  virtual ~StateDependent(){}
  virtual void CreateState(const StateType& l_state){}
  virtual void ChangeState(const StateType& l_state) = 0;
  virtual void RemoveState(const StateType& l_state) = 0;
protected:
  void SetState(const StateType& l_state){m_currentState=l_state;}
  StateType m_currentState;
};
```

Because classes that deal with things such as sounds, GUI elements, or entity management need to support different states, they must also define what happens inside them as a state is created, changed, or removed, in order to properly allocate/de-allocate resources, stop updating data that is not in the same state, and so on.

Loading state

So, how exactly are we going to implement this loading state? Well, for flexibility and easy progress tracking by means of rendering fancy loading bars, threads are going to prove invaluable. Data that needs to be loaded into memory can be loaded in a separate thread, while the loading state itself continues to get updated and rendered in order to show us that things are indeed happening. Just knowing that the application did not hang on us should create a warm and fuzzy feeling.

First, let us implement the very basics of this system by providing an interface any threaded worker can use:

```
class Worker {
public:
  Worker() : m_thread(&Worker::Work, this), m_done(false),
    m_started(false) {}
  void Begin() {
    if(m_done || m_started) { return; }
    m_started = true;
    m_thread.launch();
```

```
    }
    bool IsDone() const { return m_done; }
    bool HasStarted() const { return m_started; }
  protected:
    void Done() { m_done = true; }
    virtual void Work() = 0;
    sf::Thread m_thread;
    bool m_done;
    bool m_started;
};
```

It has its own thread, which is bound to the pure virtual method called `Work`. The thread is launched whenever the `Begin()` method is invoked. In order to protect the data from being accessed from multiple threads at once, a `sf::Mutex` class is used by creating a lock during sensitive calls. Everything else within this very basic class is simply there to provide information to the outside world about the worker's state.

File loader

With threads out of the way, we can focus on actually loading some files now. This method is going to focus on working with text files. However, using binary formats should work in pretty much the exact same way, minus all the text processing.

Let's take a look at the base class for any file loading class we can think of:

```
using LoaderPaths = std::vector<std::pair<std::string, size_t>>;

class FileLoader : public Worker {
public:
  FileLoader();
  void AddFile(const std::string& l_file);
  virtual void SaveToFile(const std::string& l_file);
  size_t GetTotalLines() const;
  size_t GetCurrentLine() const;
protected:
  virtual bool ProcessLine(std::stringstream& l_stream) = 0;
  virtual void ResetForNextFile();
  void Work();
  void CountFileLines();

  LoaderPaths m_files;
  size_t m_totalLines;
  size_t m_currentLine;
};
```

It's a distinct possibility that two or more files may need to be loaded at some point. The `FileLoader` class keeps track of all of the paths that get added to it, along with a number that represents the number of lines within that file. This is useful for determining the amount of progress that has been made while loading. In addition to the line count for each individual file, a total line count is also kept track of.

This class provides a single purely virtual method, called `ProcessLine`. It will be the way derivatives can define exactly how the file is loaded and processed.

First, let us get the basic stuff out of the way:

```
FileLoader::FileLoader() : m_totalLines(0), m_currentLine(0) {}
void FileLoader::AddFile(const std::string& l_file) {
  m_files.emplace_back(l_file, 0);
}
size_t FileLoader::GetTotalLines()const {
  sf::Lock lock(m_mutex);
  return m_totalLines;
}
size_t FileLoader::GetCurrentLine()const {
  sf::Lock lock(m_mutex);
  return m_currentLine;
}
void FileLoader::SaveToFile(const std::string& l_file) {}
void FileLoader::ResetForNextFile(){}
```

The `ResetForNextFile()` virtual method is optional to implement, but can be used in order to clear the state of some internal data that needs to exist while a file is being loaded. Since file loaders that implement this class will only have the ability to process one line at a time inside a single method, any temporary data that would normally be stored as a local variable within that method would instead need to go somewhere else. This is why we must make sure that there is actually a way to know when we're done with one file and start loading another, as well as to perform some sort of action, if necessary.

 Note the mutex locks in the two getter methods above. They're there to make sure those variables aren't written to and read from at the same time.

Now, let's get into the code that is going to be executed in a different thread:

```cpp
void FileLoader::Work() {
  CountFileLines();
  if (!m_totalLines) { Done(); return; }
  for (auto& path : m_files) {
    ResetForNextFile();
    std::ifstream file(path.first);
    std::string line;
    std::string name;
    auto linesLeft = path.second;
    while (std::getline(file, line)) {
      {
        sf::Lock lock(m_mutex);
        ++m_currentLine;
        --linesLeft;
      }
      if (line[0] == '|') { continue; }
      std::stringstream keystream(line);
      if (!ProcessLine(keystream)) {
        std::cout <<
          "File loader terminated due to an internal error."
          << std::endl;
        {
          sf::Lock lock(m_mutex);
          m_currentLine += linesLeft;
        }
        break;
      }
    }
    file.close();
  }
  Done();
}
```

A private method for counting all the lines in whatever files are about to be loaded is called first. If, for any reason, the total line count is zero, there is no purpose in proceeding, so the `Worker::Done()` method is invoked just before a return. This little bit of code is really easy to forget, but is extremely important in order for this to work. All it does is set the m_done flag of the `Worker` base class to `true`, which lets outside code know that the process is finished. Since there is currently no way to check if an SFML thread is actually finished, this is pretty much the only option.

We begin looping through different files that need to get loaded and invoke the reset method before work begins. Note the lack of checking as we're attempting to open a file. This will be explained when we cover the next method.

As each line of the file is being read, it's important to make sure that all the line count information is updated. A temporary lock for the current thread is established, in order to prevent two threads from accessing the line count as its modified. In addition to that, lines that start with a pipe symbol are excluded, since this is our standard comment pragma.

Finally, a `stringstream` object is constructed for the current line, and passed into the `ProcessLine()` method. For extra points, it returns a *boolean* value that can signal an error and stop the current file from being processed any further. If that happens, the remaining lines within that specific file are added to the total count, and the loop is broken.

The final piece of the puzzle is this chunk of code, responsible for verifying file validity and determining the amount of work ahead of us:

```
void FileLoader::CountFileLines() {
  m_totalLines = 0;
  m_currentLine = 0;
  for (auto path = m_files.begin(); path != m_files.end();) {
    if (path->first.empty()) { m_files.erase(path); continue; }
    std::ifstream file(path->first);
    if (!file.is_open()) {
      std::cerr << "Failed to load file: " << path->first
        << std::endl;
      m_files.erase(path);
      continue;
    }
    file.unsetf(std::ios_base::skipws);
    {
      sf::Lock lock(m_mutex);
      path->second = static_cast<size_t>(std::count(
        std::istreambuf_iterator<char>(file),
        std::istreambuf_iterator<char>(), '\n'));
      m_totalLines += path->second;
    }
    ++path;
    file.close();
  }
}
```

After initial zero values for line counts are set up, all added paths are iterated over and checked. We first trim out any paths that are empty. Each path is then attempted to be opened, and erased if that operation fails. Finally, in order to achieve accurate results, the file input stream is ordered to ignore empty lines. After a lock is established, `std::count` is used to count the amount of lines in a file. That number is then added to the amount of total lines we have, the path iterator is advanced, and the file is properly closed.

Since this method eliminates files that were either non-existent or unable to be opened, there is no reason to check for that again anywhere else.

Implementing the loading state

Everything is now in place in order for us to successfully implement the loading state:

```
using LoaderContainer = std::vector<FileLoader*>;

class State_Loading : public BaseState {
public:
  ...
  void AddLoader(FileLoader* l_loader);
  bool HasWork() const;
  void SetManualContinue(bool l_continue);
  void Proceed(EventDetails* l_details);
private:
  void UpdateText(const std::string& l_text, float l_percentage);
  float CalculatePercentage();
  LoaderContainer m_loaders;
  sf::Text m_text;
  sf::RectangleShape m_rect;
  unsigned short m_percentage;
  size_t m_originalWork;
  bool m_manualContinue;
};
```

The state itself will keep a vector of pointers to different file loader classes, which will have lists of their own files respectively. It also provides a way for these objects to be added. Also, note the `Proceed()` method. This is another call-back that will be used in the event manager we're about to cover soon.

For the visual portion, we will be using the bare essentials of graphics: a bit of text for the progress percentage, and a rectangle shape that represents a loading bar.

Let's take a look at all of the setup this class will do once it's constructed:

```
void State_Loading::OnCreate() {
  auto context = m_stateMgr->GetContext();
  context->m_fontManager->RequireResource("Main");
  m_text.setFont(*context->m_fontManager->GetResource("Main"));
  m_text.setCharacterSize(14);
  m_text.setStyle(sf::Text::Bold);

  sf::Vector2u windowSize = m_stateMgr->GetContext()->
    m_wind->GetRenderWindow()->getSize();
```

```
m_rect.setFillColor(sf::Color(0, 150, 0, 255));
m_rect.setSize(sf::Vector2f(0.f, 32.f));
m_rect.setOrigin(0.f, 16.f);
m_rect.setPosition(0.f, windowSize.y / 2.f);

EventManager* evMgr = m_stateMgr->GetContext()->m_eventManager;
evMgr->AddCallback(StateType::Loading, "Key_Space",
    &State_Loading::Proceed, this);
}
```

First, a font manager is obtained through the shared context. The font with a name `"Main"` is required and used to set up the text instance. After all of the visual bits are set up, the event manager is used to register a call-back for the loading state. This will be covered soon, but it's quite easy to deduce what's happening by simply looking at the arguments. Whenever the spacebar is pressed, the `Proceed` method of the `State_Loading` class is going to be invoked. The actual instance of the class is passed in as the last argument.

Remember that, by design, the resources we require must also be released. A perfect place to do that for the loading state is exactly as it is destroyed:

```
void State_Loading::OnDestroy() {
    auto context = m_stateMgr->GetContext();
    EventManager* evMgr = context->m_eventManager;
    evMgr->RemoveCallback(StateType::Loading, "Key_Space");
    context->m_fontManager->ReleaseResource("Main");
}
```

In addition to the font being released, the call-back for the spacebar is also removed.

Next, let us actually write some code that's going to bring the pieces together into a cohesive, functional whole:

```
void State_Loading::Update(const sf::Time& l_time)
    if (m_loaders.empty()) {
        if (!m_manualContinue) { Proceed(nullptr); }
        return;
    }
    auto windowSize = m_stateMgr->GetContext()->
        m_wind->GetRenderWindow()->getSize();
    if (m_loaders.back()->IsDone()) {
        m_loaders.back()->OnRemove();
        m_loaders.pop_back();
        if (m_loaders.empty()) {
            m_rect.setSize(sf::Vector2f(
                static_cast<float>(windowSize.x), 16.f));
            UpdateText(".Press space to continue.", 100.f);
            return;
```

```
      }
    }
    if (!m_loaders.back()->HasStarted()) {
      m_loaders.back()->Begin();
    }

    auto percentage = CalculatePercentage();
    UpdateText("", percentage);
    m_rect.setSize(sf::Vector2f(
      (windowSize.x / 100) * percentage, 16.f));
  }
```

The first check is used to determine if all of the file loaders have been removed from the vector due to finishing. The m_manualContinue flag is used to let the loading state know if it should wait for the spacebar to be pressed, or if it should just dispel itself automatically. If, however, we still have some loaders in the vector, the top one is checked for having concluded its work. Given that's the case, the loader is popped and the vector is checked again for being empty, which would require us to update the loading text to represent completion.

To keep this process fully automated, we need to make sure that after the top file loader is removed, the next one is started, which is where the following check comes in. Finally, the progress percentage is calculated, and the loading text is updated to represent that value, just before the loading bar's size is adjusted to visually aid us.

Drawing is going to be extremely straightforward for this state:

```
void State_Loading::Draw() {
  sf::RenderWindow* wind = m_stateMgr->GetContext()->
    m_wind->GetRenderWindow();
  wind->draw(m_rect);
  wind->draw(m_text);
}
```

The render window is first obtained through the shared context, and then used to draw the text and rectangle shape that represent the loading bar together.

The Proceed call-back method is equally straightforward:

```
void State_Loading::Proceed(EventDetails* l_details){
  if (!m_loaders.empty()) { return; }
  m_stateMgr->SwitchTo(m_stateMgr->GetNextToLast());
}
```

It has to make a check first, to make sure that we don't switch states before all the work is through. If that's not the case, the state manager is used to switch to a state that was created **before** the loading commenced.

All of the other loading state logic pretty much consists of single lines of code for each method:

```
void State_Loading::AddLoader(FileLoader* l_loader) {
 m_loaders.emplace_back(l_loader);
   l_loader->OnAdd();
}
bool State_Loading::HasWork() const { return !m_loaders.empty(); }
void State_Loading::SetManualContinue(bool l_continue) {
   m_manualContinue = l_continue;
}
void State_Loading::Activate(){m_originalWork = m_loaders.size();}
```

Although this looks fairly simple, the `Activate()` method holds a fairly important role. Since the loading state is treated as a special case here, one thing has to be kept in mind: it is *never* going to be removed before the application is closed. This means that every time we want to use it again, some things have to be reset. In this case, it's the `m_originalWork` data member, that's simply the count of all the loader classes. This number is used to calculate the progress percentage accurately, and the best place to reset it is inside the method, which gets called every time the state is activated again.

Managing application events

Event management is one of the cornerstones that provide us with fluid control experience. Any key presses, window changes, or even custom events created by the GUI system we'll be covering later are going to be processed and handled by this system. In order to effectively unify event information coming from different sources, we first must unify their types by enumerating them correctly:

```
enum class EventType {
   KeyDown = sf::Event::KeyPressed,
   KeyUp = sf::Event::KeyReleased,
   MButtonDown = sf::Event::MouseButtonPressed,
   MButtonUp = sf::Event::MouseButtonReleased,
   MouseWheel = sf::Event::MouseWheelMoved,
   WindowResized = sf::Event::Resized,
   GainedFocus = sf::Event::GainedFocus,
   LostFocus = sf::Event::LostFocus,
   MouseEntered = sf::Event::MouseEntered,
   MouseLeft = sf::Event::MouseLeft,
```

```
    Closed = sf::Event::Closed,
    TextEntered = sf::Event::TextEntered,
    Keyboard = sf::Event::Count + 1, Mouse, Joystick,
    GUI_Click, GUI_Release, GUI_Hover, GUI_Leave
};

enum class EventInfoType { Normal, GUI };
```

SFML events come first, since they are the only ones following a strict enumeration scheme. They are then followed by the live SFML input types and four GUI events. We also enumerate event information types, which are going to be used inside this structure:

```
struct EventInfo {
  EventInfo() : m_type(EventInfoType::Normal), m_code(0) {}
  EventInfo(int l_event) : m_type(EventInfoType::Normal),
    m_code(l_event) {}
  EventInfo(const GUI_Event& l_guiEvent):
    m_type(EventInfoType::GUI), m_gui(l_guiEvent) {}
  EventInfo(const EventInfoType& l_type) {
    if (m_type == EventInfoType::GUI) { DestroyGUIStrings(); }
    m_type = l_type;
    if (m_type == EventInfoType::GUI){ CreateGUIStrings("", ""); }
  }

  EventInfo(const EventInfo& l_rhs) { Move(l_rhs); }

  EventInfo& operator=(const EventInfo& l_rhs) {
    if (&l_rhs != this) { Move(l_rhs); }
    return *this;
  }

  ~EventInfo() {
    if (m_type == EventInfoType::GUI) { DestroyGUIStrings(); }
  }
  union {
    int m_code;
    GUI_Event m_gui;
  };
  EventInfoType m_type;
private:
  void Move(const EventInfo& l_rhs) {
    if (m_type == EventInfoType::GUI) { DestroyGUIStrings(); }
    m_type = l_rhs.m_type;
    if (m_type == EventInfoType::Normal){ m_code = l_rhs.m_code; }
    else {
      CreateGUIStrings(l_rhs.m_gui.m_interface,
        l_rhs.m_gui.m_element);
      m_gui = l_rhs.m_gui;
```

```
        }
    }

    void DestroyGUIStrings() {
        m_gui.m_interface.~basic_string();
        m_gui.m_element.~basic_string();
    }

    void CreateGUIStrings(const std::string& l_interface,
        const std::string& l_element)
    {
        new (&m_gui.m_interface) std::string(l_interface);
        new (&m_gui.m_element) std::string(l_element);
    }
};
```

Because we care about more than just the event type that took place, there needs to be a good way of storing additional data that comes with it. C++11's unrestricted union is a perfect candidate for that. The only downside is that now we have to worry about manually managing the data inside the union, which comes complete with data allocations and direct invocation of destructors.

As event call-backs are being invoked, it's a good idea to provide them with the actual event information. Because it's possible to construct more complex requirements for specific call-backs, we can't get away with unions this time. Any possible information that may be relevant needs to be stored, and that's precisely what is done here:

```
struct EventDetails {
    EventDetails(const std::string& l_bindName) : m_name(l_bindName){
        Clear();
    }
    std::string m_name;
    sf::Vector2i m_size;
    sf::Uint32 m_textEntered;
    sf::Vector2i m_mouse;
    int m_mouseWheelDelta;
    int m_keyCode; // Single key code.

    std::string m_guiInterface;
    std::string m_guiElement;
    GUI_EventType m_guiEvent;

    void Clear() { ... }
};
```

This structure is filled with every single bit of information that is available as the events are processed, and then passed as an argument to the call-back that gets invoked. It also provides a `Clear()` method, because instead of being created only for the time during the call-back, it lives inside the binding structure:

```
using Events = std::vector<std::pair<EventType, EventInfo>>;

struct Binding {
    Binding(const std::string& l_name) : m_name(l_name),
        m_details(l_name), c(0) {}
    void BindEvent(EventType l_type, EventInfo l_info = EventInfo())
    { ... }

    Events m_events;
    std::string m_name;
    int c; // Count of events that are "happening".

    EventDetails m_details;
};
```

A binding is what actually allows events to be grouped together in order to form more complex requirements. Think of it in terms of multiple keys needing to be pressed at once in order to perform an action, such as *Ctrl + C* for copying a piece of text. A binding for that type of situation would have two events it's waiting for: the *Ctrl* key and the *C* key.

Event manager interface

With all of the key pieces being covered, all that's left is actually managing everything properly. Let's start with some type definitions:

```
using Bindings = std::unordered_map<std::string,
    std::unique_ptr<Binding>>;
using CallbackContainer = std::unordered_map<std::string,
    std::function<void(EventDetails*)>>;
enum class StateType;
using Callbacks = std::unordered_map<StateType,
    CallbackContainer>;
```

All bindings are attached to specific names that get loaded from a `keys.cfg` file when the application is started. It follows a basic format like this:

```
Window_close 0:0
Fullscreen_toggle 5:89
Intro_Continue 5:57
Mouse_Left 9:0
```

[36]

Of course these are very basic examples. More complex bindings would have multiple events separated by white spaces.

Call-backs are also stored in an *unordered map,* as well as tied to the name of a binding that they're watching. The actual call-back containers are then grouped by state, in order to avoid multiple functions/methods getting called when similar keys are pressed. As you can imagine, the event manager is going to be inheriting from a StateDependent class for this very reason:

```cpp
class EventManager : public StateDependent{
public:
  ...
  bool AddBinding(std::unique_ptr<Binding> l_binding);
  bool RemoveBinding(std::string l_name);
  void ChangeState(const StateType& l_state);
  void RemoveState(const StateType& l_state);
  void SetFocus(bool l_focus);
  template<class T>
  bool AddCallback(const StateType& l_state,
    const std::string& l_name,
    void(T::*l_func)(EventDetails*), T* l_instance)
  { ... }
  template<class T>
  bool AddCallback(const std::string& l_name,
    void(T::*l_func)(EventDetails*), T* l_instance)
  { ... }

  bool RemoveCallback(const StateType& l_state,
    const std::string& l_name){ ... }
  void HandleEvent(sf::Event& l_event);
  void HandleEvent(GUI_Event& l_event);
  void Update();
  sf::Vector2i GetMousePos(sf::RenderWindow* l_wind = nullptr)
    const { ... }
private:
  ...
  Bindings m_bindings;
  Callbacks m_callbacks;
};
```

Once again, this is quite simple. Since this is a state-dependent class, it needs to implement the `ChangeState()` and `RemoveState()` methods. It also keeps track of when the window focus is obtained/lost, in order to avoid polling events of minimized/unfocused windows. Two versions of `AddCallback` are provided: one for a specified state, and one for the current state. Separate `HandleEvent()` methods are also available for every event type supported. So far, we only have two: SFML events, and GUI events. The latter is going to be used in the upcoming section.

Use of graphical user interfaces

A friendly way of interfacing with applications in a day and age where computers are basically a necessity inside every household is a must. The entire subject of GUIs could fill multiple books by itself, so for the sake of keeping this simple, we are only going to scratch the surface of what we have to work with:

```cpp
class GUI_Manager : public StateDependent{
  friend class GUI_Interface;
public:
  ...
  bool AddInterface(const StateType& l_state,
    const std::string& l_name);
  bool AddInterface(const std::string& l_name);
  GUI_Interface* GetInterface(const StateType& l_state,
    const std::string& l_name);
  GUI_Interface* GetInterface(const std::string& l_name);
  bool RemoveInterface(const StateType& l_state,
    const std::string& l_name);
  bool RemoveInterface(const std::string& l_name);
  bool LoadInterface(const StateType& l_state,
    const std::string& l_interface, const std::string& l_name);
  bool LoadInterface(const std::string& l_interface,
    const std::string& l_name);
  void ChangeState(const StateType& l_state);
  void RemoveState(const StateType& l_state);
  SharedContext* GetContext() const;
  void DefocusAllInterfaces();
  void HandleClick(EventDetails* l_details);
  void HandleRelease(EventDetails* l_details);
  void HandleTextEntered(EventDetails* l_details);
  void AddEvent(GUI_Event l_event);
  bool PollEvent(GUI_Event& l_event);
  void Update(float l_dT);
  void Render(sf::RenderWindow* l_wind);
  template<class T>
```

```
    void RegisterElement(const GUI_ElementType& l_id){ ... }
private:
    ...
};
```

Interface management, quite predictably, is also dependent on application states. The interfaces themselves are also assigned names, which is how they are loaded and stored. Mouse input, as well as text enter events, are both utilized in making the GUI system work, which is why this class actually uses the event manager and registers three call-backs with it. Not unlike other classes we have discussed, it also uses the factory method, in order to be able to dynamically create different types of elements that populate our interfaces.

Interfaces are described as groups of elements, like so:

```
Interface MainMenu MainMenu.style 0 0 Immovable NoTitle "Main menu"
Element Label Title 100 0 MainMenuTitle.style "Main menu:"
Element Label Play 0 32 MainMenuLabel.style "PLAY"
Element Label Credits 0 68 MainMenuLabel.style "CREDITS"
Element Label Quit 0 104 MainMenuLabel.style "EXIT"
```

Each element also supports styles for the three different states it can be in: neutral, hovered, and clicked. A single style file describes what an element would look like under all of these conditions:

```
State Neutral
Size 300 32
BgColor 255 0 0 255
TextColor 255 255 255 255
TextSize 14
Font Main
TextPadding 150 16
TextOriginCenter
/State

State Hover
BgColor 255 100 0 255
/State

State Clicked
BgColor 255 150 0 255
/State
```

The `Neutral` style serves as a base for the other two, which is why they only define attributes that are different from it. Using this model, interfaces of great complexity can be constructed and customized to do almost anything.

Representing a 2D map

Maps are another crucial part of having a decently complex game. For our purposes, we're going to be representing 2D maps that support different layers in order to fake 3D depth:

```cpp
class Map : public FileLoader{
public:
  ...
  Tile* GetTile(unsigned int l_x, unsigned int l_y,
    unsigned int l_layer);
  TileInfo* GetDefaultTile();
  TileSet* GetTileSet();
  unsigned int GetTileSize()const;
  sf::Vector2u GetMapSize()const;
  sf::Vector2f GetPlayerStart()const;
  int GetPlayerId()const;
  void PurgeMap();
  void AddLoadee(MapLoadee* l_loadee);
  void RemoveLoadee(MapLoadee* l_loadee);
  void Update(float l_dT);
  void Draw(unsigned int l_layer);
protected:
  bool ProcessLine(std::stringstream& l_stream);
  ...
};
```

As you can see, this class is actually inheriting from the `FileLoader`, which we covered earlier. It also supports something that's referred to as `MapLoadee*`, which are simply classes that will store certain data inside map files, and need to be notified when such data is encountered during the loading process. It's simply an interface that they have to implement:

```cpp
class MapLoadee {
public:
  virtual void ReadMapLine(const std::string& l_type,
    std::stringstream& l_stream) = 0;
};
```

The map files themselves are fairly straightforward:

```
SIZE 64 64
DEFAULT_FRICTION 1.0 1.0
|ENTITY|Name|x|y|elevation|
ENTITY Player 715 360 1
ENTITY Skeleton 256.0 768.0 1
|TILE|ID|x|y|layer|solid|
TILE 0 0 0 0 0
```

```
TILE 0 0 1 0 0
TILE 0 0 2 0 0
...
```

A good candidate for a `MapLoadee` here would be a class that handles entities being spawned. The two entity lines would be directly handled by it, which creates a nice level of separation between codes that shouldn't really overlap.

Sprite system

Since we're working on a 2D game, the most likely candidate for the way graphics are going to be done is a sprite sheet. Unifying the way sprite sheet cropping and animations are handled is key to not only minimizing code, but also creating a simple, neat interface that's easy to interact with. Let us take a look at how that can be done:

```
class SpriteSheet{
public:
  ...
  void CropSprite(const sf::IntRect& l_rect);
  const sf::Vector2u& GetSpriteSize()const;
  const sf::Vector2f& GetSpritePosition()const;
  void SetSpriteSize(const sf::Vector2u& l_size);
  void SetSpritePosition(const sf::Vector2f& l_pos);
  void SetDirection(const Direction& l_dir);
  Direction GetDirection() const;
  void SetSheetPadding(const sf::Vector2f& l_padding);
  void SetSpriteSpacing(const sf::Vector2f& l_spacing);
  const sf::Vector2f& GetSheetPadding()const;
  const sf::Vector2f& GetSpriteSpacing()const;
  bool LoadSheet(const std::string& l_file);
  void ReleaseSheet();
  Anim_Base* GetCurrentAnim();
  bool SetAnimation(const std::string& l_name,
    bool l_play = false, bool l_loop = false);
  void Update(float l_dT);
  void Draw(sf::RenderWindow* l_wnd);
private:
  ...
  Animations m_animations;
};
```

The `SpriteSheet` class itself isn't really that complex. It offers helper methods for cropping the sheet down to a specific rectangle, altering the stored direction, defining different attributes, such as spacing, padding, and so on, and manipulating the animation data.

Animations are stored in this class by name:

```
using Animations = std::unordered_map<std::string,
    std::unique_ptr<Anim_Base>>;
```

The interface of an animation class looks like this:

```
class Anim_Base{
  friend class SpriteSheet;
public:
  ...
  void SetSpriteSheet(SpriteSheet* l_sheet);
  bool SetFrame(Frame l_frame);
  void SetStartFrame(Frame l_frame);
  void SetEndFrame(Frame l_frame);
  void SetFrameRow(unsigned int l_row);
  void SetActionStart(Frame l_frame);
  void SetActionEnd(Frame l_frame);
  void SetFrameTime(float l_time);
  void SetLooping(bool l_loop);
  void SetName(const std::string& l_name);
  SpriteSheet* GetSpriteSheet();
  Frame GetFrame() const;
  Frame GetStartFrame() const;
  Frame GetEndFrame() const;
  unsigned int GetFrameRow() const;
  int GetActionStart() const;
  int GetActionEnd() const;
  float GetFrameTime() const;
  float GetElapsedTime() const;
  bool IsLooping() const;
  bool IsPlaying() const;
  bool IsInAction() const;
  bool CheckMoved();
  std::string GetName() const;
  void Play();
  void Pause();
  void Stop();
  void Reset();
  virtual void Update(float l_dT);
  friend std::stringstream& operator >>(
    std::stringstream&l_stream, Anim_Base& a){ ... }
protected:
  virtual void FrameStep() = 0;
```

```
    virtual void CropSprite() = 0;
    virtual void ReadIn(std::stringstream& l_stream) = 0;
    ...
};
```

First, the `Frame` data type is simply a type definition of an integer. This class keeps track of all necessary animation data, and even provides a way to set up specific frame ranges (also referred to as actions), which can be used for something such as an entity only *attacking* something if the attack animation is within that specific action range.

The obvious thing about this class is that it does not represent any single type of animation, but rather all the common elements of every type. This is why three different purely virtual methods are provided, so that different types of animation can define how the frame step is handled, define the specific method, the location of cropping, and the exact process of the animation being loaded from a file. This helps us separate directional animations, where every row represents a character facing a different way, from simple, sequential animations of frames following each other in a linear order.

Sound system

Last, but definitely not least, the sound system deserves a brief overview. It probably would be a surprise to nobody at this point to learn that sounds are also reliant upon application states, which is why we're inheriting from `StateDependent` again:

```
class SoundManager : public StateDependent{
public:
  SoundManager(AudioManager* l_audioMgr);
  ~SoundManager();

  void ChangeState(const StateType& l_state);
  void RemoveState(const StateType& l_state);

  void Update(float l_dT);

  SoundID Play(const std::string& l_sound,
    const sf::Vector3f& l_position,
    bool l_loop = false, bool l_relative = false);
  bool Play(const SoundID& l_id);
  bool Stop(const SoundID& l_id);
  bool Pause(const SoundID& l_id);

  bool PlayMusic(const std::string& l_musicId,
    float l_volume = 100.f, bool l_loop = false);
  bool PlayMusic(const StateType& l_state);
```

```
    bool StopMusic(const StateType& l_state);
    bool PauseMusic(const StateType& l_state);

    bool SetPosition(const SoundID& l_id,
      const sf::Vector3f& l_pos);
    bool IsPlaying(const SoundID& l_id) const;
    SoundProps* GetSoundProperties(const std::string& l_soundName);

    static const int Max_Sounds = 150;
    static const int Sound_Cache = 75;
private:
    ...
    AudioManager* m_audioManager;
};
```

The `AudioManager` class is responsible for managing auditory resources, in the same way textures and fonts are managed elsewhere. One of the bigger differences here is that we can actually play sounds in 3D space, hence the use of a `sf::Vector3f` structure wherever a position needs to be represented. Sounds are also grouped by specific names, but there is a slight twist to this system. SFML can only handle about 255 different sounds playing all at once, which includes `sf::Music` instances as well. It's because of this that we have to implement a recycling system that utilizes discarded instances of sounds, as well as a static limit of the maximum number of sounds allowed all at once.

Every different sound that is loaded and played has specific set up properties that can be tweaked. They are represented by this data structure:

```
struct SoundProps{
    SoundProps(const std::string& l_name): m_audioName(l_name),
      m_volume(100), m_pitch(1.f), m_minDistance(10.f),
      m_attenuation(10.f){}
    std::string m_audioName;
    float m_volume;
    float m_pitch;
    float m_minDistance;
    float m_attenuation;
};
```

`audioName` is simply the identifier of the audio resource that is loaded in memory. The volume of a sound can obviously be tweaked, as well as its pitch. The last two properties are slightly more intricate. A sound at a point in space would begin to grow quieter and quieter, as we begin to move away from it. The minimum distance property describes the unit distance from the sound source, after which the sound begins to lose its volume. The rate at which this volume is lost after that point is reached is described by the attenuation factor.

Summary

That was quite a lot of information to take in. In the span of around forty pages we have managed to summarize the better part of the entire code base that would make any basic to intermediate complexity game tick. Keep in mind that although many topics got covered here, all of the information was rather condensed. Feel free to look through the code files we provide until you feel comfortable to proceed to actually building a game, which is precisely what's coming in the next chapter. See you there!

2
Its Game Time! - Designing the Project

In the previous chapter, we covered the essential parts of our pre-established code base that is going to be used while creating a game. The time has come to take what we have learned and build upon it, by focusing on project-specific code that will be unique to the game we are making.

In this chapter, we are going to be covering the following topics:

- Implementing key entity components and systems for minimal gameplay
- Creating a couple of states for navigating the game
- Arranging all of our code into a cohesive, working project

We have a whole game to design, so let us get to it!

Use of copyrighted resources

In this chapter, and for the entire length of this book, we are going to be using these resources:

- *Mage City Arcanos* by *Hyptosis* under the **CC0** license (public domain): http://op engameart.org/content/mage-city-arcanos
- *[LPC] Leaf Recolor* by *William. Thompsonj* under the **CC-BY-SA 3.0** and **GPL 3.0** licenses: http://opengameart.org/content/lpc-leaf-recolor
- *[LPC] Medieval fantasy character sprites* by *Wulax* under **CC-BY-SA 3.0** and **GPL 3.0** licenses: http://opengameart.org/content/lpc-medieval-fantasy-character-sprites

- *Fantasy UI Elements* by *Ravenmore* at `http://dycha.net/` under the **CC-BY 3.0** license: `http://opengameart.org/content/fantasy-ui-elements-by-ravenmore`
- *Vegur font* by *Arro* under the **CC0** license (public domain): `http://www.fontspace.com/arro/vegur`
- *Fantozzi's Footsteps (Grass/Sand & Stone)* by *Fantozzi* under the **CC0** license (public domain): `http://opengameart.org/content/fantozzis-footsteps-grasssand-stone`
- *Electrix* (NES Version) by *Snabisch* under the **CC-BY 3.0** license: `http://opengameart.org/content/electrix-nes-version`
- *Town Theme RPG* by *cynicmusic* under the **CC-BY 3.0** license: `http://opengameart.org/content/town-theme-rpg`

Information about all of the licenses that apply to these resources can be found here:

- `http://creativecommons.org/publicdomain/zero/1.0/`
- `http://creativecommons.org/licenses/by/3.0/`
- `http://creativecommons.org/licenses/by-sa/3.0/`
- `http://www.gnu.org/licenses/gpl-3.0.html`

Entity placement and rendering

Let us start with the basics. Most (if not all) entities in any game we build are going to be positioned within the world. Let us ignore the corner cases of special types of entities for now. In order to represent the entity position, we are going to be creating a position component like so:

```cpp
class C_Position : public C_Base{
public:
  C_Position(): C_Base(Component::Position), m_elevation(0){}

  void ReadIn(std::stringstream& l_stream){
    l_stream >> m_position.x >> m_position.y >> m_elevation;
  }

  sf::Vector2f GetPosition() const { ... }
  sf::Vector2f GetOldPosition() const { ... }
  unsigned int GetElevation() const { ... }
  void SetPosition(float l_x, float l_y){ ... }
  void SetPosition(const sf::Vector2f& l_vec){ ... }
  void SetElevation(unsigned int l_elevation){ ... }
  void MoveBy(float l_x, float l_y){ ... }
```

```
    void MoveBy(const sf::Vector2f& l_vec){ ... }
private:
  sf::Vector2f m_position;
  sf::Vector2f m_positionOld;
  unsigned int m_elevation;
};
```

Only two things are worthy of noting here. First, the component type has to be set up through the `C_Base` constructor. That can be changed in the future if we are going to be re-designing this system, but for now this is the way to do it. We must also implement the `ReadIn` method, in order to be able to de-serialize component data properly. This means that every time an entity file is being loaded and the position data is encountered, it is going to read in the *x* coordinate, the *y* coordinate, and the elevation in this exact order.

The component itself only holds the data that is relevant to its cause. Two different data members for entity position are being stored here: the current position `m_position`, and the position of the entity one game tick ago, `m_positionOld`. That can be useful, should any system need to rely on position changes between updates.

The drawable side of things

The visual side of things is not that different to represent within the ECS paradigm. Because we may be dealing with more than one type of renderable objects, it helps out to have an interface that they all have to honor and implement:

```
class C_Drawable : public C_Base{
public:
  C_Drawable(const Component& l_type) : C_Base(l_type){}
  virtual ~C_Drawable(){}

  virtual void UpdatePosition(const sf::Vector2f& l_vec) = 0;
  virtual sf::Vector2u GetSize() const = 0;
  virtual void Draw(sf::RenderWindow* l_wind) = 0;
};
```

Depending on the type and implementation of drawable components, they may rely on different ways of representing their position, size, and the particular method of being drawn. All three of these aspects need to be defined when a new drawable type is created, much like this:

```
class C_SpriteSheet : public C_Drawable{
public:
  C_SpriteSheet(): C_Drawable(Component::SpriteSheet),
    m_spriteSheet(nullptr){}
```

```
    void ReadIn(std::stringstream& l_stream){l_stream>>m_sheetName;}
    void Create(TextureManager* l_textureMgr,
      const std::string& l_name = "")
    {
      if (m_spriteSheet) { m_spriteSheet.release(); }
      m_spriteSheet = std::make_unique<SpriteSheet>(l_textureMgr);
      m_spriteSheet->LoadSheet("media/Spritesheets/" +
        (!l_name.empty() ? l_name : m_sheetName) + ".sheet");
    }

    SpriteSheet* GetSpriteSheet(){ ... }
    void UpdatePosition(const sf::Vector2f& l_vec){ ... }
    sf::Vector2u GetSize() const { ... }
    void Draw(sf::RenderWindow* l_wind){ ... }
  private:
    std::unique_ptr<SpriteSheet> m_spriteSheet;
    std::string m_sheetName;
};
```

A sprite-sheet component utilizes one of the classes we have covered back in `Chapter 1`, *Under the Hood – Setting up the Backend*. De-serialization for this component is quite simple. All it requires is the name of the sheet file, which contains all size, padding, space, and animation information. Because this class relies on the texture manager for loading its assets, a special `Create()` method is used in order to set up this relationship post-loading.

Rendering system

With the data aspect all taken care of and out of the way, we can now focus on actually drawing entities on screen. This is where the very first type of system comes in:

```
S_Renderer::S_Renderer(SystemManager* l_systemMgr)
  :S_Base(System::Renderer, l_systemMgr)
{
  Bitmask req;
  req.TurnOnBit((unsigned int)Component::Position);
  req.TurnOnBit((unsigned int)Component::SpriteSheet);
  m_requiredComponents.push_back(req);
  req.Clear();

  m_drawableTypes.TurnOnBit((unsigned int)Component::SpriteSheet);
  // Other types...

  m_systemManager->GetMessageHandler()->
    Subscribe(EntityMessage::Direction_Changed,this);
}
```

The renderer system operates on two different types of component for now: position and sprite sheet. Given a wider variety of drawable component types, it would, of course, need to include them as well. This is precisely why a bitmask data member with the name `m_drawableTypes` is kept around. It keeps track of all possible drawable component types, and will be used later to fetch actual component data. All of those types should be registered here.

This system also needs to be notified when an entity changes its direction, in order to enforce those changes on a given sprite sheet.

All of the components a system uses usually need to be updated like so:

```
void S_Renderer::Update(float l_dT){
    EntityManager* entities = m_systemManager->GetEntityManager();
    for(auto &entity : m_entities)
    {
        auto position = entities->
            GetComponent<C_Position>(entity, Component::Position);
        C_Drawable* drawable = GetDrawableFromType(entity);
        if (!drawable) { continue; }
        drawable->UpdatePosition(position->GetPosition());
    }
}
```

It's pretty straightforward. Any and all drawable components need to have their positions updated in order for the simulation to be accurate. We use a private method to obtain a pointer to whatever drawable type the current entity has, check if it's not `nullptr`, and then update its position.

Event handling is also utilized in this system in order to achieve a *depth* effect by sorting entities:

```
void S_Renderer::HandleEvent(const EntityId& l_entity,
    const EntityEvent& l_event)
{
    if (l_event == EntityEvent::Moving_Left ||
        l_event == EntityEvent::Moving_Right ||
        l_event == EntityEvent::Moving_Up ||
        l_event == EntityEvent::Moving_Down ||
        l_event == EntityEvent::Elevation_Change ||
        l_event == EntityEvent::Spawned)
    {
        SortDrawables();
    }
}
```

All we have to do here is invoke another private method that's going to sort all entities this system has along the *y* axis. This only needs to happen if an entity is moving, changing elevations, or has just spawned.

As far as entity messages go, we're only interested in one single type, as should be evident from the constructor of S_Renderer:

```
void S_Renderer::Notify(const Message& l_message){
  if(HasEntity(l_message.m_receiver)){
    EntityMessage m=static_cast<EntityMessage>(l_message.m_type);
    switch(m){
    case EntityMessage::Direction_Changed:
      SetSheetDirection(l_message.m_receiver,
        (Direction)l_message.m_int);
      break;
    }
  }
}
```

Another private method comes to the rescue. It will be covered shortly, but the basic gist of it is that sprite sheets need to be informed of any direction changes, in order to reflect them visually.

Since the whole point of this system is rendering our entities on screen, let's do just that:

```
void S_Renderer::Render(Window* l_wind, unsigned int l_layer)
{
  EntityManager* entities = m_systemManager->GetEntityManager();
  for(auto &entity : m_entities){
    auto position = entities->
      GetComponent<C_Position>(entity, Component::Position);
    if(position->GetElevation() < l_layer){ continue; }
    if(position->GetElevation() > l_layer){ break; }
    C_Drawable* drawable = GetDrawableFromType(entity);
    if (!drawable) { continue; }
    sf::FloatRect drawableBounds;
    drawableBounds.left = position->GetPosition().x -
      (drawable->GetSize().x / 2);
    drawableBounds.top = position->GetPosition().y -
      drawable->GetSize().y;
    drawableBounds.width =
      static_cast<float>(drawable->GetSize().x);
    drawableBounds.height =
      static_cast<float>(drawable->GetSize().y);
    if (!l_wind->GetViewSpace().intersects(drawableBounds)){
      continue;
    }
```

```
      drawable->Draw(l_wind->GetRenderWindow());
   }
 }
```

Once again, it's fairly simple. The actual rendering is layer-based, so an argument is taken in for the specific layer we're currently drawing. The position component is obtained first in order to check if the entity's elevation matches the current layer being rendered. Because the game entities are always kept sorted, we know it's okay to break out of the loop if any given entity's elevation goes beyond the layer we're working with.

Finally, the drawable component of the entity is obtained, as well as checked for being outside the screen area, in order to minimize unnecessary drawing.

All we have left now are the private helper methods, starting with SetSheetDirection:

```
void S_Renderer::SetSheetDirection(const EntityId& l_entity,
   const Direction& l_dir)
{
   EntityManager* entities = m_systemManager->GetEntityManager();
   if (!entities->HasComponent(l_entity, Component::SpriteSheet))
   { return; }
   auto sheet = entities->
     GetComponent<C_SpriteSheet>(l_entity,Component::SpriteSheet);
   sheet->GetSpriteSheet()->SetDirection(l_dir);
}
```

There's nothing we haven't seen before. The entity is checked for having a sprite-sheet component, which then gets obtained and informed of direction changes.

This system heavily relies on entities being sorted, based on their *y* coordinate and elevation. For that, we use this bit of code:

```
void S_Renderer::SortDrawables(){
   EntityManager* e_mgr = m_systemManager->GetEntityManager();
   std::sort(m_entities.begin(), m_entities.end(),
     [e_mgr](unsigned int l_1, unsigned int l_2)
   {
     auto pos1 = e_mgr->
       GetComponent<C_Position>(l_1, Component::Position);
     auto pos2 = e_mgr->
       GetComponent<C_Position>(l_2, Component::Position);
     if (pos1->GetElevation() == pos2->GetElevation()){
       return pos1->GetPosition().y < pos2->GetPosition().y;
     }
     return pos1->GetElevation() < pos2->GetElevation();
   });
}
```

Because entity identifiers are stored inside an STL container, `std::sort` comes to the rescue. The actual sorting gives priority to elevation; however, if two entities share that in common, they're sorted according to the *y* coordinate, going from smallest to largest.

To wrap this up, here's a method that's going to save us some typing, should additional drawable component types be added in the future:

```
C_Drawable* S_Renderer::GetDrawableFromType(
  const EntityId& l_entity)
{
  auto entities = m_systemManager->GetEntityManager();
  for (size_t i = 0; i < static_cast<size_t>(Component::COUNT);
    ++i)
  {
    if (!m_drawableTypes.GetBit(i)) { continue; }
    auto component = static_cast<Component>(i);
    if (!entities->HasComponent(l_entity, component)){ continue; }
    return entities->GetComponent<C_Drawable>(l_entity,component);
  }
  return nullptr;
}
```

All it does is simply iterate through all component types, looking for one that matches drawable types registered in the constructor of this system. Once one is found, the entity is checked for having that component. If it does, a pointer to it gets returned.

Entity kinematics

The code we have written so far would only produce a static, unmoving scene. Since that isn't very exciting, let's work on adding potential for entity movement. Since it calls for more data being stored, we need another component type to work with:

```
class C_Movable : public C_Base{
public:
  C_Movable() : C_Base(Component::Movable),
    m_velocityMax(0.f), m_direction((Direction)0){}

  void ReadIn(std::stringstream& l_stream){
    l_stream >> m_velocityMax >> m_speed.x >> m_speed.y;
    unsigned int dir = 0;
    l_stream >> dir;
    m_direction = static_cast<Direction>(dir);
  }
  ...
  void SetVelocity(const sf::Vector2f& l_vec){ ... }
```

```
   void SetMaxVelocity(float l_vel){ ... }
   void SetSpeed(const sf::Vector2f& l_vec){ ... }
   void SetAcceleration(const sf::Vector2f& l_vec){ ... }
   void SetDirection(const Direction& l_dir){ ... }
   void AddVelocity(const sf::Vector2f& l_vec){ ... }
   void ApplyFriction(const sf::Vector2f& l_vec){ ... }
   void Accelerate(const sf::Vector2f& l_vec){ ... }
   void Accelerate(float l_x, float l_y){ ... }
   void Move(const Direction& l_dir){ ... }
private:
   sf::Vector2f m_velocity;
   sf::Vector2f m_speed;
   sf::Vector2f m_acceleration;
   float m_velocityMax;
   Direction m_direction;
};
```

Our movement is going to be modeled by the relationships between velocity, speed, and acceleration. For purposes of controlling entities, a maximum velocity value is going to be imposed as well, in order to prevent endless acceleration. We also store direction with this component in order to reduce certain complexities and inter-component relationships; however, it could be its own separate component.

Movement system

To kick this into gear, let us first take a look at what the movement system needs in order to work:

```
S_Movement::S_Movement(SystemManager* l_systemMgr)
   : S_Base(System::Movement,l_systemMgr)
{
   Bitmask req;
   req.TurnOnBit((unsigned int)Component::Position);
   req.TurnOnBit((unsigned int)Component::Movable);
   m_requiredComponents.push_back(req);
   req.Clear();

   m_systemManager->GetMessageHandler()->
     Subscribe(EntityMessage::Is_Moving,this);

   m_gameMap = nullptr;
}
```

The entity's kinematic state is going to directly control its position, so we need both position and movable components here. An entity message type of `Is_Moving` is also subscribed to. The way it is named should be a clue that this message is going to be used as a request for information, and its sender will be expecting an answer. Since this system is responsible for everything related to motion, it will be handling requests like this.

Next, let us update the component data:

```
void S_Movement::Update(float l_dT){
  if (!m_gameMap){ return; }
  EntityManager* entities = m_systemManager->GetEntityManager();
  for(auto &entity : m_entities){
    auto position = entities->
      GetComponent<C_Position>(entity, Component::Position);
    auto movable = entities->
      GetComponent<C_Movable>(entity, Component::Movable);
    MovementStep(l_dT, movable, position);
    position->MoveBy(movable->GetVelocity() * l_dT);
  }
}
```

After both components are obtained, they are passed into a private method that handles a movement step. We will be covering this later, but it's important to note that it takes the position component pointer in as a `const` value, which implies that it will be read only. This is why the position of the entity is modified separately one line down, by invoking its `MoveBy()` method. It simply advances the position by a vector, provided as the sole argument.

With a more complex system task, we obviously have more events to deal with:

```
void S_Movement::HandleEvent(const EntityId& l_entity,
  const EntityEvent& l_event)
{
  switch(l_event){
  case EntityEvent::Colliding_X:
    StopEntity(l_entity, Axis::x); break;
  case EntityEvent::Colliding_Y:
    StopEntity(l_entity, Axis::y); break;
  case EntityEvent::Moving_Left:
    SetDirection(l_entity, Direction::Left); break;
  case EntityEvent::Moving_Right:
    SetDirection(l_entity, Direction::Right); break;
  case EntityEvent::Moving_Up:
    {
      auto mov = m_systemManager->GetEntityManager()->
        GetComponent<C_Movable>(l_entity,Component::Movable);
      if(mov->GetVelocity().x == 0){
```

```
                SetDirection(l_entity, Direction::Up);
            }
        }
    break;
    case EntityEvent::Moving_Down:
        {
            auto mov = m_systemManager->GetEntityManager()->
              GetComponent<C_Movable>(l_entity,Component::Movable);
            if(mov->GetVelocity().x == 0){
                SetDirection(l_entity, Direction::Down);
            }
        }
    break;
    }
}
```

We will want to stop our entity on a given axis, if it is actually colliding with a solid. The collision event emission will be discussed when we are covering the collision system, so all we have to remember now is that if an entity is colliding on a specific axis, it needs to have its velocity reduced to 0 on that axis.

Since we are also in charge of the entity's direction, movement events are handled and used to update it. Direction priority is given to horizontal movement, while up and down directions are only set if the velocity on the *x* axis is zero.

Back in the constructor of this system, we have subscribed to a message that requests movement information. Let us take a look at how that can be handled:

```
void S_Movement::Notify(const Message& l_message){
    EntityManager* eMgr = m_systemManager->GetEntityManager();
    EntityMessage m = static_cast<EntityMessage>(l_message.m_type);
    switch(m){
    case EntityMessage::Is_Moving:
        {
        if (!HasEntity(l_message.m_receiver)){ return; }
        auto movable = eMgr->
          GetComponent<C_Movable>(l_message.m_receiver,
          Component::Movable);
        if (movable->GetVelocity() != sf::Vector2f(0.f, 0.f)){return;}
        m_systemManager->AddEvent(l_message.m_receiver,
            (EventID)EntityEvent::Became_Idle);
        }
    break;
    }
}
```

[57]

If the entity information was requested about isn't even part of this system, the message gets ignored. Otherwise, the movable component is obtained and its velocity gets checked for not being an absolute zero. If it is, an entity event `Became_Idle` is sent out. This will be useful later, when we're dealing with entity animations.

Once again, all the hard lifting exists inside our helper methods. Let's start with a simple one, used to obtain tile friction for a specific coordinate in space:

```
sf::Vector2f S_Movement::GetTileFriction(unsigned int l_elevation,
  unsigned int l_x, unsigned int l_y)
{
  Tile* t = nullptr;
  while (!t && l_elevation >= 0){
    t = m_gameMap->GetTile(l_x, l_y, l_elevation);
    --l_elevation;
  }

  return(t ? t->m_properties->m_friction :
    m_gameMap->GetDefaultTile()->m_friction);
}
```

A `null` pointer to a tile is established first. A `while` loop is then used to attempt to obtain an actual tile, starting with the original elevation and moving down until it reaches *0*. We finally return either the friction of the tile that was found, or the default friction of the map if it wasn't. It comes into play when we're trying to process the movement step of an entity here:

```
void S_Movement::MovementStep(float l_dT, C_Movable* l_movable,
  const C_Position* l_position)
{
  sf::Vector2f f_coefficient = GetTileFriction(
    l_position->GetElevation(),
    static_cast<unsigned int>(floor(l_position->GetPosition().x /
      Sheet::Tile_Size)),
    static_cast<unsigned int>(floor(l_position->GetPosition().y /
      Sheet::Tile_Size)));

  sf::Vector2f friction(l_movable->GetSpeed().x * f_coefficient.x,
    l_movable->GetSpeed().y * f_coefficient.y);

  l_movable->AddVelocity(l_movable->GetAcceleration() * l_dT);
  l_movable->SetAcceleration(sf::Vector2f(0.0f, 0.0f));
  l_movable->ApplyFriction(friction * l_dT);

  float magnitude = sqrt(
    (l_movable->GetVelocity().x * l_movable->GetVelocity().x) +
    (l_movable->GetVelocity().y * l_movable->GetVelocity().y));
```

```
  if (magnitude <= l_movable->GetMaxVelocity()){ return; }
  float max_V = l_movable->GetMaxVelocity();
  l_movable->SetVelocity(sf::Vector2f(
    (l_movable->GetVelocity().x / magnitude) * max_V,
    (l_movable->GetVelocity().y / magnitude) * max_V));
}
```

After the friction coefficient is obtained from the current tile an entity is standing on, speed loss due to friction is calculated, velocity due to acceleration is added, acceleration itself is zeroed out, and friction is applied. In order to account for diagonal movement, a velocity magnitude is calculated and checked for exceeding the maximum allowed value. If it does, the entity's velocity is re-calculated based on the ratios between its current velocity and the total magnitude, and adjusted to fit within the provided boundaries.

Stopping an entity simply comes down to zeroing its velocity out on a provided axis, like so:

```
void S_Movement::StopEntity(const EntityId& l_entity,
  const Axis& l_axis)
{
  auto movable = m_systemManager->GetEntityManager()->
    GetComponent<C_Movable>(l_entity,Component::Movable);
  if(l_axis == Axis::x){
    movable->SetVelocity(sf::Vector2f(
      0.f, movable->GetVelocity().y));
  } else if(l_axis == Axis::y){
    movable->SetVelocity(sf::Vector2f(
      movable->GetVelocity().x, 0.f));
  }
}
```

Updating the entity's direction is equally as simple, but it can't go unnoticed by other systems:

```
void S_Movement::SetDirection(const EntityId& l_entity,
  const Direction& l_dir)
{
  auto movable = m_systemManager->GetEntityManager()->
    GetComponent<C_Movable>(l_entity,Component::Movable);
  movable->SetDirection(l_dir);

  Message msg((MessageType)EntityMessage::Direction_Changed);
  msg.m_receiver = l_entity;
  msg.m_int = static_cast<int>(l_dir);
  m_systemManager->GetMessageHandler()->Dispatch(msg);
}
```

After the direction is updated, a new message is constructed and dispatched, letting the relevant systems know about the direction changes of an entity. This will also prove to be incredibly useful when handling entity animations.

Handling collisions

In order to make the game we're making feel like more than just entities moving across a static background with no consequences, collisions have to be checked for and handled. Within the ECS paradigm, this can be achieved by implementing a collidable component. For more flexibility, let's define multiple points that the collision box can be attached to:

```
enum class Origin{ Top_Left, Abs_Centre, Mid_Bottom };
```

The **TOP_LEFT** origin simply places the collision rectangle's top-left corner to the position provided. **ABS_CENTRE** moves that rectangle's centre to the position, and the **MIDDLE_BOTTOM** origin places it halfway through the *x* axis and all the way down the *y* axis. Consider the following illustration:

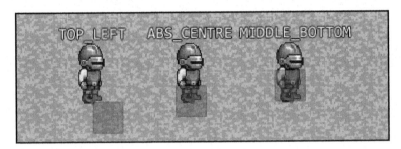

With this information, let us work on implementing the collidable component:

```
class C_Collidable : public C_Base{
public:
  C_Collidable(): C_Base(Component::Collidable),
    m_origin(Origin::Mid_Bottom), m_collidingOnX(false),
    m_collidingOnY(false){}

  void ReadIn(std::stringstream& l_stream){
    unsigned int origin = 0;
    l_stream >> m_AABB.width >> m_AABB.height >> m_offset.x
      >> m_offset.y >> origin;
    m_origin = static_cast<Origin>(origin);
  }
  const sf::FloatRect& GetCollidable() const { ... }
  bool IsCollidingOnX() const { ... }
```

```
      bool IsCollidingOnY() const { ... }
      void CollideOnX(){ m_collidingOnX = true; }
      void CollideOnY(){ m_collidingOnY = true; }
      void ResetCollisionFlags(){ ... }
      void SetCollidable(const sf::FloatRect& l_rect){ ... }
      void SetOrigin(const Origin& l_origin){ ... }
      void SetSize(const sf::Vector2f& l_vec){ ... }

      void SetPosition(const sf::Vector2f& l_vec){
        switch(m_origin){
        case(Origin::Top_Left) :
          m_AABB.left    = l_vec.x + m_offset.x;
          m_AABB.top     = l_vec.y + m_offset.y;
          break;
        case(Origin::Abs_Centre):
          m_AABB.left    = l_vec.x - (m_AABB.width / 2) + m_offset.x;
          m_AABB.top     = l_vec.y - (m_AABB.height / 2) + m_offset.y;
          break;
        case(Origin::Mid_Bottom):
          m_AABB.left    = l_vec.x - (m_AABB.width / 2) + m_offset.x;
          m_AABB.top     = l_vec.y - m_AABB.height + m_offset.y;
          break;
        }
      }
  private:
    sf::FloatRect m_AABB;
    sf::Vector2f m_offset;
    Origin m_origin;

    bool m_collidingOnX;
    bool m_collidingOnY;
};
```

First, let us look at the data we are keeping. `sf::FloatRect` represents the basic **AABB** bounding box around the entity that will be used as our collider. We also want to be able to offset it by some value, which is going to be loaded from the entity file. Obviously, the origin point is stored as well, along with two flags that indicate whether a collision is happening on each axis.

The `SetPosition()` method incorporates the use of an origin point and adjusts the rectangle to be positioned properly, since the native `sf::FloatRect` doesn't support origins by itself.

Collision system

In order to work with and handle collisions, we only need two components:

```
S_Collision::S_Collision(SystemManager* l_systemMgr)
  : S_Base(System::Collision,l_systemMgr)
{
  Bitmask req;
  req.TurnOnBit((unsigned int)Component::Position);
  req.TurnOnBit((unsigned int)Component::Collidable);
  m_requiredComponents.push_back(req);
  req.Clear();

  m_gameMap = nullptr;
}
```

Note the `m_gameMap` data member. We're going to need to provide the collision system with a pointer to the game map at some point, in order to be able to handle map collisions.

Next, let's handle updating our component data:

```
void S_Collision::Update(float l_dT){
  if (!m_gameMap){ return; }
  EntityManager* entities = m_systemManager->GetEntityManager();
  for(auto &entity : m_entities){
    auto position = entities->
      GetComponent<C_Position>(entity, Component::Position);
    auto collidable = entities->
      GetComponent<C_Collidable>(entity, Component::Collidable);
    CheckOutOfBounds(position);
    collidable->SetPosition(position->GetPosition());
    collidable->ResetCollisionFlags();
    MapCollisions(entity, position, collidable);
  }
  EntityCollisions();
}
```

First, the entity's position is checked to see whether it's outside the map's boundaries. After it potentially has been adjusted, the `collidable` component is updated with the new position information, and its collision flags are reset. Both components are then passed into a private method that handles map collisions.

After all of the entities are checked against the map, we must check them for collisions against each other:

```
void S_Collision::EntityCollisions(){
  EntityManager* entities = m_systemManager->GetEntityManager();
```

```
for(auto itr = m_entities.begin(); itr!=m_entities.end(); ++itr)
{
    for(auto itr2=std::next(itr); itr2!=m_entities.end(); ++itr2){
        auto collidable1 = entities->
            GetComponent<C_Collidable>(*itr, Component::Collidable);
        auto collidable2 = entities->
            GetComponent<C_Collidable>(*itr2, Component::Collidable);
        if(collidable1->GetCollidable().intersects(
            collidable2->GetCollidable()))
        {
            // Entity-on-entity collision!
        }
    }
}
}
```

So far, we don't really need to handle entity-on-entity collisions in any way, but this is an entry point for later features.

The out-of-bounds check is fairly simple:

```
void S_Collision::CheckOutOfBounds(C_Position* l_pos){
    unsigned int TileSize = m_gameMap->GetTileSize();

    if (l_pos->GetPosition().x < 0){
        l_pos->SetPosition(0.0f, l_pos->GetPosition().y);
    } else if (l_pos->GetPosition().x >
        m_gameMap->GetMapSize().x * TileSize)
    {
        l_pos->SetPosition(
            static_cast<float>(m_gameMap->GetMapSize().x * TileSize),
            l_pos->GetPosition().y);
    }

    if (l_pos->GetPosition().y < 0){
        l_pos->SetPosition(l_pos->GetPosition().x, 0.0f);
    } else if (l_pos->GetPosition().y >
        m_gameMap->GetMapSize().y * TileSize)
    {
        l_pos->SetPosition(
            l_pos->GetPosition().x,
            static_cast<float>(m_gameMap->GetMapSize().y * TileSize));
    }
}
```

It simply checks the position for being either in negative coordinates, or outside the map's boundaries.

Processing actual map collisions is further broken down into more readable bits:

```
void S_Collision::MapCollisions(const EntityId& l_entity,
  C_Position* l_pos, C_Collidable* l_col)
{
  Collisions c;
  CheckCollisions(l_pos, l_col, c);
  HandleCollisions(l_entity, l_pos, l_col, c);
}
```

After a `Collisions` data type is set up, it, along with the position and collidable components, is passed to two private methods, which actually perform collision checks, and later handle them. The `Collisions` data type is just a container for collision information:

```
struct CollisionElement{
  CollisionElement(float l_area, TileInfo* l_info,
    const sf::FloatRect& l_bounds) :m_area(l_area), m_tile(l_info),
    m_tileBounds(l_bounds){}
  float m_area;
  TileInfo* m_tile;
  sf::FloatRect m_tileBounds;
};

using Collisions = std::vector<CollisionElement>;
```

Let us focus on actually filling this structure out with useful collision information next:

```
void S_Collision::CheckCollisions(C_Position* l_pos,
  C_Collidable* l_col, Collisions& l_collisions)
{
  unsigned int TileSize = m_gameMap->GetTileSize();
  sf::FloatRect EntityAABB = l_col->GetCollidable();
  int FromX = static_cast<int>(floor(EntityAABB.left / TileSize));
  int ToX = static_cast<int>(floor((EntityAABB.left +
    EntityAABB.width) / TileSize));
  int FromY = static_cast<int>(floor(EntityAABB.top / TileSize));
  int ToY = static_cast<int>(floor((EntityAABB.top +
    EntityAABB.height) / TileSize));

  for (int x = FromX; x <= ToX; ++x) {
    for (int y = FromY; y <= ToY; ++y) {
      for (size_t l = l_pos->GetElevation(); l <
        l_pos->GetElevation() + 1; ++l)
      {
        auto t = m_gameMap->GetTile(x, y, l);
        if (!t) { continue; }
        if (!t->m_solid) { continue; }
        sf::FloatRect TileAABB = static_cast<sf::FloatRect>(
```

```
           sf::IntRect(x*TileSize, y*TileSize,TileSize,TileSize));
        sf::FloatRect Intersection;
        EntityAABB.intersects(TileAABB, Intersection);
        float S = Intersection.width * Intersection.height;
        l_collisions.emplace_back(S, t->m_properties, TileAABB);
        break;
      }
    }
   }
  }
}
```

This method uses the entity collision box and the map tile size to establish a range of tiles that are intersecting with it. We then use that range to obtain tiles one by one, check if they exist and are solid, construct their bounding boxes, measure the areas of intersection, and add all of that information to the collision container. So far, so good!

The grand finale of this system is, of course, handling all of the collision information that got collected:

```
void S_Collision::HandleCollisions(const EntityId& l_entity,
  C_Position* l_pos, C_Collidable* l_col,Collisions& l_collisions)
{
  sf::FloatRect EntityAABB = l_col->GetCollidable();
  unsigned int TileSize = m_gameMap->GetTileSize();

  if (l_collisions.empty()) { return; }
  std::sort(l_collisions.begin(), l_collisions.end(),
    [](CollisionElement& l_1, CollisionElement& l_2) {
      return l_1.m_area > l_2.m_area;
    }
  );

  for (auto &col : l_collisions) {
    EntityAABB = l_col->GetCollidable();
    if (!EntityAABB.intersects(col.m_tileBounds)) { continue; }
    float xDiff = (EntityAABB.left + (EntityAABB.width / 2)) -
      (col.m_tileBounds.left + (col.m_tileBounds.width / 2));
    float yDiff = (EntityAABB.top + (EntityAABB.height / 2)) -
      (col.m_tileBounds.top + (col.m_tileBounds.height / 2));
    float resolve = 0;
    if (std::abs(xDiff) > std::abs(yDiff)) {
      if (xDiff > 0) {
        resolve=(col.m_tileBounds.left+TileSize)-EntityAABB.left;
      } else {
        resolve = -((EntityAABB.left + EntityAABB.width) -
          col.m_tileBounds.left);
      }
      l_pos->MoveBy(resolve, 0);
```

```
          l_col->SetPosition(l_pos->GetPosition());
        m_systemManager->AddEvent(
          l_entity, (EventID)EntityEvent::Colliding_X);
        l_col->CollideOnX();
      } else {
        if (yDiff > 0) {
          resolve=(col.m_tileBounds.top + TileSize)-EntityAABB.top;
        } else {
          resolve = -((EntityAABB.top + EntityAABB.height) -
            col.m_tileBounds.top);
        }
        l_pos->MoveBy(0, resolve);
        l_col->SetPosition(l_pos->GetPosition());
        m_systemManager->AddEvent(
          l_entity, (EventID)EntityEvent::Colliding_Y);
        l_col->CollideOnY();
      }
    }
  }
}
```

The collision container is first checked for being empty. If it isn't, we sort the collision information to flow in a descending order, and use the size of the intersecting area for the comparison. This ensures that the collision(s) with the largest area of intersection come first, and thus gets handled first.

During the processing of this information, we must first check if the entity's bounding box is still colliding with the tile. In case of multiple collisions, the first collision that got processed may have moved an entity in such a way that it no longer collides with anything at all.

The xDiff and yDiff variables are used to hold the penetration information of each axis, and the resolve variable will be used to store exact distance by which the entity is going to be pushed to resolve the collision. The first two variables are then compared, in order to decide which axis to resolve the collision on. Our resolve variable is used to calculate the exact distance of the push based on whether it's a left-to-right or right-to-left collision.

Finally, the position is adjusted by the resolve distance on the relevant axis, the collidable component's position is updated to match the changes, a colliding event is sent out, and the collidable component's `CollideOnX` or `CollideOnY` method is invoked to update the collision flags. These events then get handled by other systems, such as `S_Movement`, which we have already covered.

Controlling entities

Since we have already laid down the code foundation, it's now possible to focus on controlling the entities on the screen. Whether they're being controlled as player avatars by means of a keyboard, or through some sort of **artificial intelligence (AI)**, they still need to have this basic component:

```
class C_Controller : public C_Base{
public:
  C_Controller() : C_Base(Component::Controller){}
  void ReadIn(std::stringstream& l_stream){}
};
```

As you can tell, we have absolutely no data that gets stored here so far. For now, it can simply be considered just a specific signature that lets the ECS know it can be controlled.

Control system

In order for entities to be controlled, they must have three basic component types:

```
S_Control::S_Control(SystemManager* l_systemMgr)
  : S_Base(System::Control,l_systemMgr)
{
  Bitmask req;
  req.TurnOnBit((unsigned int)Component::Position);
  req.TurnOnBit((unsigned int)Component::Movable);
  req.TurnOnBit((unsigned int)Component::Controller);
  m_requiredComponents.push_back(req);
  req.Clear();
}
```

Actual control happens through the event system:

```
void S_Control::HandleEvent(const EntityId& l_entity,
  const EntityEvent& l_event)
{
  switch(l_event){
  case EntityEvent::Moving_Left:
    MoveEntity(l_entity, Direction::Left); break;
  case EntityEvent::Moving_Right:
    MoveEntity(l_entity, Direction::Right); break;
  case EntityEvent::Moving_Up:
    MoveEntity(l_entity, Direction::Up); break;
  case EntityEvent::Moving_Down:
    MoveEntity(l_entity, Direction::Down); break;
  }
}
```

The movement itself is just a modification of the movable component, as shown here:

```
void S_Control::MoveEntity(const EntityId& l_entity,
  const Direction& l_dir)
{
  auto mov = m_systemManager->GetEntityManager()->
    GetComponent<C_Movable>(l_entity, Component::Movable);
  mov->Move(l_dir);
}
```

The C_Movable component type takes care of actually modifying its data. All we need to do is pass in a valid direction.

Entity states

Having entities that are able to move around now implies they can either be standing still or moving. This quickly brings about the issue of entity states. Luckily, we have an elegant way of dealing with that, by introducing another component type and a system. Let's start by enumerating all possible entity states, and using the enumeration to establish a component type:

```
enum class EntityState{ Idle, Walking, Attacking, Hurt, Dying };

class C_State : public C_Base{
public:
  C_State(): C_Base(Component::State){}
  void ReadIn(std::stringstream& l_stream){
    unsigned int state = 0;
```

```
    l_stream >> state;
    m_state = static_cast<EntityState>(state);
  }

  EntityState GetState() const { ... }
  void SetState(const EntityState& l_state){ ... }
private:
  EntityState m_state;
};
```

That's all we have to keep track of inside the component class. Time to move on to the system!

State system

Because state is not directly tethered to any other data, we can only require one component type to be present in order to work with states:

```
S_State::S_State(SystemManager* l_systemMgr)
  : S_Base(System::State,l_systemMgr)
{
  Bitmask req;
  req.TurnOnBit((unsigned int)Component::State);
  m_requiredComponents.push_back(req);

  m_systemManager->GetMessageHandler()->
    Subscribe(EntityMessage::Move,this);
  m_systemManager->GetMessageHandler()->
    Subscribe(EntityMessage::Switch_State,this);
}
```

This system also needs to subscribe to two different message types: Move and Switch_State. The action of movement is obviously state-dependent, since, for example, an entity shouldn't be able to move if it is dead.

Updating entities with a state is fairly basic, since we're about to utilize the movement system indirectly:

```
void S_State::Update(float l_dT){
  EntityManager* entities = m_systemManager->GetEntityManager();
  for(auto &entity : m_entities){
    auto state = entities->
      GetComponent<C_State>(entity, Component::State);
    if(state->GetState() == EntityState::Walking){
      Message msg((MessageType)EntityMessage::Is_Moving);
      msg.m_receiver = entity;
```

```
        m_systemManager->GetMessageHandler()->Dispatch(msg);
    }
  }
}
```

All we care about so far is if the state of the current entity is `Walking`, but the entity has gone idle. For that, we can send out the `Is_Moving` message, which the `S_Movement` is going to respond to with an event, given that the entity has stopped. That event is then handled here:

```
void S_State::HandleEvent(const EntityId& l_entity,
  const EntityEvent& l_event)
{
  switch(l_event){
  case EntityEvent::Became_Idle:
    ChangeState(l_entity,EntityState::Idle,false);
    break;
  }
}
```

A private method for changing an entity's state is invoked, setting it to `Idle`. Kids' stuff!

Next, let us handle the message types this system is subscribed to:

```
void S_State::Notify(const Message& l_message){
  if (!HasEntity(l_message.m_receiver)){ return; }
  EntityMessage m = static_cast<EntityMessage>(l_message.m_type);
  switch(m){
  case EntityMessage::Move:
    {
      auto state = m_systemManager->GetEntityManager()->
        GetComponent<C_State>(l_message.m_receiver,
        Component::State);

      if (state->GetState() == EntityState::Dying){ return; }
      EntityEvent e;
      Direction dir = static_cast<Direction>(l_message.m_int);
      if (dir==Direction::Up){e=EntityEvent::Moving_Up;}
      else if (dir==Direction::Down){e=EntityEvent::Moving_Down;}
      else if(dir==Direction::Left){e=EntityEvent::Moving_Left;}
      else if(dir==Direction::Right){e=EntityEvent::Moving_Right;}

      m_systemManager->AddEvent(l_message.m_receiver,
        static_cast<EventID>(e));
      ChangeState(l_message.m_receiver,
        EntityState::Walking,false);
    }
    break;
```

```
  case EntityMessage::Switch_State:
    ChangeState(l_message.m_receiver,
      (EntityState)l_message.m_int,false);
    break;
  }
}
```

Since actual entity movement depends on its state, this is the system that decides whether there is movement or not. The entity's state is first checked, to make sure it can't move if it's dying. An `EntityEvent` structure is then constructed and set to match the direction of the `Move` message. After the event is dispatched, the entity's state is changed to `Walking`.

Other systems within the ECS may care about the state of an entity changing. For that, we need to handle these changes accordingly:

```
void S_State::ChangeState(const EntityId& l_entity,
  const EntityState& l_state, bool l_force)
{
  EntityManager* entities = m_systemManager->GetEntityManager();
  auto state = entities->
    GetComponent<C_State>(l_entity, Component::State);
  if (!l_force && state->GetState()==EntityState::Dying){return;}
  state->SetState(l_state);
  Message msg((MessageType)EntityMessage::State_Changed);
  msg.m_receiver = l_entity;
  msg.m_int = static_cast<int>(l_state);
  m_systemManager->GetMessageHandler()->Dispatch(msg);
}
```

Note the last argument of this method. It indicates whether the state change should be forced or not. This is done to ensure that certain state changes can be defined as non-critical, and should be ignored if an entity is dying.

If the state ends up getting changed, the component data is updated, and a new `State_Changed` message is dispatched to inform other systems.

Sheet animation system

One of the objects sensitive to state changes is the sprite sheet animation system. Knowing an entity's state is of paramount importance, if we desire to apply animations that describe its current action:

```
S_SheetAnimation::S_SheetAnimation(SystemManager* l_systemMgr)
  : S_Base(System::SheetAnimation,l_systemMgr)
{
```

```
    Bitmask req;
    req.TurnOnBit((unsigned int)Component::SpriteSheet);
    req.TurnOnBit((unsigned int)Component::State);
    m_requiredComponents.push_back(req);

    m_systemManager->GetMessageHandler()->
        Subscribe(EntityMessage::State_Changed,this);
}
```

As you can see, all we need are two component types and a subscription to a message type of `State_Changed`. So far, so good!

Updating the sprite sheets can get a little involved, so let us delve right into it:

```
void S_SheetAnimation::Update(float l_dT){
    EntityManager* entities = m_systemManager->GetEntityManager();
    for(auto &entity : m_entities){
        auto sheet = entities->
            GetComponent<C_SpriteSheet>(entity, Component::SpriteSheet);
        auto state = entities->
            GetComponent<C_State>(entity, Component::State);

        sheet->GetSpriteSheet()->Update(l_dT);

        const std::string& animName = sheet->
            GetSpriteSheet()->GetCurrentAnim()->GetName();
        if(animName == "Attack"){
            if(!sheet->GetSpriteSheet()->GetCurrentAnim()->IsPlaying())
            {
                Message msg((MessageType)EntityMessage::Switch_State);
                msg.m_receiver = entity;
                msg.m_int = static_cast<int>(EntityState::Idle);
                m_systemManager->GetMessageHandler()->Dispatch(msg);
            } else if(sheet->GetSpriteSheet()->
                GetCurrentAnim()->IsInAction())
            {
                Message msg((MessageType)EntityMessage::Attack_Action);
                msg.m_sender = entity;
                m_systemManager->GetMessageHandler()->Dispatch(msg);
            }
        } else if(animName == "Death" &&
            !sheet->GetSpriteSheet()->GetCurrentAnim()->IsPlaying())
        {
            Message msg((MessageType)EntityMessage::Dead);
            msg.m_receiver = entity;
            m_systemManager->GetMessageHandler()->Dispatch(msg);
        }
        if (sheet->GetSpriteSheet()->GetCurrentAnim()->CheckMoved()){
```

```
    int frame = sheet->GetSpriteSheet()->
      GetCurrentAnim()->GetFrame();
    Message msg((MessageType)EntityMessage::Frame_Change);
    msg.m_receiver = entity;
    msg.m_int = frame;
    m_systemManager->GetMessageHandler()->Dispatch(msg);
    }
  }
}
```

After the sprite sheet and state components are obtained, the sheet gets updated. The name of its current animation is then obtained. Keep in mind that certain entity states are dependent on the current animation, and as soon as that animation is over, we want to switch back to an idle state. For example, the attack animation is first checked for no longer playing. If that's the case, a message is sent to the state system, letting it know that this entity's state needs to be switched to idle. Additionally, the animation's action range is checked, which is used to determine whether, for example, the current frames of the attack animation are of the character swinging the sword just right, where we can inflict damage.

The exact same principle applies to the death animation, except the message that gets sent out once that is finished is different.

Finally, every single animation has to be checked for frame progression, in which case a message gets sent out, notifying systems interested in that type that the animation frame has changed.

As mentioned before, sprite sheets need to know if the entity's state has changed. This is where we handle that:

```
void S_SheetAnimation::Notify(const Message& l_message){
  if (!HasEntity(l_message.m_receiver)) { return; }
  EntityMessage m = static_cast<EntityMessage>(l_message.m_type);
  switch(m){
  case EntityMessage::State_Changed:
    {
      EntityState s = static_cast<EntityState>(l_message.m_int);
      switch(s){
      case EntityState::Idle:
        ChangeAnimation(l_message.m_receiver,"Idle",true,true);
        break;
      case EntityState::Walking:
        ChangeAnimation(l_message.m_receiver,"Walk",true,true);
        break;
      case EntityState::Attacking:
        ChangeAnimation(l_message.m_receiver,"Attack",true,false);
        break;
```

```
        case EntityState::Hurt: break;
        case EntityState::Dying:
          ChangeAnimation(l_message.m_receiver,"Death",true,false);
          break;
      }
    }
    break;
  }
}
```

This essentially just maps the name of a specific animation to a state. The private method used to set that up is quite simple:

```
void S_SheetAnimation::ChangeAnimation(const EntityId& l_entity,
  const std::string& l_anim, bool l_play, bool l_loop)
{
  auto sheet = m_systemManager->GetEntityManager()->
    GetComponent<C_SpriteSheet>(l_entity,Component::SpriteSheet);
  sheet->GetSpriteSheet()->SetAnimation(l_anim,l_play,l_loop);
}
```

It takes in the entity identifier, the name of the animation, a flag for whether the animation should be played automatically, and another flag for whether it should loop. The sprite sheet that sits inside the component is then requested to play the animation provided.

Entity sounds

Just like states, an entity can emit multiple different types of sound. Each different type must also have certain parameters associated with it:

```
enum class EntitySound{ None = -1, Footstep, Attack,
  Hurt, Death, COUNT };

struct SoundParameters{
  static const int Max_SoundFrames = 5;
  SoundParameters(){
    for (int i = 0; i < Max_SoundFrames; ++i){ m_frames[i] = -1; }
  }
  std::string m_sound;
  std::array<int, Max_SoundFrames> m_frames;
};
```

struct SoundParameters simply stores the name of the sound, as well as an array of integers for the maximum number of sound frames. A sound frame is the glue between sounds and sprite sheets, as it defines during which animation frames the sound is emitted.

- Having defined the previous data structure allows us to successfully create a sound emitter component type:

```
class C_SoundEmitter : public C_Base{
public:
  C_SoundEmitter():C_Base(Component::SoundEmitter),m_soundID(-1){}
  void ReadIn(std::stringstream& l_stream){
    std::string main_delimiter = ":";
    std::string frame_delimiter = ",";
    for (size_t i=0;i<static_cast<size_t>(EntitySound::COUNT);++i)
    {
      std::string chunk;
      l_stream >> chunk;
      if (chunk.empty()){ break; }

      std::string sound = chunk.substr(0,
        chunk.find(main_delimiter));
      std::string frames = chunk.substr(chunk.find(main_delimiter)
        +main_delimiter.length());
      m_params[i].m_sound = sound;
      size_t pos = 0;
      unsigned int frameNum = 0;
      while (frameNum < SoundParameters::Max_SoundFrames){
        pos = frames.find(frame_delimiter);
        int frame = -1;
        if (pos != std::string::npos){
          frame = stoi(frames.substr(0, pos));
          frames.erase(0, pos + frame_delimiter.length());
        } else {
          frame = stoi(frames);
          m_params[i].m_frames[frameNum] = frame;
          break;
        }
        m_params[i].m_frames[frameNum] = frame;
        ++frameNum;
      }
    }
  }

  SoundID GetSoundID() const { ... }
  void SetSoundID(const SoundID& l_id){ ... }
  const std::string& GetSound(const EntitySound& l_snd) const{...}
  bool IsSoundFrame(const EntitySound& l_snd, int l_frame) const
```

```
  { ... }
  SoundParameters* GetParameters() { ... }
private:
  std::array<SoundParameters,
    static_cast<size_t>(EntitySound::COUNT)> m_params;
  SoundID m_soundID;
};
```

The only data we are storing here is an array of `SoundParameter` objects for each type of `EntitySound` enum, and a `SoundID` data member, which is going to be used in the sound system, in order to make sure only one entity sound is playing at the same time. The large method for de-serialization simply deals with correctly loading in the sound frames.

Another, much more basic component type we need before we can proceed is a sound listener:

```
class C_SoundListener : public C_Base{
public:
  C_SoundListener() : C_Base(Component::SoundListener){}
  void ReadIn(std::stringstream& l_stream){}
};
```

This, much like `C_Controller`, is basically just a flag that lets the sound system know that the entity that has it should be treated as the listener. We need to be careful with this, since there should only ever be one sound listener present at a time.

Sound system

The system in charge of managing entity sounds uses the component signature bitmask in a way that allows multiple different compositions to be recognized:

```
S_Sound::S_Sound(SystemManager* l_systemMgr)
  : S_Base(System::Sound, l_systemMgr),
  m_audioManager(nullptr), m_soundManager(nullptr)
{
  Bitmask req;
  req.TurnOnBit((unsigned int)Component::Position);
  req.TurnOnBit((unsigned int)Component::SoundEmitter);
  m_requiredComponents.push_back(req);
  req.ClearBit((unsigned int)Component::SoundEmitter);
  req.TurnOnBit((unsigned int)Component::SoundListener);
  m_requiredComponents.push_back(req);

  m_systemManager->GetMessageHandler()->
    Subscribe(EntityMessage::Direction_Changed, this);
```

```
    m_systemManager->GetMessageHandler()->
      Subscribe(EntityMessage::Frame_Change, this);
}
```

We want entities with a position component, as well as an emitter and/or listener component. The message of type `Direction_Changed` is also subscribed to, as well as `Frame_Change`.

Updating these components looks like this:

```
void S_Sound::Update(float l_dT){
  EntityManager* entities = m_systemManager->GetEntityManager();
  for (auto &entity : m_entities){
    auto c_pos = entities->
      GetComponent<C_Position>(entity, Component::Position);
    auto position = c_pos->GetPosition();
    auto elevation = c_pos->GetElevation();

    auto IsListener = entities->
      HasComponent(entity, Component::SoundListener);
    if (IsListener){
      sf::Listener::setPosition(
        MakeSoundPosition(position, elevation));
    }

    if (!entities->HasComponent(entity, Component::SoundEmitter))
    { continue; }
    auto c_snd = entities->
     GetComponent<C_SoundEmitter>(entity,Component::SoundEmitter);
    if (c_snd->GetSoundID() == -1){ continue; }
    if (!IsListener){
      if (!m_soundManager->SetPosition(c_snd->GetSoundID(),
        MakeSoundPosition(position, elevation)))
      { c_snd->SetSoundID(-1); }
    } else {
      if (!m_soundManager->IsPlaying(c_snd->GetSoundID())){
        c_snd->SetSoundID(-1);
      }
    }
  }
}
```

The entity is checked for being a sound listener. If it is, the SFML's sound listener position is set to the position of the entity, with elevation included. We utilize a private helper method here, to construct a 3D vector, which will be covered shortly.

If the entity has a sound emitter component, and its sound identifier isn't equal to −1, which would indicate that no sounds are playing, the sound's position is attempted to be updated, provided the entity isn't a sound listener. If either the position update fails, or the sound is no longer playing, its identifier is set back to −1.

Next up is message handling:

```
void S_Sound::Notify(const Message& l_message){
  if (!HasEntity(l_message.m_receiver)){ return; }
  EntityManager* entities = m_systemManager->GetEntityManager();
  auto IsListener = entities->
    HasComponent(l_message.m_receiver, Component::SoundListener);
  EntityMessage m = static_cast<EntityMessage>(l_message.m_type);
  switch (m){
  case EntityMessage::Direction_Changed:
  {
    if (!IsListener){ return; }
    Direction dir = static_cast<Direction>(l_message.m_int);
    switch (dir){
    case Direction::Up:
      sf::Listener::setDirection(0, 0, -1); break;
    case Direction::Down:
      sf::Listener::setDirection(0, 0, 1); break;
    case Direction::Left:
      sf::Listener::setDirection(-1, 0, 0); break;
    case Direction::Right:
      sf::Listener::setDirection(1, 0, 0); break;
    }
  }
    break;
  case EntityMessage::Frame_Change:
    if (!entities->
      HasComponent(l_message.m_receiver,Component::SoundEmitter))
    { return; }
    auto state = entities->
      GetComponent<C_State>(l_message.m_receiver,Component::State)
      ->GetState();
    auto sound = EntitySound::None;
    if(state ==EntityState::Walking){sound=EntitySound::Footstep; }
    else if (state == EntityState::Attacking){
      sound = EntitySound::Attack;
    } else if (state == EntityState::Hurt){
      sound = EntitySound::Hurt;
    } else if (state == EntityState::Dying){
      sound = EntitySound::Death;
    }
    if (sound == EntitySound::None){ return; }
```

```
    EmitSound(l_message.m_receiver, sound, false,
      IsListener, l_message.m_int);
    break;
  }
}
```

We should only care about the direction change message if our entity is a sound listener, in which case the global sound listener direction is simply updated to reflect the changes.

If a frame is changed, we make sure the entity is a sound emitter first. If it is, its current state is matched to a sound type that would play. The private EmitSound method is then invoked:

```cpp
void S_Sound::EmitSound(const EntityId& l_entity,
  const EntitySound& l_sound, bool l_useId, bool l_relative,
  int l_checkFrame)
{
  if (!HasEntity(l_entity)){ return; }
  if (!m_systemManager->GetEntityManager()->
    HasComponent(l_entity, Component::SoundEmitter))
  { return; }
  EntityManager* entities = m_systemManager->GetEntityManager();
  auto c_snd = entities->GetComponent<C_SoundEmitter>(
    l_entity, Component::SoundEmitter);
  if (c_snd->GetSoundID() != -1 && l_useId){ return; }
  if (l_checkFrame != -1 &&
    !c_snd->IsSoundFrame(l_sound, l_checkFrame))
  { return; }
  auto c_pos = entities->
    GetComponent<C_Position>(l_entity, Component::Position);
  auto pos = (l_relative ?
   sf::Vector3f(0.f, 0.f, 0.f) :
   MakeSoundPosition(c_pos->GetPosition(),c_pos->GetElevation()));
  if (l_useId){
    c_snd->SetSoundID(m_soundManager->Play(
      c_snd->GetSound(l_sound), pos));
  } else {
    m_soundManager->Play(c_snd->GetSound(l_sound),
      pos, false, l_relative);
  }
}
```

After all the component and entity checks have passed, the sound emitter is checked for not emitting another sound already in case we want to use the existing ID. The sound frame is then checked, and the position for the sound is calculated based on whether the entity is a listener or not. Finally, based on whether we're using the sound ID or not, the sound manager's `Play` method is invoked, and its return sound ID is possibly stored.

To conclude the sound topic within ECS, as well as the entire ECS portion of this chapter, let's look at how we construct a 3D sound position based on the entity's x and y positions, as well as its elevation:

```
sf::Vector3f S_Sound::MakeSoundPosition(
    const sf::Vector2f& l_entityPos, unsigned int l_elevation)
{
    return sf::Vector3f(
        l_entityPos.x,
        static_cast<float>(l_elevation * Sheet::Tile_Size),
        l_entityPos.y
    );
}
```

The `z` member of `sf::Vector3f` is used to store the *height*, which is simply the elevation multiplied by the tile size.

Implementing the menu state

With most of the backend already covered, we're ready to move towards the front, and start working on more interactive aspects of the project, such as interfaces. Let's start by creating a main menu:

```
void State_MainMenu::OnCreate(){
    auto context = m_stateMgr->GetContext();
    GUI_Manager* gui = context->m_guiManager;
    gui->LoadInterface("MainMenu.interface", "MainMenu");
    gui->GetInterface("MainMenu")->SetPosition(
        sf::Vector2f(250.f, 168.f));
    EventManager* eMgr = context->m_eventManager;
    eMgr->AddCallback("MainMenu_Play", &State_MainMenu::Play, this);
    eMgr->AddCallback("MainMenu_Quit", &State_MainMenu::Quit, this);
}
```

All of these classes have already been covered in `Chapter 1`, *Under the Hood – Setting up the Backend*, but let us have a quick rundown of what this does once more. After we obtain the shared context, a main menu interface is loaded and positioned on screen. The `m_eventManager` is then used to bind the main menu button clicks to methods of this class.

These resources/bindings obviously have to be removed when the state is destroyed:

```
void State_MainMenu::OnDestroy(){
  m_stateMgr->GetContext()->m_guiManager->
    RemoveInterface(StateType::Game, "MainMenu");
  EventManager* eMgr = m_stateMgr->GetContext()->m_eventManager;
  eMgr->RemoveCallback(StateType::MainMenu, "MainMenu_Play");
  eMgr->RemoveCallback(StateType::MainMenu, "MainMenu_Quit");
}
```

Upon activation of the main menu state, we are going to want to check if a game state has already been added:

```
void State_MainMenu::Activate(){
  auto& play = *m_stateMgr->GetContext()->m_guiManager->
    GetInterface("MainMenu")->GetElement("Play");
  if (m_stateMgr->HasState(StateType::Game)){
    // Resume
    play.SetText("Resume");
  } else {
    // Play
    play.SetText("Play");
  }
}
```

This ensures that the first button in the menu accurately reflects the existence/lack of a game state.

Finally, here are the callbacks of the main menu buttons:

```
void State_MainMenu::Play(EventDetails* l_details){
  m_stateMgr->SwitchTo(StateType::Game);
}
void State_MainMenu::Quit(EventDetails* l_details){
  m_stateMgr->GetContext()->m_wind->Close();
}
```

In case of the play button being clicked, we switch to a game state, whether or not it exists yet. The quit button, on the other hand, would reach the window class and close it.

Implementing the game state

Now it's getting more interesting. The game state is where all of the fun happens, so we need to make sure it's set up properly. Let us start, as per usual, with the creation of the state:

```
void State_Game::OnCreate() {
  auto context = m_stateMgr->GetContext();
  EventManager* evMgr = context->m_eventManager;

  evMgr->AddCallback("Key_Escape", &State_Game::MainMenu, this);
  evMgr->AddCallback("Player_MoveLeft",
    &State_Game::PlayerMove, this);
  evMgr->AddCallback("Player_MoveRight",
    &State_Game::PlayerMove, this);
  evMgr->AddCallback("Player_MoveUp",
    &State_Game::PlayerMove, this);
  evMgr->AddCallback("Player_MoveDown",
    &State_Game::PlayerMove, this);

  sf::Vector2u size = context->m_wind->GetWindowSize();
  m_view.setSize(static_cast<float>(size.x),
    static_cast<float>(size.y));
  m_view.setCenter(static_cast<float>(size.x) / 2,
    static_cast<float>(size.y) / 2);
  m_view.zoom(0.6f);

  auto loading = m_stateMgr->
    GetState<State_Loading>(StateType::Loading);
  context->m_gameMap->AddFile(
    Utils::GetWorkingDirectory() + "media/Maps/map1.map");
  loading->AddLoader(context->m_gameMap);
  loading->SetManualContinue(true);
  context->m_soundManager->PlayMusic("TownTheme", 50.f, true);
}
```

First, all of the relevant events we're interested in are bound to methods of this class. This includes the escape key, which simply switches back to the menu state, and four player movement keys. The view of this state is then set up to be zoomed in slightly more, just to be able to see the character better.

The last couple of lines obtain the loading state, and add the game map and the tile set to it as loaders right after the map and tile set files to be loaded are added.

Naturally, these callbacks are going to need to be unbound upon the destruction of the state:

```
void State_Game::OnDestroy(){
    auto context = m_stateMgr->GetContext();
    EventManager* evMgr = context->m_eventManager;
    evMgr->RemoveCallback(StateType::Game, "Key_Escape");
    evMgr->RemoveCallback(StateType::Game, "Key_O");
    evMgr->RemoveCallback(StateType::Game, "Player_MoveLeft");
    evMgr->RemoveCallback(StateType::Game, "Player_MoveRight");
    evMgr->RemoveCallback(StateType::Game, "Player_MoveUp");
    evMgr->RemoveCallback(StateType::Game, "Player_MoveDown");
    context->m_gameMap->PurgeMap();
    context->m_gameMap->GetTileSet()->Purge();
}
```

 Note that both the game map and the tile set are both purged here as well.

Updating the game state only comes down to updating its own camera, alongside the game map and the ECS system manager:

```
void State_Game::Update(const sf::Time& l_time){
    auto context = m_stateMgr->GetContext();
    UpdateCamera();
    context->m_gameMap->Update(l_time.asSeconds());
    context->m_systemManager->Update(l_time.asSeconds());
}
```

The camera (or the view) of the state is updated like so:

```
void State_Game::UpdateCamera(){
    if (m_player == -1){ return; }
    SharedContext* context = m_stateMgr->GetContext();
    auto pos = m_stateMgr->GetContext()->m_entityManager->
        GetComponent<C_Position>(m_player, Component::Position);

    m_view.setCenter(pos->GetPosition());
    context->m_wind->GetRenderWindow()->setView(m_view);

    sf::FloatRect viewSpace = context->m_wind->GetViewSpace();
    if (viewSpace.left <= 0){
```

```
        m_view.setCenter(viewSpace.width / 2, m_view.getCenter().y);
        context->m_wind->GetRenderWindow()->setView(m_view);
    } else if (viewSpace.left + viewSpace.width >
        (context->m_gameMap->GetMapSize().x) * Sheet::Tile_Size)
    {
        m_view.setCenter(
            ((context->m_gameMap->GetMapSize().x) * Sheet::Tile_Size) -
              (viewSpace.width / 2),
            m_view.getCenter().y);
        context->m_wind->GetRenderWindow()->setView(m_view);
    }

    if (viewSpace.top <= 0){
        m_view.setCenter(m_view.getCenter().x, viewSpace.height / 2);
        context->m_wind->GetRenderWindow()->setView(m_view);
    } else if (viewSpace.top + viewSpace.height >
        (context->m_gameMap->GetMapSize().y) * Sheet::Tile_Size)
    {
        m_view.setCenter(
            m_view.getCenter().x,
            ((context->m_gameMap->GetMapSize().y) * Sheet::Tile_Size) -
              (viewSpace.height / 2));
        context->m_wind->GetRenderWindow()->setView(m_view);
    }
}
```

This can look like a lot, but the basic gist of it is first obtaining the position of our player, and then using those coordinates to either centre the view on, or position it in such a way that the very edge of the map is at the edge of the view. The idea is not moving the state view beyond the borders of the map.

Drawing is also fairly straightforward:

```
void State_Game::Draw(){
    auto context = m_stateMgr->GetContext();
    for (unsigned int i = 0; i < Sheet::Num_Layers; ++i){
        context->m_gameMap->Draw(i);
        m_stateMgr->GetContext()->m_systemManager->Draw(
            m_stateMgr->GetContext()->m_wind, i);
    }
}
```

A loop is started for each layer/elevation the game map supports. The map data of that layer is drawn first, and is followed by the system manager drawing entities on that layer.

Let us take a look at the callback method for our player movement:

```
void State_Game::PlayerMove(EventDetails* l_details){
  Message msg((MessageType)EntityMessage::Move);
  if (l_details->m_name == "Player_MoveLeft"){
    msg.m_int = static_cast<int>(Direction::Left);
  } else if (l_details->m_name == "Player_MoveRight"){
    msg.m_int = static_cast<int>(Direction::Right);
  } else if (l_details->m_name == "Player_MoveUp"){
    msg.m_int = static_cast<int>(Direction::Up);
  } else if (l_details->m_name == "Player_MoveDown"){
    msg.m_int = static_cast<int>(Direction::Down);
  }
  msg.m_receiver = m_player;
  m_stateMgr->GetContext()->m_systemManager->
    GetMessageHandler()->Dispatch(msg);
}
```

Whenever this is invoked, a new `Move` message is constructed. The direction it carries is set, based on the actual event name. After the receiving entity (the player) is stored, the message is dispatched.

Lastly, we have one callback and the state's activation method:

```
void State_Game::MainMenu(EventDetails* l_details){
  m_stateMgr->SwitchTo(StateType::MainMenu);
}

void State_Game::Activate() {
  auto map = m_stateMgr->GetContext()->m_gameMap;

  m_player = map->GetPlayerId();
  map->Redraw();
}
```

If the *Esc* key is pressed, we simply switch to the main menu state. If the state is then switched back to `Game`, the `Activate` method of it is invoked. We use that functionality to re-obtain the player ID, in case it changed.

The main game class

All we have left to do now is to put everything together. We're going to be using a Game class for that, so let's take a look at it:

```
class Game{
public:
  Game();
  ~Game();
  void Update();
  void Render();
  void LateUpdate();
  sf::Time GetElapsed();
  Window* GetWindow();
private:
  void SetUpClasses();
  void SetUpECS();
  void SetUpStates();
  void RestartClock();
  sf::Clock m_clock;
  sf::Time m_elapsed;
  SharedContext m_context;
  RandomGenerator m_rand;
  Window m_window;
  TextureManager m_textureManager;
  FontManager m_fontManager;
  AudioManager m_audioManager;
  SoundManager m_soundManager;
  GUI_Manager m_guiManager;
  SystemManager m_systemManager;
  EntityManager m_entityManager;
  Map m_gameMap;
  std::unique_ptr<StateManager> m_stateManager;
};
```

This class holds all of the classes that we covered, so let us begin setting them up in the constructor:

```
Game::Game()
  : m_window("Chapter 2", sf::Vector2u(800, 600), false),
  m_entityManager(&m_systemManager, &m_textureManager),
  m_guiManager(m_window.GetEventManager(), &m_context),
  m_soundManager(&m_audioManager),
  m_gameMap(&m_window, &m_entityManager, &m_textureManager)
{
  SetUpClasses();
  SetUpECS();
```

```
    SetUpStates();

    m_fontManager.RequireResource("Main");
    m_stateManager->SwitchTo(StateType::Intro);
}


Game::~Game(){ m_fontManager.ReleaseResource("Main"); }
```

The initializer list is used to set up whatever dependencies our classes have that need to be satisfied inside their constructors. The rest of the constructor body is used to invoke three private *setup* methods, as well as to require the main font that is to be used throughout the game, and switch to the Intro state.

We're going to need a couple of basic setters and getters from this class as well:

```
sf::Time Game::GetElapsed(){ return m_clock.getElapsedTime(); }
void Game::RestartClock(){ m_elapsed = m_clock.restart(); }
Window* Game::GetWindow(){ return &m_window; }
```

With that out of the way, let us actually update all of our code:

```
void Game::Update(){
  m_window.Update();
  m_stateManager->Update(m_elapsed);
  m_guiManager.Update(m_elapsed.asSeconds());
  m_soundManager.Update(m_elapsed.asSeconds());

  GUI_Event guiEvent;
  while (m_context.m_guiManager->PollEvent(guiEvent)){
    m_window.GetEventManager()->HandleEvent(guiEvent);
  }
}
```

After the relevant managers are updated, the GUI events are polled and passed to the event manager to be handled.

Next, let us take a look at what needs to happen during the Render call:

```
void Game::Render(){
  m_window.BeginDraw();
  // Render here.
  m_stateManager->Draw();
  m_guiManager.Render(m_window.GetRenderWindow());
  m_window.EndDraw();
}
```

This is fairly basic as well. Since we're going to always want to draw states, the state manager's `Draw` call is placed here. On top of that (quite literally), we're going to always draw the GUIs.

A nice little feature to have is a late update that can be used to process anything that can't go into regular updates:

```
void Game::LateUpdate(){
    m_stateManager->ProcessRequests();
    RestartClock();
}
```

The state manager's removal requests are processed here, in addition to the game clock being restarted.

One of the three private methods invoked in the constructor that helps us set up all the classes can be implemented like so:

```
void Game::SetUpClasses() {
    m_clock.restart();
    m_context.m_rand = &m_rand;
    srand(static_cast<unsigned int>(time(nullptr)));
    m_systemManager.SetEntityManager(&m_entityManager);

    m_context.m_wind = &m_window;
    m_context.m_eventManager = m_window.GetEventManager();
    m_context.m_textureManager = &m_textureManager;
    m_context.m_fontManager = &m_fontManager;
    m_context.m_audioManager = &m_audioManager;
    m_context.m_soundManager = &m_soundManager;
    m_context.m_gameMap = &m_gameMap;
    m_context.m_systemManager = &m_systemManager;
    m_context.m_entityManager = &m_entityManager;
    m_context.m_guiManager = &m_guiManager;

    m_stateManager = std::make_unique<StateManager>(&m_context);
    m_gameMap.SetStateManager(m_stateManager.get());
}
```

After the random number generator is seeded, we need to make sure to bind every single class to the shared context, in order to be able to access them anywhere a service locator pattern is relied upon.

Another set up function we invoked deals with setting up the entity component system:

```
void Game::SetUpECS() {
  m_entityManager.AddComponentType<C_Position>(
    Component::Position);
  m_entityManager.AddComponentType<C_SpriteSheet>(
    Component::SpriteSheet);
  m_entityManager.AddComponentType<C_State>(Component::State);
  m_entityManager.AddComponentType<C_Movable>(Component::Movable);
  m_entityManager.AddComponentType<C_Controller>(
    Component::Controller);
  m_entityManager.AddComponentType<C_Collidable>(
    Component::Collidable);
  m_entityManager.AddComponentType<C_SoundEmitter>(
    Component::SoundEmitter);
  m_entityManager.AddComponentType<C_SoundListener>(
    Component::SoundListener);

  m_systemManager.AddSystem<S_State>(System::State);
  m_systemManager.AddSystem<S_Control>(System::Control);
  m_systemManager.AddSystem<S_Movement>(System::Movement);
  m_systemManager.AddSystem<S_Collision>(System::Collision);
  m_systemManager.AddSystem<S_SheetAnimation>(
    System::SheetAnimation);
  m_systemManager.AddSystem<S_Sound>(System::Sound);
  m_systemManager.AddSystem<S_Renderer>(System::Renderer);

  m_systemManager.GetSystem<S_Collision>(System::Collision)->
    SetMap(&m_gameMap);
  m_systemManager.GetSystem<S_Movement>(System::Movement)->
    SetMap(&m_gameMap);
  m_systemManager.GetSystem<S_Sound>(System::Sound)->
    SetUp(&m_audioManager, &m_soundManager);
}
```

Here, all of the component types and systems are added and set up for use. The collision and movement systems need to have access to the game map, while the sound system relies on the audio and sound managers.

The last bit of setup is related to states and their dependents:

```
void Game::SetUpStates() {
  m_stateManager->AddDependent(m_context.m_eventManager);
  m_stateManager->AddDependent(&m_guiManager);
  m_stateManager->AddDependent(&m_soundManager);
  m_stateManager->RegisterState<State_Intro>(StateType::Intro);
  m_stateManager->RegisterState<State_MainMenu>(
    StateType::MainMenu);
  m_stateManager->RegisterState<State_Game>(StateType::Game);
}
```

The event, GUI, and sound managers all rely on being kept up to date on all state changes, so they must be registered as dependents. Also, our three main state types that we will be using are registered as well, so that they can be created using the factory method inside the state manager.

The final bit of code

Lastly, the main entry point of our application is defined inside the main function, like so:

```
void main(int argc, void** argv[]){
  // Program entry point.
  {
    Game game;
    while(!game.GetWindow()->IsDone()){
      game.Update();
      game.Render();
      game.LateUpdate();
    }
  }
}
```

After an instance of `Game` is set up, we begin a `while` loop that keeps running until the `Window` instance is closed. Inside the loop, we update the game, render it, and call the late update method as well, for all of those post-rendering tasks.

Summary

With that, it's a good time to wrap up. If you have followed through to the end, congratulations! You have just built a basic, fully functioning game out of nothing but a couple of states, some components, and systems. This chapter, much like the one before, is quite condensed, so feel free to look through the code and feel comfortable with its structure.

In the next chapter, we're going to be focusing solely on implementing and using particle systems in order to really add some life to the bare-bones game we have made. See you there!

3
Make It Rain! - Building a Particle System

Having the right amount of interactivity in any given game is incredibly important. Whether it amuses the player by having their consequences start chain reactions that eventually impact their state, or it simply means that the controls and input management feel just right, one cannot deny that this is one of the few things that can either make or break a game. While the latter is quite important, it's not the smooth navigation of menus that draw most gamers in, which is why in this chapter we are going to be focusing on environmental interactions, as well as stylization through the means of particle systems.

In this chapter, we're going to be covering the following topics:

- Benefits of the **Structure of Arrays** storage pattern
- Architecture and implementation of a flexible particle system
- Creation of different types of generator and updater objects that allow a wide variety of effects to be created

There is quite a bit to learn, so let us not waste any time and dive right in!

Use of copyrighted resources

As always, let us begin by acknowledging all of the generous artists out there, who make all of this possible by providing assets under incredibly flexible licenses:

- *misc png* by *dbszabo1* under the **CC0** license (public domain): http://dbszabo1.d
  eviantart.com/art/misc-png-316228902

- *Jillcreation-overlay-cloud* by *Juan Story* under the **CC0** license (public domain): `http://www.effecthub.com/item/5358`
- *[LPC] Leaf Recolor* by *William.Thompsonj* under the **CC-BY-SA 3.0** and **GPL 3.0** licenses: `http://opengameart.org/content/lpc-leaf-recolor`

Particle system basics

There are quite a few things we first need to cover in order to get to the more meaty parts of implementing the particle system. Understanding certain concepts is key to making our system work as intended, starting with the way data is stored.

Array of structs versus struct of arrays

It may be tempting at first to simply stick all of the data a particle has into a single class, give it some custom methods for handling certain situations, and store all of these objects in some generic container, as shown here:

```
                            S myArray[50];

struct S{                struct S{                struct S{
    int m_x;                 int m_x;                 int m_x;
    int m_y;                 int m_y;                 int m_y;
    std::string m_name;      std::string m_name;      std::string m_name;
    ...                      ...                      ...           • • •
};                       };                       };
```

While it's certainly easier this way, it doesn't help with performance at all. Keep in mind that we're probably going to be dealing with thousands, if not tens of thousands of instances of particles, all of which need to be updated in a variety of different ways. A simple update loop that works with particles may end up making the cache look like this:

0			1			2		
m_x	m_y	m_name	m_x	m_y	m_name	m_x	m_y	m_name	...

This is terrible as far as performance is concerned, because if we only need to work with positions, that means all of the additional space in the cache that could be used to store positions of other particles now holds useless data that will not be used at all, at least not now. In turn, when it's time to update another particle and its position is requested, it will most likely not be found inside the cache, resulting in a cache miss and time wasted.

A much better scenario would look like this:

This is much better in terms of performance, as all of the data that exists in the cache is guaranteed to be used. How do we achieve such a result? By storing different particle properties in their own containers, where the memory is ensured to be contiguous, as shown here:

```
struct S{
    int m_x[50];
    int m_y[50];
    std::string m_name[50];
    ...
};
```

Storage, however, isn't everything. We must also make sure that whenever we are working with structures such as this, only the relevant and necessary data is being used. That part, however, will be addressed later down the line.

Storing particles

With the key concept out of the way, let us take a look at how particles can be stored using the **SoA** pattern:

```
class ParticleContainer {
public:
    ...
    const static size_t Max_Particles = 3000;
```

```
    sf::Vector3f m_position[Max_Particles];
    sf::Vector3f m_velocity[Max_Particles];
    sf::Vector3f m_acceleration[Max_Particles];
    sf::Vector2f m_startSize[Max_Particles];
    sf::Vector2f m_currentSize[Max_Particles];
    sf::Vector2f m_finalSize[Max_Particles];
    sf::Color m_startColor[Max_Particles];
    sf::Color m_currentColor[Max_Particles];
    sf::Color m_finalColor[Max_Particles];
    std::string m_texture[Max_Particles];
    sf::RectangleShape m_drawable[Max_Particles];
    float m_startRotation[Max_Particles];
    float m_currentRotation[Max_Particles];
    float m_finalRotation[Max_Particles];
    float m_lifespan[Max_Particles];
    float m_maxLifespan[Max_Particles];
    bool m_gravity[Max_Particles];
    bool m_addBlend[Max_Particles];
    bool m_alive[Max_Particles];

    size_t m_countAlive;
    TextureManager* m_textureManager;
protected:
    ...
};
```

There are a couple of ways particle properties can be stored and accounted for. Here, we're using C-style arrays along with a static constant that denotes their sizes. All of these properties, as well as their purposes, will be covered in later segments of the chapter.

A few extra things that are beneficial to keep track of here are the count of particles that are still alive and a pointer to the texture manager, since some of these suckers may be using textures that need to be grabbed and released. They are, of course, set up properly inside the constructor:

```
ParticleContainer(TextureManager* l_textureManager)
  : m_textureManager(l_textureManager), m_countAlive(0)
{ Reset(); }

~ParticleContainer(){
  for (size_t i = 0; i < Max_Particles; ++i){
    if (m_texture[i].empty()) { continue; }
    m_textureManager->ReleaseResource(m_texture[i]);
  }
}
```

The destructor of this container class has a fairly simple job. All it needs to do, in order to not leave any loose ends, is loop through every particle stored and check if it is using a texture, which is just a string identifier. If it is, the texture is released.

Another fairly important task that was left up to the constructor is resetting all of the allocated memory for the particles. This is left to the `Reset()` method:

```
void Reset(){
    for (size_t i = 0; i < Max_Particles; ++i) { ResetParticle(i); }
    m_countAlive = 0;
}
```

The `ResetParticle` private method is invoked for each single particle in the list. It is responsible for actually zeroing all of the data out to make sure the next particle that gets the same identifier will not possess certain properties carried over from the previous particle that owned it.

In order to actually manage the SoA structure efficiently, we're going to be using these two key methods for enabling and disabling a particular ID:

```
void Enable(size_t l_id){
    if (m_countAlive >= Max_Particles) { return; }
    m_alive[l_id] = true;
    Swap(l_id, m_countAlive);
    ++m_countAlive;
}

void Disable(size_t l_id){
    if (!m_countAlive) { return; }
    ResetParticle(l_id);
    Swap(l_id, m_countAlive - 1);
    --m_countAlive;
}
```

A sanity check is performed first in order to make sure we're not enabling any particles if the maximum amount already exists, or disabling any if there are no active ones. Enabling a particle simply requires its *alive* flag to be set to *true*, while disabling calls for a complete reset. All of the data stored at l_id is then swapped with either the element after the last active particle when enabling in order to make it last, or with the very last particle when disabling. Consider the following illustration:

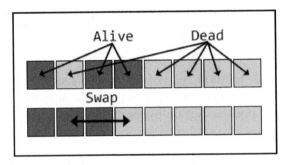

Although it covers the scenario of disabling a particle, the same basic principle holds up for enabling as well.

Actual data swapping isn't a very complicated process:

```
void Swap(size_t l_first, size_t l_second) {
  std::swap(m_position[l_first], m_position[l_second]);
  std::swap(m_velocity[l_first], m_velocity[l_second]);
  std::swap(m_acceleration[l_first], m_acceleration[l_second]);
  std::swap(m_startSize[l_first], m_startSize[l_second]);
  ...
}
```

It simply invokes std::swap on every single particle property at the l_first and l_second indices.

Finally, we get to the actual reset code for a single particle:

```
void ResetParticle(size_t l_id){
  m_alive[l_id] = false;
  m_gravity[l_id] = false;
  m_addBlend[l_id] = false;
  m_lifespan[l_id] = 0.f;
  m_maxLifespan[l_id] = 0.f;
  m_position[l_id] = { 0.f, 0.f, 0.f };
  m_velocity[l_id] = { 0.f, 0.f, 0.f };
  m_acceleration[l_id] = { 0.f, 0.f, 0.f };
  m_startRotation[l_id] = 0.f;
```

```
m_currentRotation[l_id] = 0.f;
m_finalRotation[l_id] = 0.f;
m_startSize[l_id] = { 0.f, 0.f };
m_currentSize[l_id] = { 0.f, 0.f };
m_finalSize[l_id] = { 0.f, 0.f };
m_startColor[l_id] = { 0, 0, 0, 0 };
m_currentColor[l_id] = { 0, 0, 0, 0 };
m_finalColor[l_id] = { 0, 0, 0, 0 };
if (!m_texture[l_id].empty()){
    m_textureManager->ReleaseResource(m_texture[l_id]);
    m_texture[l_id].clear();
    m_drawable[l_id].setTexture(nullptr);
}
}
```

Predictably, every single particle parameter is reset to an appropriate default value at the provided index. If the texture identifier is not empty, the resource also gets released, since it is no longer needed.

Particle system architecture

In order to cater for the way particles are stored and still provide a means of updating, interaction, and flexibility to the system, we must carefully address its architecture. Let's begin by breaking it down into smaller parts that will be easier to manage on their own:

- **Emitter:**an object that exists in the world and acts as a particle spawner. It has access to a list of generators that each emitted particle is fed through before it gets spawned.
- **Generator:**this belongs to a list of other similar objects that have direct access to particle properties and modify them according to their own, pre-defined rules in order to achieve a certain look.
- **Updater:**one of many objects owned by the particle system, and designed to only use the data it needs for a specific task, which is always related to updating particles in a specific way.
- **Force applicator:**a small data structure, used by one of the updaters in order to create *forces* in the world, which physically interact with the particles.

Let us take some time and look at each individual piece in more depth.

The generator

A generator within this context is going to act as a stamp in a way. It will take in a range of particles, the properties of which are going to be adjusted according to the type of generator that received them. Consider this illustration:

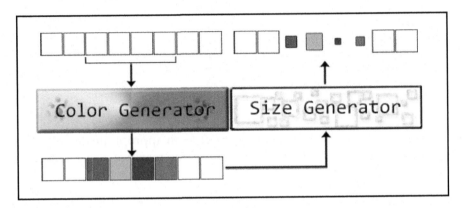

A specific generator can be almost considered as a stamp of sorts. Some of the properties it imprints on a particle can be random, while others are constant. Either way, once a few particles are fed into it, they come out *stamped* with the properties that the generator is responsible for.

All the generators we're going to be implementing need to be generalized, which is why they all must obey by the provided interface:

```
class BaseGenerator {
public:
  virtual ~BaseGenerator() {}
  virtual void Generate(Emitter* l_emitter,
    ParticleContainer* l_particles, size_t l_from, size_t l_to)=0;
  friend std::stringstream& operator >> (
    std::stringstream& l_stream, BaseGenerator& b)
  {
    b.ReadIn(l_stream);
    return l_stream;
  }

  virtual void ReadIn(std::stringstream& l_stream) {}
};
```

First, the `Generate()` method needs some explaining. It takes in a pointer to the `Emitter` instance that owns it. It also takes a pointer to the particle container it's going to be working with. The last two arguments are particle IDs that form a range, which represents particles that will be enabled inside the container. The range itself is going to be calculated inside the emitter that owns the generator.

This base class also allows derivative generators to implement how their properties are loaded from files. This will be important later, when we start actually creating different types of generators.

The emitter

As mentioned previously, an emitter is simply a class that owns a list of generators in order to spawn a specific type of particle. It can be positioned within the world, and is responsible for calculating particle ID ranges for emission by keeping track of its emit rate. Let's take a look at the header of the `Emitter` class:

```
class Emitter {
public:
  Emitter(const sf::Vector3f& l_position,int l_maxParticles = -1);
  void Update(float l_dT, ParticleContainer* l_particles);
  void SetPosition(const sf::Vector3f& l_position);
  sf::Vector3f GetPosition() const;
  size_t GetEmitRate() const;
  void SetEmitRate(size_t l_nPerSecond);
  void SetParticleSystem(ParticleSystem* l_system);
  void SetGenerators(const std::string& l_generators);
  std::string GetGenerators() const;
  ParticleSystem* GetParticleSystem() const;
private:
  std::string m_generators;
  size_t m_emitRate;
  int m_maxParticles;
  sf::Vector3f m_position;
  float m_accumulator;
  ParticleSystem* m_system;
};
```

As you can see, this class doesn't actually store a list of generator instances. Instead, it stores a string identifier that will be used to obtain the list for a specific style of particles from the particle system.

All of the setters and getters in this class are simple one-line methods that perform exactly as advertised, so we won't be covering them.

Aside all of the other obvious data members, it stores a floating point value named `m_accumulator`, which is going to be used in conjunction with the emit rate. We'll go over it more very shortly. It also stores an `m_maxParticles` data member in order to know if particles should be emitted indefinitely, or if the emitter needs to stop after a certain amount have been created.

Implementing emitter

Let's start with the basics of simply initializing all data members to their default values:

```
Emitter::Emitter(const sf::Vector3f& l_position,
    int l_maxParticles) : m_position(l_position),
  m_maxParticles(l_maxParticles), m_emitRate(0),
  m_accumulator(0.f), m_system(nullptr){}
```

The only real method of importance in this class is obviously the `Update()` method. It's responsible for actually doing all of the heavy lifting when it comes to particle emission:

```
void Emitter::Update(float l_dT, ParticleContainer* l_particles){
  if (m_generators.empty()) { return; }
  auto generatorList = m_system->GetGenerators(m_generators);
  if (!generatorList) { return; }
  m_accumulator += l_dT * m_emitRate;
  if (m_accumulator < 1.f) { return; }
  auto num_particles = static_cast<int>(m_accumulator);
  m_accumulator -= num_particles;
  if (m_maxParticles != -1) {
    if (num_particles > m_maxParticles) {
      num_particles = m_maxParticles;
      m_maxParticles = 0;
    }
    else { m_maxParticles -= num_particles; }
  }
  size_t from = l_particles->m_countAlive;
  size_t to = (l_particles->m_countAlive + num_particles >
    l_particles->Max_Particles ? l_particles->Max_Particles - 1
    : l_particles->m_countAlive + num_particles - 1);

  for (auto& generator : *generatorList){
    generator->Generate(this, l_particles, from, to);
  }
  for (auto i = from; i <= to; ++i){ l_particles->Enable(i); }
  if (!m_maxParticles) { m_system->RemoveEmitter(this); }
}
```

Naturally, the updating is not going to happen if either the generator identifier is empty, or we were unable to obtain the list of generators from the particle system. Provided that isn't the case, the `m_accumulator` data member is added to based on the emit rate and **delta time**. It holds the total number of particles that have yet to be emitted. Since we obviously can't emit half of a particle, or any other fraction for that matter, the accumulator data member is checked to see whether it's less than one. If that's the case, there is nothing to emit/update.

The number of particles to be emitted is then calculated by simply converting the accumulator value to an integer. It is then subtracted from the accumulator, which retains whatever fraction of a particle is left for the next tick.

The way we know an emitter should keep on spitting particles out indefinitely is if its `m_maxParticles` data member is set to -1. If it isn't, the number of particles to be emitted this tick is checked for not having exceeded the limit.

Finally, we get to the interesting part. First, the range of IDs that will be brought back to life is calculated, making sure it doesn't go beyond the maximum number of particles allowed. The generator list for the type of particle the emitter is spitting out is then iterated over, with pointers to the current emitter, and the particle list being passed into their `Generate()` methods, alongside the calculated ranges. The range of particles is then iterated over and re-enabled to be displayed again, and the emitter is checked to see if it needs to be removed, should the `m_maxParticles` data member reach zero.

The updater

In order to breathe life into our particle system, we must constantly keep it updated. Keeping performance in mind, we must stay true to the SoA pattern and only work with the data that is absolutely necessary for a particular scenario, as shown here:

```
sf::Vector3f m_position[50];        Spatial Updater  position += velocity;
sf::Vector3f m_velocity[50];
sf::RectangleShape m_RS[50];        Drawable Updater drawable.setPosition(position);
```

With that in mind, a very basic interface for all updaters can be put together, looking something like this:

```
class BaseUpdater {
public:
  virtual ~BaseUpdater() {}
  virtual void Update(float l_dT,
    ParticleContainer* l_particles) = 0;
};
```

All updaters should ever care about, as you can see, is the delta time and having a pointer to the particle container they are operating on. There is no need to provide it with ranges, as it will be operating on all *alive* particles.

Force applicators

Because we don't want our character to be running around a static, dead environment, some interactivity between events and particles is required. This relationship is established via the means of forces, which impact the kinematic states of particles within reach, as shown here:

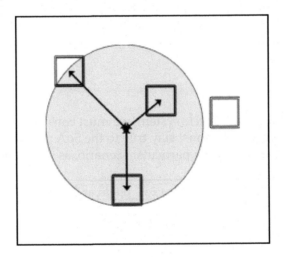

Force applicators are not fundamental to particle systems. All we need to do in order to generalize them is store some data, and let the appropriate updater(s) take care of the logic. Having said that, let us take a look at what we need to store:

```
struct ForceApplicator {
  ForceApplicator(const sf::Vector3f& l_center,
    const sf::Vector3f& l_force, float l_radius)
    : m_center(l_center), m_force(l_force), m_radius(l_radius){}
  sf::Vector3f m_center;
  sf::Vector3f m_force;
  float m_radius;
};
```

Forces can be positioned in the world, so their centers need to be stored. Additionally, a radius of the force is also necessary, in order to figure out the area of impact. Lastly, there can be no impact without first knowing how strong it is. This is where m_force comes in, by allowing force to be defined in all three axes.

Building the particle system class

With all of the building blocks in place, it's time to actually build the particle system class. Let's start with some type definitions:

```
using Updaters = std::unordered_map<std::string,
  std::unique_ptr<BaseUpdater>>;
using EmitterList = std::vector<std::unique_ptr<Emitter>>;
using Emitters = std::unordered_map<StateType, EmitterList>;
using GeneratorList = std::vector<std::unique_ptr<BaseGenerator>>;
using Generators = std::unordered_map<std::string,GeneratorList>;
using RemovedEmitters = std::vector<Emitter*>;
using Particles = std::unordered_map<StateType,
  std::unique_ptr<ParticleContainer>>;
using ForceApplicatorList = std::vector<ForceApplicator>;
using ForceApplicators = std::unordered_map<StateType,
  ForceApplicatorList>;

using GeneratorFactory = std::unordered_map<std::string,
  std::function<BaseGenerator*(void)>>;
```

In order to access any updater we want, we can map them to `string` identifiers. While the updaters aren't state-specific, emitters are. Their lists have to be associated with specific states in order to maintain particles across the entire application. Generators, just like updaters, aren't unique to any particular state, and we want to be able to access them via a string identifier from `Emitter` classes. Speaking of which, as evident from the code we've already covered, emitters can request removal of themselves in case they should stop emitting particles. Since that happens during the update cycle while the class is still in use, a separate list of emitter pointers must be kept for later removal.

Particles themselves are obviously stored within the designated `ParticleContainer` class, but these containers can, obviously, be possessed by different states. A similar idea applies as before, where we mapped state types to different particle containers in order to maintain application-wide particle support. The same exact principle also applies to force applicators.

The last data type we have should be a dead giveaway for the fact that we're going to be using the factory design pattern for producing different types of particle generator. These types will also be tied to string identifiers.

With all of that in mind, it's time to discuss how the `ParticleSystem` class can be implemented, starting with its header:

```
class ParticleSystem : public FileLoader, public StateDependent,
  public MapLoadee
{
public:
  ParticleSystem(StateManager* l_stateManager,
    TextureManager* l_textureMgr, RandomGenerator* l_rand,
    Map* l_map);
  void AddEmitter(std::unique_ptr<Emitter> l_emitter,
    const StateType& l_state = StateType(0));
  void AddForce(ForceApplicator l_force,
    const StateType& l_state = StateType(0));
  void RemoveEmitter(Emitter* l_emitter);

  GeneratorList* GetGenerators(const std::string& l_name);

  TextureManager* GetTextureManager() const;
  RandomGenerator* GetRand() const;

  void CreateState(const StateType& l_state);
  void ChangeState(const StateType& l_state);
  void RemoveState(const StateType& l_state);

  void ReadMapLine(const std::string& l_type,
    std::stringstream& l_stream);
```

```
    void Update(float l_dT);
    void ApplyForce(const sf::Vector3f& l_center,
      const sf::Vector3f& l_force, float l_radius);
    void Draw(Window* l_window, int l_elevation);
private:
    bool ProcessLine(std::stringstream& l_stream);
    void ResetForNextFile();

    template<class T>
    void RegisterGenerator(const std::string& l_name) { ... }

    std::string m_loadingGenerator;
    Particles m_container;
    Particles::iterator m_stateItr;
    Emitters::iterator m_emitterItr;
    Updaters m_updaters;
    Emitters m_emitters;
    Generators m_generators;
    GeneratorFactory m_factory;
    ForceApplicators m_forces;
    RemovedEmitters m_removedEmitters;
    TextureManager* m_textureMgr;
    RandomGenerator* m_rand;
    Map* m_map;
};
```

First, let us examine the inheritance subtleties of this class. Because we are going to have properties of particles saved inside text files, inheritance from `FileLoader` is useful, not to mention we get to offload the work to a separate thread. Also, recall that different states will need to be provided access to our particle system, which means the particle manager must implement methods for adding, changing, and removing states. Lastly, keep in mind that particle emitters and the different forces that impact them may be something game maps contain, so we're also inheriting from the `MapLoadee` class.

The class itself obviously needs access to the texture manager, a pointer to which is later passed down to the classes that need it. The same is true for the random number generator, as well as a pointer to the map instance.

Lastly, note the two highlighted data members of this class, which are both iterators. These are kept around for easier access to data that is state-specific while updating/rendering particles.

Implementing the particle system

Let's start by taking a look at the constructor of this class:

```
ParticleSystem::ParticleSystem(StateManager* l_stateManager,
    TextureManager* l_textureManager, RandomGenerator* l_rand,
    Map* l_map)
    : m_stateManager(l_stateManager),m_textureMgr(l_textureManager),
    m_rand(l_rand), m_map(l_map)
{
    m_updaters.emplace("Lifespan",
        std::make_unique<LifespanUpdater>());
    ...
    RegisterGenerator<PointPosition>("PointPosition");
    ...
}
```

Outside the initializer list that performs all of the data member set-up duties, there is only one other purpose for the constructor here: setting up all of the updaters and generator types. The code we have above is heavily abridged, but the idea remains the same. All of the updaters we want to use are inserted into their container with the appropriate string identifier attached. On the generator side, we invoke a private template method that ties a specific type of a generator to a string identifier. Once again, we are using the factory pattern here.

Adding emitter objects to our particle system is relatively straightforward:

```
void ParticleSystem::AddEmitter(
    std::unique_ptr<Emitter> l_emitter, const StateType& l_state)
{
    l_emitter->SetParticleSystem(this);
    if (!GetGenerators(l_emitter->GetGenerators())) {
        return;
    }
    if (l_state == StateType(0)) {
        if (m_emitterItr == m_emitters.end()) { return; }
        m_emitterItr->second.emplace_back(std::move(l_emitter));
        return;
    }
    auto itr = m_emitters.find(l_state);
    if (itr == m_emitters.end()) { return; }
    itr->second.emplace_back(std::move(l_emitter));
}
```

First, the emitter is provided with a pointer to the particle system for later access. We then check if the emitter's generator list name is valid. It's pointless to have an emitter that is going to be spawning *empty* particles.

As evident from the class header, a default value to the second argument of this method is provided. This gives us a nice way to differentiate whether a user of this class wants to add an emitter to a specific state, or just the current state that is selected. Both of these possibilities are then handled in the remaining chunk of the code.

Force applicators are dealt with in a very similar fashion:

```
void ParticleSystem::AddForce(ForceApplicator l_force,
  const StateType& l_state)
{
  if (l_state == StateType(0)) {
    if (m_stateItr == m_container.end()) { return; }
    m_forces[m_currentState].emplace_back(l_force);
    return;
  }
  auto itr = m_forces.find(l_state);
  if(itr == m_forces.end()) { return; }
  itr->second.emplace_back(l_force);
}
```

Once again, the second argument has a default value, so we handle both the possibilities before attempting to insert the force applicator data inside the appropriate container.

Removal of emitters, as mentioned in the data type section, has two stages. The first stage is simply putting a pointer to the emitter in a designated list:

```
void ParticleSystem::RemoveEmitter(Emitter* l_emitter) {
  m_removedEmitters.push_back(l_emitter);
}
```

The actual removal is handled elsewhere. We will be covering that shortly.

Obtaining the generator list is important for the emission process, so naturally, we must have a method for that as well:

```
GeneratorList* ParticleSystem::GetGenerators(
  const std::string& l_name)
{
  auto& itr = m_generators.find(l_name);
  if (itr == m_generators.end()) {
    return nullptr;
  }
  return &itr->second;
}
```

Now, we stumble upon the state-dependent part of the particle system, starting with state creation:

```
void ParticleSystem::CreateState(const StateType& l_state) {
  if (m_container.find(l_state) != m_container.end()) { return; }
  m_container.emplace(l_state,
    std::make_unique<ParticleContainer>(m_textureMgr));
  m_emitters.emplace(l_state, EmitterList());
  m_forces.emplace(l_state, ForceApplicatorList());
  ChangeState(l_state);
}
```

First, a determination needs to be made whether the state being created doesn't already, for some reason, have its own particle container allocated. If it doesn't, one is created and inserted into the state's particle container, as well as an emitter list, and a force applicator list for that same state.

 The CreateState() method of the StateDependent class is the only piece of code that needs to be invoked manually, in case certain states don't need to utilize that particular state dependent resource.

Next, let's discuss how a state can be changed inside a particle system:

```
void ParticleSystem::ChangeState(const StateType& l_state) {
  SetState(l_state);
  m_stateItr = m_container.find(m_currentState);
  m_emitterItr = m_emitters.find(m_currentState);

  auto c = static_cast<CollisionUpdater*>(
    m_updaters["Collision"].get());
  if (l_state == StateType::Game) { c->SetMap(m_map); }
  else { c->SetMap(nullptr); }
  auto f = static_cast<ForceUpdater*>(m_updaters["Force"].get());
```

```
    auto& forceItr = m_forces.find(m_currentState);
    if (forceItr == m_forces.end()) {
      f->SetApplicators(nullptr); return;
    }
    f->SetApplicators(&forceItr->second);
  }
```

After a private method for changing its own internal state is invoked, the data member that holds an iterator to the particles of the current state is updated. The same exact thing is done to the emitter iterator.

The next few lines of code may not make much sense within this context, since we have not worked on any updaters yet, but let us cover them anyway. Further down the line, we are going to have updaters for particle collisions and forces. As far as collisions go, the updater only needs to have a pointer to the game map, presuming the current state is Game. ForceUpdater, on the other hand, needs to have access to a list of force applicators for the current state. Both of these types of updater are accommodated here.

Let's wrap up the state modification subject by taking a look at what happens inside a particle system when a state is removed:

```
void ParticleSystem::RemoveState(const StateType& l_state) {
  if (m_stateItr->first == l_state) {
    m_stateItr = m_container.end();
    m_emitterItr = m_emitters.end();
  }
  m_emitters.erase(l_state);
  m_forces.erase(l_state);
  m_container.erase(l_state);
}
```

All we do here is erase data from state-bound containers. Since there are two iterator data members kept around, those too must be reset in case the state being removed matches the current state. Because of the way our state system works, and the order of ChangeState and RemoveState, we don't need to worry about iterators being invalidated.

Our particle system will definitely have plenty of data to load from text files, which is why it inherits from a file loader class. Let us take a look at the method that every single line stream will be fed into:

```
bool ParticleSystem::ProcessLine(std::stringstream& l_stream) {
  std::string type;
  l_stream >> type;
  if (type == "Name") {
    if (!(l_stream >> m_loadingGenerator)) { return false; }
    auto generators = GetGenerators(m_loadingGenerator);
```

```
          if (generators) { return false; }
      } else {
          if (m_loadingGenerator.empty()) { return false; }
          auto itr = m_factory.find(type);
          if (itr == m_factory.end()) { return true; }
          std::unique_ptr<BaseGenerator> generator(itr->second());
          l_stream >> *generator;
          m_generators[m_loadingGenerator].emplace_back(
              std::move(generator));
      }
      return true;
  }
```

The first string of each line, later referred to as type, is extracted. If we have a name, another string is attempted to be extracted, and later checked for matches inside the generator list, in order to avoid duplicates. The name of the generator list is stored inside the `m_loadingGenerator` data member.

If any other type is encountered, it is safe to assume we are dealing with a specific type of generator. If that is the case, the generator list name is first checked that it isnt't being empty, which would indicate a file format problem. The generator factory is then searched for the generator with the type loaded from the file. If it is found, a new generator instance is created through it, the stream object is passed to it to do its own loading via the >> operator, and the final instance is inserted into the generator list for the current type of `m_loadingGenerator`.

Because we're using a data member to keep file information around, it must be reset before attempting to load another file. Our `FileLoader` interface provides such functionality, given this method is overloaded:

```
  void ParticleSystem::ResetForNextFile() {
    m_loadingGenerator.clear();
  }
```

The final base class the particle system is inheriting from, `MapLoadee`, requires us to implement a single method that will handle map file entries with its own custom types:

```
  void ParticleSystem::ReadMapLine(const std::string& l_type,
    std::stringstream& l_stream)
{
  if (l_type == "ParticleEmitter") {
    sf::Vector3f position;
    size_t emitRate;
    std::string generatorType;
    l_stream >> generatorType >> position.x >> position.y >>
      position.z >> emitRate;
```

```
      auto emitter = std::make_unique<Emitter>(position);
      emitter->SetEmitRate(emitRate);
      emitter->SetGenerators(generatorType);
      AddEmitter(std::move(emitter), StateType::Game);
    } else if (l_type == "ForceApplicator") {
      sf::Vector3f position;
      sf::Vector3f force;
      float radius;
      l_stream >> position.x >> position.y >> position.z >>
        force.x >> force.y >> force.z >> radius;
      AddForce(ForceApplicator(position, force, radius),
        StateType::Game);
    }
  }
}
```

As you can see, two different types of map entry are supported by the particle system: `ParticleEmitter` and `ForceApplicator`. In both cases, all of the appropriate data is streamed in and applied to the newly constructed objects, which are then added to the Game state.

Next, let's focus on the method that *makes it all move*, so of speak. It's time to take a look at the Update() method:

```
void ParticleSystem::Update(float l_dT) {
  if (m_stateItr == m_container.end()) { return; }
  for (auto& emitter : m_emitterItr->second) {
    emitter->Update(l_dT, m_stateItr->second.get());
  }
  for (auto& updater : m_updaters){
    updater.second->Update(l_dT, m_stateItr->second.get());
  }
  if (!m_removedEmitters.size()) { return; }
  for (auto& removed : m_removedEmitters) {
    m_emitterItr->second.erase(
      std::remove_if(
        m_emitterItr->second.begin(),
        m_emitterItr->second.end(),
        [removed](std::unique_ptr<Emitter>& emitter) {
          return emitter.get() == removed;
        }
    ));
  }
  m_removedEmitters.clear();
}
```

It really only consists of three basic parts: updating emitters, updating all the different `BaseUpdater` instances, and processing removed emitters. None of this happens if the current state iterator is not valid. Having no particles to work with means we have no work at all.

The updating of emitters and updaters is fairly straightforward. Removal of disposed emitters is not anything too complex either. The container of removed emitter pointers is iterated over, and for each entry, an emitter that is still within the world and has the same memory address is removed from the container.

Finally, we get to the code responsible for getting all of our beautiful particles out on the screen:

```
void ParticleSystem::Draw(Window* l_window, int l_elevation) {
  if (m_stateItr == m_container.end()) { return; }
  auto container = m_stateItr->second.get();
  auto& drawables = container->m_drawable;
  auto& positions = container->m_position;
  auto& blendModes = container->m_addBlend;
  auto view = l_window->GetRenderWindow()->getView();
  auto renderer = l_window->GetRenderer();

  auto state = m_stateManager->GetCurrentStateType();
  if (state == StateType::Game || state == StateType::MapEditor) {
    renderer->UseShader("default");
  } else {
    renderer->DisableShader();
  }

  for (size_t i = 0; i < container->m_countAlive; ++i) {
    if (l_elevation >= 0) {
      if (positions[i].z < l_elevation * Sheet::Tile_Size) {
        continue;
      }
      if (positions[i].z >= (l_elevation + 1) * Sheet::Tile_Size){
        continue;
      }
    } else if (positions[i].z <
      Sheet::Num_Layers * Sheet::Tile_Size)
    { continue; }
    renderer->AdditiveBlend(blendModes[i]);
    renderer->Draw(drawables[i]);
  }
  renderer->AdditiveBlend(false);
}
```

Naturally, if we're in a state that does not have a particle container, no drawing needs to be done. Otherwise, we obtain references to arrays of drawables, their positions and blend modes. Since we want particles to support layering in order to add depth, the second argument of this method takes in the current layer being drawn.

> Note the state checking and use of shaders in this portion of the code. We're essentially controlling which states the particles are shaded in here. The map editor state will be covered in the next two chapters.

If the layer/elevation tests pass, there's one more check we need to make in order to be able to render a particle, and that is whether the particle is currently within the view of the screen.

> This simple AABB collision check obviously does **not** account for particles being rotated. Although the bounds that are checked still contain the entire body of a particle, certain corner-case scenarios may result in it being rendered, while it is rotated in such a way that it should be invisible, yet where the bounding box is still within the view. This can be solved by applying a more sophisticated collision check algorithm, but it isn't going to be covered here.

Finally, after all of the tests have passed, it is time to render the particle. Keep in mind that it is in our best interest here to support two blending modes when it comes to rendering: additive and alpha blending. Luckily, SFML makes it easy for us, and it's only necessary to pass an additional argument to the draw method of a window instance to determine how something is drawn.

Having the ability to switch between blending modes can be useful when rendering some particle types, since they would look more realistic that way. For example, take a look at the same type of particles being rendered with additive blending, versus alpha blending, which is the default mode:

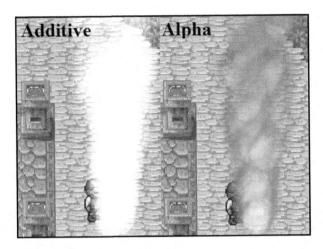

While not all particles are going to take advantage of this blending mode, it's definitely a nice option to have for those that need that extra oomph.

Creating updaters

With the core particle system all built up, it is time to focus on individual bits and pieces that will give our system its functionality and polish. By the time we are done, these are some of the effects that will be possible:

The only way to get there is to keep going, so let us get to it!

Spatial updater

First, and probably the most obvious task is adjusting particle positions based on their kinematic states. As small as they may be, they still operate based on changes in velocity, acceleration, and position:

```
class SpatialUpdater : public BaseUpdater {
public:
  void Update(float l_dT, ParticleContainer* l_particles) {
    auto& velocities = l_particles->m_velocity;
    auto& accelerations = l_particles->m_acceleration;
    for (size_t i = 0; i < l_particles->m_countAlive; ++i) {
      velocities[i] += accelerations[i] * l_dT;
    }
    auto& positions = l_particles->m_position;
    for (size_t i = 0; i < l_particles->m_countAlive; ++i) {
      positions[i] += velocities[i] * l_dT;
    }
  }
};
```

So far, so good! Some of these updaters will have rather small footprints since they perform incredibly simple tasks. All we do here is obtain references to velocity, acceleration and position containers. The data is then manipulated in two separate loops in order to minimize cache misses.

Drawable updater

Next, let's update the drawable bits of our particles. This is where the appropriately named DrawableUpdater comes in:

```
class DrawableUpdater : public BaseUpdater {
public:
  void Update(float l_dT, ParticleContainer* l_particles) {
    auto& positions = l_particles->m_position;
    auto& drawables = l_particles->m_drawable;
    for (size_t i = 0; i < l_particles->m_countAlive; ++i) {
      drawables[i].setPosition(positions[i].x, positions[i].y);
    }
    auto& sizes = l_particles->m_currentSize;
    for (size_t i = 0; i < l_particles->m_countAlive; ++i) {
      drawables[i].setSize(sizes[i]);
    }
    for (size_t i = 0; i < l_particles->m_countAlive; ++i) {
      float ScaleFactor = std::max(
```

```
        (positions[i].z / Sheet::Tile_Size) *
        ScaleToElevationRatio, 1.f);
      drawables[i].setScale(ScaleFactor, ScaleFactor);
    }
    auto& colors = l_particles->m_currentColor;
    for (size_t i = 0; i < l_particles->m_countAlive; ++i) {
      drawables[i].setFillColor(colors[i]);
    }
    auto& rotations = l_particles->m_currentRotation;
    for (size_t i = 0; i < l_particles->m_countAlive; ++i) {
      drawables[i].setRotation(rotations[i]);
    }

    for (size_t i = 0; i < l_particles->m_countAlive; ++i) {
      drawables[i].setOrigin(
        drawables[i].getLocalBounds().width / 2,
        drawables[i].getLocalBounds().height / 2);
    }
  }
  static const float ScaleToElevationRatio;
};

const float DrawableUpdater::ScaleToElevationRatio = 1.5f;
```

This is quite a bit of code, but its essence is incredibly simple. Separate loops are utilized in order to set all of the relevant drawable properties up. We do, however, have something more interesting going on. Note the highlighted portions of the code, all of which are related to scale. As you have probably figured out by now, SFML deals with only two dimensions when it comes to visuals. In order to fake 3D particles flying around, we can utilize drawable scaling. The scale factor itself is capped at *1.f*, so we don't go any smaller than the default particle size. The scale to elevation ratio here is set to *1.5f*, which is debatably the best value, but is obviously up for tweaking. All it is is a simple ratio that the supposed *elevation* of a particle gets multiplied by in order to obtain a scale value, which, when used, should create the illusion of a particle flying towards the camera.

Lifespan updater

Since computer resources, at least during the time of writing this book, are limited, we need to have a good way of disposing of particles when it's time. One good idea is attaching a lifespan to particles, so that after it's supposed to have expired, the particle is gracefully removed from the population:

```
class LifespanUpdater : public BaseUpdater {
public:
```

```
    void Update(float l_dT, ParticleContainer* l_particles) {
      auto& lifespans = l_particles->m_lifespan;
      auto& maxLifespans = l_particles->m_maxLifespan;
      for (size_t i = 0; i < l_particles->m_countAlive;) {
        lifespans[i] += l_dT;
        if (lifespans[i] < maxLifespans[i]) { ++i; continue; }
        l_particles->Disable(i);
      }
    }
};
```

This is a quite simple little updater. The delta time is added to each live particle, which then is checked for having exceeded its lifespan. If it has, the particle is disabled. Keep in mind that disabling the particle will decrease the `m_countAlive` data member of a particle container. For this very reason, we must be careful when incrementing the `i` local variable, in order to not skip any data in the process.

Interpolator

Tons of particle properties are not going to be static throughout their lifetime. Take, for example, the particle color. We may want to fade a particle to complete transparency, or even cycle through a range of colors. All of this can be achieved by interpolating. This process is a good candidate for its own updater class:

```
class Interpolator : public BaseUpdater {
public:
  void Update(float l_dT, ParticleContainer* l_particles) {
    auto& startColors = l_particles->m_startColor;
    auto& currentColors = l_particles->m_currentColor;
    auto& finalColors = l_particles->m_finalColor;
    auto& lifespans = l_particles->m_lifespan;
    auto& maxLifespans = l_particles->m_maxLifespan;
    for (size_t i = 0; i < l_particles->m_countAlive; ++i) {
      if (startColors[i] == finalColors[i]) { continue; }
      currentColors[i].r = Utils::Interpolate<sf::Uint8>(0.f,
        maxLifespans[i], startColors[i].r, finalColors[i].r,
        lifespans[i]);
      currentColors[i].g = Utils::Interpolate<sf::Uint8>(0.f,
        maxLifespans[i], startColors[i].g, finalColors[i].g,
        lifespans[i]);
      currentColors[i].b = Utils::Interpolate<sf::Uint8>(0.f,
        maxLifespans[i], startColors[i].b, finalColors[i].b,
        lifespans[i]);
      currentColors[i].a = Utils::Interpolate<sf::Uint8>(0.f,
        maxLifespans[i], startColors[i].a, finalColors[i].a,
```

```
            lifespans[i]);
    }

    auto& startRotations = l_particles->m_startRotation;
    auto& currentRotations = l_particles->m_currentRotation;
    auto& finalRotations = l_particles->m_finalRotation;

    for (size_t i = 0; i < l_particles->m_countAlive; ++i) {
        if (startRotations[i] == finalRotations[i]) { continue; }
        currentRotations[i] = Utils::Interpolate<float>(0.f,
            maxLifespans[i], startRotations[i], finalRotations[i],
            lifespans[i]);
    }

    auto& startSizes = l_particles->m_startSize;
    auto& currentSizes = l_particles->m_currentSize;
    auto& finalSizes = l_particles->m_finalSize;

    for (size_t i = 0; i < l_particles->m_countAlive; ++i) {
        if (startSizes[i] == finalSizes[i]) { continue; }
        currentSizes[i] = sf::Vector2f(
            Utils::Interpolate<float>(0.f, maxLifespans[i],
                startSizes[i].x, finalSizes[i].x, lifespans[i]),
            Utils::Interpolate<float>(0.f, maxLifespans[i],
                startSizes[i].y, finalSizes[i].y, lifespans[i]));
    }
    }
};
```

Once again, we have lots of code, but the essence of it is basically the same all throughout. The `Interpolate` function, stored within our `Utilities.h` header, takes in a range of time values throughout which we need interpolation, the range of values that are supposed to be interpolated, and the current time value, which determines the output.

The interpolated properties are particle colors, rotations, and sizes. For all three of them, we first check if the starting value is the same as the final value in order to avoid useless computations.

Force updater

During the planning stages of this particle system, we have discussed having different forces in the world that would affect particles. Outside the possibility of having custom forces, we also want to have basic gravity, so that particles with any sort of elevation begin falling down, provided they have the property of being affected by gravity. Let us implement an updater that will allow us to do that:

```cpp
class ForceUpdater : public BaseUpdater {
  friend class ParticleSystem;
public:
  ForceUpdater() : m_applicators(nullptr) {}

  void Update(float l_dT, ParticleContainer* l_particles) {
    auto& velocities = l_particles->m_velocity;
    auto& gravity = l_particles->m_gravity;
    for (size_t i = 0; i < l_particles->m_countAlive; ++i) {
      if (!gravity[i]) { continue; }
      velocities[i].z -= Gravity * l_dT;
    }

    if (!m_applicators) { return; }
    auto& positions = l_particles->m_position;
    for (size_t i = 0; i < l_particles->m_countAlive; ++i) {
      for (auto& force : *m_applicators) {
        Force(force.m_center, force.m_force * l_dT,
          force.m_radius, positions[i], velocities[i]);
      }
    }
  }

  void SetApplicators(ForceApplicatorList* l_list) {
    m_applicators = l_list;
  }

  static const float Gravity;
private:
  void Force(const sf::Vector3f& l_center,
    const sf::Vector3f& l_force, float l_radius,
    sf::Vector3f& l_position, sf::Vector3f& l_velocity)
  { ... }

  ForceApplicatorList* m_applicators;
};

const float ForceUpdater::Gravity = 128.f;
```

The first, and arguably the most important, function of this particular updater is applying gravity to all of the particles that need it. We want to be able to give certain types of particles, such as smoke or fire, the ability to not be affected by the gravitational force, so it's all left up to a flag that can be set. The actual gravitational force is defined as a static `const` data member, and set up underneath the class definition.

Next is the business we have with the force applicators within the world. If the force updater has no pointer to a force applicator list, there is obviously nothing left to do, so we return from the update method. Otherwise, a private `Force()` method is invoked with the force's center, the amount of force adjusted for delta time, its radius, and references to the position and velocity of the particle passed in as arguments:

```
void Force(const sf::Vector3f& l_center,
  const sf::Vector3f& l_force, float l_radius,
  sf::Vector3f& l_position, sf::Vector3f& l_velocity)
{
  sf::Vector3f from(l_center.x - l_radius,
    l_center.y - l_radius, l_center.z - l_radius);
  sf::Vector3f to(l_center.x + l_radius,
    l_center.y + l_radius, l_center.z + l_radius);
  if (l_position.x < from.x) { return; }
  if (l_position.y < from.y) { return; }
  if (l_position.z < from.z) { return; }
  if (l_position.x > to.x) { return; }
  if (l_position.y > to.y) { return; }
  if (l_position.z > to.z) { return; }

  sf::Vector3f distance = l_center - l_position;
  sf::Vector3f a_distance = sf::Vector3f(std::abs(distance.x),
    std::abs(distance.y), std::abs(distance.z));
  float magnitude = std::sqrt(std::pow(a_distance.x, 2) +
    std::pow(a_distance.y, 2) + std::pow(a_distance.z, 2));
  sf::Vector3f normal = sf::Vector3f(
    a_distance.x / magnitude,
    a_distance.y / magnitude,
    a_distance.z / magnitude
  );
  sf::Vector3f loss = sf::Vector3f(
    std::abs(l_force.x) / (l_radius / a_distance.x),
    std::abs(l_force.y) / (l_radius / a_distance.y),
    std::abs(l_force.z) / (l_radius / a_distance.z)
  );
  sf::Vector3f applied = sf::Vector3f(
    (l_force.x > 0 ? l_force.x - loss.x : l_force.x + loss.x),
    (l_force.y > 0 ? l_force.y - loss.y : l_force.y + loss.y),
    (l_force.z > 0 ? l_force.z - loss.z : l_force.z + loss.z)
  );
```

```
applied.x *= normal.x;
applied.y *= normal.y;
applied.z *= normal.z;
if (distance.x < 0) { applied.x = -applied.x; }
if (distance.y < 0) { applied.y = -applied.y; }
if (distance.z < 0) { applied.z = -applied.z; }

l_velocity += applied;
}
```

After the distance ranges are calculated using the center and radius of the force, the position of the particle is tested to see whether it is within the force-affected area. Provided all of the tests pass, the distance is calculated between the center of the force and the particle. It's then used to calculate the absolute distance between them, determine the magnitude of the force, and normalize the vector. Force loss is calculated based on the radii and distances on all three axes, and subtracted from the actual applied force, which is then multiplied by the normal in order to yield the finished product. Depending on the distance sign, we can determine which direction the force should be applied to, which is what the next three lines are for. Finally, after all of that work, we're ready to add the applied force to the particle's velocity.

With the help of this updater, we can actually apply forces to particles even from outside classes, like so:

```
void ParticleSystem::ApplyForce(const sf::Vector3f& l_center,
  const sf::Vector3f& l_force, float l_radius)
{
  if (m_stateItr == m_container.end()) { return; }
  auto f = static_cast<ForceUpdater*>(m_updaters["Force"].get());
  auto container = m_stateItr->second.get();
  auto& positions = container->m_position;
  auto& velocities = container->m_velocity;
  for (size_t i = 0; i < container->m_countAlive; ++i) {
    f->Force(l_center, l_force, l_radius,
      positions[i], velocities[i]);
  }
}
```

While this isn't as useful as, say, having constant forces inside the world, it can still be used for testing purposes.

Collision updater

Another important aspect of particles interacting with the world is handling their collisions. So far, the only real collision we need to worry about is particles hitting the floor; however, actual map collisions could be implemented quite easily with the help of this class:

```
class CollisionUpdater : public BaseUpdater {
public:
  void Update(float l_dT, ParticleContainer* l_particles) {
    auto& positions = l_particles->m_position;
    auto& velocities = l_particles->m_velocity;
    for (size_t i = 0; i < l_particles->m_countAlive; ++i) {
      if (positions[i].z > 0.f) { continue; }
      positions[i].z = 0.f;
      velocities[i].z = 0.f;
    }

    if (!m_map) { return; }
    for (size_t i = 0; i < l_particles->m_countAlive; ++i) {
      if (positions[i].z > 0.f) { continue; }
      ApplyFriction(l_dT, positions[i], velocities[i]);
    }
  }
  void SetMap(Map* l_map) { m_map = l_map; }
private:
  void ApplyFriction(float l_dT, sf::Vector3f& l_position,
    sf::Vector3f& l_velocity) { ... }
  Map* m_map;
};
```

All we have to worry about here is checking whether the position of a particle on the z axis is below zero. If it is, the position on that axis is reset back to zero, as well as its velocity. Additionally, if the updater has been provided with a pointer to a map instance, we want to handle particle friction against the map, provided they are touching the ground. Provided that's the case, the delta time is passed into a private `ApplyFriction()` method, along with the position and velocity vectors of the particle:

```
void ApplyFriction(float l_dT, sf::Vector3f& l_position,
  sf::Vector3f& l_velocity)
{
  sf::Vector2i tileCoords = sf::Vector2i(
    static_cast<int>(floor(l_position.x / Sheet::Tile_Size)),
    static_cast<int>(floor(l_position.y / Sheet::Tile_Size)));
  auto tile = m_map->GetTile(tileCoords.x, tileCoords.y, 0);
  sf::Vector2f friction;
  if (!tile) { friction = m_map->GetDefaultTile()->m_friction; }
  else { friction = tile->m_properties->m_friction; }
```

```
friction.x *= std::abs(l_velocity.x);
friction.y *= std::abs(l_velocity.y);
friction *= l_dT;
if (l_velocity.x != 0.f && friction.x != 0.f) {
  if (std::abs(l_velocity.x) - std::abs(friction.x) < 0.f) {
    l_velocity.x = 0.f;
  } else {
    l_velocity.x += (l_velocity.x > 0.f ?
      friction.x * -1.f : friction.x);
  }
}

if (l_velocity.y != 0.f && friction.y != 0.f) {
  if (std::abs(l_velocity.y) - std::abs(friction.y) < 0.f) {
    l_velocity.y = 0.f;
  } else {
    l_velocity.y += (l_velocity.y > 0.f ?
      friction.y * -1.f : friction.y);
  }
}
}
```

After the tile coordinates a particle is touching are determined, the tile is checked to see whether it exists in the first place. If it does not, the default friction is used. Once all of that is sorted out, the velocity **lost to friction** is calculated, and then multiplied by delta time to get accurate results for the current frame. Everything else after this point is related to making sure the values being added have the right sign, and don't result in going past absolute zero into the opposite sign domain.

Particle generators

Having all of these updaters really does nothing unless certain base values are generated for the particles. Whether it is the initial position of a particle, the range of colors, or the name of a texture that gets attached to our flying little data structures, having that initial data set based on some pre-conceived notion is important. There are quite a few generators we support, not to mention tons of candidates for new generators, and thus new types of particles. Having said that, let us take a look at a couple of basics that we need to get some basic effects going.

Point position

The simplest generator we can possibly have in this entire system is a point position. Essentially, it just sets all positions of fed-in particles to a static point in space:

```
class PointPosition : public BaseGenerator {
public:
  void Generate(Emitter* l_emitter,ParticleContainer* l_particles,
    size_t l_from, size_t l_to)
  {
    auto& positions = l_particles->m_position;
    auto center = l_emitter->GetPosition();
    for (auto i = l_from; i <= l_to; ++i) {positions[i] = center;}
  }
};
```

The center point all particles are positioned at is taken from the emitter. Its position will always be used to determine where a particle should be spawned.

Area position

Setting all particle positions to the same point can get rather boring, not to mention visually odd. If we're dealing with particles such as smoke or fire, it may make more sense to scatter the particles within a specified area. This is where AreaPosition comes in:

```
class AreaPosition : public BaseGenerator {
public:
  AreaPosition() = default;
  AreaPosition(const sf::Vector3f& l_deviation)
    : m_deviation(l_deviation) {}
  void Generate(Emitter* l_emitter,ParticleContainer* l_particles,
    size_t l_from, size_t l_to)
  {
    auto& positions = l_particles->m_position;
    auto center = l_emitter->GetPosition();
    auto rangeFrom = sf::Vector3f(center.x - m_deviation.x,
      center.y - m_deviation.y, center.z - m_deviation.z);
    auto rangeTo = sf::Vector3f(center.x + m_deviation.x,
      center.y + m_deviation.y, center.z + m_deviation.z);
    auto& rand = *l_emitter->GetParticleSystem()->GetRand();
    for (auto i = l_from; i <= l_to; ++i) {
      positions[i] = sf::Vector3f(
        rand(rangeFrom.x, rangeTo.x),
        rand(rangeFrom.y, rangeTo.y),
        rand(rangeFrom.z, rangeTo.z)
```

```
        );
      }
    }

    void ReadIn(std::stringstream& l_stream) {
      l_stream >> m_deviation.x >> m_deviation.y >> m_deviation.z;
    }
private:
    sf::Vector3f m_deviation;
};
```

This particular position generator still uses the emitter position as the center point, but also applies a random deviation range to it. The deviation value can be read directly from the particle file, or simply set through the constructor of this generator.

Line position

A slight variation on the area position is a line position. It works in the same basic way as the area position does, except only for one axis, which is either provided through the constructor or loaded in from the particle file:

```
enum class LineAxis{ x, y, z };

class LinePosition : public BaseGenerator {
public:
    LinePosition() : m_axis(LineAxis::x), m_deviation(0.f) {}
    LinePosition(LineAxis l_axis, float l_deviation)
      : m_axis(l_axis), m_deviation(l_deviation) {}
    void Generate(Emitter* l_emitter,ParticleContainer* l_particles,
      size_t l_from, size_t l_to)
    {
      auto& positions = l_particles->m_position;
      auto center = l_emitter->GetPosition();
      auto& rand = *l_emitter->GetParticleSystem()->GetRand();
      for (auto i = l_from; i <= l_to; ++i) {
        if (m_axis == LineAxis::x) {
          center.x = rand(center.x - m_deviation,
            center.x + m_deviation);
        } else if (m_axis == LineAxis::y) {
          center.y = rand(center.y - m_deviation,
            center.y + m_deviation);
        } else {
          center.z = rand(center.z - m_deviation,
            center.z + m_deviation); }
        positions[i] = center;
      }
```

```
    }

    void ReadIn(std::stringstream& l_stream) {
      std::string axis;
      l_stream >> axis >> m_deviation;
      if (axis == "x") { m_axis = LineAxis::x; }
      else if (axis == "y") { m_axis = LineAxis::y; }
      else if (axis == "z") { m_axis = LineAxis::z; }
      else { std::cout << "Faulty axis: " << axis << std::endl; }
    }
  private:
    LineAxis m_axis;
    float m_deviation;
};
```

The random deviation here is only applied to one of the axes. The same effect could arguably be achieved with an area position generator, but it doesn't hurt to have a little variety.

Particle properties

Certain properties particles possess would really not call for their own generators. For example, gravity and blending mode flags for particles could just be pooled to exist within a single type of generator:

```
class PropGenerator : public BaseGenerator {
public:
  PropGenerator(bool l_gravity = true, bool l_additive = false)
    : m_gravity(l_gravity), m_additive(l_additive) {}
  void Generate(Emitter* l_emitter,ParticleContainer* l_particles,
    size_t l_from, size_t l_to)
  {
    auto& gravity = l_particles->m_gravity;
    for (auto i = l_from; i <= l_to; ++i) {
      gravity[i] = m_gravity;
    }
    auto& additive = l_particles->m_addBlend;
    for (auto i = l_from; i <= l_to; ++i) {
      additive[i] = m_additive;
    }
  }

  void ReadIn(std::stringstream& l_stream) {
    int gravity = 1;
    int additive = 0;
    l_stream >> gravity >> additive;
```

```
      m_gravity = (gravity != 0);
      m_additive = (additive != 0);
    }
  private:
    bool m_gravity;
    bool m_additive;
};
```

Both the gravity and blending mode flags can, as with all the previous generators, be loaded in from the file, or set through the constructor of the class.

Random color

Randomizing the color of all emitted particles may be something one may want to do, whether the random variations are slight for something such as differently shaded water particles, or completely random for a fountain of skittles. All of that and more can be done by this class:

```
class RandomColor : public BaseGenerator {
public:
  RandomColor() = default;
  RandomColor(const sf::Vector3i& l_from, const sf::Vector3i& l_to)
    : m_from(l_from), m_to(l_to) {}
  void Generate(Emitter* l_emitter, ParticleContainer* l_particles,
    size_t l_from, size_t l_to)
  {
    auto& rand = *l_emitter->GetParticleSystem()->GetRand();
    auto& colors = l_particles->m_currentColor;
    for (auto i = l_from; i <= l_to; ++i) {
      sf::Color target{
        static_cast<sf::Uint8>(rand(m_from.x, m_to.x)),
        static_cast<sf::Uint8>(rand(m_from.y, m_to.y)),
        static_cast<sf::Uint8>(rand(m_from.z, m_to.z)),
        255
      };
      colors[i] = target;
    }
  }
   void ReadIn(std::stringstream& l_stream) {
    l_stream >> m_from.x >> m_to.x >> m_from.y >> m_to.y >>
      m_from.z >> m_to.z;
  }
private:
  sf::Vector3i m_from;
  sf::Vector3i m_to;
};
```

The generator stores ranges, which are going to be used to generate random results. They can either be loaded in from the particle file, or set through the constructor. Since the ranges can be different for each one of the three color channels, they are randomized separately.

Color range

While the random color generator simply assigns the current color of the particle, a color range provides a range of colors that the particle will fade through during its lifespan, thanks to interpolation. This process is as simple as assigning those values:

```cpp
class ColorRange : public BaseGenerator {
public:
  ColorRange() = default;
  ColorRange(const sf::Color& l_start, const sf::Color& l_finish)
    : m_start(l_start), m_finish(l_finish) {}
  void Generate(Emitter* l_emitter,ParticleContainer* l_particles,
    size_t l_from, size_t l_to)
  {
    auto& beginning = l_particles->m_startColor;
    auto& current = l_particles->m_currentColor;
    auto& ending = l_particles->m_finalColor;
    for (auto i = l_from; i <= l_to; ++i) {
      beginning[i] = m_start;
      current[i] = m_start;
      ending[i] = m_finish;
    }
  }
  void ReadIn(std::stringstream& l_stream) {
    int s_r = 0, s_g = 0, s_b = 0, s_a = 0;
    int f_r = 0, f_g = 0, f_b = 0, f_a = 0;
    l_stream >> s_r >> s_g >> s_b >> s_a;
    l_stream >> f_r >> f_g >> f_b >> f_a;

    m_start = {
      static_cast<sf::Uint8>(s_r), static_cast<sf::Uint8>(s_g),
      static_cast<sf::Uint8>(s_b), static_cast<sf::Uint8>(s_a)
    };
    m_finish = {
      static_cast<sf::Uint8>(f_r), static_cast<sf::Uint8>(f_g),
      static_cast<sf::Uint8>(f_b), static_cast<sf::Uint8>(f_a)
    };
  }
private:
  sf::Color m_start;
  sf::Color m_finish;
};
```

Just as before, the ranges can be read in from the particle file or set up by using the constructor. Both the initial and the current colors of a particle are set to match the starting color.

Note the de-serialization method. Because we're reading integers from the text file, the variable type must reflect that at first. After all the values are read in, they're then converted to `sf::Uint8` and stored as ranges. This obviously includes the alpha channel, in order to give particles the means of fading out when they're about to de-spawn.

Random lifespan

Generating the lifespan for particles is fairly similar to everything else we've done so far, so let's just jump straight into it:

```cpp
class RandomLifespan : public BaseGenerator {
public:
  RandomLifespan() : m_from(0.f), m_to(0.f) {}
  RandomLifespan(float l_from, float l_to)
    : m_from(l_from), m_to(l_to) {}
  void Generate(Emitter* l_emitter,ParticleContainer* l_particles,
    size_t l_from, size_t l_to)
  {
    auto& rand = *l_emitter->GetParticleSystem()->GetRand();
    auto& lifespans = l_particles->m_maxLifespan;
    for (auto i = l_from; i <= l_to; ++i) {
      lifespans[i] = rand(m_from, m_to);
    }
  }

  void ReadIn(std::stringstream& l_stream) {
    l_stream >> m_from >> m_to;
  }
private:
  float m_from;
  float m_to;
};
```

Predictably, lifespans are also stored as ranges, which can be loaded from the particle file or set up by using the constructor. Afterwards, the life of a particle is randomized within the specified range. This can provide certain effects with visual variety by eliminating the *line of death* that tends to visually stick out.

Random size

Randomizing the particle size is another useful tool to have in our visual arsenal. Let us take a look:

```
class RandomSize : public BaseGenerator {
public:
  RandomSize() : m_from(0), m_to(0) {}
  RandomSize(int l_from, int l_to): m_from(l_from), m_to(l_to) {}

  void Generate(Emitter* l_emitter,ParticleContainer* l_particles,
    size_t l_from, size_t l_to)
  {
    auto& rand = *l_emitter->GetParticleSystem()->GetRand();
    auto& sizes = l_particles->m_currentSize;
    for (auto i = l_from; i <= l_to; ++i) {
      float size = static_cast<float>(rand(m_from, m_to));
      sizes[i] = sf::Vector2f(size, size);
    }
  }

  void ReadIn(std::stringstream& l_stream) {
    l_stream >> m_from >> m_to;
  }
private:
  int m_from;
  int m_to;
};
```

As always, ranges are stored as data members, and can be read in from a file, or set up via the constructor. The size itself is randomized once, and then applied as the same size for both axes. As of yet, we have no reason to generate rectangular particles with non-matching dimensions.

Random velocity

All of the effort we have put into the system so far would literally be at a standstill if we did not give these particles a push from their birth. Applying random velocity values can achieve just that:

```
class RandomVelocity : public BaseGenerator {
public:
  RandomVelocity() = default;
  RandomVelocity(const sf::Vector3f& l_from,
    const sf::Vector3f& l_to) : m_from(l_from), m_to(l_to) {}
```

```
    void Generate(Emitter* l_emitter,ParticleContainer* l_particles,
      size_t l_from, size_t l_to)
    {
      auto& rand = *l_emitter->GetParticleSystem()->GetRand();
      auto& velocities = l_particles->m_velocity;
      for (auto i = l_from; i <= l_to; ++i) {
        sf::Vector3f target{
          rand(m_from.x, m_to.x),
          rand(m_from.y, m_to.y),
          rand(m_from.z, m_to.z)
        };
        velocities[i] = target;
      }
    }

    void ReadIn(std::stringstream& l_stream) {
      l_stream >> m_from.x >> m_to.x >> m_from.y >> m_to.y >>
      m_from.z >> m_to.z;
    }
  private:
    sf::Vector3f m_from;
    sf::Vector3f m_to;
};
```

Velocities, as covered earlier, work in three dimensions, so that is precisely how we must store them. Their ranges are either loaded from particle files, or set up through the constructor of this generator. They are then individually randomized and applied.

Rotation range

Rotation of particles can be nice for a number of different effects we can think of. Rotating them slightly over their lifetimes can provide some nice variety, so let us reflect that in this next generator:

```
class RotationRange : public BaseGenerator {
public:
  RotationRange() : m_start(0.f), m_finish(0.f) {}
  RotationRange(float l_start, float l_finish)
    : m_start(l_start), m_finish(l_finish) {}
  void Generate(Emitter* l_emitter,ParticleContainer* l_particles,
    size_t l_from, size_t l_to)
  {
    auto& beginning = l_particles->m_startRotation;
    auto& ending = l_particles->m_finalRotation;
    for (auto i = l_from; i <= l_to; ++i) {
      beginning[i] = m_start;
```

```
        ending[i] = m_finish;
      }
    }

    void ReadIn(std::stringstream& l_stream) {
      l_stream >> m_start >> m_finish;
    }
  private:
    float m_start;
    float m_finish;
  };
```

Since the rotation values are going to be interpolated over the particle's lifetime, we use beginning and ending values to reflect that.

Size range

Particle sizes are no different from any other data we have been dealing with so far, so let's take a look:

```
class SizeRange : public BaseGenerator {
public:
  SizeRange() : m_start(0), m_finish(0) {}
  SizeRange(float l_start, float l_finish)
    : m_start(l_start), m_finish(l_finish) {}
  void Generate(Emitter* l_emitter,ParticleContainer* l_particles,
    size_t l_from, size_t l_to)
  {
    if (m_start == m_finish) {
      auto& sizes = l_particles->m_currentSize;
      for (auto i = l_from; i <= l_to; ++i) {
        sizes[i] = sf::Vector2f(m_start, m_start);
      }
    } else {
      auto& beginning = l_particles->m_startSize;
      auto& ending = l_particles->m_finalSize;
      for (auto i = l_from; i <= l_to; ++i) {
        beginning[i] = sf::Vector2f(m_start, m_start);
        ending[i] = sf::Vector2f(m_finish, m_finish);
      }
    }
  }

  void ReadIn(std::stringstream& l_stream) {
    l_stream >> m_start >> m_finish;
  }
```

```
private:
  float m_start;
  float m_finish;
};
```

The ranges provided to this generator are first checked to see whether they're not equal. If that is the case, however, we can treat the size of a particle as constant and simply set its current size to it to save the interpolator some work. Otherwise, the beginning and ending values of the size are filled out.

Texture generator

Last, but definitely not least, we can make our particles about a million times more appealing to the eye by texturing them. Luckily, our system makes it fairly easy to do at this point. Let's take a look:

```
class TextureGenerator : public BaseGenerator {
public:
  TextureGenerator() = default;
  TextureGenerator(const std::string& l_texture)
    : m_texture(l_texture) {}
  void Generate(Emitter* l_emitter,ParticleContainer* l_particles,
    size_t l_from, size_t l_to)
  {
    if (m_texture.empty()) { return; }
    TextureManager* manager = l_emitter->
      GetParticleSystem()->GetTextureManager();
    if (!manager->RequireResource(m_texture)) { return; }
    auto& textures = l_particles->m_texture;
    auto& drawables = l_particles->m_drawable;
    auto resource = manager->GetResource(m_texture);
    auto size = resource->getSize();
    for (auto i = l_from; i <= l_to; ++i) {
      textures[i] = m_texture;
      manager->RequireResource(m_texture);
      drawables[i].setTexture(resource);
      drawables[i].setTextureRect(sf::IntRect(0,0,size.x,size.y));
    }
    manager->ReleaseResource(m_texture);
  }

  void ReadIn(std::stringstream& l_stream){l_stream >> m_texture;}
private:
  std::string m_texture;
};
```

The string identifier of the texture that needs to be used for the particle type is first either loaded in from a file, or passed in via the constructor. The string is then checked inside the `Generate` method in order to make sure it is not empty. After a pointer to the texture manager is obtained, the resource handle is checked for validity by an attempt to require it.

 Remember that the `RequireResource` line actually claims the resource is being used, until it's released.

All particles that are being generated are then provided with the resource handle of the texture. For each particle, the resource is required one more time, and then finally passed into the drawable object of the particle, as well as properly cropped based on the particle size.

Finally, note the last highlighted line of code inside the `Generate()` method. Because we have increased the internal resource counter once by requiring it at the very beginning for verification purposes, as well as to obtain a reference to the resource, it must now be released, leaving the internal resource counter with the same value as the number of particles that actually use this texture.

Using the particle system

Before we can start using our particle system, some basic setting up is in order. First, since the particle system is dependent on both states and map loading, their relationship must be set up inside the main `Game` class like so:

```
void Game::SetUpStates() {
   ...
   m_stateManager->AddDependent(m_particles.get());
   ...
}

void Game::SetUpClasses() {
   ...
   m_gameMap.AddLoadee(m_particles.get());
}
```

Next, let's build an actual type of particle that will be used inside the main menu to make it look spectacular:

```
Name MenuFlame
PointPosition
```

```
SizeRange 32 8
|ColorRange 255 255 0 100 0 255 255 0
RandomColor 100 255 100 255 100 255
RandomLifespan 6 6
RandomVelocity -10 10 -50 -80 5 10
RotationRange 0 45
Texture Flame
Properties 0 1
```

All of these generator parameters have already been covered, so if this format looks questionable, it may be prudent to review the generator section once again.

Let us add all of these spectacular visuals to the menu state, in order to make it much more impressive than it currently is. We can start by first setting up a couple of emitters:

```cpp
void State_MainMenu::OnCreate() {
  ...
  auto w_size = context->m_wind->GetWindowSize();
  context->m_particles->CreateState(StateType::MainMenu);
  auto emitter = std::make_unique<Emitter>(sf::Vector3f(
    static_cast<float>(w_size.x) / 3.f,
    static_cast<float>(w_size.y) - 64.f,
    33.f));
  emitter->SetEmitRate(25);
  emitter->SetGenerators("MenuFlame");
  context->m_particles->AddEmitter(std::move(emitter));
  emitter = std::make_unique<Emitter>(sf::Vector3f(
    (static_cast<float>(w_size.x) / 3.f) * 2.f,
    static_cast<float>(w_size.y) - 64.f,
    33.f));
  emitter->SetEmitRate(25);
  emitter->SetGenerators("MenuFlame");
  context->m_particles->AddEmitter(std::move(emitter));
  emitter = std::make_unique<Emitter>(sf::Vector3f(
    0.f,
    static_cast<float>(w_size.y) / 2.f,
    0.f));
  emitter->SetEmitRate(60);
  emitter->SetGenerators("MenuSmoke");
  context->m_particles->AddEmitter(std::move(emitter));
  auto f = ForceApplicator(
    sf::Vector3f(static_cast<float>(w_size.x) / 2.f,
      static_cast<float>(w_size.y) / 2.f, 64.f),
    sf::Vector3f(500.f, 500.f, 500.f), 256.f);
  context->m_particles->AddForce(f);
}
```

Note the highlighted line of the code. A state must be created inside the particle system in order for us to be able to use it. Next, two emitters are created. One is positioned at one third of the width of the screen, and the other, two thirds. Both of them are added to the system, as well as another emitter, positioned off to the left, which will be emitting smoke. Finally, a force applicator, positioned right in between the two flames, is added to the particle system as well. With this thoughtful positioning, we're going to be creating a really good-looking effect that will be showcased shortly.

Our particles obviously need to be updated in order to function properly:

```
void State_MainMenu::Update(const sf::Time& l_dT) {
  m_stateMgr->GetContext()->m_particles->Update(l_dT.asSeconds());
}
```

Finally, let's draw them on screen:

```
void State_MainMenu::Draw() {
  auto context = m_stateMgr->GetContext();
  for (unsigned int i = 0; i < Sheet::Num_Layers; ++i) {
    m_stateMgr->GetContext()->m_particles->Draw(
      *m_stateMgr->GetContext()->m_wind, i);
  }
  m_stateMgr->GetContext()->m_particles->Draw(
    *m_stateMgr->GetContext()->m_wind, -1);
}
```

Since the `Draw()` method takes in the layer we are currently drawing, and for this state layers are irrelevant, we simply iterate over the number of layers, invoking the `Draw()` method for each one. At the end, the `Draw()` method is invoked one last time with the argument `-1`, signifying that we want to draw all of the particles that are outside the maximum layer.

The final result, along with the smoke effect, looks a little like this:

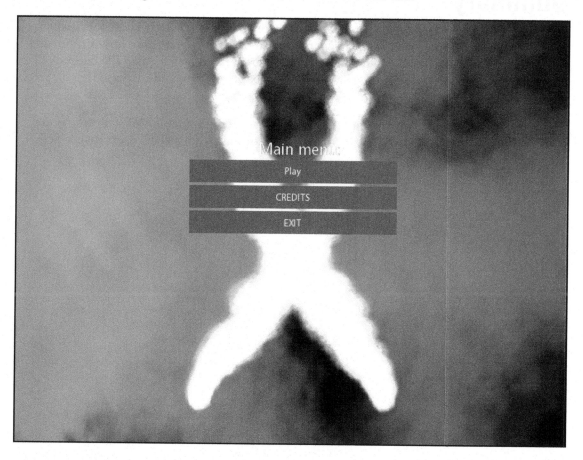

This is far from showcasing what the particle system can really do. The code in this chapter includes examples that exist within the game state, and can be easily found by compiling the project and simply taking a stroll through the scenery.

Summary

There may have been quite a bit to take in, but if you are here, congratulations! With some careful architecting, calculated decisions, and a dash of taste, we have not only produced a particle system that makes the game look ten times better, but also formed the bedrock of knowledge that serves as a stepping stone towards better design, and increased performance.

In the next few chapters, we are going to be covering the fundamentals of sculpting your own tools for actually designing the game we are working with, as well as its assets. See you there!

4
Have Thy Gear Ready - Building Game Tools

Making games is a fine art. It is entirely possible, of course, to make art with the most basic of tools, but most commonly, developers need a strong toolkit supporting them in order to efficiently and professionally create quick, painless edits to their game. Building the said toolkit is arguably on a par with the difficulty of building the actual game, but the work spent on proper tools offsets the difficulty and frustrations that come with direct file edits.

In this chapter, we're going to be covering these topics:

- Building a graphical means of file management
- File loading in a separate thread
- Establishing a state and means of controls for map editing

There's lots of ground to cover, so let's get started!

Use of copyrighted resources

As usual, let us give proper thanks to the artists and their assets that made this possible:

- *Folder Orange* by *sixsixfive* under the **CC0** license (public domain): `https://openc lipart.org/detail/212337/folder-orange`
- *Generic Document* by *isendrak* under the **CC0** license (public domain): `https://openclipart.org/detail/212798/generic-document`
- *Tango Media Floppy* by *warszawianka* under the **CC0** license (public domain): `https://openclipart.org/detail/34579/tango-media-floppy`

- *Close* by *danilo* under the **CC0** license (public domain): `https://openclipart.org/detail/215431/close`
- *Hand Prints* by *kattekrab* under the **CC0** license (public domain): `https://openclipart.org/detail/16340/hand-prints`
- *Paint Brush with Dark Red Dye* by *Astro* under the **CC0** license (public domain): `https://openclipart.org/detail/245360/Paint-Brush-with-Dye-11`
- *Primary Eraser* by *dannya* under the **CC0** license (public domain): `https://openclipart.org/detail/199463/primary-eraser`
- *Mono Tool Rect Selection* by *dannya* under the **CC0** license (public domain): `https://openclipart.org/detail/198758/mono-tool-rect-selection`
- *Color Bucket Red* by *frankes* under the **CC0** license (public domain): `https://openclipart.org/detail/167327/color-bucket-red`

File management

The success and usability of the map editor tool is going to rely heavily on one specific interfacing element here, which is file access and management. In order to provide efficient means of file access, loading and saving, we are going to work on developing the means of visually guiding our user through the file system. The entire system consists of a few moving parts. For now, let us solely focus on the interface aspect of this idea.

File manager interface

Before we can successfully work with any kind of map data, it is important to have a comfortable means of loading and saving. This can be offloaded to a file manager interface, which is going to be responsible for displaying directory information. Let us take a look at what ours is going to look like:

With this goal in mind, let us begin planning a class for it, starting with the header:

```cpp
class GUI_FileManager {
public:
  GUI_FileManager(std::string l_name, GUI_Manager* l_guiMgr,
    StateManager* l_stateMgr);
  ~GUI_FileManager();

  void SetDirectory(std::string l_dir);
  void ParentDirCallback(EventDetails* l_details);
  void HandleEntries(EventDetails* l_details);
  void ActionButton(EventDetails* l_details);
  void CloseButton(EventDetails* l_details);
  void Hide();
  void Show();
  void LoadMode();
  void SaveMode();
  bool IsInSaveMode() const;

  template<class T>
  void SetActionCallback(
    void(T::*l_method)(const std::string&), T* l_instance)
  {...}
private:
  void ListFiles();
```

```
    GUI_Interface* m_interface;
    std::string m_name;
    std::string m_dir;

    std::string m_folderEntry;
    std::string m_fileEntry;

    GUI_Manager* m_guiManager;
    StateManager* m_stateMgr;
    StateType m_currentState;
    std::function<void(std::string)> m_actionCallback;
    bool m_saveMode;
};
```

Evidently, this class is a slightly more complex manifestation of a wrapper for a `GUI_Interface` instance. It is responsible for keeping track of the current directory we are in, as well as invoking a callback function/method when a file is selected to be loaded or saved. The callback function only takes a string argument, which carries the full path to the file that was selected to be loaded or saved, and can be registered like this:

```
void SetActionCallback(
    void(T::*l_method)(const std::string&), T* l_instance)
{
    m_actionCallback =
        [l_instance, l_method](const std::string& l_str) -> void
        { (l_instance->*l_method)(l_str); };
}
```

Nothing too complicated yet. Let us move on to actually implementing the class!

Implementing the file manager

With the class definition out of the way, it is time to take a look at the actual code that makes the file manager tick. Let's start by implementing the constructor of this class:

```
GUI_FileManager::GUI_FileManager(std::string l_name,
    GUI_Manager* l_guiMgr, StateManager* l_stateMgr):
    m_guiManager(l_guiMgr), m_stateMgr(l_stateMgr), m_name(l_name),
    m_saveMode(false)
{
    m_guiManager->LoadInterface(""FileManager.interface"", l_name);
    m_interface = m_guiManager->GetInterface(l_name);
    m_currentState = m_stateMgr->GetCurrentStateType();
    m_folderEntry = m_interface->GetElement("FolderEntry")->
        GetStyleName();
    m_fileEntry = m_interface->GetElement("FileEntry")->
```

```
    GetStyleName();
  m_interface->RemoveElement("FolderEntry");
  m_interface->RemoveElement("FileEntry");
  m_interface->SetContentRectSize({ 300, 260 });
  m_interface->SetContentOffset({ 0.f, 16.f });
  m_interface->PositionCenterScreen();

  auto mgr = m_stateMgr->GetContext()->m_eventManager;

  mgr->AddCallback<GUI_FileManager>("FileManager_Parent",
    &GUI_FileManager::ParentDirCallback, this);
  mgr->AddCallback<GUI_FileManager>("FileManager_Entries",
    &GUI_FileManager::HandleEntries, this);
  mgr->AddCallback<GUI_FileManager>("FileManager_ActionButton",
    &GUI_FileManager::ActionButton, this);
  mgr->AddCallback<GUI_FileManager>("FileManager_Close",
    &GUI_FileManager::CloseButton, this);

  SetDirectory(Utils::GetWorkingDirectory());
}
```

First, we load the interface and store its pointer in the designated data member. We also want to store the current state of the application, and obtain the style names of the elements, called `FolderEntry` and `FileEntry`, which are then removed. This makes the interface file a sort of template that gets filled in with all the right information later.

Once the appropriate content size and offset are set, the interface is positioned in the centre of the screen. We then subscribe to relevant GUI interface events and set our file manager directory as the current directory the application is in.

The callbacks and interfaces created in this class obviously need to be removed once they are no longer in use. This is where the destructor comes in:

```
GUI_FileManager::~GUI_FileManager() {
  m_guiManager->RemoveInterface(m_currentState, m_name);
  auto events = m_stateMgr->GetContext()->m_eventManager;
  events->RemoveCallback(m_currentState, ""FileManager_Parent"");
  events->RemoveCallback(m_currentState, ""FileManager_Entries"");
  events->RemoveCallback(m_currentState,
    ""FileManager_ActionButton"");
  events->RemoveCallback(m_currentState, ""FileManager_Close"");
}
```

Next, it is important for the file manager class to have a way to easily change its current directory:

```
void GUI_FileManager::SetDirectory(std::string l_dir) {
  m_dir = l_dir;
  std::replace(m_dir.begin(), m_dir.end(), '''', ''/'');
  m_interface->RemoveElementsContaining(""Entry_"");
  ListFiles();
}
```

A couple of interesting things happened. Right after the argument is stored; all of the backward slashes in the directory string are replaced with forward slashes, in order to maintain compatibility with multiple other operating systems that do not play well with the former. The interface is then instructed to destroy all elements it has that begin with the ""Entry_"" string. This is done in order to clear out all file and directory entries that may already exist. Finally, `ListFiles()` method is invoked, which populates the file manager with all of the files and folders inside the new directory. Let' us take a look at how that can be done:

```
void GUI_FileManager::ListFiles() {
  m_interface->GetElement(""Directory"")->SetText(m_dir);
  auto list = Utils::GetFileList(m_dir, ""*.*"", true);
  Utils::SortFileList(list);
  auto ParentDir = m_interface->GetElement(""ParentDir"");
  float x = ParentDir->GetPosition().x;
  float y = ParentDir->GetPosition().y+ParentDir->GetSize().y+1.f;
  size_t i = 0;
  for (auto& file : list) {
    if (file.first == ""."" || file.first == "".."") { continue; }
    std::string entry = (file.second ? "FEntry_"" : ""Entry_");
    m_interface->AddElement(GUI_ElementType::Label,
      entry + std::to_string(i));
    auto element = m_interface->GetElement(
      entry + std::to_string(i));
    element->SetText(file.first);
    element->SetPosition({ x, y });
    m_guiManager->LoadStyle((file.second ?
      m_folderEntry : m_fileEntry), element);
    y += ParentDir->GetSize().y + 4.f;
    ++i;
  }
}
```

First, the `Directory` element is obtained in order to change its text. It represents the full path of the current working directory. The complete file list inside that directory is then obtained, including other folders. After it gets sorted alphabetically and by type, the parent directory element is obtained to calculate the starting coordinates of the first element on the list, which is, in turn, iterated over. Non-physical directories, such as " . " or " . . ", are dismissed. A new element is then added to the interface, with an appropriate name that varies depending on whether we are working with a file or a folder. That same element is then updated to have the entry name, be in the right position and have a correct style attached to it. Finally, the *y* coordinate is incremented for the next element on the list.

With the directory structure being visually represented, let us take a look at what needs to happen when one of its entries is actually clicked:

```
void GUI_FileManager::HandleEntries(EventDetails* l_details) {
    if(l_details->m_guiElement.find("FEntry_") != std::string::npos){
        std::string path = m_dir +
            m_interface->GetElement(l_details->m_guiElement)->GetText()
            + "";
        SetDirectory(path);
        m_interface->UpdateScrollVertical(0);
    } else if (l_details->m_guiElement.find("Entry_") !=
        std::string::npos)
    {
        m_interface->GetElement("FileName")->SetText(
          m_interface->GetElement(l_details->m_guiElement)->GetText());
    }
}
```

The first check here lets us know whether the item clicked on was a directory or a file. In case of a folder click, we want to be able to traverse the filesystem by taking its name and adding it onto our existing directory path. The vertical scroll of the interface is then set back to zero, in order to move the content back up to the top if any scrolling has been done.

A file click is a simpler matter. All we need to do in that case is obtain the text-field element that holds the filename, and change its contents to the name of the file that was just clicked on.

All of this works perfectly for forward-traversal, but what if we want to go backwards? The parent directory element helps us out here:

```
void GUI_FileManager::ParentDirCallback(EventDetails* l_details) {
  auto i = m_dir.find_last_of("/", m_dir.length() - 2);
  if (i != std::string::npos) {
    std::string dir = m_dir.substr(0U, i + 1);
    SetDirectory(dir);
  }
}
```

Here, it simply comes down to basic string manipulation. The very last instance of the forward slash character is first attempted to be located inside the directory string. If one is found, the string is simply *clipped* at that point, in order to drop everything that comes after it. The shortened path is then set as the current directory, where the rest of the magic that we've already covered happens.

The last piece of the puzzle in making this work is handling the button press action:

```
void GUI_FileManager::ActionButton(EventDetails* l_details) {
  if (m_actionCallback == nullptr) { return; }
  auto filename = m_interface->GetElement("FileName")->GetText();
  m_actionCallback(m_dir + filename);
}
```

First, we need to make sure the action callback is actually set. If it is, it gets invoked with the path to the currently selected file as its argument. The only other action button we have to worry about after this point is the close button:

```
void GUI_FileManager::CloseButton(EventDetails* l_details){
  Hide();
}
```

It simply invokes the `Hide()` method, which is covered here, along with its counterpart:

```
void GUI_FileManager::Hide() { m_interface->SetActive(false); }

void GUI_FileManager::Show() {
  m_interface->SetActive(true);
  m_interface->PositionCenterScreen();
  ListFiles();
  m_interface->Focus();
}
```

When an interface is hidden, it's simply set to inactive. Showing it requires setting it back to being active, except we also want to position it in the absolute centre of the screen in this instance. In addition to that, it is a good idea to refresh its content, as the file structure may have changed while it was hidden. Lastly, the interface is focused, in order to bring it to the front of the drawing queue.

The final bits of helpful code for this class consist of these methods:

```
bool GUI_FileManager::IsInSaveMode() const { return m_saveMode; }
void GUI_FileManager::LoadMode() {
  m_interface->GetElement("ActionButton")->SetText("Load");
  m_saveMode = false;
}
void GUI_FileManager::SaveMode() {
  m_interface->GetElement("ActionButton")->SetText("Save");
  m_saveMode = true;
}
```

They help our other classes interface with this one more easily, by allowing them to determine if the file manager is in `Save` or `Load` mode, and to switch between the two.

Loading files in a separate thread

We have covered the threaded worker base class previously in `Chapter 1`, *Under the Hood – Setting up the Backend*. This is exactly where it will come in handy. In order to make the application seem more user-friendly, we want to render a nice loading bar that shows progress while the files are being loaded. Let us start by first defining a data type, used to store file paths that need to be loaded:

```
using LoaderPaths = std::vector<std::pair<std::string, size_t>>;
```

The `size_t` here represents the number of lines that are in the file, which makes it easy for us to determine the current loading progress. With that out of the way, let us work on the header file:

```
class FileLoader : public Worker {
public:
  FileLoader();
  void AddFile(const std::string& l_file);
  virtual void SaveToFile(const std::string& l_file);

  size_t GetTotalLines() const;
  size_t GetCurrentLine() const;
private:
  virtual bool ProcessLine(std::stringstream& l_stream) = 0;
```

```
    virtual void ResetForNextFile();
    void Work();
    void CountFileLines();

    LoaderPaths m_files;
    size_t m_totalLines;
    size_t m_currentLine;
};
```

Any `FileLoader` class in our code base needs to implement the `ProcessLine` method, which simply defines what needs to happen as each individual line of the file is being parsed. If necessary, it can also take advantage of `SaveToFile`, which, as the name states, defines the process of writing the class data out, and `ResetForNextFile`. The latter method is invoked after every file that has finished loading, in order to give derivative classes a chance to clean up their internal state.

As far as data members go, we have a list of loader paths that are to be loaded, the number of total lines of all files that are supposed to be parsed, and the number of the current line being read.

Implementing the file loader

Let us start simply, and cover the one-liner methods first:

```
FileLoader::FileLoader() : m_totalLines(0), m_currentLine(0) {}
void FileLoader::AddFile(const std::string& l_file) {
  m_files.emplace_back(l_file, 0);
}
size_t FileLoader::GetTotalLines() const{ return m_totalLines; }
size_t FileLoader::GetCurrentLine() const{ return m_currentLine; }
void FileLoader::SaveToFile(const std::string& l_file) {}
void FileLoader::ResetForNextFile() {}
```

The constructor simply initializes a few of the class data members to their default values. The `AddFile()` method inserts the argument to the file container with the line count *zero*. The next two methods are simple getters, while the last two are not even implemented, as they are optional.

Next, let us work on the method that will actually be running in a thread and parse the file information:

```
void FileLoader::Work() {
  CountFileLines();
  if (!m_totalLines) { return; }
  for (auto& path : m_files) {
```

```
        ResetForNextFile();
        std::ifstream file(path.first);
        std::string line;
        std::string name;
        auto linesLeft = path.second;
        while (std::getline(file, line)) {
            {
                sf::Lock lock(m_mutex);
                ++m_currentLine;
                --linesLeft;
            }
            if (line[0] == '|') { continue; }
            std::stringstream keystream(line);
            if (!ProcessLine(keystream)) {
                {
                    sf::Lock lock(m_mutex);
                    m_currentLine += linesLeft;
                }
                break;
            }
        }
        file.close();
    }
    m_files.clear();
    Done();
}
```

First, a private method for counting all file lines is invoked. This is necessary, as we want to be able to calculate our progress, and knowing how much work there is in total is needed for that. If after this method is called, the total number of lines is zero, we simply return as there is nothing to process.

We then enter a loop that runs once for each file on the list. The class is reset for new file iteration, and a line from the input stream is created. The number of lines remaining to be processed is created, and another loop is entered that will execute once for each line in the file. Our sf::Mutex object is then locked in order to safely manipulate the two line data members that are used for progress tracking.

If the first character of our line is a pipe, |, it means we ran into a commented line and should just skip the current iteration. Otherwise, an std::stringstream of the current line is created and passed into the pure virtual ProcessLine() method, which is encapsulated in an if statement to catch a possible failure, in which case the remainder of lines inside the current file are simply added to the current line counter and the loop is broken out of.

Once the processing of all files is complete, the `Done()` method is invoked in order to terminate the thread and let the outside code know we've finished.

Another equally as important process is counting the lines of all file entries inside this class:

```cpp
void FileLoader::CountFileLines() {
  m_totalLines = 0;
  m_currentLine = 0;
  for (auto path = m_files.begin(); path != m_files.end();) {
    if (path->first.empty()) {
      path = m_files.erase(path);
      continue;
    }
    std::ifstream file(path->first);
    if (!file.is_open()) {
      path = m_files.erase(path);
      continue;
    }
    file.unsetf(std::ios_base::skipws);
    {
      sf::Lock lock(m_mutex);
      path->second = static_cast<size_t>(std::count(
        std::istreambuf_iterator<char>(file),
        std::istreambuf_iterator<char>(),
        '\n'));
      m_totalLines += path->second;
    }
    ++path;
    file.close();
  }
}
```

This one is fairly straightforward. After the two counters are zeroed out, we begin iterating over each path inside the file list. If the name of it is empty, the element is removed. Otherwise, we attempt to open the files. If that fails, the path is also erased. Otherwise, the file stream is requested to not skip whitespaces, and we enter a `sf::Mutex` lock, where the number of lines in the file stream is calculated using `std::count`, and added to the total line counter. The path iterator is then moved forward, and the file is closed.

The loading state

The last piece of the threaded file loading puzzle is the loading state. In order to avoid other logic going on and simply focus on the graphical progress representation, it's a good idea to just switch to a dedicated state that will handle all loading logic inside it. Let us begin by defining a data type for holding pointers to `FileLoader*` instances:

```
using LoaderContainer = std::vector<FileLoader*>;
```

The actual loading state header will end up looking something like this:

```
class State_Loading : public BaseState {
public:
    ... // Other typical state methods.
    void SetManualContinue(bool l_continue);
    void Proceed(EventDetails* l_details);
private:
    void UpdateText(const std::string& l_text, float l_percentage);
    float CalculatePercentage();
    LoaderContainer m_loaders;
    sf::Text m_text;
    sf::RectangleShape m_rect;
    unsigned short m_percentage;
    size_t m_originalWork;
    bool m_manualContinue;
};
```

As you can see, we have one event callback method, a couple of helper methods, the container for loader pointers, an instance of `sf::Text` and `sf::RectangleShape` to represent the loading bar, a number to represent the progress percentage, and the number of lines inside all files we originally started with.

Implementing the loading state

All of this data needs to be initialized before it being used, so let us take a look at the `OnCreate()` method:

```
void State_Loading::OnCreate() {
    auto context = m_stateMgr->GetContext();
    context->m_fontManager->RequireResource("Main");
    m_text.setFont(*context->m_fontManager->GetResource("Main"));
    m_text.setCharacterSize(14);
    m_text.setStyle(sf::Text::Bold);

    sf::Vector2u windowSize = m_stateMgr->GetContext()->
```

```
      m_wind->GetRenderWindow()->getSize();

   m_rect.setFillColor(sf::Color(0, 150, 0, 255));
   m_rect.setSize(sf::Vector2f(0.f, 16.f));
   m_rect.setOrigin(0.f, 8.f);
   m_rect.setPosition(0.f, windowSize.y / 2.f);

   EventManager* evMgr = m_stateMgr->GetContext()->m_eventManager;
   evMgr->AddCallback(StateType::Loading,
      "Key_Space", &State_Loading::Proceed, this);
}
```

Because we are going to be using text, we need to have a font to work with. After one is acquired and all of the stylistic text settings are handled, we set up the rectangle to be exactly in the centre of the screen and register an event callback for proceeding out of the loading state, if the manual continue flag is set to `true`.

Destroying this state also means the event callback and the font need to be released:

```
void State_Loading::OnDestroy() {
   auto context = m_stateMgr->GetContext();
   EventManager* evMgr = context->m_eventManager;
   evMgr->RemoveCallback(StateType::Loading, "Key_Space");
   context->m_fontManager->ReleaseResource("Main");
}
```

Next, let us take a look at the updated logic:

```
void State_Loading::Update(const sf::Time& l_time) {
   if (m_loaders.empty()) {
      if (!m_manualContinue) { Proceed(nullptr); }
      return;
   }
   auto windowSize = m_stateMgr->GetContext()->
      m_wind->GetRenderWindow()->getSize();
   if (m_loaders.back()->IsDone()) {
      m_loaders.back()->OnRemove();
      m_loaders.pop_back();
      if (m_loaders.empty()) {
         m_rect.setSize(sf::Vector2f(
            static_cast<float>(windowSize.x), 16.f));
         UpdateText(".Press space to continue.", 100.f);
         return;
      }
   }
   if (!m_loaders.back()->HasStarted()) {m_loaders.back()->Begin();}

   auto percentage = CalculatePercentage();
```

```
    UpdateText("", percentage);
    m_rect.setSize(sf::Vector2f(
        (windowSize.x / 100) * percentage, 16.f));
}
```

First, a check is made to determine if we are ready to exit the state, given all of the work that has been done. If the manual continue flag is set to `false`, we simply invoke the Proceed callback directly by passing `nullptr` as the `EventDetails` pointer, since it is not used there anyway. The update method is then returned from.

If we still have some work to do, the first element on the loader list is checked to see if it's done. If it is, the loader is removed, and if it was the last one, the size of the rectangle is set to match the full size of the window on the x axis, which shows full completion. The text in the middle is also updated to let the user know they need to press the spacebar key to continue. Finally, the update method is returned from once again, to prevent further logic from executing.

If none of those conditions were met, the first element on the loader list is checked to see if it has started its work. If it has not yet started, its `Begin` method is invoked. This is quickly followed by the percentage calculation, which is then used to update the text in the middle of the screen and adjust the size of the progress bar rectangle to match said percentage.

Drawing in this state simply comes down to two calls:

```
void State_Loading::Draw() {
    sf::RenderWindow* wind = m_stateMgr->
        GetContext()->m_wind->GetRenderWindow();
    wind->draw(m_rect);
    wind->draw(m_text);
}
```

All we need to do here is render the rectangle and the text instances.

Next, let us take a look at the helper method that updates our text instance:

```
void State_Loading::UpdateText(const std::string& l_text,
    float l_percentage)
{
    m_text.setString(std::to_string(
        static_cast<int>(l_percentage)) + "%" + l_text);
    auto windowSize = m_stateMgr->GetContext()->
        m_wind->GetRenderWindow()->getSize();
    m_text.setPosition(windowSize.x / 2.f, windowSize.y / 2.f);
    Utils::CenterSFMLText(m_text);
}
```

After the text string is updated, its position is updated to be directly in the middle of the screen. Since updating its contents may change the bounding box, and thus how it is centered, a helper function inside our `Utils` namespace is used to center it properly.

Next, let us calculate the actual progress of the loading procedure:

```
float State_Loading::CalculatePercentage() {
  float absolute = 100.f;
  if (m_loaders.back()->GetTotalLines()) {
    float d = (100.f * (m_originalWork - m_loaders.size()))) /
      static_cast<float>(m_originalWork);
    float current = (100.f * m_loaders.back()->GetCurrentLine()) /
      static_cast<float>(m_loaders.back()->GetTotalLines());
    float totalCurrent = current /
      static_cast<float>(m_originalWork);
    absolute = d + totalCurrent;
  }
  return absolute;
}
```

After an absolute value of `100.f` is created, the current progress is calculated by first determining the progress of how many files have been already loaded out of the number we began with, followed by the progress of the current file being calculated and used to determine absolute progress, which is then returned.

Once all of the work is done, the `Proceed()` method is invoked to return to the previous state:

```
void State_Loading::Proceed(EventDetails* l_details) {
  if (!m_loaders.empty()) { return; }
  m_stateMgr->SwitchTo(m_stateMgr->GetNextToLast());
}
```

Obviously it needs to check if the list of file loaders is actually empty first. If it is, the state manager is instructed to switch to the state that comes just before this one, which means it is the one that initiated the loading procedure.

Finally, what would a class be without some helper methods? Let us take a look at them now:

```
void State_Loading::AddLoader(FileLoader* l_loader) {
  m_loaders.emplace_back(l_loader);
  l_loader->OnAdd();
}
bool State_Loading::HasWork() const { return !m_loaders.empty(); }
void State_Loading::Activate() {
  m_originalWork = m_loaders.size();
}
```

Creating the map editor state

Now we're finally ready to actually tackle the state, in which all of the map editing is going to take place. Let us take a gander at its header file:

```
class State_MapEditor : public BaseState {
public:
  ...
  void ResetSavePath();
  void SetMapRedraw(bool l_redraw);
  void MainMenu(EventDetails* l_details);
  void MapEditorNew(EventDetails* l_details);
  void MapEditorLoad(EventDetails* l_details);
  void MapEditorSave(EventDetails* l_details);
  void MapEditorSaveAs(EventDetails* l_details);
  void MapEditorExit(EventDetails* l_details);
  void MapAction(const std::string& l_name);
private:
  void SaveMap(const std::string& l_path);
  void LoadMap(const std::string& l_path);
  GUI_FileManager m_files;
  MapControls m_mapControls;
  std::string m_mapSavePath;
  bool m_mapRedraw;
};
```

This `State_MapEditor` class is going to be the frontier that deals with the most general editor events. Note the highlighted data member here. We have not yet covered this class, but it is responsible for handling the finer aspects of control for this application. It will be covered in the next chapter.

Aside from the `MapControls` class, we also have the file manager, a string for the path to a file that is currently being worked on, and a *boolean* flag that keeps track of whether the game map should be redrawn or not.

Implementing the state

As always, let us begin by tackling the construction of all the important data inside this state:

```
void State_MapEditor::OnCreate() {
  auto context = m_stateMgr->GetContext();
  auto evMgr = context->m_eventManager;
  evMgr->AddCallback("Key_Escape",
    &State_MapEditor::MainMenu, this);
  evMgr->AddCallback("MapEditor_New",
    &State_MapEditor::MapEditorNew, this);
  evMgr->AddCallback("MapEditor_Load",
    &State_MapEditor::MapEditorLoad, this);
  evMgr->AddCallback("MapEditor_Save",
    &State_MapEditor::MapEditorSave, this);
  evMgr->AddCallback("MapEditor_SaveAs",
    &State_MapEditor::MapEditorSaveAs, this);
  evMgr->AddCallback("MapEditor_Exit",
    &State_MapEditor::MapEditorExit, this);

  m_files.SetActionCallback(&State_MapEditor::MapAction, this);
  m_files.SetDirectory(Utils::GetWorkingDirectory() +
    "media/maps/");
  m_files.Hide();
  context->m_guiManager->LoadInterface(
    "MapEditorTop.interface", "MapEditorTop");
  context->m_guiManager->GetInterface("MapEditorTop")->
    SetPosition({ 200, 0 });

  context->m_particles->CreateState(StateType::MapEditor);
}
```

After all of the event callbacks are set up, the file manager class is provided with its own callback for either loading or saving a file, as well as the starting directory it needs to be in. In this case, appropriately enough, it is the maps folder. The manager is then hidden, and another interface is loaded and positioned on screen. MapEditorTop is the control strip on the very top of the screen that has buttons for creating a new map, loading, saving, and exiting the application:

Once the state is finished and is about to be destroyed, it needs to remove all call-backs that it set up. This can be done in the OnDestroy() method:

```
void State_MapEditor::OnDestroy() {
  auto context = m_stateMgr->GetContext();
  auto textureMgr = context->m_textureManager;
  auto evMgr = context->m_eventManager;
  evMgr->RemoveCallback(StateType::MapEditor, "Key_Escape");
  evMgr->RemoveCallback(StateType::MapEditor, "MapEditor_New");
  evMgr->RemoveCallback(StateType::MapEditor, "MapEditor_Load");
  evMgr->RemoveCallback(StateType::MapEditor, "MapEditor_Save");
  evMgr->RemoveCallback(StateType::MapEditor, "MapEditor_SaveAs");
  evMgr->RemoveCallback(StateType::MapEditor, "MapEditor_Exit");
  context->m_gameMap->PurgeMap();
  context->m_gameMap->GetTileMap()->SetMapSize({ 0,0 });
}
```

In addition to callbacks, the map is also purged just before its size is set back to absolute zero. Since we are on the subject of callbacks, let us just cover most of them in a single go:

```
void State_MapEditor::MapEditorNew(EventDetails* l_details) {
  m_mapControls.NewMap();
}
void State_MapEditor::MapEditorLoad(EventDetails* l_details) {
  m_files.LoadMode();
  m_files.Show();
}

void State_MapEditor::MapEditorSave(EventDetails* l_details) {
  if (m_mapSavePath.empty()) { MapEditorSaveAs(nullptr); return; }
  SaveMap(m_mapSavePath);
}
void State_MapEditor::MapEditorSaveAs(EventDetails* l_details) {
  m_files.SaveMode();
  m_files.Show();
}
```

```
void State_MapEditor::MapEditorExit(EventDetails* l_details) {
  m_stateMgr->SwitchTo(StateType::MainMenu);
  m_stateMgr->Remove(StateType::MapEditor);
}
```

When the **New** map button is clicked, we want to invoke a special method of the
`MapControls` class that will handle it. If the **Load** button is clicked, we simply switch the
mode of the file manager to load, and show it on screen.

Clicking the **Save** button can have two behaviors. First, if we are dealing with a fresh, new
map that has not been saved yet, it is the same as clicking the **Save As...** button, which
switches the file manager to save mode and shows it on screen. However, if we have loaded
a map or have previously saved a new one, the state remembers where it was saved, as well
as its name. Prompting the user to enter a filename again would be pointless here, so the
map is simply written to the exact same location, with the exact same name.

Finally, if the **Exit** button is clicked, we simply switch back to the main menu state and
remove this one.

With the UI code out of the way, let us take a look at what needs to happen when a map is
being loaded:

```
void State_MapEditor::LoadMap(const std::string& l_path) {
  auto context = m_stateMgr->GetContext();
  auto loading = m_stateMgr->
    GetState<State_Loading>(StateType::Loading);
  context->m_particles->PurgeCurrentState();
  context->m_gameMap->PurgeMap();
  context->m_gameMap->ResetWorker();
  context->m_gameMap->GetTileMap()->GetTileSet().ResetWorker();
  context->m_gameMap->AddFile(l_path);
  loading->AddLoader(context->m_gameMap);
  loading->SetManualContinue(false);
  m_mapRedraw = true;
  m_mapSavePath = l_path;
  m_stateMgr->SwitchTo(StateType::Loading);
}
```

Since we want a nice loading bar to appear as a map is being read in, we are going to be using the loading state. After it is obtained, both the particle system and the map are purged. The map, which inherits from the `FileLoader` class, is then reset. The file path that was provided as an argument is then added to it to be loaded, and the loading state itself is set up to automatically dismiss itself once the loading is done. At the same time, we make sure that the map is going to be re-drawn as the map editor state resumes, and that it remembers the path of the map if it is to be saved later. Finally, we can switch to the loading state.

Next, let us work on the code that is responsible for saving the map:

```
void State_MapEditor::SaveMap(const std::string& l_path) {
  m_stateMgr->GetContext()->m_gameMap->SaveToFile(l_path);
  m_mapSavePath = l_path;
}
```

This is much simpler than the previous method. The path is simply passed to the `SaveToFile` method of the game map class, and stored for later use.

The actual callback of the file manager that mediates between the load and save methods can be implemented like :

```
void State_MapEditor::MapAction(const std::string& l_path) {
  if(m_files.IsInSaveMode()) { SaveMap(l_path); }
  else { LoadMap(l_path); }
  m_files.Hide();
}
```

Depending on the mode the file manager is in, the appropriate method is called with the path being passed in as the argument. The actual interface is then hidden.

Because we want to re-draw the map after it was loaded, the perfect place for that logic is inside the `Activate()` method, as it gets called right when a state is switched to:

```
void State_MapEditor::Activate() {
  if (!m_mapRedraw) { return; }
  auto map = m_stateMgr->GetContext()->m_gameMap;
  map->Redraw();
  m_mapControls.SetTileSheetTexture(
    map->GetTileSet()->GetTextureName());
  m_mapRedraw = false;
}
```

If the `m_mapRedraw` flag is not on, there is no need to do anything at this point. Otherwise, we want to redraw the map and provide the `mapControls` class with the tile-sheet texture name, so that it can perform its own logic, such as, for example, tile selection.

Next, let us take a look at what needs to be updated while the application is in this state:

```
void State_MapEditor::Update(const sf::Time& l_time) {
    auto context = m_stateMgr->GetContext();
    m_mapControls.Update(l_time.asSeconds());
    context->m_gameMap->Update(l_time.asSeconds());
    context->m_systemManager->Update(l_time.asSeconds());
    context->m_particles->Update(l_time.asSeconds());
}
```

Alongside the `mapControls` class, the game map, ECS system manager, and the particle system also need to be updated, because we are going to be using all of these classes while building maps. Predictably enough, these are the same objects that also need to be drawn:

```
void State_MapEditor::Draw() {
    auto context = m_stateMgr->GetContext();
    auto window = context->m_wind->GetRenderWindow();
    auto from = (m_mapControls.DrawSelectedLayers() ?
        m_mapControls.GetSelectionOptions()->GetLowestLayer() : 0);
    auto to = (m_mapControls.DrawSelectedLayers() ?
        m_mapControls.GetSelectionOptions()->GetHighestLayer()
        : Sheet::Num_Layers - 1);
    for (auto i = from; i <= to; ++i) {
        context->m_gameMap->Draw(i);
        context->m_systemManager->Draw(context->m_wind, i);
        context->m_particles->Draw(*window, i);
    }
    if(!m_mapControls.DrawSelectedLayers()) {
        context->m_particles->Draw(*window, -1);
    }
    m_mapControls.Draw(window);
}
```

Note the `from` and `to` variables. The `mapControl` class is going to provide us with a way to switch between layers/elevations, so we need to obtain that information before anything is rendered, in order to make sure only the appropriate layers are drawn on screen. `DrawSelectedLayers` simply returns a *boolean* value that determines whether or not all layers should be drawn, or just the selected ones. Once the loop has iterated over the appropriate elevations, we make sure to draw the remaining particles that are above the maximum elevation, provided, of course, everything needs to be rendered. This is topped off by the map controls being drawn over everything else.

For other outside communications with this class, we provide two basic setter methods:

```
void State_MapEditor::ResetSavePath() { m_mapSavePath = ""; }
void State_MapEditor::SetMapRedraw(bool l_redraw) {
  m_mapRedraw = l_redraw;
}
```

These are going to be used inside the control classes to communicate events, such as a new map being created, or it needing to be re-drawn.

Building the control mechanism

While building maps, the user tends to run into situations where they need more than just a tile being placed where the mouse clicks. It would definitely be useful to have tools that would enable them to freely pan around, select chunks of the map for deletion or copying, erase them and so on. Our control class is going to serve this exact purpose. It will provide a set of tools that can be used for multiple different situations:

```
enum class ControlMode{None, Pan, Brush, Bucket, Eraser, Select};
```

The preceding control mode enumeration represents a couple of the most common tools that come in a variety of different pieces of software. We're going to implement some of them here, and leave the rest up to you! In the end, we should have a control interface that looks a little like this:

Let us get to actually writing out the header for the control class. For clarity, we are going to be discussing its methods and data members separately, starting with the member functions:

```
class MapControls {
public:
  MapControls(Window* l_window, EventManager* l_eventManager,
    StateManager* l_stateManager, Map* l_map, GUI_Manager* l_gui,
    EntityManager* l_entityMgr, ParticleSystem* l_particles,
```

```
    sf::View& l_view);
  ~MapControls();

  void Update(float l_dT);
  void Draw(sf::RenderWindow* l_window);

  void NewMap();
  void SetTileSheetTexture(const std::string& l_sheet);
  ControlMode GetMode() const;
  bool IsInAction() const;
  bool IsInSecondary() const;
  GUI_SelectionOptions* GetSelectionOptions();

  sf::Vector2i GetMouseTileStart()const;
  sf::Vector2i GetMouseTile()const;
  sf::Vector2f GetMouseDifference()const;

  bool DrawSelectedLayers()const;
  void ToggleDrawingSelectedLayers();

  void MouseClick(EventDetails* l_details);
  void MouseRelease(EventDetails* l_details);
  void MouseWheel(EventDetails* l_details);
  void ToolSelect(EventDetails* l_details);
  void DeleteTiles(EventDetails* l_details);
  void NewMapCreate(EventDetails* l_details);
  void NewMapClose(EventDetails* l_details);

  void SelectMode(ControlMode l_mode);
  void RedrawBrush();
private:
  void UpdateMouse();
  void PanUpdate();
  void BrushUpdate();
  void BucketUpdate();
  void EraserUpdate();
  void SelectionUpdate();
  void PlaceBrushTiles();
  void ResetZoom();
  void ResetTools();
  ...
};
```

In addition to all of the helper methods for setting and getting the class parameters, we have a whole bunch of event callbacks, as well as individual update methods for every kind of map tool we're going to be working with. Next, let us take a look at the data members we are going to be working with:

```cpp
class MapControls {
private:
    ...
    // Mode and mouse/layer flags.
    ControlMode m_mode;
    bool m_action;
    bool m_secondaryAction;
    bool m_rightClickPan;
    bool m_drawSelectedLayers;
    // Mouse information.
    sf::Vector2i m_mousePosition;
    sf::Vector2i m_mouseStartPosition;
    sf::Vector2f m_mouseDifference;
    sf::Vector2i m_mouseTilePosition;
    sf::Vector2i m_mouseTileStartPosition;
    float m_zoom;
    // Brush information, and map bounds.
    TileMap m_brush;
    sf::RenderTexture m_brushTexture;
    sf::RectangleShape m_brushDrawable;
    sf::RectangleShape m_mapBoundaries;
    // Other interfaces used here.
    GUI_MapTileSelector m_tileSelector;
    GUI_SelectionOptions m_selectionOptions;
    GUI_Interface* m_mapSettings;
    // Ties to other classes.
    Window* m_window;
    EventManager* m_eventManager;
    StateManager* m_stateManager;
    Map* m_map;
    GUI_Manager* m_guiManager;
    EntityManager* m_entityManager;
    ParticleSystem* m_particleSystem;
    sf::View& m_view;
};
```

Alongside the `ControlMode` that this class is currently in, we are also going to be storing a couple of flags. The `m_action` flag will be used with tools, as well as `m_secondaryAction`. The former simply denotes whether the left mouse button is pressed or not, while the latter is used with an action that can only happen once the mouse position has changed. This will prove useful when we are trying to optimize certain things to not happen, unless they absolutely have to. The last two flags signify whether we are currently right-click panning, and whether only the selected layers should be drawn on screen.

Below that, there are a couple of 2D vectors, used to store mouse information, such as its current position, where a left-click first happened, the difference between the current and last frame in the mouse position, its current position in tile coordinates, and its starting position in tile coordinates. Additionally, we also have a floating point value for the current zoom factor.

For the brush that will be used to paint with, we simply use a `TileMap` structure, just like the game map class does. Since the brush is going to have to be drawn on screen, we need to store a texture for it, as well as another drawable object that will be used to show it. Finally, a `sf::RectangleShape` type is going to more than suffice for showing the boundaries of the map on screen.

Additional code separation, especially when code is becoming quite lengthy, is always a good idea. For this purpose, other non-general-control logic is going to be spread out into two additional interface classes: a tile selector, and the selection options. A tile selector is a simple window that shows the entire tile-sheet and allows the user to select tiles they want to paint with, while selection options is a separate interface that provides us with a myriad of settings that can be tweaked when specific things on screen are selected. Both of these classes are going to be covered in the next chapter.

Lastly, we have another interface, named `m_mapSettings`, the logic of which is going to be handled within the `MapControls` class. When creating new maps, we need a neat little window that is going to allow us to configure the size of the map, its default friction value, and the name of the tile-sheet it is going to be using. This is exactly the purpose the map settings interface is going to serve.

Implementing controls

There are quite a few data members to initialize, so let us take a look at how the constructor manages it:

```
MapControls::MapControls(Window* l_window, EventManager* l_eventManager,
    StateManager* l_stateManager, Map* l_map, GUI_Manager* l_gui,
    EntityManager* l_entityMgr, ParticleSystem* l_particles,
    sf::View& l_view):
    /* Storing arguments first. */
    m_window(l_window), m_eventManager(l_eventManager),
    m_stateManager(l_stateManager), m_map(l_map),
    m_guiManager(l_gui), m_entityManager(l_entityMgr),
    m_particleSystem(l_particles), m_view(l_view),
    /* Setting up initial data member values. */
    m_mode(ControlMode::Pan), m_action(false),
    m_secondaryAction(false), m_rightClickPan(false),
    m_zoom(1.f), m_brush(sf::Vector2u(1, 1), *l_map->GetTileSet()),
    m_drawSelectedLayers(false),
    /* Initializing other interface classes. */
    m_tileSelector(l_eventManager, l_gui,
        l_gui->GetContext()->m_textureManager),
    m_mapSettings(nullptr),
    m_selectionOptions(l_eventManager, l_gui, this,
        &m_tileSelector, l_map, &m_brush, l_entityMgr, l_particles)
{ ... }
```

As you can see, there is quite a lot going on here. Let us zip through it section by section. Right after the arguments of the constructor are processed, we set up the data members of this class to hold their initial values. Shortly after that, the custom interface classes get set up, with all the necessary arguments being passed to their constructors. For now, we are not going to be worrying about them, as they will be covered in the next chapter.

Let us take a look at the actual constructor body next:

```
MapControls::MapControls(...)
{
    ... // All of the callbacks gets set up.
    m_guiManager->LoadInterface("MapEditorTools.interface",
        "MapEditorTools");
    m_guiManager->GetInterface("MapEditorTools")->
        SetPosition({ 0.f, 16.f });
    m_guiManager->LoadInterface("MapEditorNewMap.interface",
        "MapEditorNewMap");
    m_mapSettings = m_guiManager->GetInterface("MapEditorNewMap");
    m_mapSettings->PositionCenterScreen();
    m_mapSettings->SetActive(false);
```

```
m_brush.SetTile(0, 0, 0, 0);
m_brushDrawable.setFillColor({ 255, 255, 255, 200 });
m_brushDrawable.setOutlineColor({ 255, 0, 0, 255 });
m_brushDrawable.setOutlineThickness(-1.f);
m_mapBoundaries.setPosition({ 0.f, 0.f });
m_mapBoundaries.setFillColor({ 0,0,0,0 });
m_mapBoundaries.setOutlineColor({255, 50, 50, 255});
m_mapBoundaries.setOutlineThickness(-1.f);

auto dropdown = static_cast<GUI_DropDownMenu*>(
  m_mapSettings->GetElement("SheetDropdown"))->GetMenu();
dropdown->PurgeEntries();
auto names = Utils::GetFileList(Utils::GetWorkingDirectory() +
  "media/Tilesheets/", "*.tilesheet");
for (auto& entity : names) {
  dropdown->AddEntry(entity.first.substr(
    0, entity.first.find(".tilesheet")));
}
dropdown->Redraw();
}
```

Right after all event callbacks get set up, we begin working on the interfaces. The actual tools interface is loaded and positioned on screen, as well as the new map settings window, which we are going to keep track of by storing its pointer as one of our data members. It gets positioned in the centre of the screen and set as inactive for the time being.

The next segment simply deals with the stylistic aspects of the brush drawable, as well as the map boundaries rectangle. These values can obviously be customized to look completely different.

Lastly, we need to make sure to populate the drop-down element for sheet selection inside the new map settings interface. After the element is obtained and cleared of all other entries, the list of all filenames that are of type `.tilesheet` inside the appropriate location is obtained and iterated over, stripping away the file format from each one and adding it to the drop-down list, which is then re-drawn to reflect all changes.

Keep in mind that all interfaces and callbacks that were created here need to be removed, which is all that happens in the destructor. For that specific reason, we are not going to be covering that here, as it is redundant.

Let us take a look at what needs to happen when this class is being updated:

```
void MapControls::Update(float l_dT) {
  m_mapBoundaries.setSize(sf::Vector2f(
    m_map->GetTileMap()->GetMapSize() *
    static_cast<unsigned int>(Sheet::Tile_Size)));
```

```
    UpdateMouse();
    if (m_mode == ControlMode::Pan || m_rightClickPan){PanUpdate();}
    else if (m_mode == ControlMode::Brush) { BrushUpdate(); }
    else if (m_mode == ControlMode::Bucket) { BucketUpdate(); }
    else if (m_mode == ControlMode::Eraser) { EraserUpdate(); }
    else if (m_mode == ControlMode::Select) { SelectionUpdate(); }
}
```

First, we handle any possible changes in size of the map class. The map boundary rectangle is updated here to reflect them. Next, we must make sure the mouse is updated properly. All of that logic is contained within the `UpdateMouse` method, which is invoked here. Finally, depending on the current `ControlMode`, we need to invoke the appropriate update method for the specific tool that is selected. The pan tool is special in a way, because it will be updated when it is selected as a tool, and when the right mouse button is being pressed as well.

Drawing all of these objects may be simpler than you think:

```
void MapControls::Draw(sf::RenderWindow* l_window) {
    l_window->draw(m_mapBoundaries);
    if (m_mode == ControlMode::Brush) {
        l_window->draw(m_brushDrawable);
    }
    m_selectionOptions.Draw(l_window);
}
```

In this specific instance, all we need to render is the rectangle of the mapBoundaries, the brush, if the `ControlMode` is set to `Brush`, and the `SelectionOptions` class, which has its own `Draw` method. More on that will be covered in the next chapter.

Next, let us implement everything necessary to keep track of all the relevant mouse information:

```
void MapControls::UpdateMouse() {
    auto mousePos = m_eventManager->GetMousePos(
        m_window->GetRenderWindow());
    m_mouseDifference = sf::Vector2f(mousePos - m_mousePosition);
    m_mouseDifference *= m_zoom;
    m_mousePosition = mousePos;
    auto view = m_window->GetRenderWindow()->getView();
    auto viewPos = view.getCenter() - (view.getSize() * 0.5f);
    auto mouseGlobal=viewPos+(sf::Vector2f(m_mousePosition)*m_zoom);
    auto newPosition = sf::Vector2i(
        floor(mouseGlobal.x / Sheet::Tile_Size),
        floor(mouseGlobal.y / Sheet::Tile_Size)
    );
```

[169]

```
    if (m_mouseTilePosition != newPosition && m_action) {
      m_secondaryAction = true;
    }
    m_mouseTilePosition = newPosition;
}
```

After the current mouse position is obtained, it is used to compute the coordinate difference between the current frame and the previous one.

 Since the mouse difference is expressed in **global coordinates**, we must remember to multiply them by the *zoom factor*.

The mouse position is then stored for the next frame, so this process can take place all over again. The current `sf::View` is then obtained for calculating the current **global** position of the camera. From this, we can calculate the global mouse position (adjusted for zoom, of course), and the mouse tile position, which is simply the tile that's being pointed at.

The current mouse tile position is then checked against the calculated result for being different. If it is, and the left mouse button is currently being pressed (as shown by the `m_action` data member), the secondary action flag is turned on. The mouse tile position is then stored for the next frame.

The next method in the mouse variety deals with left and right clicks, and can be implemented like so:

```
void MapControls::MouseClick(EventDetails* l_details) {
  if (l_details->m_hasBeenProcessed) { return; }
  if (l_details->m_keyCode !=
    static_cast<int>(MouseButtonType::Left))
  {
    m_rightClickPan = true;
    return;
  }
  m_mousePosition = m_eventManager->GetMousePos(
    m_window->GetRenderWindow());
  m_mouseStartPosition = m_mousePosition;

  auto view = m_window->GetRenderWindow()->getView();
  auto viewPos = view.getCenter() - (view.getSize() * 0.5f);
  auto mouseGlobal = viewPos + (sf::Vector2f(m_mousePosition)
    * m_zoom);
  m_mouseTileStartPosition = sf::Vector2i(
    floor(mouseGlobal.x / Sheet::Tile_Size),
    floor(mouseGlobal.y / Sheet::Tile_Size)
```

```
    );

    if (!m_selectionOptions.MouseClick(mouseGlobal)) { return; }

    m_action = true;
    m_secondaryAction = true;
}
```

Because something else may have already processed a mouse event, we need to check for the event details that get submitted as an argument. We do not want to accidentally paint some tiles on the map if we are simply interacting with an interface, for example. Next, the key code of the event is checked to see whether it is the left mouse button. If it is not, all we need to worry about is setting the right-click pan flag to true and returning.

If we indeed have a left-click, on the other hand, the current mouse position is stored as both the starting and the current positions. A very similar process to updating the mouse takes place here, leading to the calculation of the global mouse coordinates. They are then passed into the MouseClick() method of the selection options class, which returns a *boolean* flag, signifying whether any entities or particle emitters have been selected. We will be dealing with that in the next chapter. If that is not the case, however, both the action and secondary action flags are set to true in order to use the currently selected tool.

In the same way that for every action there is an equal and opposite reaction, for each click we need to have a release:

```
void MapControls::MouseRelease(EventDetails* l_details) {
    if (l_details->m_keyCode !=
        static_cast<int>(MouseButtonType::Left))
    {
        m_rightClickPan = false;
        return;
    }
    m_action = false;
    m_secondaryAction = false;
    m_selectionOptions.MouseRelease();
}
```

All we need to worry about here is resetting all of the action flags that are used while the mouse is active. This includes the right-click panning, and both action flags. The selection options interface also needs to be notified of a release.

A neat little feature that is going to help out a lot is being able to zoom in and out. It is handled here as an event:

```
void MapControls::MouseWheel(EventDetails* l_details) {
    if (l_details->m_hasBeenProcessed) { return; }
```

```
    float factor = 0.05f;
    factor *= l_details->m_mouseWheelDelta;
    factor = 1.f - factor;
    m_view.zoom(factor);
    m_zoom *= factor;
}
```

If this event has not already been processed by something else, we proceed to calculate the amount of zoom that needs to happen. A `float factor` value is defined here, and is multiplied by the change in the mouse wheel position. In order for it to be treated as a scale factor, it is subtracted from `1.f`, and then used to zoom in the view. Finally, in order to keep track of the current zoom value, we must multiply it by the said scale factor.

The next event we need to worry about is one of the tools being selected:

```
void MapControls::ToolSelect(EventDetails* l_details) {
    auto mode = ControlMode::None;
    if (l_details->m_name == "MapEditor_PanTool") {
        mode = ControlMode::Pan;
    } else if (l_details->m_name == "MapEditor_BrushTool") {
        mode = ControlMode::Brush;
    } else if (l_details->m_name == "MapEditor_PaintTool") {
        mode = ControlMode::Bucket;
    } else if (l_details->m_name == "MapEditor_EraserTool") {
        mode = ControlMode::Eraser;
    } else if (l_details->m_name == "MapEditor_SelectTool") {
        mode = ControlMode::Select;
    }
    SelectMode(mode);
}
```

This is quite simple, as we basically map the names of elements to their `ControlMode` counter-parts. The appropriate mode is then selected on the bottom.

Speaking of tools, each one of them has their own individual update method. Let us begin by taking a look at how the pan tool is updated:

```
void MapControls::PanUpdate() {
    if (!m_action && !m_rightClickPan) { return; }
    if (m_mouseDifference == sf::Vector2f(0.f, 0.f)) { return; }
    m_view.setCenter(m_view.getCenter() +
        (sf::Vector2f(0.f, 0.f) - sf::Vector2f(m_mouseDifference)));
}
```

We obviously do not want the screen to move if the mouse is not being clicked, or if the mouse position delta between frames is absolute zero. Given that both those conditions are satisfied, however, all we need to do is move the centre of the view to a different location. This location is calculated by adding its current position with the mouse position difference, which has to have its sign flipped. We do this, because as the mouse is clicked and moved left, for example, the view needs to shift right in order to feel natural. The same is true for the *x* axis.

In the case of a brush tool, the logic goes like this:

```
void MapControls::BrushUpdate() {
  auto tilePos = sf::Vector2f(
    static_cast<float>(m_mouseTilePosition.x * Sheet::Tile_Size),
    static_cast<float>(m_mouseTilePosition.y * Sheet::Tile_Size)
  );
  m_brushDrawable.setPosition(tilePos);
  PlaceBrushTiles();
}
```

First, the global position of the tile the mouse is over currently is calculated, which the brush drawable is set to match. Doing it like this creates a feel of the brush being locked to a grid. Another method is then invoked for placing the tiles:

```
void MapControls::PlaceBrushTiles() {
  if (!m_action || !m_secondaryAction) { return; }
  m_map->GetTileMap()->PlotTileMap(m_brush,
    m_mouseTilePosition, m_selectionOptions.GetLowestLayer());
  auto size = m_brush.GetMapSize();
  auto from = sf::Vector3i(m_mouseTilePosition.x,
    m_mouseTilePosition.y, m_selectionOptions.GetLowestLayer());
  auto to = sf::Vector3i(m_mouseTilePosition.x + size.x - 1,
    m_mouseTilePosition.y + size.y - 1,
    m_selectionOptions.GetHighestLayer());
  m_map->Redraw(from, to);
  m_secondaryAction = false;
  // Set it to false in order to avoid multiple placements.
}
```

The first and most obvious check here is to make sure that both the primary and secondary actions are on. We do not want to be placing tiles if the mouse is not being clicked, or if it already has been clicked, but is still at the same location. Otherwise, we are good to go on painting, which begins by the brush tile map being placed on the game maps tile map at the current mouse tile position, starting at the lowest layer currently selected by the selection options. Even though we may be able to shift through elevations at ease, we still need to tell this method about the lowest current elevation selected, because the brush tile map itself still begins at elevation *0*.

After the map has been updated, the tile coordinate range to be redrawn is calculated and passed to the `MapControls` class to be rendered on screen. We do not want to re-draw the whole map, as that would take more time and introduce latency. Lastly, the secondary action flag is set to `false` in order to indicate that a placement has been made at these coordinates already.

The next tool we need to update is the selection box:

```
void MapControls::SelectionUpdate() {
  m_selectionOptions.SelectionUpdate();
}
```

As you can see, all of that logic is handled by the `SelectionOptions` class. For now, we simply need to worry about invoking this method

The same `SelectionOptions` interface may be responsible for manipulating our brush, which means we need to have a method for redrawing it to reflect changes:

```
void MapControls::RedrawBrush() {
  auto brushSize = m_brush.GetMapSize();
  auto brushRealSize = brushSize *
    static_cast<unsigned int>(Sheet::Tile_Size);
  auto textureSize = m_brushTexture.getSize();
  if (brushRealSize.x != textureSize.x ||
    brushRealSize.y != textureSize.y)
  {
    if (!m_brushTexture.create(brushRealSize.x, brushRealSize.y))
    { /* Error Message. */ }
  }

  m_brushTexture.clear({ 0, 0, 0, 0 });

  for (auto x = 0; x < brushSize.x; ++x) {
    for (auto y = 0; y < brushSize.y; ++y) {
      for (auto layer = 0; layer < Sheet::Num_Layers; ++layer) {
        auto tile = m_brush.GetTile(x, y, layer);
        if (!tile) { continue; }
```

```
        auto info = tile->m_properties;
        if (!info) { continue; }
        info->m_sprite.setPosition(sf::Vector2f(
          x * Sheet::Tile_Size, y * Sheet::Tile_Size));
        m_brushTexture.draw(info->m_sprite);
      }
    }
  }

  m_brushTexture.display();
  m_brushDrawable.setTexture(&m_brushTexture.getTexture());
  m_brushDrawable.setSize(sf::Vector2f(brushRealSize));
  m_brushDrawable.setTextureRect(
    sf::IntRect(sf::Vector2i(0, 0), sf::Vector2i(brushRealSize)));
}
```

First, the real pixel brush size is calculated from the size of its tile map. If it does not match the current dimensions of the texture that represents it, the texture needs to be re-created. Once that is taken care of, the texture is cleared to all transparent pixels, and we begin iterating over each tile and layer inside said brush. Given it is a valid tile that has proper ties to an information structure that holds its sprite for rendering, the latter is set to the correct position on the texture and drawn to it.

Once this is done, the texture's display method is invoked to show all the changes, and the drawable object of the brush is bound to the texture again. The drawables size and texture rectangle is also reset, because the dimensions of the texture could have changed.

In this type of an application, it's important to have a quick and easy way of deleting something that's currently selected. For this, we're going to be processing the event that's bound to the *Delete* key on your keyboard:

```
void MapControls::DeleteTiles(EventDetails* l_details) {
  if (m_mode != ControlMode::Select) { return; }
  m_selectionOptions.RemoveSelection(l_details);
}
```

This is a very simple callback. It simply checks if the current `ControlMode` is selected, and passes its details to another callback that belongs to the `selectionOptions` class. It will be dealing with all removals.

When a new tool is being selected, we must reset all data members we work with to their initial values in order to avoid weird bugs. This is where the `ResetTools()` method comes in:

```
void MapControls::ResetTools() {
    auto defaultVector = sf::Vector2i(-1, -1);
    m_mouseTilePosition = defaultVector;
    m_mouseTileStartPosition = defaultVector;
    m_selectionOptions.Reset();
    m_tileSelector.Hide();
}
```

It simply resets certain mouse data to a default uninitialized state. The `m_selectionOptions Reset()` method is also invoked, so that it can deal with its own resetting. Lastly, the `tileSelector` interface is hidden here as well.

Another useful little method is for resetting the zoom of the current view to a normal level:

```
void MapControls::ResetZoom() {
    m_view.zoom(1.f / m_zoom);
    m_zoom = 1.f;
}
```

By dividing `1.f` by the current zoom factor, we obtain a scale value, which, when scaled by, the view returns to its normal state.

Next, let us see what needs to happen in order for this class to change its `ControlMode`:

```
void MapControls::SelectMode(ControlMode l_mode) {
    ResetTools();
    m_mode = l_mode;
    if (m_mode == ControlMode::Brush) { RedrawBrush(); }
    m_selectionOptions.SetControlMode(m_mode);
}
```

After the tools are reset, the mode passed in as the argument is stored. If the mode being applied is a brush, it needs to be re-drawn. Lastly, the `selectionOptions` class is notified of the mode change, so that it can perform its own logic.

Finally, one of the last key pieces of code is the creation of a new map:

```
void MapControls::NewMapCreate(EventDetails* l_details) {
    auto s_x = m_mapSettings->GetElement("Size_X")->GetText();
    auto s_y = m_mapSettings->GetElement("Size_Y")->GetText();
    auto friction = m_mapSettings->
        GetElement("Friction")->GetText();
    auto selection = static_cast<GUI_DropDownMenu*>(
```

```
        m_mapSettings->GetElement("SheetDropdown"))->
        GetMenu()->GetSelected();
    if (selection.empty()) { return; }

    auto context = m_guiManager->GetContext();
    auto editorState = m_stateManager->
        GetState<State_MapEditor>(StateType::MapEditor);
    m_particleSystem->PurgeCurrentState();
    m_map->PurgeMap();
    editorState->ResetSavePath();

    m_map->GetTileMap()->SetMapSize
        sf::Vector2u(std::stoi(s_x), std::stoi(s_y)));
    m_map->GetDefaultTile()->m_friction =
        sf::Vector2f(std::stof(friction), std::stof(friction));
    m_map->GetTileSet()->ResetWorker();
    m_map->GetTileSet()->AddFile(Utils::GetWorkingDirectory() +
        "media/Tilesheets/" + selection + ".tilesheet");
    m_map->GetTileSet()->SetName(selection + ".tilesheet");

    auto loading = m_stateManager->
        GetState<State_Loading>(StateType::Loading);
    loading->AddLoader(context->m_gameMap->GetTileSet());
    loading->SetManualContinue(false);
    editorState->SetMapRedraw(true);
    m_mapSettings->SetActive(false);
    m_stateManager->SwitchTo(StateType::Loading);
}
```

First, we obtain the size values from the text-fields of the map settings interface. In addition to that, we also grab the friction value, as well as the current selection of the tile-sheet drop–down menu. If the latter is empty, we simply return, as no tile-sheet has been selected.

If we do proceed, the particle system and the map both need to be purged. The MapEditor state is then notified to reset its save path, which forces the user to re-enter a filename when saving.

The map's size is then set up, alongside the default friction value. The selected tile-sheet file is added for further loading in a separate thread, and its name is registered inside the game map's internal TileSet data member.

Finally, the loading state is obtained, the tile-set is added to it, and the manual continue flag is set to false, in order to make the loading screen simply go back to the current state after it is done. The new map settings interface is then hidden, and we can finally switch to the loading state.

In case a mistake happens, the user must have a way to close the new `m_mapSettings` interface:

```
void MapControls::NewMapClose(EventDetails* l_details) {
  m_mapSettings->SetActive(false);
}
```

This callback gets invoked when the **close** button of the interface is pressed. All it does is simply hiding it.

Finally, we have a bunch of setters and getters that do not add up to much on their own, but are useful in the long run:

```
void MapControls::NewMap() { m_mapSettings->SetActive(true); }
void MapControls::SetTileSheetTexture(const std::string& l_sheet) {
  m_tileSelector.SetSheetTexture(l_sheet);
}
ControlMode MapControls::GetMode() const { return m_mode; }
bool MapControls::IsInAction() const { return m_action; }
bool MapControls::IsInSecondary() const{return m_secondaryAction;}
GUI_SelectionOptions* MapControls::GetSelectionOptions() {
  return &m_selectionOptions;
}
sf::Vector2i MapControls::GetMouseTileStart() const {
  return m_mouseTileStartPosition;
}
sf::Vector2i MapControls::GetMouseTile() const {
  return m_mouseTilePosition;
}
sf::Vector2f MapControls::GetMouseDifference() const {
  return m_mouseDifference;
}
bool MapControls::DrawSelectedLayers() const {
  return m_drawSelectedLayers;
}
void MapControls::ToggleDrawingSelectedLayers() {
  m_drawSelectedLayers = !m_drawSelectedLayers;
}
```

You may have noticed that we have not yet covered the bucket and eraser tools. This is what is usually referred to as homework, which should serve as good practice:

```
void MapControls::BucketUpdate() { /* IMPLEMENT */ }
void MapControls::EraserUpdate() { /* IMPLEMENT */ }
```

Keep in mind that as we have not yet implemented everything that makes the map editor tick, this should probably wait until the next chapter is wrapped up.

Summary

In this chapter, we have introduced and implemented the concept of graphical file management, as well as laid the foundations for one of the most important tools a small RPG-style game uses. There is still a lot left to do before we can start reaping the benefits of having proper tools. In the next chapter, we will be covering the finishing touches of the map editor, as well as implementing a different tool for managing entities. See you there!

5
Filling the Tool Belt - a few More Gadgets

The last chapter established a firm ground for us to build on. It is time to take full advantage of it and finish what we started, by building a robust set of tools, ready to take on a wide variety of design problems.

In this chapter, we are going to be covering these topics:

- Implementation of selection options
- Design and programming of a tile selection window
- Management of entities

There is quite a lot of code to cover, so let us just jump into it!

Planning the selection options

Versatile selection options are important when creating a responsive and useful application. Without them, any sort of software can feel unintuitive, clunky, or unresponsive at best. In this particular case, we are going to be dealing with selecting, copying, and placing tiles, entities, and particle emitters.

Let us see what such an interface might look like:

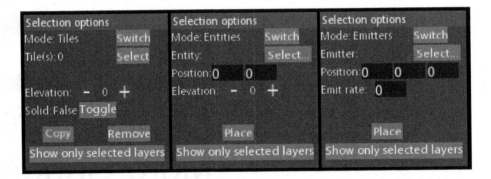

In order to get there, we need to create a flexible class, designed to be able to handle any possible combination of options and controls. Let us start by going over the most basic data types that are going to come in handy when developing this system:

```
enum class SelectMode{ Tiles, Entities, Emitters };
using NameList = std::vector<std::pair<std::string, bool>>;
```

First, the selection mode needs to be enumerated. As shown in the preceding snippet, there are three modes we are going to be working with at the moment, although this list can easily be expanded in the future. The `NameList` data type is going to be used to store the contents of entity and particle directories. This is simply the return format for the utility function we are going to be relying on.

With the data types out of the way, let us take a stab at creating the blueprint of our `SelectionOptions` class:

```
class GUI_SelectionOptions {
public:
  GUI_SelectionOptions(EventManager* l_eventManager,
    GUI_Manager* l_guiManager, MapControls* l_controls,
    GUI_MapTileSelector* l_selector, Map* l_map, TileMap* l_brush,
    EntityManager* l_entityMgr, ParticleSystem* l_particles);
  ~GUI_SelectionOptions();

  void Show();
  void Hide();
  void SetControlMode(ControlMode l_mode);
  void SetSelectMode(SelectMode l_mode);
  SelectMode GetSelectMode() const;
  void SelectEntity(int l_id);
  void SelectEmitter(Emitter* l_emitter);
```

```
    sf::Vector2i GetSelectXRange() const;
    sf::Vector2i GetSelectYRange() const;
    unsigned int GetLowestLayer() const;
    unsigned int GetHighestLayer() const;

    void Update();
    void Draw(sf::RenderWindow* l_window);
    bool MouseClick(const sf::Vector2f& l_pos);
    void MouseRelease();
    void Reset();

    void SelectModeSwitch(EventDetails* l_details);
    void OpenTileSelection(EventDetails* l_details);
    void SolidToggle(EventDetails* l_details);
    void CopySelection(EventDetails* l_details);
    void PlaceSelection(EventDetails* l_details);
    void RemoveSelection(EventDetails* l_details);
    void ToggleLayers(EventDetails* l_details);
    void SelectionOptionsElevation(EventDetails* l_details);
    void SaveOptions(EventDetails* l_details);
private:
    void SelectionElevationUpdate();
    void UpdateSelectDrawable();
    void UpdateTileSelection();
    void UpdateEntitySelection();
    void UpdateEmitterSelection();
    void DeleteSelection(bool l_deleteAll);
    ...
};
```

In order to keep things simple, let us focus on talking about the methods we need first, before covering data members. As far as public methods go, we have pretty much the assortment anyone would expect. Alongside the `Show()` and `Hide()` methods, which are going to be used to manipulate the interface this class encapsulates, we pretty much only have a few setters and getters, used to manipulate the `ControlMode` and `SelectMode`, select specific entities or particle emitters, and obtain tile selection ranges, as well as the range of layer visibility/selection. Additionally, this class also needs to provide plenty of callback methods for numerous controls of the interface we are working with.

The private methods mainly consist of code used to update the interface and the visual representation of its selection onscreen, as well as methods for updating each possible mode the selection interface can be in. It's topped off by a private method `DeleteSelection()`, which is going to be useful when removing tiles, entities, or particle emitters.

Finally, let us take a gander at all of the data members that are going to be used to preserve the state of this class:

```
class GUI_SelectionOptions {
private:
    ...
    // Selection data.
    SelectMode m_selectMode;
    sf::RectangleShape m_selectDrawable;
    sf::Color m_selectStartColor;
    sf::Color m_selectEndColor;
    sf::Color m_entityColor;
    sf::Color m_emitterColor;
    sf::Vector2i m_selectRangeX;
    sf::Vector2i m_selectRangeY;
    bool m_selectUpdate;
    // Entity and emitter select info.
    int m_entityId;
    C_Position* m_entity;
    Emitter* m_emitter;
    NameList m_entityNames;
    NameList m_emitterNames;
    // Selection range.
    unsigned int m_layerSelectLow;
    unsigned int m_layerSelectHigh;
    // Interfaces.
    GUI_Interface* m_selectionOptions;
    MapControls* m_mapControls;
    GUI_MapTileSelector* m_tileSelector;
    // Class ties.
    EventManager* m_eventManager;
    GUI_Manager* m_guiManager;
    Map* m_map;
    TileMap* m_brush;
    EntityManager* m_entityManager;
    ParticleSystem* m_particleSystem;
};
```

We start by storing the current selection mode, alongside the RectangleShape object, used to visually represent the selection being made. In order to make our tools feel more responsive and lively, we are going to be providing a number of different colors, used to represent different states of selection. For example, the m_selectStartColor and m_selectEndColor data members are used to differentiate the tile selection that's still being made, and its final state, when the mouse button is released. In addition to colors, we also have two vector types that store the tile selection range for both axes, and a *boolean* flag, used to determine when the rectangle shape should be updated.

For the other two states, we need to store the entity identifier and its position component, given we are in an entity selection mode, and a pointer to the particle emitter, provided we are currently working with particles. This is also where the contents of particle and entity directories are going to be stored, in order to populate the drop-down list with the appropriate values.

Additionally, we need to keep track of the layer selection range, as well as pointers to the selectionOptions interface, the MapControl class that was covered in the previous chapter, and a map tile selector class, which will be covered shortly. Keep in mind that only the m_selectionOptions interface is technically owned by this class. The other two classes encapsulate their own interfaces, thus managing their destruction.

Lastly, we need to have access to the eventManager, guimanager, the game map instance, the tile brush, entityManager, and the particleSystem.

Implementing selection options

With all of this data to properly initialize, we have quite a lot of work to do in the constructor:

```
GUI_SelectionOptions::GUI_SelectionOptions(
  EventManager* l_eventManager, GUI_Manager* l_guiManager,
  MapControls* l_controls, GUI_MapTileSelector* l_selector,
  Map* l_map, TileMap* l_brush, EntityManager* l_entityMgr,
  ParticleSystem* l_particles) :
  /* Processing arguments. */
  m_eventManager(l_eventManager), m_guiManager(l_guiManager),
  m_mapControls(l_controls), m_tileSelector(l_selector),
  m_map(l_map), m_brush(l_brush), m_entityManager(l_entityMgr),
  m_particleSystem(l_particles),
  /* Initializing default values of data members. */
  m_selectRangeX(-1, -1), m_selectRangeY(-1, -1),
  m_layerSelectLow(0), m_layerSelectHigh(0),
  m_selectMode(SelectMode::Tiles), m_entityId(-1),
  m_entity(nullptr), m_emitter(nullptr), m_selectUpdate(true)
{...}
```

After all of the arguments are properly stored away, the default values of all data members are set up. This ensures that the initial state of the selection is defined. The body of the constructor is used to appropriately deal with other tasks:

```
GUI_SelectionOptions::GUI_SelectionOptions(...)
{
  ... // Setting up callbacks.
  m_guiManager->LoadInterface(
    "MapEditorSelectionOptions.interface",
    "MapEditorSelectionOptions");
  m_selectionOptions =
    m_guiManager->GetInterface("MapEditorSelectionOptions");
  m_selectionOptions->SetPosition({ 0.f, 164.f });
  m_selectionOptions->SetActive(false);
  m_selectStartColor = sf::Color(0, 0, 150, 120);
  m_selectEndColor = sf::Color(0, 0, 255, 150);
  m_entityColor = sf::Color(255, 0, 0, 150);
  m_emitterColor = sf::Color(0, 255, 0, 150);

  m_entityNames = Utils::GetFileList(Utils::GetWorkingDirectory()
    + "media/Entities/", "*.entity");
  m_emitterNames = Utils::GetFileList(Utils::GetWorkingDirectory()
    + "media/Particles/", "*.particle");
}
```

Here, all of the proper callbacks are set up, the interface the class owns is loaded, positioned and hidden, and the color values are initialized. Finally, the contents of the entity and particle emitter directories are obtained and stored.

We're not going to be covering the destructor here, because it simply deals with removing all callbacks and the interface that is set up.

Speaking of interfaces, the outside code needs to be able to easily show and hide the selectionOptions window:

```
void GUI_SelectionOptions::Show() {
  m_selectionOptions->SetActive(true);
  m_guiManager->BringToFront(m_selectionOptions);
}
void GUI_SelectionOptions::Hide() {
  m_selectionOptions->SetActive(false);
}
```

The desired effect is achieved by either setting the interface as active or inactive. In the former case, the `guiManager` is also used in order to position the `selectionOptions` interface above everything else, by bringing it to the front.

Because this interface/class is a sort of helper, it depends on the control mode of our editor. This relationship requires the `selectionOptions` class to be notified of `controlMode` changes:

```
void GUI_SelectionOptions::SetControlMode(ControlMode l_mode) {
    if (l_mode != ControlMode::Brush && l_mode
      != ControlMode::Select)
    { return; }
    SetSelectMode(SelectMode::Tiles);
    if (l_mode == ControlMode::Brush) {
        m_selectionOptions->SetActive(true);
        m_selectionOptions->Focus();
        m_selectionOptions->GetElement("TileSelect")->SetActive(true);
    } else if (l_mode == ControlMode::Select) {
        m_selectionOptions->SetActive(true);
        m_selectionOptions->Focus();
        m_selectionOptions->GetElement("SolidToggle")->
            SetActive(true);
        m_selectionOptions->GetElement("CopySelection")->
            SetActive(true);
    }
}
```

It's only necessary to worry about the `Brush` and `Select` modes, as this interface is not even needed for anything else. In case a `Brush` is selected, the interface is enabled and focused, while its `TileSelect` element is also enabled. This ensures we can select tiles we want to paint with. If the selection tool is picked, we want the buttons for solidity toggling and selection copying to be enabled instead.

The actual selection mode switching needs to be handled too, and can be done like so:

```
void GUI_SelectionOptions::SetSelectMode(SelectMode l_mode) {
    Reset();
    m_selectMode = l_mode;
    m_selectionOptions->SetActive(true);
    m_selectionOptions->Focus();

    if (l_mode == SelectMode::Tiles) {
        ... // GUI Element manipulation.
    } else if(l_mode == SelectMode::Entities) {
        ... // GUI Element manipulation.
        auto dropdown = static_cast<GUI_DropDownMenu*>(
          m_selectionOptions->GetElement("SelectDropdown"))->
```

[187]

```
        GetMenu();
      dropdown->PurgeEntries();
      for (auto& entity : m_entityNames) {
        dropdown->AddEntry(
          entity.first.substr(0, entity.first.find(".entity")));
      }
      dropdown->Redraw();
  } else if (l_mode == SelectMode::Emitters) {
      ... // GUI Element manipulation.
      auto dropdown = static_cast<GUI_DropDownMenu*>(
        m_selectionOptions->GetElement("SelectDropdown"))->
        GetMenu();
      dropdown->PurgeEntries();
      for (auto& emitter : m_emitterNames) {
        dropdown->AddEntry(
          emitter.first.substr(0, emitter.first.find(".particle")));
      }
      dropdown->Redraw();
  }
}
```

First, the `Reset()` method is invoked. It is used to disable all unnecessary interface elements and zero out the selection data members to their default values. After the actual selection mode is stored and the interface is set to active, we begin dealing with the actual mode-specific logic.

If we are in the tile selection mode, it simply involves enabling a number of interface elements, as well as setting their text to match the context. For the sake of simplicity, all of the element manipulation in this method is omitted.

Dealing with entity and emitter modes is similar, yet includes an additional step, which is populating the drop-down menu with appropriate values. In both cases, the drop-down element is obtained and purged of its current entries. The appropriate directory list is then iterated over; adding each entry to the drop-down, making sure the file type is removed. Once this is done, the drop-down menu is instructed to be re-drawn.

Let us take a look at what needs to happen when our selection options class is instructed to select a particular entity:

```
void GUI_SelectionOptions::SelectEntity(int l_id) {
  if (l_id == -1) {
    m_entityId = -1;
    m_selectionOptions->GetElement("CopySelection")->
      SetActive(false);
    m_selectionOptions->GetElement("PlaceSelection")->
      SetText("Place");
```

```
    m_selectionOptions->GetElement("RemoveSelection")->
      SetActive(false);
    m_entity = nullptr;
    return;
  }
  auto pos = m_entityManager->
    GetComponent<C_Position>(l_id, Component::Position);
  if (!pos) {
    m_entityId = -1;
    m_selectionOptions->GetElement("CopySelection")->
      SetActive(false);
    m_selectionOptions->GetElement("PlaceSelection")->
      SetText("Place");
    m_selectionOptions->GetElement("RemoveSelection")->
      SetActive(false);
    m_entity = nullptr;
    return;
  }
  m_selectionOptions->GetElement("CopySelection")->
    SetActive(true);
  m_selectionOptions->GetElement("PlaceSelection")->
    SetText("Edit");
  m_selectionOptions->GetElement("RemoveSelection")->
    SetActive(true);
  m_entityId = l_id;
  m_entity = pos;
  m_selectionOptions->GetElement("InfoText")->
    SetText(std::to_string(m_entityId));
  m_selectUpdate = true;
}
```

First, the argument could be used to de-select an entity, as well as select it. If the appropriate de-select value is passed, or an entity position component with the provided identifier has not been found, the related interface elements are adjusted to match the situation.

If an entity with the provided ID does exist, the proper elements are enabled and adjusted. The entity position component as well as its identifier is stored for later use, and the information text element of the selection options interface is changed to reflect the ID of the entity selected. It is also marked to be updated, by manipulating the *boolean* flag m_selectUpdate.

A very similar process takes place when selecting an emitter:

```
void GUI_SelectionOptions::SelectEmitter(Emitter* l_emitter) {
  m_emitter = l_emitter;
  if (!l_emitter) {
```

```
        m_selectionOptions->GetElement("CopySelection")->
          SetActive(false);
        m_selectionOptions->GetElement("PlaceSelection")->
          SetText("Place");
        m_selectionOptions->GetElement("RemoveSelection")->
          SetActive(false);
        return;
    }
    m_selectionOptions->GetElement("CopySelection")->
      SetActive(true);
    m_selectionOptions->GetElement("PlaceSelection")->
      SetText("Edit");
    m_selectionOptions->GetElement("RemoveSelection")->
      SetActive(true);
    m_selectionOptions->GetElement("InfoText")->SetText(m_emitter->
      GetGenerators());
    m_selectionOptions->GetElement("EmitRate")->
      SetText(std::to_string(m_emitter->GetEmitRate()));
    m_selectUpdate = true;
}
```

It is simpler in a sense that we are only working with a pointer to a particle emitter. If `nullptr` is passed in, proper elements are disabled and adjusted. Otherwise, the interface is updated to reflect the information of the emitter that is selected, while also marking the `selectionOptions` interface is properly updated afterwards.

We obviously also need a way to switch between the different selection modes, hence this callback:

```
void GUI_SelectionOptions::SelectModeSwitch(
  EventDetails* l_details)
{
  if (m_selectMode == SelectMode::Tiles) {
    if (m_mapControls->GetMode() != ControlMode::Select) {
      m_mapControls->SelectMode(ControlMode::Select);
    }
    SetSelectMode(SelectMode::Entities);
  } else if (m_selectMode == SelectMode::Entities) {
    SetSelectMode(SelectMode::Emitters);
  } else { SetSelectMode(SelectMode::Tiles); }
}
```

It simply cycles through all of the options for selection. One thing worthy of pointing out here is that if the interface before cycling is in tile mode, we want to make sure that the `ControlMode` is switched to `Select`.

Another feature we want to work on is opening up and dealing with tiles being selected from the tile-sheet:

```
void GUI_SelectionOptions::OpenTileSelection(
  EventDetails* l_details)
{
  if (!m_tileSelector->IsActive()) {
    m_tileSelector->Show();
    return;
  }
  m_mapControls->SelectMode(ControlMode::Brush);
  if (m_tileSelector->CopySelection(*m_brush)) {
    m_selectionOptions->GetElement("Solidity")->SetText("False");
    m_mapControls->RedrawBrush();
  }
  m_selectionOptions->GetElement("InfoText")->SetText(
    std::to_string(m_brush->GetTileCount()));
}
```

First, we deal with just opening the `tileSelector` interface, provided it is not set to active yet. On the other hand, if the interface is open, the select button being pressed indicates the user attempting to copy their selection to the brush. The `mapControls` class is instructed to switch its mode to `Brush`, which is then passed into the `tileSelector` class's `CopySelection()` method, responsible for copying actual tile data. Since it returns a *boolean* value that indicates its success, the method is invoked inside an `if` statement, which allows us to update the solidity element of the interface and request a brush re-draw, provided the copying procedure was successful. At any rate, the information text element of the `selectionOptions` interface is then updated to hold the total count of tiles that have been selected and copied to the brush.

Toggling the solidity of the current portion of the map being selected or the brush itself is also possible in our tile editor:

```
void GUI_SelectionOptions::SolidToggle(EventDetails* l_details) {
  auto mode = m_mapControls->GetMode();
  if (m_mapControls->GetMode() != ControlMode::Brush
    && mode != ControlMode::Select)
  { return; }
  auto element = m_selectionOptions->GetElement("Solidity");
  auto state = element->GetText();
  bool solid = false;
  std::string newText;
  if (state == "True") { newText = "False"; }
  else { solid = true; newText = "True"; }
  element->SetText(newText);
  sf::Vector2u start;
```

```
sf::Vector2u finish;
TileMap* map = nullptr;
if (mode == ControlMode::Brush) {
  map = m_brush;
  start = sf::Vector2u(0, 0);
  finish = map->GetMapSize() - sf::Vector2u(1, 1);
} else if (mode == ControlMode::Select) {
  map = m_map->GetTileMap();
  start = sf::Vector2u(m_selectRangeX.x, m_selectRangeY.x);
  finish = sf::Vector2u(m_selectRangeX.y, m_selectRangeY.y);
}

for (auto x = start.x; x <= finish.x; ++x) {
  for (auto y = start.y; y <= finish.y; ++y) {
    for (auto layer = m_layerSelectLow;
      layer < m_layerSelectHigh; ++layer)
    {
      auto tile = map->GetTile(x, y, layer);
      if (!tile) { continue; }
      tile->m_solid = solid;
    }
  }
}
```

First, we obviously can not toggle the solidity of a selection, if the control mode is not set to either the `Brush` or `Select` mode. With that being covered, the solidity state label is obtained, as well as its text. After flipping its value to its opposite and updating the element's text, we establish a range of tiles that will be modified. In the case of a brush having its solidity toggled, the range encapsulates the entire structure. On the other hand, the map selection range is used when dealing with the select mode.

The `m_selectRangeX` and `m_selectRangeY` data members represent the selection range of the map tiles. Each range is responsible for its own axis. For example, `m_selectRangeX.x` is the **starting** X coordinate, and `m_selectRangeX.y` is the **ending** X coordinate.

After the range is properly established, we simply need to iterate over it and obtain tiles from the appropriate `TileMap`, setting their solidity to the appropriate value.

Copying a certain portion of the map to the brush could also prove to be a useful feature:

```cpp
void GUI_SelectionOptions::CopySelection(EventDetails* l_details)
{
  if (m_selectRangeX.x == -1) { return; }
  auto size = sf::Vector2u(
    m_selectRangeX.y - m_selectRangeX.x,
    m_selectRangeY.y - m_selectRangeY.x);
  size.x += 1;
  size.y += 1;
  m_brush->Purge();
  m_brush->SetMapSize(size);
  unsigned int b_x = 0, b_y = 0, b_l = 0;
  bool solid = false, mixed = false;
  unsigned short changes = 0;
  for (auto x = m_selectRangeX.x; x <= m_selectRangeX.y; ++x) {
    for (auto y = m_selectRangeY.x; y <= m_selectRangeY.y; ++y) {
      for (auto layer = m_layerSelectLow;
        layer <= m_layerSelectHigh; ++layer)
      {
        auto tile = m_map->GetTile(x, y, layer);
        if (!tile) { ++b_l; continue; }
        auto newTile = m_brush->SetTile(
          b_x, b_y, b_l, tile->m_properties->m_id);
        if (!newTile) { continue; }
        if (!mixed) {
          if (tile->m_solid && !solid) {
            solid = true; ++changes;
          } else if (solid) {
            solid = false; ++changes;
          }
          if (changes >= 2) { mixed = true; }
        }
        *newTile = *tile;
        ++b_l;
      }
      b_l = 0;
      ++b_y;
    }
    b_y = 0;
    ++b_x;
  }
  m_layerSelectHigh = m_layerSelectLow +
    m_brush->GetHighestElevation();
  if (m_layerSelectHigh >= Sheet::Num_Layers) {
    auto difference = (m_layerSelectHigh - Sheet::Num_Layers) + 1;
    m_layerSelectHigh = Sheet::Num_Layers - 1;
    m_layerSelectLow -= difference;
```

```
        }
        SelectionElevationUpdate();
        m_mapControls->SelectMode(ControlMode::Brush);
        m_selectionOptions->GetElement("InfoText")->
            SetText(std::to_string(m_brush->GetTileCount()));
        m_selectionOptions->GetElement("Solidity")->
            SetText((mixed ? "Mixed" : (solid ? "True" : "False")));
    }
```

We begin by checking if a selection actually was made, which can be done by checking any of the select range data members. Afterwards, the size of the selection is calculated by subtracting the start-points of the selection from the end-points, and increasing the size by one unit on both axes. This is done in order to compensate for inclusive ranges that start and end on the same exact tile number.

Once the brush tile map is purged and resized, some local variables are set up in order to aid the rest of the code. The three *unsigned integers* are going to be used as index coordinates for the brush tile map, in order to map the copied tiles correctly. The two *boolean* flags and the *unsigned short* changes are going to keep track of solidity changes, in order to update the GUI element that denotes what solidity state the selection is in.

Next, the tile loops are entered. After the map tile at the specific coordinates is obtained and passes the validity check, the brush tile at the current coordinates denoted by b_x, b_y, and b_l is set to hold the same tile ID. The solidity changes of the tile are then detected and noted, in order to determine if we have a mixed selection of solidities. Finally, all other tile properties are transferred to the brush, by utilizing the overloaded = operator.

In order to keep the interface up-to-date with our actions, the current layer selection range is checked for exceeding the actual range of total layers supported by the application. If, for example, we support four total layers and the current selected layer is two while the brush has all of its layers filled, we want to adjust the current layer selection to honour that by calculating the layer difference, adjusting the highest layer selected to match the maximum layer supported by the application, and subtract the difference from the lowest layer, hence preserving the proper range of the brush.

Lastly, a method for updating the selection options elevation selection text is invoked, the map controls class is instructed to switch to the Brush mode, and the selection options interface is updated with the information of the brush tile count and solidity.

Let us drift away from the topic of placing, editing, or copying tiles for a second, and talk about actually placing entities or emitters when the **Place** button is pressed:

```
void GUI_SelectionOptions::PlaceSelection(EventDetails* l_details)
{
  if (m_selectMode == SelectMode::Tiles) { return; }
  auto dropdownValue = static_cast<GUI_DropDownMenu*>(
    m_selectionOptions->GetElement("SelectDropdown"))->
    GetMenu()->GetSelected();
  if (dropdownValue.empty()) { return; }
  if (m_selectMode == SelectMode::Entities) {
    if (!m_entity || m_entityId == -1) {
      // New entity.
      auto id = m_entityManager->AddEntity(dropdownValue);
      if (id == -1) { return; }
      SelectEntity(id);
    }
    SaveOptions(nullptr);
  } else if (m_selectMode == SelectMode::Emitters) {
    if (!m_emitter) {
      // New emitter.
      auto text = m_selectionOptions->
        GetElement("EmitRate")->GetText();
      auto rate = std::stoi(text);
      auto emitter = m_particleSystem->AddEmitter(
        sf::Vector3f(0.f, 0.f, 0.f), dropdownValue, rate,
        StateType::MapEditor);
      SelectEmitter(emitter);
    }
    SaveOptions(nullptr);
  }
}
```

We are not going to be using this functionality to do anything with tiles, because that is what the mouse is designated for. If the selectionOptions interface is in the proper Select mode, the value of the drop-down menu is obtained and checked for not being empty. The **Place** button can also act as the **Edit** button under appropriate circumstances, such as when an entity or particle emitter is selected, so in both cases, the appropriate values are checked for representing a selection, or lack thereof. If nothing is selected, the drop-down value is used to add a new entity or emitter of the selected type. The SaveOptions() method is then invoked, so in either case, the information currently stored in the selectionOptions interface is saved to either the newly created object, or one that was already selected.

Pressing the **Remove** button can be handled like so:

```
void GUI_SelectionOptions::RemoveSelection(
    EventDetails* l_details)
{
    DeleteSelection(l_details->m_shiftPressed);
}
```

As you can see, a different method is invoked here, with a *boolean* flag being passed to it, denoting whether the *Shift* key is being held down, controlling how much of the current selection is removed. Let us take a look at the actual delete method:

```
void GUI_SelectionOptions::DeleteSelection(bool l_deleteAll) {
    if (m_selectMode == SelectMode::Tiles) {
        if (m_selectRangeX.x == -1) { return; }
        auto layerRange = (l_deleteAll ?
            sf::Vector2u(0, Sheet::Num_Layers - 1) :
            sf::Vector2u(m_layerSelectLow, m_layerSelectHigh));

        m_map->GetTileMap()->RemoveTiles(
            sf::Vector2u(m_selectRangeX),
            sf::Vector2u(m_selectRangeY),
            layerRange);
        m_map->ClearMapTexture(
            sf::Vector3i(m_selectRangeX.x,
                m_selectRangeY.x, layerRange.x),
            sf::Vector3i(m_selectRangeX.y,
                m_selectRangeY.y, layerRange.y));
    } else if (m_selectMode == SelectMode::Entities) {
        if (!m_entity || m_entityId == -1) { return; }
        m_entityManager->RemoveEntity(m_entityId);
        SelectEntity(-1);
    } else if (m_selectMode == SelectMode::Emitters) {
        if (!m_emitter) { return; }
        m_particleSystem->RemoveEmitter(m_emitter);
        SelectEmitter(nullptr);
    }
}
```

Once again, we deal with all three different selection types: tile, entity, and particle emitters. If we are working with tiles, the selection range is checked. Provided something actually is selected, the layer range is defined, based on whether the argument says everything should be deleted. The map is then instructed to remove the tiles and cleat its render texture within the calculated ranges.

In the cases of entities and particle emitters, it's much less complicated. The selected entity/emitter is simply removed, and the appropriate `SelectX` method is invoked shortly after, passing in a value for nothing being selected.

Next, let us handle the + and – buttons that control the elevation selection being pressed:

```
void GUI_SelectionOptions::SelectionOptionsElevation(
  EventDetails* l_details)
{
  int low = 0, high = 0;
  bool shift = sf::Keyboard::isKeyPressed(sf::Keyboard::LShift);
  if (l_details->m_name == "MapEditor_SelectOptionsPlus") {
    if (shift) { high = 1; } else { low = 1; }
  } else if(l_details->m_name == "MapEditor_SelectOptionsMinus") {
    if (shift) { high = -1; } else { low = -1; }
  }

  auto mode = m_mapControls->GetMode();

  if (mode == ControlMode::Brush) {
    if (high != 0) { return; } // only working with low values.
    int l = m_layerSelectLow + low;
    if (l < 0 || l >= Sheet::Num_Layers) { return; }
    if (l + m_brush->GetHighestElevation() >=
      Sheet::Num_Layers)
    { return; }
    m_layerSelectLow = l;
    m_layerSelectHigh = l + m_brush->GetHighestElevation();
    SelectionElevationUpdate();
  } else if (mode == ControlMode::Select) {
    int l = m_layerSelectLow + low;
    int h = m_layerSelectHigh + high;
    if (l < 0 || l >= Sheet::Num_Layers) { return; }
    if (h < 0 || h >= Sheet::Num_Layers) { return; }
    if (m_layerSelectLow == m_layerSelectHigh && !shift) {
      m_layerSelectLow += low;
      m_layerSelectLow += high;
      m_layerSelectHigh = m_layerSelectLow;
    } else {
      m_layerSelectLow = l;
      m_layerSelectHigh = h;
    }
    if (m_layerSelectLow > m_layerSelectHigh) {
      std::swap(m_layerSelectLow, m_layerSelectHigh);
    }
    SelectionElevationUpdate();
  }
}
```

Here, we want to handle the button clicks in a specific way. Keep in mind that support for selecting ranges of layers is also something of great importance. Consider the following illustration:

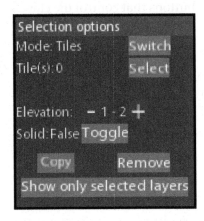

Simply clicking either a plus or a minus would affect the low number, which represents the lowest elevation selected. Holding a *Shift* key would increase the high number, controlling the highest elevation. For this, two integers, `low` and `high`, are set up, alongside a *boolean* flag that determines if a *Shift* key is being held or not. Based on that and the event name, the numbers are adjusted to represent the changes in elevation.

Next, we branch out the logic once again. If a `Brush` mode is selected, we do not want to deal with any changes of the high elevation at all. Instead, only the low layer selection is used here. After a new value for it is established by adding the layer delta to the already selected low elevation, the range is checked for exceeding the boundaries of [0;`Sheet::NumLayers`). Provided that passes, the low elevation selection is updated with the new value, as is the high value, which simply takes the low elevation and adds the thickness of the brush to it, represented by the brush's highest elevation.

The `Select` mode follows the same basic principle, with one exception: it also handles the high elevation. With the deltas properly added to the current values, the range is checked for exceeding the allowed limits. The next check deals with how we control shift-clicks depending on whether both the low and high values are the same. If they are, the deltas are simply added to the low value, which is copied over to the high elevation, preserving the equality. Otherwise, both low and high values are simply overwritten with the preceding newly calculated range.

In both cases, it is also important to invoke the `SelectionElevationUpdate()` method, which makes sure the interface elements are kept up-to-date, like so:

```
void GUI_SelectionOptions::SelectionElevationUpdate() {
  if (!m_selectionOptions->IsActive()) { return; }
  m_selectionOptions->GetElement("Elevation")->SetText(
    std::to_string(m_layerSelectLow) +
    (m_layerSelectLow != m_layerSelectHigh ?
    " - " + std::to_string(m_layerSelectHigh) : "")
  );
  SaveOptions(nullptr);
}
```

After making sure the selection options interface is actually active, the elevation label is updated with the proper layer range. The `SaveOptions()` callback is then invoked with `nullptr` for its argument. It is responsible for actually saving the interface's information to whatever object happens to be selected. Let us take a look at this method now:

```
void GUI_SelectionOptions::SaveOptions(EventDetails* l_details) {
  if (m_selectMode == SelectMode::Tiles) { return; }

  auto x = m_selectionOptions->GetElement("Pos_X")->GetText();
  auto y = m_selectionOptions->GetElement("Pos_Y")->GetText();
  auto z = m_selectionOptions->GetElement("Pos_Z")->GetText();

  auto c_x = std::stoi(x);
  auto c_y = std::stoi(y);
  auto c_z = std::stoi(z);

  if (m_selectMode == SelectMode::Entities) {
    if (!m_entity || m_entityId == -1) { return; }
    m_entity->SetPosition(sf::Vector2f(c_x, c_y));
    m_entity->SetElevation(m_layerSelectLow);
  } else if (m_selectMode == SelectMode::Emitters) {
    if (!m_emitter) { return; }
    auto emitRate = m_selectionOptions->
      GetElement("EmitRate")->GetText();
    auto c_rate = std::stoi(emitRate);
    m_emitter->SetPosition(sf::Vector3f(c_x, c_y, c_z));
    m_emitter->SetEmitRate(c_rate);
  }
}
```

The most obvious first check is to make sure we are not in tile mode, because there is nothing to save there. Afterwards, the values from the text-fields representing X, Y, and Z coordinates are obtained and converted to numbers. This is where our logic branches out once again.

In the case of dealing with an entity, we must first make sure one is selected. If it is, its position is changed to that of the values just obtained from the interface. We do not need to use the Z coordinate here, because that is replaced by the elevation.

The Z coordinate is, however, used when dealing with particle emitters. After obtaining the additional value of the emit rate from the interface and converting it to a proper number, all of these values are applied to the current particle emitter selected.

Now, the piece of code that makes everything else tick:

```
void GUI_SelectionOptions::Update() {
  if (m_selectUpdate) { UpdateSelectDrawable(); }
  if (!m_mapControls->IsInAction()) { return; }
  if (m_selectMode == SelectMode::Tiles) {UpdateTileSelection();}
  else if (m_selectMode == SelectMode::Entities) {
    UpdateEntitySelection();
  } else if (m_selectMode == SelectMode::Emitters) {
    UpdateEmitterSelection();
  }
}
```

At this point, we want to make sure the selection drawable is updated, provided the `m_selectUpdate` flag is enabled. The rest of the code can be skipped if the `mapControls` class is not letting us know that the left mouse button is pressed. However, if it is, an appropriate update method is invoked, depending on what `selectMode` the interface is in.

A good way to keep an application looking neat and responsive is having neat indicators of certain selections being made, like so:

Let us take a look at how the selection rectangle can be updated for entities and emitters:

```cpp
void GUI_SelectionOptions::UpdateSelectDrawable() {
  if (m_selectMode == SelectMode::Entities) {
    if (m_entityId == -1) { return; }
    if (!m_entity) { return; }
    if (m_entityManager->HasComponent(m_entityId,
      Component::Collidable))
    {
      auto col = m_entityManager->
        GetComponent<C_Collidable>(m_entityId,
        Component::Collidable);
      auto primitive = col->GetCollidable();
      m_selectDrawable.setPosition(primitive.left, primitive.top);
      m_selectDrawable.setSize(
        sf::Vector2f(primitive.width, primitive.height));
    } else if (m_entityManager->HasComponent(m_entityId,
      Component::SpriteSheet))
    {
      auto drawable = m_entityManager->
        GetComponent<C_SpriteSheet>(m_entityId,
        Component::SpriteSheet);
      auto pos = drawable->GetSpriteSheet()->GetSpritePosition();
      auto size = drawable->GetSpriteSheet()->GetSpriteSize();
      m_selectDrawable.setPosition(pos);
      m_selectDrawable.setSize(sf::Vector2f(size));
    } else {
      m_selectDrawable.setPosition(
        m_entity->GetPosition() - sf::Vector2f(16.f, 16.f));
      m_selectDrawable.setSize(sf::Vector2f(32.f, 32.f));
    }
  } else if (m_selectMode == SelectMode::Emitters) {
    if (!m_emitter) { return; }
    auto pos = sf::Vector2f(
      m_emitter->GetPosition().x, m_emitter->GetPosition().y);
    m_selectDrawable.setPosition(pos - sf::Vector2f(16.f, 16.f));
    m_selectDrawable.setSize(sf::Vector2f(32.f, 32.f));
  }
}
```

As always, our logic branches out, depending on the selection mode we are in. Provided we are working with entities, a few checks are necessary in order to make sure one is selected. If it is, the next problem at hand is giving the rectangle a proper size, origin, and position. The easiest way to do that is by obtaining the colloidal component of an entity and manipulating it based on the collision primitive. If the entity doesn't have that type of component, we attempt to use the next best thing – its sprite sheet. Finally, if there's only a position component to work with, the rectangle is centered at the entity's position and given a fixed size of *32×32*.

Dealing with emitters is quite similar, minus the entire component headache. Provided one is selected, its 2D position is obtained and used to centre the rectangle, while giving it a static size of *32×32*.

Let us move on to updating the tile selection next:

```cpp
void GUI_SelectionOptions::UpdateTileSelection() {
  auto& tileStart = m_mapControls->GetMouseTileStart();
  auto& mouseTile = m_mapControls->GetMouseTile();

  auto start = sf::Vector2f(
    (tileStart.x + (tileStart.x > mouseTile.x ? 1 : 0))
      * Sheet::Tile_Size,
    (tileStart.y + (tileStart.y > mouseTile.y ? 1 : 0))
      * Sheet::Tile_Size
  );

  auto end = sf::Vector2f(
    (mouseTile.x + (tileStart.x <= mouseTile.x ? 1 : 0))
      * Sheet::Tile_Size,
    (mouseTile.y + (tileStart.y <= mouseTile.y ? 1 : 0))
      * Sheet::Tile_Size
  );

  m_selectDrawable.setPosition(
    (start.x <= end.x ? start.x : end.x),
    (start.y <= end.y ? start.y : end.y)
  );

  m_selectDrawable.setFillColor(m_selectStartColor);
  m_selectDrawable.setSize({
    std::abs(end.x - start.x),
    std::abs(end.y - start.y)
  });
  m_selectRangeX = sf::Vector2i(
    std::min(tileStart.x, mouseTile.x),
    std::max(tileStart.x, mouseTile.x)
```

```
  );
  m_selectRangeY = sf::Vector2i(
     std::min(tileStart.y, mouseTile.y),
     std::max(tileStart.y, mouseTile.y)
  );
}
```

This is the actual method that handles tile selection logic. First, the coordinates of the starting tile that got clicked are obtained along with the current mouse position in tile coordinates. This information is used to calculate absolute global coordinates for the rectangle that will be used to represent the selection. The actual rectangle is then updated with this information, as well as set to have the m_selectStartColor color. Finally, all that is left to do is save this information as the current selection range, making sure it is in ascending order.

Next, updating entity selection deserves a peek:

```
void GUI_SelectionOptions::UpdateEntitySelection() {
    if (!m_mapControls->IsInAction()) { return; }
    if (!m_entity) { return; }
    m_entity->MoveBy(m_mapControls->GetMouseDifference());
    auto elevation = m_entity->GetElevation();
    m_selectionOptions->GetElement("Pos_X")->
       SetText(std::to_string(static_cast<int>(
          m_entity->GetPosition().x)));
    m_selectionOptions->GetElement("Pos_Y")->
       SetText(std::to_string(static_cast<int>(
          m_entity->GetPosition().y)));
    m_selectionOptions->GetElement("Elevation")->
       SetText(std::to_string(elevation));
    m_layerSelectLow = elevation;
    m_layerSelectHigh = elevation;
    m_selectUpdate = true;
}
```

A check is needed to make sure the mapControls are in action in the same fashion as tile updating. Also, we obviously cannot update an entity that is not even selected, so a check is needed for that as well. The final bit of logic simply deals with moving the entity by the mouse position difference and updating our selectionOptions interface to hold its current position and elevation. The layer selection range is also updated to hold the elevation information. Finally, the select update flag is set to true, which requests the selection rectangle to be updated.

It's time to wrap up the updating logic. The only remaining mode left to update is the particle emitter selection:

```
void GUI_SelectionOptions::UpdateEmitterSelection() {
  if (!m_mapControls->IsInAction()) { return; }
  if (!m_emitter) { return; }
  auto emitPos = m_emitter->GetPosition();
  auto position = sf::Vector2f(emitPos.x, emitPos.y);
  position += m_mapControls->GetMouseDifference();
  m_emitter->SetPosition(
    { position.x, position.y, m_emitter->GetPosition().z });
  m_selectionOptions->GetElement("Pos_X")->
    SetText(std::to_string(static_cast<int>(emitPos.x)));
  m_selectionOptions->GetElement("Pos_Y")->
    SetText(std::to_string(static_cast<int>(emitPos.y)));
  m_selectionOptions->GetElement("Pos_Z")->
    SetText(std::to_string(static_cast<int>(emitPos.z)));
  m_selectUpdate = true;
}
```

Just as before, the map control primary action flag is checked before proceeding, as well as the actual selection being made. The X and Y attributes of the particle emitter position are pushed by the mouse delta, while the Z coordinate is preserved as is. Afterwards, it is only a matter of updating the interface with the most recent position of the particle emitter, and marking the selection drawable for updating.

The last few pieces of the puzzle involve us dealing with mouse input correctly:

```
bool GUI_SelectionOptions::MouseClick(const sf::Vector2f& l_pos) {
  if (m_selectMode == SelectMode::Tiles) { return true; }
  bool madeSelection = false;
  if (m_selectMode == SelectMode::Entities) {
    int entity = -1;
    if (m_mapControls->DrawSelectedLayers()) {
      entity = m_entityManager->FindEntityAtPoint(l_pos,
        m_layerSelectLow, m_layerSelectHigh);
    } else {
      entity = m_entityManager->FindEntityAtPoint(l_pos);
    }
    SelectEntity(entity);
    madeSelection = entity != -1;
  } else if (m_selectMode == SelectMode::Emitters) {
    Emitter* emitter = nullptr;
    if (m_mapControls->DrawSelectedLayers()) {
      emitter = m_particleSystem->FindEmitter(l_pos,
        sf::Vector2f(32.f, 32.f), m_layerSelectLow,
          m_layerSelectHigh);
```

```
    } else {
      emitter = m_particleSystem->FindEmitter(
        l_pos, sf::Vector2f(32.f, 32.f));
    }
    SelectEmitter(emitter);
    madeSelection = emitter != nullptr;
  }
  if (!madeSelection) {
    m_selectionOptions->GetElement("Pos_X")->
      SetText(std::to_string(static_cast<int>(l_pos.x)));
    m_selectionOptions->GetElement("Pos_Y")->
      SetText(std::to_string(static_cast<int>(l_pos.y)));
  }
  return madeSelection;
}
```

As you recall from the previous chapter, this method is invoked by the `mapControls` class. It is required to return a *boolean* value that denotes whether a selection has been made or not, so that the `mapControls` class can deal with its own logic if the set of tools can give the artist a boost they have been looking for
latter is true. When dealing with tiles, this method always needs to return `true`, allowing the control class to know that an action is taking place regardless.

While in entity mode, the `FindEntityAtPoint` method of the `entityManager` class is invoked, with the global position, as well as the layer selection range being passed in as arguments. The latter is only true if the user of the tile editor has decided to only make selected layers visible. It will return an entity ID if an entity has been found at a specific point in space, which is then used to call `SelectEntity`. To determine whether an entity has been selected, the ID is checked for not being equal to a known value for *not found*.

A very similar procedure is used to select a particle emitter. Because most emitters are single points in space, a `sf::Vector2f` needs to be used here simply to define the area around the position that can be clicked in order to select it.

Lastly, if a selection hasn't been made, the position text-fields of the selection options interface are filled in with the global coordinates of the click. This allows easier positioning of objects in the world before placement.

Surprisingly, quite a lot needs to happen when a mouse button is released. Let's take a look:

```
void GUI_SelectionOptions::MouseRelease() {
  if (m_selectMode == SelectMode::Tiles) {
    m_selectDrawable.setFillColor(m_selectEndColor);
    m_selectionOptions->GetElement("CopySelection")->
      SetActive(true);
    m_selectionOptions->GetElement("RemoveSelection")->
```

```
        SetActive(true);

    bool solid = false, mixed = false;
    unsigned short changes = 0;
    for (auto x = m_selectRangeX.x; x <= m_selectRangeX.y
      && !mixed; ++x)
    {
      for (auto y = m_selectRangeY.x; y <= m_selectRangeY.y
        && !mixed; ++y)
      {
        for (auto layer = m_layerSelectLow;
          layer <= m_layerSelectHigh && !mixed; ++layer)
        {
          auto tile = m_map->GetTile(x, y, layer);
          if (!tile) { continue; }
          if (tile->m_solid && !solid) {
            solid = true;
            ++changes;
          } else if (tile->m_solid && !solid) {
            solid = false;
            ++changes;
          }
          if (changes >= 2) { mixed = true; }
        }
      }
    }
    m_selectionOptions->GetElement("Solidity")->
      SetText((mixed ? "Mixed" : (solid ? "True" : "False")));
  } else if (m_selectMode == SelectMode::Entities) {
    m_selectDrawable.setFillColor(m_entityColor);
  } else if (m_selectMode == SelectMode::Emitters) {
    m_selectDrawable.setFillColor(m_emitterColor);
  }
}
```

Most of this logic is concerned with dealing with tile selection. The first thing we need to worry about is setting the selection rectangle to its final color, indicating the selection is made. After that, the interface buttons for copying and removing the selection are made visible, and a loop is used to check the selection in order to determine the solidity situation of the entire chunk, which is then saved to the appropriate interface element.

The entity and emitter modes do not need quite as much maintenance for such a simple task. All we need to worry about here is setting the selection rectangle colors appropriately.

As modes are being switched, all of the important data needs to be reset in order to avoid strange bugs:

```
void GUI_SelectionOptions::Reset() {
  auto defaultVector = sf::Vector2i(-1, -1);
  m_selectRangeX = defaultVector;
  m_selectRangeY = defaultVector;
  m_entityId = -1;
  m_entity = nullptr;
  m_emitter = nullptr;
  static_cast<GUI_DropDownMenu*>(
    m_selectionOptions->GetElement("SelectDropdown"))->
    GetMenu()->ResetSelected();
  ... // GUI Element manipulation.
}
```

In addition to ranges and IDs being reset, the actual selection of the `DropDownMenu` of entities/emitters needs zeroing-out. Finally, all of the mode-specific GUI elements we have been working with need to be disabled and/or set to their neutral values.

Finally, we are left with only one essential chunk of code left to cover – the `Draw()` method:

```
void GUI_SelectionOptions::Draw(sf::RenderWindow* l_window) {
  auto mode = m_mapControls->GetMode();
  if (mode == ControlMode::Select) {
    if (m_selectMode == SelectMode::Tiles &&
      m_selectRangeX.x == -1)
    { return; }
    if (m_selectMode == SelectMode::Entities && !m_entity)
    { return; }
    if (m_selectMode == SelectMode::Emitters && !m_emitter)
    { return; }
    l_window->draw(m_selectDrawable);
  }
}
```

The only thing that we really need to draw is the selection rectangle. As it is quite evident here, it does not need to be drawn if no selection of any kind has been made. This includes checking all three select modes.

For the sake of completion, we only have a couple of getter methods left to look over:

```
unsigned int GUI_SelectionOptions::GetLowestLayer() const{
  return m_layerSelectLow;
}
unsigned int GUI_SelectionOptions::GetHighestLayer() const{
  return m_layerSelectHigh;
}
SelectMode GUI_SelectionOptions::GetSelectMode() const{
  return m_selectMode;
}
sf::Vector2i GUI_SelectionOptions::GetSelectXRange() const{
  return sf::Vector2i(
    std::min(m_selectRangeX.x, m_selectRangeX.y),
    std::max(m_selectRangeX.x, m_selectRangeX.y));
}
sf::Vector2i GUI_SelectionOptions::GetSelectYRange() const{
  return sf::Vector2i(
    std::min(m_selectRangeY.x, m_selectRangeY.y),
    std::max(m_selectRangeY.x, m_selectRangeY.y));
}
```

This concludes the `selectionOptions` class.

Building the tile selector

When working with tile maps, it is important to have a fast and intuitive way of accessing the tile-sheet, selecting its contents and painting them directly onto the game map. A good set of tools can give the artist the boost they have been looking for, while an unmanageable application is only a hindrance. Let us take a peek at what we are going to be building:

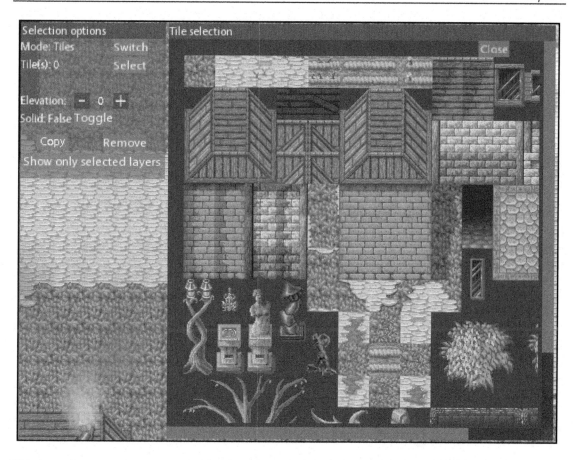

This interface, just like most others we have been working with, is going to be much easier to manage when wrapped in a class of its own:

```
class GUI_MapTileSelector {
public:
  GUI_MapTileSelector(EventManager* l_eventManager,
    GUI_Manager* l_guiManager, TextureManager* l_textureManager);
  ~GUI_MapTileSelector();
  void Show();
  void Hide();
  bool IsActive() const;
  void SetSheetTexture(const std::string& l_texture);
  void UpdateInterface();
  bool CopySelection(TileMap& l_tileMap) const;
  void TileSelect(EventDetails* l_details);
  void Close(EventDetails* l_details);
private:
```

```
    EventManager* m_eventManager;
    GUI_Manager* m_guiManager;
    TextureManager* m_textureManager;
    GUI_Interface* m_interface;
    sf::RenderTexture m_selectorTexture;
    sf::Sprite m_tileMapSprite;
    sf::RectangleShape m_shape;
    std::string m_sheetTexture;

    sf::Vector2u m_startCoords;
    sf::Vector2u m_endCoords;
    bool m_selected;
};
```

Just like before, we have `Show()` and `Hide()` methods to manage its visibility, as well as a couple of callbacks. Note the highlighted method. It is going to be used for setting the texture of the tile-sheet the map is using.

The data members are quite predictable for a class like this. Alongside the classes that this object relies on, we keep track of a pointer to the actual interface it is going to be manipulating, an instance of a `sf::RenderTexture` that we are going to be drawing to, the sprite that will be used to display the render texture, a rectangle shape, start and end coordinates, and a *boolean* flag for the actual selection drawable. Lastly, `m_sheetTexture` is going to simply keep track of the texture identifier until it is time to release it.

Implementing the tile selector

Let us begin by setting all of this data up inside the constructor:

```
GUI_MapTileSelector::GUI_MapTileSelector(
    EventManager* l_eventManager, GUI_Manager* l_guiManager,
    TextureManager* l_textureManager) :
    m_eventManager(l_eventManager), m_guiManager(l_guiManager),
    m_textureManager(l_textureManager), m_selected(false)
{
    m_eventManager->AddCallback(StateType::MapEditor,
        "MapEditor_TileSelectClick",
        &GUI_MapTileSelector::TileSelect, this);
    m_eventManager->AddCallback(StateType::MapEditor,
        "MapEditor_TileSelectRelease",
        &GUI_MapTileSelector::TileSelect, this);
    m_eventManager->AddCallback(StateType::MapEditor,
        "MapEditor_TileSelectClose",
        &GUI_MapTileSelector::Close, this);
```

```
m_guiManager->LoadInterface("MapEditorTileSelect.interface",
  "MapEditorTileSelect");
m_interface = m_guiManager->GetInterface("MapEditorTileSelect");
m_interface->SetContentRectSize(
  sf::Vector2i(m_interface->GetSize()-sf::Vector2f(32.f,32.f)));
m_interface->SetContentOffset({ 16.f, 16.f });
m_interface->PositionCenterScreen();
m_interface->SetActive(false);

m_shape.setFillColor({ 0, 0, 150, 150 });
m_shape.setSize({ Sheet::Tile_Size, Sheet::Tile_Size });
m_shape.setPosition(0.f, 0.f);
}
```

After the arguments are taken care of, the three callback methods we need are set up. The interface is then loaded and stored as one of the data members, just before its content rectangle size and offset are changed in order to allow space for control elements, such as the close button to be positioned comfortably. The interface is then centered on–screen and set to inactive. Finally, the rectangle shape used to represent tile selection is initialized to its default state as well.

Let us take a look at the destructor of this class next, in order to make sure we are not forgetting to release certain resources:

```
GUI_MapTileSelector::~GUI_MapTileSelector() {
  ... // Callbacks and interface removal.
  if (!m_sheetTexture.empty()) {
    m_textureManager->ReleaseResource(m_sheetTexture);
  }
}
```

After all three callbacks are released, it is imperative to make sure the tile-sheet texture is removed as well, provided its identifier is not empty.

Speaking of the tile-sheet texture, let us see how one can be assigned to this class:

```
void GUI_MapTileSelector::SetSheetTexture(
  const std::string& l_texture)
{
  if (!m_sheetTexture.empty()) {
    m_textureManager->ReleaseResource(m_sheetTexture);
  }
  m_sheetTexture = l_texture;
  m_textureManager->RequireResource(m_sheetTexture);
  m_tileMapSprite.setTexture(
    *m_textureManager->GetResource(m_sheetTexture));
  m_tileMapSprite.setPosition({ 0.f, 0.f });
```

```
    auto size = m_tileMapSprite.getTexture()->getSize();
    m_selectorTexture.create(size.x, size.y);
    m_selectorTexture.clear({ 0,0,0,0 });
    m_selectorTexture.draw(m_tileMapSprite);
    m_selectorTexture.display();

    auto element = static_cast<GUI_Sprite*>(
      m_interface->GetElement("TileSprite"));
    element->SetTexture(m_selectorTexture);
  }
```

After the current tile-sheet texture is properly released, the new one is assigned and retrieved. Because of this, the actual selector texture that will be passed to the main GUI element of our interface needs to be re-drawn and passed into said element.

A similar procedure takes place when the interface needs to be updated:

```
    void GUI_MapTileSelector::UpdateInterface() {
      m_selectorTexture.clear({ 0,0,0,0 });
      m_selectorTexture.draw(m_tileMapSprite);
      m_selectorTexture.draw(m_shape);
      m_selectorTexture.display();

      m_interface->RequestContentRedraw();
    }
```

It simply consists of the tile-sheet, as well as the selector rectangle being drawn to the render texture. The interface is then instructed to re-draw its content, as it was changed.

Next, let us provide a way for outside classes to copy the current tile-sheet selection to a `TileMap` structure:

```
    bool GUI_MapTileSelector::CopySelection(TileMap& l_tileMap) const{
      if (!m_selected) { return false; }
      l_tileMap.Purge();
      auto TileCoordsStart = m_startCoords /
        static_cast<unsigned int>(Sheet::Tile_Size);
      auto TileCoordsEnd = m_endCoords /
        static_cast<unsigned int>(Sheet::Tile_Size);
      auto size = TileCoordsEnd - TileCoordsStart;
      l_tileMap.SetMapSize(size + sf::Vector2u(1,1));

      auto sheetSize = m_textureManager->GetResource(
        l_tileMap.GetTileSet().GetTextureName())->getSize();
      auto nPerRow = sheetSize.x / Sheet::Tile_Size;

      auto t_x = 0, t_y = 0;
      for (auto x = TileCoordsStart.x; x <= TileCoordsEnd.x; ++x) {
```

```
      for (auto y = TileCoordsStart.y; y <= TileCoordsEnd.y; ++y) {
        auto coordinate = (y * nPerRow) + x;
        auto tile = l_tileMap.SetTile(t_x, t_y, 0, coordinate);
        // Always layer 0.
        if (!tile) { ++t_y; continue; }
        tile->m_solid = false;
        ++t_y;
      }
      t_y = 0;
      ++t_x;
    }
    return true;
}
```

Obviously, we cannot copy anything if nothing has been selected. The first check takes care of that. The `TileMap` passed in as the argument is then purged in preparation for being overwritten. The tile coordinate range is then calculated, and the `TileMap` argument is resized to match the size of the selection. After a couple of local variables are established to help us calculate the *1D* coordinate index, we begin iterating over the calculated range of tiles one by one, adding them to the tile map. Because we're not working with any sort of depth when dealing with a tile-sheet, the layer is always going to be set to the value 0.

The following code deals with the mouse-click and mouse-release events, which are vital when making a selection:

```
void GUI_MapTileSelector::TileSelect(EventDetails* l_details) {
  if (l_details->m_name == "MapEditor_TileSelectClick") {
    m_startCoords = sf::Vector2u(l_details->m_mouse);
    m_endCoords = sf::Vector2u(l_details->m_mouse);
    m_selected = false;
  } else {
    if (l_details->m_mouse.x < 0 || l_details->m_mouse.y < 0) {
      m_endCoords = sf::Vector2u(0, 0);
      return;
    }
    m_endCoords = sf::Vector2u(l_details->m_mouse);
    m_selected = true;
  }

  if (m_startCoords.x > m_endCoords.x) {
    std::swap(m_startCoords.x, m_endCoords.x);
  }
  if (m_startCoords.y > m_endCoords.y) {
    std::swap(m_startCoords.y, m_endCoords.y);
  }

  auto start = sf::Vector2i(m_startCoords.x / Sheet::Tile_Size,
```

```
        m_startCoords.y / Sheet::Tile_Size);
    start *= static_cast<int>(Sheet::Tile_Size);
    auto end = sf::Vector2i(m_endCoords.x / Sheet::Tile_Size,
        m_endCoords.y / Sheet::Tile_Size);
    end *= static_cast<int>(Sheet::Tile_Size);

    m_shape.setPosition(sf::Vector2f(start));
    m_shape.setSize(sf::Vector2f(end - start) +
        sf::Vector2f(Sheet::Tile_Size, Sheet::Tile_Size));
    UpdateInterface();
}
```

If we are dealing with a mouse-left click, we simply need to make note of the mouse coordinates at this point in time, as well as reset the m_selected flag to false. On the other hand, if the left mouse button has been released, the final mouse position is first checked for not going into negative values on both axes. The end coordinates are then stored, and the m_selected flag is set to true.

The remaining chunk of code simply deals with making sure the start and end coordinates are stored in an ascending order, and calculating the proper position and size of the selector rectangle. The UpdateInterface() method is then invoked, which makes sure everything is re-drawn.

Let us wrap this up by quickly looking over some of the helper methods of this class:

```
void GUI_MapTileSelector::Close(EventDetails* l_details){ Hide(); }
void GUI_MapTileSelector::Show() {
    m_interface->SetActive(true);
    m_interface->Focus();
}
void GUI_MapTileSelector::Hide() {m_interface->SetActive(false); }
bool GUI_MapTileSelector::IsActive() const{
    return m_interface->IsActive();
}
```

The Show() and Hide() methods simply manipulate the interfaces activity, while the Close callback just invokes Hide. Just like that, all of the pieces fit together and we are left with a fully functional map editor!

Summary

Building tools for a game may not be the easiest or the most pleasant task in the world, but in the end, it always pays off. Dealing with text files, endless copy-pasting, or other botch-like solutions may work fine in the short term, but nothing beats a fully equipped set of tools, ready to take on any project with the click of a button! Although the editor we have built is geared towards a very specific task, the idea behind it can, with enough time and energy, be applied to any set of production problems.

In the next chapter, we are going to be covering the basics and general uses of shaders in SFML. The OpenGL shading language, along with SFML's built in support for shaders, is going to allow us to create a very basic day and night cycle. See you there!

6
Adding Some Finishing Touches - Using Shaders

Having good art is important for any game, as it greatly compliments the content game designers bring to the table. However, simply tacking on any and all graphics to some logic and calling it a day just does not cut it anymore. Good visual aesthetics of a game are now formed by hand-in-hand cooperation of amazing art and the proper post-processing that follows. Dealing with graphics as if they are paper cut-outs feels dated, while incorporating them in the dynamic universe of your game world and making sure they react to their surroundings by properly shading them has become the new standard. For a brief moment, let us put aside gameplay and discuss the technique of that special kind of post-processing, known as shading.

In this chapter, we are going to be covering:

- The basics of the SFML shader class
- Implementing a unified way of drawing objects
- Adding a day-night cycle to the game

Let us get started with giving our project that extra graphical enhancement!

Understanding shaders

In the modern world of computer graphics, many different calculations are offloaded to the GPU. Anything from simple pixel colour calculations, to complex lighting effects can and should be handled by hardware that is specifically designed for this purpose. This is where shaders come in.

A **shader** is a little program that runs on your graphics card instead of the CPU, and controls how each pixel of a shape is rendered. The main purpose of a shader, as the name suggests, is performing lighting and shading calculations, but they can be used for much more than that. Because of the power modern GPUs have, libraries exist that are designed to perform calculations on the GPU that would usually be executed on the CPU, in order to cut down the computation time significantly. Anything from physics computations to cracking password hashes can be done on the GPU, and the entry point to that horsepower is a shader.

 GPUs are good at performing tons of very specific calculations in parallel at once. Using less predictable or unparallel algorithms is very inefficient on the GPU, which is what the CPU excels at. However, as long as the data can be processed exactly the same in parallel, the task is deemed worthy of being pushed to the GPU for further handling.

There are two main types of shader that SFML provides: **vertex** and **fragment**. Newer versions of SFML (*2.4.0* and up) have added support for geometry shaders as well, but it is not necessary to cover this for our purposes.

A **vertex shader** is executed once per vertex. This process is commonly referred to as **per-vertex** shading. For example, any given triangle has three vertices. This means that the shader would be executed once for each vertex for a grand total of three times.

A **fragment shader** is executed once per pixel (otherwise known as a fragment), which results in the process being referred to as **per-pixel** shading. This is much more taxing than simply performing per-vertex calculations, but is much more accurate and generally produces better visual results.

Both types of shader can be used at once on a single piece of geometry being drawn, and can also communicate with each other.

Shader examples

The **OpenGL Shading Language** (**GLSL**) is extremely similar to C or C++. It even uses the same basic syntax, as seen in this vertex shader example:

```
#version 450

void main()
{
    gl_Position = gl_ProjectionMatrix * gl_ModelViewMatrix
        * gl_Vertex;
    gl_FrontColor = gl_Color; // Send colour to fragment shader.
}
```

Notice the version on the very first line. The number 450 indicates the version of OpenGL that should be used, in this case 4.5. Newer versions of SFML support OpenGL versions 3.3+; however the success of running it also depends on the capabilities of your graphics card.

For now, simply ignore the first line of the main function. It has to do with positions transformations from one coordinate system to another, and is specific to a few possible approaches to shading. These concepts will be covered in the next chapter.

GLSL provides quite a few *hooks* that allow direct control of vertex and pixel information, such as gl_Position and gl_Color. The former is simply the position of the vertex that will be used in further calculations down the line, while the latter is the vertex colour, which is being assigned to gl_FrontColor, ensuring the colour is passed down the pipeline to the fragment shader.

Speaking of the fragment shader, here is a very minimal example of what it may look like:

```
#version 450

void main()
{
    gl_FragColor = vec4(1.0, 1.0, 1.0, 1.0); // White pixel.
}
```

In this particular case, gl_FragColor is used to set a static value of the pixel being rendered. Any shape being rendered while using this shader will come out white.

The values of this vector are normalized, meaning they have to fall in the range of *0.f < n <= 1.0f.*

Keep in mind that `gl_Color` can be used here to sample the colour that is passed down from the vertex shader. However, because there may be multiple pixels in between vertices, the colour for each fragment is interpolated. In a case where each vertex of a triangle is set to colours red, green, and blue, the interpolated result would look like this:

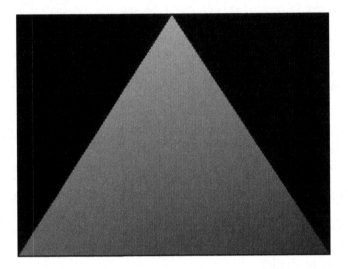

One last thing to note about any shader is that they support communication from outside sources. This is done by using the `uniform` keyword, followed by the variable type and capped off by its name like so:

```
#version 450
uniform float r;
uniform float g;
uniform float b;

void main()
{
    gl_FragColor = vec4(r, g, b, 1.0);
}
```

In this particular example, outside code passes in three `float` that will be used as color values for the fragment. Uniforms are simply **global** variables that can be manipulated by outside code before a shader is used.

SFML and shaders

Storing and using shaders in SFML is made simple by introducing the `sf::Shader` class. Although shaders are generally supported by most devices out there, it is still a good idea to perform a check that determines if the system the code is being executed on supports shaders as well:

```
if(!sf::Shader::isAvailable()){ // Shaders not available! }
```

This shader class can hold either one of the two types of shader just by itself or a single instance of each type at the same time. Shaders can be loaded in one of two ways. The first is by simply reading a text file:

```
sf::Shader shader; // Create a shader instance.

// Loading a single type of shader.
if (!shader.loadFromFile("shader.vert", sf::Shader::Vertex)) {
  // Failed loading.
}
// OR
if (!shader.loadFromFile("shader.frag", sf::Shader::Fragment)) {
  // Failed loading.
}

// load both shaders
if (!shader.loadFromFile("shader.vert", "shader.frag")) {
  // Failed loading.
}
```

 File extensions of these shaders do not have to match the preceding ones. Because we are working with text files, the extension simply exists for clarity.

The second way to load a shader is by parsing a string loaded in memory:

```
sf::Shader shader;
const std::string code = "...";
// String that contains all shader code.

if (!shader.loadFromMemory(code, sf::Shader::Vertex)) {
  // Failed loading.
}
```

Using a shader is fairly straightforward as well. Its address simply needs to be passed in to a render targets `draw()` call as the second argument when something is being rendered to it:

```
window.draw(drawable, &shader);
```

Since our shaders may need to be communicated with through `uniform` variables, there has to be a way to set them. Enter `sf::Shader::setUniform(...)`:

```
shader.setUniform("r", 0.5f);
```

This simple bit of code manipulates the `r` uniform inside whatever shader(s) happen to be loaded inside the `shader` instance. The method itself supports many more types besides *float*, which we will be covering in the next chapter.

Localizing rendering

Shading is a powerful concept. The only problem with injecting a stream of extra-graphical-fanciness to our game at this point is the fact that it is simply not architected to deal with using shaders efficiently. Most, if not all of our classes that do any kind of drawing do so by having direct access to the `sf::RenderWindow` class, which means they would have to pass in their own shader instances as arguments. This is not efficient, re-usable, or flexible at all. A better approach, such as a separate class dedicated to rendering, is a necessity.

In order to be able to switch from shader to shader with relative ease, we must work on storing them properly within the class:

```
using ShaderList = std::unordered_map<std::string,
  std::unique_ptr<sf::Shader>>;
```

Because the `sf::Shader` class is a non-copyable object (inherits from `sf::NonCopyable`), it is stored as a unique pointer, resulting in avoidance of any and all move semantics. This list of shaders is directly owned by the class that is going to do all of the rendering, so let us take a look at its definition:

```cpp
class Renderer {
public:
  Renderer(Window* l_window, bool l_useShaders = true);

  void AdditiveBlend(bool l_flag);
  bool UseShader(const std::string& l_name);
  void DisableShader();
  sf::Shader* GetShader(const std::string& l_name);

  void BeginDrawing();
  bool IsDrawing()const;
  void Draw(const sf::Shape& l_shape,
    sf::RenderTarget* l_target = nullptr);
  void Draw(const sf::Sprite& l_sprite,
    sf::RenderTarget* l_target = nullptr);
  void Draw(const sf::Drawable& l_drawable,
    sf::RenderTarget* l_target = nullptr);
  void EndDrawing();
private:
  void LoadShaders();

  Window* m_window;
  ShaderList m_shaders;
  sf::Shader* m_currentShader;
  bool m_addBlend;
  bool m_drawing;
  bool m_useShaders;
  unsigned int m_drawCalls; // For debug purposes.
};
```

Since shaders need to be passed in as arguments to the window `draw()` calls, it is obviously imperative for the renderer to have access to the `Window` class. In addition to that and the list of shaders that can be used at any given time, we also keep a pointer to the current shader being used in order to cut down on container access time, as well as a couple of flags that will be used when choosing the right shader to use, or determining whether the drawing is currently happening in the first place. Lastly, a fairly useful debug feature is having information about how many draw calls happen during each update. For this, a simple *unsigned integer* is going to be used.

The class itself provides the basic features of enabling/disabling additive blending instead of a regular shader, switching between all available shaders, and disabling the current shader, as well as obtaining it. The `BeginDrawing()` and `EndDrawing()` methods are going to be used by the `Window` class in order to provide us with *hooks* for obtaining information about the rendering process. Note the overloaded `Draw()` method. It is designed to take in any drawable type and draw it on either the current window, or the appropriate render target that can be provided as the second argument.

Finally, the `LoadShaders()` private method is going to be used during the initialization stage of the class. It holds all of the logic necessary to load every single shader inside the appropriate directory, and store them for later use.

Implementing the renderer

Let us begin by quickly going over the construction of the `Renderer` object, and the initialization of all of its data members:

```
Renderer::Renderer(Window* l_window, bool l_useShaders)
  : m_window(l_window), m_useShaders(l_useShaders),
    m_drawing(false), m_addBlend(false), m_drawCalls(0),
  m_currentShader(nullptr) {}
```

Once the pointer to the `Window*` instance is safely stored, all of the data members of this class are initialized to their default values. The body of the constructor simply consists of a private method call, responsible for actually loading and storing all of the shader files:

```
void Renderer::LoadShaders() {
  if(!m_useShaders) { return; }
  auto directory = Utils::GetWorkingDirectory() +"media/Shaders/";
  auto v_shaders = Utils::GetFileList(directory, "*.vert", false);
  auto f_shaders = Utils::GetFileList(directory, "*.frag", false);

  for (auto& shader : v_shaders) {
    auto& file = shader.first;
    auto name = file.substr(0, file.find(".vert"));
    auto fragShader = std::find_if(
      f_shaders.begin(), f_shaders.end(),
      [&name](std::pair<std::string, bool>& l_pair) {
        return l_pair.first == name + ".frag";
      }
    );

    auto shaderItr = m_shaders.emplace(name,
      std::move(std::make_unique<sf::Shader>()));
```

```
      auto& shader = shaderItr.first->second;
      if (fragShader != f_shaders.end()) {
        shader->loadFromFile(directory + name + ".vert",
          directory + name + ".frag");
        f_shaders.erase(fragShader);
      } else {
        shader->loadFromFile(directory + name + ".vert",
          sf::Shader::Vertex);
      }
    }

    for (auto& shader : f_shaders) {
      auto& file = shader.first;
      auto name = file.substr(0, file.find(".frag"));
      auto shaderItr = m_shaders.emplace(name,
        std::move(std::make_unique<sf::Shader>()));
      auto& shader = shaderItr.first->second;
      shader->loadFromFile(directory + name + ".frag",
        sf::Shader::Fragment);
    }
  }
```

We begin by establishing a local variable that is going to hold the path to our shader directory. It is then used to obtain two lists of files with .vert and .frag extensions respectively. These will be the vertex and fragment shaders to be loaded. The goal here is to group vertex and fragment shaders with identical names, and assign them to a single instance of sf::Shader. Any shaders that do not have a vertex or fragment counterpart will simply be loaded alone in a separate instance.

Vertex shaders are as good a place as any to begin. After the filename is obtained and stripped of its extension, a fragment shader with the same name is attempted to be located. At the same time, a new sf::Shader instance is inserted into the shader container, and a reference to it is obtained. If a fragment counterpart has been found, both files are loaded into the shader. The fragment shader name is then removed from the list, as it will no longer need to be loaded in on its own.

As the first part of the code does all of the pairing, all that is really left to do at this point is load the fragment shaders. It is safe to assume that anything on the fragment shader list is a standalone fragment shader, not associated with a vertex counterpart.

Since shaders can have uniform variables that need to be initialized, it is important that outside classes have access to the shaders they use:

```
sf::Shader* Renderer::GetShader(const std::string& l_name) {
  if(!m_useShaders) { return nullptr;  }
  auto shader = m_shaders.find(l_name);
```

```
      if (shader == m_shaders.end()) { return nullptr; }
      return shader->second.get();
  }
```

If the shader with the provided name has not been located, `nullptr` is returned. On the other hand, a raw pointer to the `sf::Shader*` instance is obtained from the smart pointer and returned instead.

The same outside classes need to be able to instruct the `Renderer` when a specific shader should be used. For this purpose, the `UseShader()` method comes in handy:

```
  bool Renderer::UseShader(const std::string& l_name) {
    if(!m_useShaders) { return false; }
    m_currentShader = GetShader(l_name);
    return (m_currentShader != nullptr);
  }
```

Since the `GetShader()` method already does the error-checking for us, it is used here as well. The value returned from it is stored as the pointer to the current shader, if any, and is then evaluated in order to return a *boolean* value, signifying success/failure.

The actual drawing of geometry is what we are all about here, so let us take a look at the overloaded `Draw()` method:

```
  void Renderer::Draw(const sf::Shape& l_shape,
    sf::RenderTarget* l_target)
  {
    if (!l_target) {
      if (!m_window->GetViewSpace().intersects(
        l_shape.getGlobalBounds()))
      { return; }
    }
    Draw((const sf::Drawable&)l_shape, l_target);
  }

  void Renderer::Draw(const sf::Sprite& l_sprite,
    sf::RenderTarget* l_target)
  {
    if (!l_target) {
      if (!m_window->GetViewSpace().intersects(
        l_sprite.getGlobalBounds()))
      { return; }
    }
    Draw((const sf::Drawable&)l_sprite, l_target);
  }
```

Whether a `sf::Sprite` or `sf::Shape` is being rendered, the actual idea behind this is exactly the same. First, we check if the intention behind the method call was indeed to render to the main window by looking at the `l_target` argument. If so, a fair thing to do here is to make sure the drawable object actually is on screen. It would be pointless to draw it if it was not. Provided the test passes, the main `Draw()` method overload is invoked, with the current arguments being passed down:

```
void Renderer::Draw(const sf::Drawable& l_drawable,
  sf::RenderTarget* l_target)
{
  if (!l_target) { l_target = m_window->GetRenderWindow(); }
  l_target->draw(l_drawable,
    (m_addBlend ? sf::BlendAdd : m_currentShader && m_useShaders ?
      m_currentShader : sf::RenderStates::Default));
  ++m_drawCalls;
}
```

This is where all of the actual magic happens. The `l_target` argument is again checked for being equal to `nullptr`. If it is, the render window is stored inside the argument pointer. Whatever the target, at this point its `Draw()` method is invoked, with the drawable being passed in as the first argument, as well as the appropriate shader or blend mode passed in as the second. The additive blending obviously takes precedence here, enabling a quicker way of switching between using a shader and the additive blending modes by simply needing to use the `AdditiveBlend()` method.

Once the drawing is done, the `m_drawCalls` data member is incremented, so that we can keep track of how many drawables have been rendered in total at the end of each cycle.

Finally, we can wrap this class up by looking at a couple of essential yet basic setter/getter code:

```
void Renderer::AdditiveBlend(bool l_flag) { m_addBlend = l_flag; }
void Renderer::DisableShader() { m_currentShader = nullptr; }
void Renderer::BeginDrawing(){ m_drawing = true; m_drawCalls = 0;}
bool Renderer::IsDrawing() const { return m_drawing; }
void Renderer::EndDrawing() { m_drawing = false; }
```

As you can see, disabling the use of shaders for whatever is being drawn currently is as simple as setting the `m_currentShader` data member to `nullptr`. Also note the `BeginDrawing()` method. It conveniently resets the `m_drawCalls` counter, which makes it easier to manage.

Integrating the Renderer class

There is obviously no point in even having the `Renderer` class, if it is not going to be in its proper place or used at all. Since its only job is to draw things on screen with the correct effect being applied, a fitting place for it would be inside the `Window` class:

```
class Window{
public:
   ...
   Renderer* GetRenderer();
   ...
private:
   ...
   Renderer m_renderer;
};
```

Because outside classes rely on it as well, it is a good idea to provide a getter method for easy retrieval of this object.

Actually integrating it into the rest of the code is surprisingly easy. A good place to start is giving the `Renderer` access to the `Window` class like so:

```
Window::Window(...) : m_renderer(this, l_useShaders) { ... }
```

The renderer also has *hooks* for knowing when we begin and end the drawing process. Luckily, the `Window` class already supports this idea, so it's really easy to tap into it:

```
void Window::BeginDraw() {
  m_window.clear(sf::Color::Black);
  m_renderer.BeginDrawing();
}
void Window::EndDraw() {
  m_window.display();
  m_renderer.EndDrawing();
}
```

Finally, in order to make use of the newest versions of OpenGL, the window needs to be instructed to create a version of the newest context available:

```
void Window::Create() {
   ...
   sf::ContextSettings settings;
   settings.depthBits = 24;
   settings.stencilBits = 8;
   settings.antialiasingLevel = 0;
   settings.majorVersion = 4;
   settings.minorVersion = 5;
```

```
m_window.create(sf::VideoMode(m_windowSize.x, m_windowSize.y,
    32), m_windowTitle, style, settings);
if (!m_shadersLoaded) {
  m_renderer.LoadShaders();
  m_shadersLoaded = true;
  }
}
```

Note the shader loading bit at the end of this code snippet. The `Renderer` class is instructed to load the shaders available in the designated directory, provided shaders are being used in the first place. These several simple additions conclude the integration of the `Renderer` class.

Adapting existing classes

Up until this point, rendering something on screen was as simple as passing it as a drawable object to a `Draw()` method of a `Window` class. While great for smaller projects, this is problematic for us, simply because that heavily handicaps any use of shaders. A good way to upgrade from there is to simply take in `Window` pointers:

```
class ParticleSystem : ... {
public:
  ...
  void Draw(Window* l_window, int l_elevation);
};

class S_Renderer : ... {
public:
  ...
  void Render(Window* l_wind, unsigned int l_layer);
};

class SpriteSheet{
public:
  ...
  void Draw(Window* l_wnd);
};
```

Let us go over each of these classes and see what needs to be changed in order to add proper support for shaders.

Updating the ParticleSystem

Going all the way back to Chapter 3, *Make it rain! – Building a particle system* we have already used a certain amount of shading trickery without even knowing it! The additive blending used for fire effects is a nice feature, and in order to preserve it without having to write a separate shader for it, we can simply use the AdditiveBlend() method of the Renderer class:

```
void ParticleSystem::Draw(Window* l_window, int l_elevation) {
  ...
  auto state = m_stateManager->GetCurrentStateType();
  if (state == StateType::Game || state == StateType::MapEditor) {
    renderer->UseShader("default");
  } else {
    renderer->DisableShader();
  }

  for (size_t i = 0; i < container->m_countAlive; ++i) {
    ...
    renderer->AdditiveBlend(blendModes[i]);
    renderer->Draw(drawables[i]);
  }
  renderer->AdditiveBlend(false);
}
```

First, note the check of the current application state. For now, we do not really need to use shaders inside any other states besides Game or MapEditor. Provided we are in one of them, the default shader is used. Otherwise, shading is disabled.

When dealing with actual particles, the AdditiveBlend() method is invoked with the blend mode flag being passed in as its argument, either enabling or disabling it. The particle drawable is then drawn on screen. After all of them have been processed, additive blending is turned off.

Updating entity and map rendering

The default shader is not only used when rendering particles. As it happens, we want to be able to apply unified shading, at least to some extent, to all world objects. Let us begin with entities:

```
void S_Renderer::Render(Window* l_wind, unsigned int l_layer)
{
  EntityManager* entities = m_systemManager->GetEntityManager();
  l_wind->GetRenderer()->UseShader("default");
  for(auto &entity : m_entities) {
    ...
    drawable->Draw(l_wind);
  }
}

void SpriteSheet::Draw(Window* l_wnd) {
  l_wnd->GetRenderer()->Draw(m_sprite);
}
```

The only real changes to the rendering system are the invocation of the `UseShader()` method, and the fact that a pointer to the `Window` class is being passed down to the sprite-sheets `Draw()` call as an argument, instead of the usual `sf::RenderWindow`. The `SpriteSheet` class, in turn, is also modified to use the `Renderer` class, even though it does not actually interact with or modify shaders at all.

The game map should be shaded in exactly the same way as well:

```
void Map::Draw(unsigned int l_layer) {
  if (l_layer >= Sheet::Num_Layers) { return; }
  ...
  m_window->GetRenderer()->UseShader("default");
  m_window->GetRenderer()->Draw(m_layerSprite);
}
```

The only real difference here is the fact that the `Map` class already has access to the `Window` class internally, so it does not have to be passed in as an argument.

Creating a day/night cycle

Unifying the shading across many different world objects in our game gave us a very nice way of manipulating how the overall scene is actually represented. Many interesting effects are now possible, but we are going to focus on a rather simple yet effective one-lighting. The actual subtleties of the lighting subject will be covered in later chapters, but what we can do now is build a system that allows us to shade the world differently, based on the current time of the day, like so:

As you can tell, this effect can add a lot to a game and make it feel very dynamic. Let us take a look at how it can be implemented.

Updating the Map class

In order to accurately represent a day/night cycle, the game must keep a clock. Because it is relative to the world, the best place to keep track of this information is the Map class:

```
class Map : ... {
  ...
protected:
  ...
  float m_gameTime;
  float m_dayLength;
};
```

For the sake of having dynamic and customizable code, two additional data members are stored: the current game time, and the overall length of the day. The latter allows the user to potentially create maps with a variable length of a day, which could offer some interesting opportunities for game designers.

Using these values is fairly simple:

```
void Map::Update(float l_dT) {
  m_gameTime += l_dT;
  if (m_gameTime > m_dayLength * 2) { m_gameTime = 0.f; }
  float timeNormal = m_gameTime / m_dayLength;
  if(timeNormal > 1.f){ timeNormal = 2.f - timeNormal; }
   m_window->GetRenderer()->GetShader("default")->
    setUniform("timeNormal", timeNormal);
}
```

The actual game time is first manipulated by adding the frame time to it. It is then checked for having exceeded the boundaries of twice the value of the length of a day, in which case the game time is set back to 0.f. This relationship represents a 1:1 proportion between the length of a day and the length of a night.

Finally, ensuring the light properly fades between day and night, a `timeNormal` local variable is established, and used to calculate the amount of darkness that should be cast over the scene. It is then checked for having exceeded the value of `1.f`, in which case it is adjusted to start moving back down, representing the fade from darkness to dawn. The value is then passed to the default shader.

 It is important to remember that shaders work with normalized values most of the time. This is why we are striving to provide it with a value between `0.f` to `1.f`.

The final piece of the puzzle is actually initializing our two additional data members to their default values:

```
Map::Map(...) : ..., m_gameTime(0.f), m_dayLength(30.f)
{ ... }
```

As you can see, we have given the day length a value of `30.f`, which means the full day/night cycle will last a minute. This is obviously not going to be very useful for a game, but can come in handy when testing the shaders.

Writing the shaders

With all of the C++ code out of the way, we can finally focus on GLSL. Let us begin by implementing the default vertex shader:

```
#version 450
void main()
{
  // transform the vertex position
  gl_Position = gl_ModelViewProjectionMatrix * gl_Vertex;
  // transform the texture coordinates
  gl_TexCoord[0] = gl_TextureMatrix[0] * gl_MultiTexCoord0;
  // forward the vertex color
  gl_FrontColor = gl_Color;
}
```

This is nothing different from the examples used during the introduction stage of this chapter. The purpose of adding the vertex shader now is simply to avoid having to write it again later, when something needs to be done in it. With that said, let us move on to the fragment shader:

```
#version 450
uniform sampler2D texture;
uniform float timeNormal;

void main()
{
  // lookup the pixel in the texture
  vec4 pixel = texture2D(texture, gl_TexCoord[0].xy);
  if(pixel == vec4(0.0, 0.0, 0.0, 1.0))
    pixel = vec4(1.0, 1.0, 1.0, 1.0);
  // multiply it by the color
  gl_FragColor = gl_Color * pixel;
  gl_FragColor[0] -= timeNormal;
  gl_FragColor[1] -= timeNormal;
  gl_FragColor[2] -= timeNormal;
  gl_FragColor[2] += 0.2;
}
```

 The `sampler2D` type in this instance is simply the texture being passed into the shader by SFML. Other textures may also be passed into the shader manually, by using the `shader.setUniform("texture", &texture);` call.

In order to properly draw a pixel, the fragment shader needs to sample the texture of the current object being drawn. If a simple shape is being drawn, the pixel being sampled from the texture is checked for being completely black. If that's the case, it's simply set to a white pixel. In addition to that, we also need the `timeNormal` value discussed earlier. After the current pixel of the texture has been sampled, it is multiplied by the colour passed in from the vertex shader and stored as `gl_FragColor`. The `timeNormal` value is then subtracted from all three colour channels. Finally, a slight tint of blue is added to the pixel in the end. This gives our scene a blue tint, and is purely an aesthetic choice.

Summary

Many argue that graphics should be a secondary concern for a game developer. While it is clear that the visual side of a project should not be its primary concern, the visuals can serve a player more than simply acting as pretty backdrops. Graphical enhancements can even help tell a story better by making the player feel more engrossed in the environment, using clever visual cues, or simply controlling the overall mood and atmosphere. In this chapter, we have taken one of our first steps towards building a system that will serve as a massive helper when conquering the world of special effects.

In the next chapter, we will be delving deeper into the lower levels of graphical enhancements. See you there!

7
One Step Forward, One Level Down - OpenGL Basics

Often times it's easy to take a library like SFML for granted. After all, the ideas and concepts offered by it seem quite intuitive. Building something rather simple can take as little as a couple of minutes, and there are no major headaches to deal with. In a perfect world, we could just offload those troubles to someone else and simply rely on increasingly higher levels of abstraction to get the job done. However, what happens when certain limitations make us slam face-first into a brick wall? In order to know the way around them, it's necessary to know the fundamentals that SFML was built on. In other words, at that point, downward is the only way forward.

In this chapter, we are going to be covering:

- Setting up and using OpenGL with a window from SFML
- Shaping and submitting data to the GPU
- Creating, building, and using shaders for rendering
- Applying textures to geometry
- Looking at various coordinate spaces and model transformations
- Implementing a camera

That is quite a laundry list of things to do, so let us not waste any time and jump right in!

Use of copyrighted resources

As always, let us acknowledge those who deserve to be acknowledged, and give credit where credit's due. These are the resources used in this chapter:

- Old wall texture by `texturelib.com` under the CC0: license:`http://texturelib.com/texture/?path=/Textures/brick/medieval/brick_medieval_0121`
- STB public domain image loader by *Sean Barrett* under the CC0 license: `https://github.com/nothings/stb/blob/master/stb_image.h`

Setting up OpenGL

- In order to have access to the latest version of OpenGL, we need to download two libraries. One is named the OpenGL Extension Wrangler Library. It loads and makes available all OpenGL extensions that are supported on the target platform. The library can be downloaded here `http://glew.sourceforge.net/`.
- The other library we need is called OpenGL Mathematics, or GLM for short. It is a header-only library that adds a lot of extra data types and functions, which come in handy more often than not. Anything from simple vector data types to functions used to calculate cross products are added in by this library. It can be found here `http://glm.g-truc.net/0.9.8/index.html`.

Setting up a Visual Studio project

Alongside the usual SFML includes, which we are still going to need for creating a window, we also need to add the GLEW and GLM `include` folders in the **Include Directories** field under **VC++ Directories**.

The GLEW **Additional Library Directory** must be added in as well in the **General** section under **Linker**. The library files are located inside the `Release` folder, which holds a couple of directories: `Win32` and `x64`. These need to be set up correctly for different build configurations.

Finally, the `glew32.lib` file has to be added to the **Additional Dependencies** field in the **Input** section under **Linker**, as well as the `OpenGL32.lib` file. It can be linked statically, in which case, `glew32s.lib` needs to be added instead of the regular `glew32.lib`. If linking statically, the `GLEW_STATIC` **Preprocessor Definition** in the **Preprocessor** section under **C/C++** needs to be added as well.

Using GLEW

The first thing we are going to need if we are working with OpenGL is a window. Luckily, window creation isn't OpenGL specific, so one can be made using almost any library out there that supports it, including SFML. For our purposes, we'll be reusing the Window class with some minor adjustments to it, including the actual SFML window type:

```
class GL_Window {
  ...
private:
  ...
  sf::Window m_window;
  ...
};
```

Note the data type of the `m_window` data member. If actual SFML is not used to draw anything, we do not need an instance of `sf::RenderWindow` and can instead work with `sf::Window`. This means that any task that does not have anything to do with the actual window has to be handled separately. This even includes clearing the window:

```
void GL_Window::BeginDraw() {
  glClearColor(0.f, 0.f, 0.f, 1.f); // BLACK
  glClear(GL_COLOR_BUFFER_BIT);
}
```

Here we get a glimpse at the first two GL functions we are going to be using. Because GLEW is a C API, code that looks like this will be quite common. There are no classes to manage, as every task is performed via function calls and a shared state. Case in point, our first function `glClearColor()` actually sets up the color that the screen will be cleared with, including the alpha channel.

This specific function, as well as many others, takes in what is known as a **normalized** vector. It is useful when representing proportion. For example, clearing the screen to the color purple would mean passing the value *0.5f* as the first and the third parameter, which would mean half of the colour is red, and the other half is blue.

The second function call actually performs the clearing with the stored value. It takes in a single argument, which is essentially just a bitmask, defined using the #define pre-processor directive. This specific implementation detail allows more masks to be passed into the function call by utilizing **bitwise** or operations, represented by the pipe | symbol. This concept will be revisited by us eventually.

With that out of the way, let us actually create the window and initialize the GLEW library:

```
Game::Game() : m_window("Chapter 7", sf::Vector2u(800, 600))
{
    ...
    std::cout << glGetString(GL_VERSION) << std::endl;
    GLenum status = glewInit();
    if (status != GLEW_OK) {
        std::cout << "GLEW failed!" << std::endl;
    }
    ...
}
```

All we need to do in order to initialize GLEW is to call a single function glewInit(). It returns a value, which represents the success/failure of the operation. Another useful function to keep around is glGetString(). It returns a static string that represents specific information about the OpenGL version that is supported by the computer it is executed on. In this case, we specifically want to check the version of OpenGL and print it out, but it can also be used to determine the OpenGL extensions, the supported GLSL version, the name of the hardware rendering platform, and so on.

The rendering pipeline

When drawing something on the screen, a certain sequence of steps must be followed in order to submit the geometry, convert it to pixels, and color them all appropriately. This particular sequence of steps is often referred to as the **rendering pipeline**. How it functions depends entirely on the version of OpenGL you are using. Versions below *3.0* use what is called a **fixed function pipeline**, while newer OpenGL releases of *3.0* + utilize the **programmable pipeline**. The former is now deprecated and is referred to as **legacy** OpenGL, while the latter is widely used and applied, even on mobile devices, and has become the standard.

Fixed function pipeline

Actually drawing things on screen with the fixed function pipeline is much easier than the modern way of doing things, but it comes at a price. Consider the following example:

```
glBegin(GL_TRIANGLES);
glColor3f(1.0f, 0.0f, 0.0f); // Red
glVertex3f(-0.5f, -0.5f, 0.5f);
glColor3f(0.0f, 1.0f, 0.0f); // Green
glVertex3f(-0.5f, 0.5f, 0.5f);
glColor3f(0.0f, 0.0f, 1.0f); // Blue
glVertex3f(0.5f, 0.5f, 0.5f);
glEnd();
```

This particular block of code is quite easily readable, which is one advantage of the legacy method. We begin by invoking the `glBegin()` method and passing in a value, which signifies how the actual vertices should be interpreted as they are being submitted. We are working with triangles, which means that every three vertices submitted in a row will be connected and turned into a triangle. Note the calls to `glColor3f` as well. The color of the vertices is set as they are being submitted, and the same can be done with texture coordinates as well. The final call to the `glEnd()` method flushes all of the submitted data to the GPU for rendering.

While this is very readable and easy to understand for newcomers, the vertex data has to be resubmitted to the GPU every frame, which heavily impacts performance. Small applications would not notice the difference, but the memory transfer overhead really starts to add up after a significant number of primitives have been submitted.

Another issue with this approach is how limited it is. Certain effects, if at all possible, can be extremely slow to pull off with the fixed function pipeline.

Programmable pipeline

Using the programmable pipeline is quite a bit more complicated for small tasks, but it proves invaluable for larger projects. Just like the fixed function pipeline, there are steps that are static and unchanging. The programmable pipeline does, however, provide a way to customize certain aspects of how the data submitted to the GPU is processed. This is where **shaders** come in. Shaders have already been briefly covered in the previous chapter; however, there is much more to them that has not yet been explained. They are the programs that can be written in a C-like language and executed on the GPU instead of the CPU. As it turns out, shaders are used to customize certain parts of the programmable pipeline. Consider the following diagram:

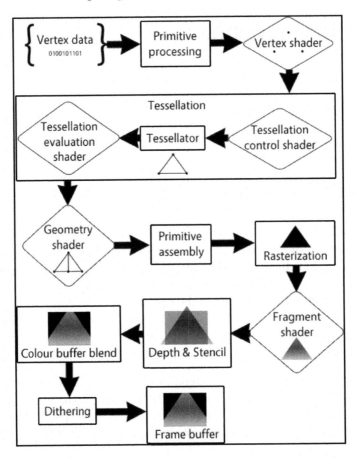

Just like the fixed-function pipeline, vertex data is submitted to the GPU. However, this data is not re-submitted every frame. Instead, the vertex data lives on the GPU and can be referred to when it needs to be rendered. Once a call has been made to draw a specific set of vertices, they're passed in to be processed and relayed to the vertex shader.

The **Vertex shader** is one of few programmable bits of this pipeline. It is often used to calculate the positions of vertices in the appropriate coordinate system, and pass these vertices down the pipeline to be processed further.

The **Tessellation** stage essentially is responsible for performing sub-divisions of our existing geometry into smaller primitives. It actually ends up connecting the vertices and passing these primitives further down the pipeline. There are two shaders in this stage that can be written and used; however, we are not going to be doing that.

All of the primitive data is then passed down to a **Geometry shader**, which just like the two tessellation shaders is optional. It can be used to generate more vertices from the existing geometry.

After the primitives have been properly assembled, they are passed further down and handled by the rasterizer.

Rasterization is the actual process of turning vertex and primitive information into pixel data. These pixels are then passed further down the pipeline.

The last programmable bit of this pipeline receives all of the pixel information from the previous stage. It is called the **Fragment shader** (that is, pixel shader), and can be used to determine the value of each individual pixel within the geometry we are rendering. Anything from assigning specific colors, to actually sampling pixels of a texture is done at this stage. These pixels are then pushed further down to be handled by other stages.

The **Depth & Stencil** stage performs various tests in order to clip unneeded pixels that should not be drawn on screen. If a pixel is outside of the window area or even behind another bit of geometry, it is dropped at this stage.

Unclipped pixels are then blended onto the existing frame buffer, which is used to draw everything on screen. Before they are blended, however, the **Dithering** process takes place, making sure pixels are correctly rounded up or down if the render image has less or more precision than the value we have.

Although it may be hard to grasp this concept at first, the programmable pipeline is a superior approach to modern rendering. Out of all of these stages covered, we only really need to write the vertex and fragment shaders to get started. We will be covering that very soon.

Storing and drawing primitives

All of our primitive data has to be represented as a set of vertices. Whether we are dealing with a triangle or a sprite on screen, or if it is a huge, complex model of a monster, it can all be broken down to this fundamental type. Let us take a look at a class that represents it:

```
enum class VertexAttribute{ Position, COUNT };

struct GL_Vertex {
  GL_Vertex(const glm::vec3& l_pos): m_pos(l_pos) {}

  glm::vec3 m_pos; // Attribute 1.
  // ...
};
```

As you can see, it is only a simple `struct` that holds a 3D vector that represents a position. Later on, we might want to store other information about a vertex, such as texture coordinates, its color, and so on. These different pieces of information about a specific vertex are usually referred to as **attributes**. For convenience, we are also enumerating different attributes to make the rest of our code more clear.

Vertex storage

Before any primitives can be drawn, their data must be stored on the GPU. In OpenGL, this task is achieved by utilizing **Vertex Array Objects (VAO)** and **Vertex Buffer Objects (VBO)**.

A vertex buffer object can simply be thought of as space that gets allocated on the GPU for storing data. That data can be anything. It could be vertex positions, colors, texture coordinates, and so on. We are going to use VBOs to store all of our primitive information.

A vertex array object is like a parent to a VBO, or even multiple VBOs. It stores information about how data that lives inside a VBO should be accessed, how information can be passed into various shader stages, and many more details that together form a state. If a VBO is the actual data pool, a VAO can be thought of as an instruction set of how to access that data.

Both VAO and VBO instances are identified by simple integers, which get returned after the space is allocated. These integers will be used to differentiate different buffers and array objects.

The model class

With that bit of information out of the way, we can finally get down to actually implementing a model class! A model, in our case, is any set of triangles that can form a shape. With enough triangles, any shape can be modelled. Let us take a look at the class header:

```
class GL_Model {
public:
  GL_Model(GL_Vertex* l_vertices, unsigned int l_vertCount);
  ~GL_Model();

  void Draw();
private:
  GLuint m_VAO;
  GLuint m_vertexVBO;
  unsigned int m_drawCount;
};
```

As you can tell, it is quite simple. The constructor takes in two arguments for now: a pointer to the first instance of a vertex, and the number of vertices we are actually submitting. This makes it easy for us to load a model quickly from a simple array of vertices, although it may not be the best way of loading more complex meshes.

Note that the class also has a `Draw()` method, which will be used later on to actually submit its vertices to the rendering pipeline and begin the drawing process.

Lastly, we have the two *GL unsigned integer* types: `m_VAO` and `m_vertexVBO`. These integers will refer to the actual vertex array object that is used with this model, as well as the vertex buffer object, used to store all of the vertex information. We also have an *unsigned integer*, `m_drawCount`, which is going to store the number of vertices this particular model has in order to draw them all.

Implementing the model class

With that out of the way, let us begin allocating and filling in our data structures! The constructor of the GL_Model class is going to be helping us with that task:

```
GL_Model::GL_Model(GL_Vertex* l_vertices,
  unsigned int l_vertCount)
{
  m_drawCount = l_vertCount;

  glGenVertexArrays(1, &m_VAO);
  glBindVertexArray(m_VAO);
  glGenBuffers(1, &m_vertexVBO);

  glBindBuffer(GL_ARRAY_BUFFER, m_vertexVBO);
  glBufferData(GL_ARRAY_BUFFER,
    l_vertCount * sizeof(l_vertices[0]),
    l_vertices, GL_STATIC_DRAW);
  glEnableVertexAttribArray(
    static_cast<GLuint>(VertexAttribute::Position));
  glVertexAttribPointer(
    static_cast<GLuint>(VertexAttribute::Position), 3, GL_FLOAT,
    GL_FALSE, 0, 0);

  glBindVertexArray(0);
}
```

We begin by copying the amount of vertices to the m_drawCount data member. This is going to be useful later, as we need to know exactly how many vertices need to be drawn before actually rendering them. Some space for a VAO is then allocated, using the glGenVertexArrays function. Its first argument is the amount of objects that need to be created, while the second one takes a pointer to a variable that is going to store the returned identifiers.

The next function call, glBindVertexArray(), actually enables a vertex array object with the provided identifier, so that any subsequent function call after this one modifies the vertex array object that was passed in as the argument. Any vertex array object manipulation from this point on will be performed on the VAO with the identifier, m_VAO.

Because GLEW is a C API, the idea of binding and unbinding something dominates most aspects of it. In order to modify or do anything with certain data that lives on the GPU, the appropriate buffer must be bound first.

Just like the VAO, the vertex buffer object also needs to be generated. The function `glGenBuffers` does just that. In this case, we only need one buffer object, which is what the first argument denotes. Once it is generated, just like the VAO, we need to bind to this buffer in order to modify it. This is where the `glBindBuffer` function comes in. As it is bound to, we also need to specify the type of buffer we are going to treat it as. Because we just want an array of data, `GL_ARRAY_BUFFER` is used.

Now that we have a buffer created, we can push some data to it! A call to `glBufferData` does just that. The first argument, just like the previous function, determines what kind of buffer we are dealing with. The second argument is the **byte** size of the data chunk we want to submit, which OpenGL has to know in order to allocate enough space for the buffer to hold all of the data. In this case, it is just the number of vertices multiplied by the number of bytes the first element takes up. The third argument is just a pointer to the actual data structure we want to submit. How much of that is read in is determined by the second argument, which, in this case, is all of it. Finally, the last argument is used as a hint for OpenGL to manage the data storage as efficiently as possible depending on its use. It stores the data differently depending on what we do with it. `GL_STATIC_DRAW` means we are not going to be modifying the data, so that it can store it a certain way that is most efficient for this situation.

With all of the data buffered, we can begin working with the VAO again and give it information about how the vertex information should be accessed. Because the vertex position has to be passed to the fragment shader, we need to enable it as an attribute and store information about how it should be processed in the VAO. This is where `glEnableVertexAttribArray()` and `glVertexAttribPointer()` functions come in.

The former function simply enables a certain attribute to be used by the vertex shader. `VertexAttribute::Position` evaluates to 0, so the *0th* attribute in the vertex shader is enabled for use. The latter, however, actually specifies how this data is read and processed before it gets piped down the vertex shader. In this case, the *0th* attribute is defined as a set of three variables, all of which are floats. The next argument can be useful if we want to normalize the data before it gets sent to the vertex shader. In this case, we do not need to do that, so `GL_FALSE` is passed in instead. The last two arguments are the byte stride and byte offset of the data we are interested in inside the buffer. Because we are only storing the vertexes position inside the `GL_Vertex` structure so far, both of these values are 0. However, what would happen if we had more attributes? Consider the following diagram:

Position	Position	Position
Color	Color	Color

Imagine we have all of the data inside a buffer, which was shown previously. For each vertex in there, its position is followed by its color, and then by another vertexes position. If we just want to filter out the position data, for example, stride and offset can be very useful. The stride argument is the number of bytes that have to be jumped from the beginning of one data segment to another. Effectively, stride can be thought of as the size of the entire vertex's data structure, which, in this case, is the sum of the size of the position vector, as well as the color vector. To put it simply, it's the number of bytes from the beginning of one vertex, to the beginning of another.

Offset, on the other hand, is just the number of bytes we need to move from the beginning of whichever structure we happen to be reading in order to reach the desired element. Accessing the color element would mean the offset would have to be the size of the position vector. To put it simply, the offset is the number of bytes from the beginning of the structure to the beginning of the desired element.

After our data is submitted and accounted for, we can use `glBindVertexArray` again to bind to *0*, which would show that we're done with the VAO.

All of this allocated data actually has to be disposed of when it's no longer needed. The destructor can help us here:

```
GL_Model::~GL_Model() {
    glDeleteBuffers(1, &m_vertexVBO);
    glDeleteVertexArrays(1, &m_VAO);
}
```

First, the vertex buffer object needs to be disposed of. We pass the number of VBOs, as well as the pointer to the first identifier to the `glDeleteBuffers` function, which purges all of the buffer data on the GPU. The VAO follows a similar procedure afterwards.

Finally, we can implement the `Draw` method of our `Model` class:

```
void GL_Model::Draw() {
    glBindVertexArray(m_VAO);
    glDrawArrays(GL_TRIANGLES, 0, m_drawCount);
    glBindVertexArray(0);
}
```

Before drawing something, we need to specify which data the pipeline should use. All of the vertex information sits safely in our buffer object that is managed by the VAO, so we bind it. The `glDrawArrays` function is then invoked. As the name states, it draws arrays of vertices. Its first argument is the type of primitive we want to draw, which in this case is triangles. Lines, points, and other types can also be drawn like this. The second argument is the starting index inside the buffer array object. Since we want to draw everything from the beginning, this is set to 0. Lastly, the number of vertices to be drawn is passed in. The call to this function actually initiates the rendering pipeline, sending all of the vertex data into the vertex shader. The final call is to the `glBindVertexArray()` function that simply unbinds our VAO.

Using shaders

The standardization of the programmable pipeline now means shaders have to be written for certain tasks, including the basic ones. This means that simply submitting our vertex data and rendering it would do nothing, as the two fundamental chunks of the rendering pipeline, the vertex and fragment shaders, are non-existent. In this section, we are going to cover how shaders are loaded, built, and applied to our virtual geometry, in turn producing those glorious pixels on the screen.

Loading shader files

Before we can use shaders, we must first discuss how they are loaded. All we technically need to create a shader is a string, containing all of its code. A very simple helper function can be written to parse a file and return it as a string, as shown here:

```
inline std::string ReadFile(const std::string& l_filename) {
  std::ifstream file(l_filename);
  if (!file.is_open()) { return ""; }
  std::string output;
  std::string line;
  while (std::getline(file, line)) {
    output.append(line + "\n");
  }
  file.close();
  return output;
}
```

This is nothing we have not seen before, when it comes to file reading and parsing. A string is created, then appended to with each new line of the file being read, and finally returned.

Creating shader programs

OpenGL shaders themselves are part of programs that are used throughout the rendering pipeline. If we have a vertex shader and a fragment shader we wish to utilize, both of them are actually joined into one program, which is then bound to so that the pipeline can use the appropriate shader at the right time. This is important, because it shapes the way the GL_Shader data structure is built:

```cpp
enum class ShaderType{ Vertex, Fragment, COUNT };

class GL_Shader {
public:
  GL_Shader(const std::string& l_fileName);
  ~GL_Shader();

  void Bind() const;
private:
  static void CheckError(GLuint l_shader, GLuint l_flag,
    bool l_program, const std::string& l_errorMsg);
  static GLuint BuildShader(const std::string& l_src,
    unsigned int l_type);

  GLuint m_program;
  GLuint m_shader[static_cast<unsigned int>(ShaderType::COUNT)];
};
```

First, we enumerate the shader types we are going to be using. For basic purposes, vertex and fragment shaders are more than enough.

The constructor of the class takes a filename of the shader(s) we are going to be loading. There is also a Bind() method, which will be used to enable a specific shader program before rendering begins.

We also have two static helper methods, used for printing out errors inside shaders, and actually building them. Yes, shaders need to be compiled and linked before they can be used, much like C/C++.

Finally, we need two *GL unsigned integer* data members, the latter of which is an array. The first integer is going to represent the shader program, which contains all attached shaders. The array of integers keeps track of identifiers of all types of shaders that are in the program.

Implementing the shader class

Let us get down to actually creating some shaders! As always, a good place to start is the constructor:

```
GL_Shader::GL_Shader(const std::string& l_fileName) {
  auto src_vert = Utils::ReadFile(l_fileName + ".vert");
  auto src_frag = Utils::ReadFile(l_fileName + ".frag");
  if (src_vert.empty() && src_frag.empty()) { return; }

  m_program = glCreateProgram(); // Create a new program.
  m_shader[static_cast<GLuint>(ShaderType::Vertex)] =
    BuildShader(src_vert, GL_VERTEX_SHADER);
  m_shader[static_cast<GLuint>(ShaderType::Fragment)] =
    BuildShader(src_frag, GL_FRAGMENT_SHADER);

  for (GLuint i = 0;
    i < static_cast<GLuint>(ShaderType::COUNT); ++i)
  {
    glAttachShader(m_program, m_shader[i]);
  }

  glBindAttribLocation(m_program,
    static_cast<GLuint>(VertexAttribute::Position), "position");

  glLinkProgram(m_program);
  CheckError(m_program, GL_LINK_STATUS, true, "Shader link error:");
  glValidateProgram(m_program);
  CheckError(m_program, GL_VALIDATE_STATUS, true, "Invalid shader:");
}
```

Before any shader compilation is done, we first need to have the actual source code loaded in memory. OpenGL does not do this for you, so we are going to be utilizing the `ReadFile` function implemented earlier. Once both types of shaders are loaded and checked for not being empty, a new shader program is created using `glCreateProgram()`. It returns an identifier that we need to keep track of if we want to use the shaders when rendering.

For the actual vertex and fragment shaders the static `BuildShader()` method is invoked, and the returned identifier is stored inside the `m_shader` array for the relevant type of shader. Note the `GL_VERTEX_SHADER` and `GL_FRAGMENT_SHADER` definitions being passed to the method call. These are the shader types OpenGL needs in order to build the shaders.

After the shaders have been built, they need to be attached to our created program. For this we can simply use a loop and invoke `glAttachShader`, which takes the ID of the program, as well as an ID of the shader to be attached to said program.

Shaders need to have some sort of input as they are being executed. Remember that our model rendering begins with a binding to a VAO, which holds the information about how certain attributes of a VBO should be accessed, followed by a draw call. In order for the data feeding to work properly, our shader class needs to bind a name and attribute location. This can be done by calling `glBindAttribLocation`, and passing in the ID of the program, the actual attribute location, which is enumerated as `VertexAttribute`, and the name of the attribute variable that's going to be used inside the shader program. This step ensures that the data being fed into the vertex shader will be accessible through a *position* variable. This will be covered more in the *Writing basic shaders* section.

After the shaders are built and have their attributes bound, all we have left is linking and validation, the latter of which determines if the shader executable can run given the current OpenGL state. Both `glLinkProgram` and `glValidateProgram` simply take the ID of the program. After each of these function calls, we also invoke the other static helper method, `CheckError`. It is responsible for actually fetching a string of information, pertaining to any sort of errors during the linking and compilation stages. This method takes in the program ID, a flag that is used to determine what stage of the shader building process we are actually interested in, a *Boolean* value that signifies whether the whole shader program is being checked or if it is just an individual shader, and a string to be split out into the console window before the actual error is printed.

Shaders, just like any resource, need to be cleaned up once we are done with them:

```
GL_Shader::~GL_Shader() {
  for (GLuint i = 0;
    i < static_cast<GLuint>(ShaderType::COUNT); ++i)
  {
    glDetachShader(m_program, m_shader[i]);
    glDeleteShader(m_shader[i]);
  }
  glDeleteProgram(m_program);
}
```

Thanks to the `ShaderType` enumeration, we know exactly how many shader types we support, and so we are able to simply run a loop for each one during cleanup. For each shader type, we must first detach it from the shader program using `glDetachShader`, which takes the program ID and the shader ID, and then deletes it using `glDeleteShader`. Once all the shaders are removed, the program itself is deleted through the `glDeleteProgram()` function call.

As discussed previously, OpenGL operates using function calls and a shared state. This means that certain resources such as shaders, for example, must be bound to before being used for rendering:

```
void GL_Shader::Bind() const { glUseProgram(m_program); }
```

In order to use a shader for a specific set of primitives to be drawn, we simply need to call `glUseProgram` and pass in the ID of the shader program.

Let us take a look at one of our helper methods, used to determine if there were any errors during the various stages of the shader program setup:

```
void GL_Shader::CheckError(GLuint l_shader, GLuint l_flag,
  bool l_program, const std::string& l_errorMsg)
{
  GLint success = 0;
  GLchar error[1024] = { 0 };
  if (l_program) { glGetProgramiv(l_shader, l_flag, &success); }
  else { glGetShaderiv(l_shader, l_flag, &success); }

  if (success) { return; }
  if (l_program) {
    glGetProgramInfoLog(l_shader, sizeof(error), nullptr, error);
  } else {
    glGetShaderInfoLog(l_shader, sizeof(error), nullptr, error);
  }
  std::cout << l_errorMsg << error << std::endl;
}
```

First, a few local variables are set up for storing the state information: a success flag, and a buffer for an error message to be put in. If the `l_program` flag is true, it means we are trying to fetch information about the actual shader program. Otherwise, we are only interested in an individual shader. To obtain the parameter that signifies success or failure of link/validation/compilation stages of a shader/program, we need to use `glGetProgramiv` or `glGetShaderiv`. Both of them take an ID to a shader or program being checked, a flag of the parameter we are interested in, and a pointer to the return value that is to be overwritten with either `GL_TRUE` or `GL_FALSE` in this case.

If whichever stage of the shader building process we are interested in finished successfully, we simply return from the method. Otherwise, we invoke either `glGetProgramInfoLog()` or `glGetShaderInfoLog()` to fetch the error information of the program or individual shader. Both of these functions take the identifier of either the program or shader being checked, the size of the error message buffer we have allocated, a pointer to a variable that would be used to store the length of the string returned, which we do not really need so `nullptr` is passed in, and a pointer to the error message buffer that is to be written to. Afterwards, it is as simple as printing out our `l_errorMsg` prefix, followed by the actual error written to the `error` message buffer.

Last, but definitely not least, let us see what it takes to build an individual shader:

```
GLuint GL_Shader::BuildShader(const std::string& l_src,
  unsigned int l_type)
{
  GLuint shaderID = glCreateShader(l_type);
  if (!shaderID) {
    std::cout << "Bad shader type!" << std::endl; return 0;
  }
  const GLchar* sources[1];
  GLint lengths[1];
  sources[0] = l_src.c_str();
  lengths[0] = l_src.length();
  glShaderSource(shaderID, 1, sources, lengths);
  glCompileShader(shaderID);
  CheckError(shaderID, GL_COMPILE_STATUS, false,
    "Shader compile error: ");
  return shaderID;
}
```

First, an individual shader has to be created using the `glCreateShader()` method. It takes in a shader type, such as `GL_VERTEX_SHADER`, which we used in the constructor of this class. If, for some reason, the shader creation failed, an error message is written to the console window and the method returns a 0. Otherwise, two arrays of GL types are set up: one for the sources of potentially multiple shaders, and one for the lengths of each source string. For now we're only going to be dealing with one source per shader, but it is possible to handle multiple sources later on, should we ever want to.

After the source code and its length have been written to the arrays we just set up, `glShaderSource` is used to submit the code to a buffer before it gets compiled. The function takes in the ID of the newly created shader, the number of source strings we're passing in, a pointer to the source array, as well as a pointer to the source length array. The shader is then actually compiled using `glCompileShader`, and the `CheckError` helper method is invoked to print out any possible compilation errors. Note the `GL_COMPILE_STATUS` flag being passed in, as well as the false flag, showing that we're interested in checking the status of an individual shader, rather than the whole shader program.

Writing basic shaders

As our `GL_Shader` class is done, we can finally get to write some basic shaders for our application! Let us get started by taking a look at a file named `basic.vert`, which is our vertex shader:

```
#version 450
attribute vec3 position;

void main(){
    gl_Position = vec4(position, 1.0);
}
```

First, we set up the `attribute` of the shader that is going to be written to by OpenGL. It is an attribute of type `vec3`, and is going to represent our **vertex position** information that gets fed into this shader one by one. This type was set up inside the `GL_Model` class constructor using the `glVertexAttribPointer`, and then named in the `GL_Shader` class constructor, using the `glBindVertexAttribLocation` function.

The body of the shader has to have a main function, where all of the magic happens. In this case, all we need to do is set the internal OpenGL variable `gl_Position` to the position we want our vertex to have. It requires a `vec4` type, so the position attribute is converted to it, with the last vector value, which is used for clipping purposes, being set to `1.0`. For now, we do not need to worry about this. Just keep in mind that the actual vertex position in normalized device coordinates (coordinates in a range of *(-1,-1)* and *(1,1)*) are set here.

Note the version number on the very first line. If your computer does not support OpenGL 4.5, this can be changed to anything else, especially because we are not doing anything that older versions do not support.

After the vertex information is processed, we also need to worry about shading the individual pixels that make up our geometry correctly. This is where the fragment shader comes in:

```
#version 450

void main(){
    gl_FragColor = vec4(1.0, 1.0, 1.0, 1.0); // White.
}
```

This shader also uses an internal OpenGL variable. This time it is named `gl_FragColor`, and, predictably enough, is used for setting the color of the pixel we are processing. For now, let us just shade all of the pixels of our geometry white.

Drawing our first triangle

We have our model class that handles all of the geometry data, as well as the shader class, which deals with processing our data at various points of the programmable rendering pipeline. With that out of the way, all we have left to do is actually set up and use these classes. Let us start by adding them as data members to the `Game` object:

```
class Game{
  ...
private:
  ...
  std::unique_ptr<GL_Shader> m_shader;
  std::unique_ptr<GL_Model> m_model;
  ...
};
```

They can then be set up in the constructor of our `Game` class:

```
Game::Game() ... {
  ...
  m_shader = std::make_unique<GL_Shader>(
    Utils::GetWorkingDirectory() + "GL/basic");

  GL_Vertex vertices[] = {
    //           |-----POSITION----|
```

```
//              X       Y       Z
GL_Vertex({ -0.5, -0.5, 0.5 }, // 0
GL_Vertex({ -0.5, 0.5, 0.5 }, // 1
GL_Vertex({ 0.5, 0.5, 0.5 }, // 2
};

    m_model = std::make_unique<GL_Model>(vertices, 3);
}
```

First, the shader class is created and a path with a filename is passed to it, so that the
basic.vert and basic.frag shaders inside the GL directory of our executable directory
can be loaded. An array of vertices is then set up, with each one being initialized to a
particular position in normalized device coordinates. This particular arrangement creates
three vertices in the middle of the screen, which will be connected into a triangle. The
coordinates here fall within the range of what is known as **normalized device coordinates**.
It is the coordinate system that the window uses, as shown here:

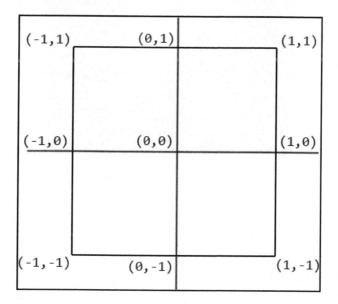

A GL_Model object is then created, with the vertex array and vertex count being passed in
as arguments. The GL_Model then goes on to push this data to the GPU, as discussed
previously.

Lastly, let us take a look at how we can render our triangle on screen:

```
void Game::Render() {
  m_window.BeginDraw();
  // Render here.
```

```
    m_shader->Bind();
    m_model->Draw();
    // Finished rendering.
    m_window.EndDraw();
}
```

After the window is cleared inside the `BeginDraw()` method, the shader program is bound to, so that the vertex and fragment shaders we wrote earlier are used when the vertex data of our `GL_Model` is being pushed through the rendering pipeline. The models `Draw()` method is then invoked, to begin the rendering process. After successful program compilation and execution, this is what we should see on screen:

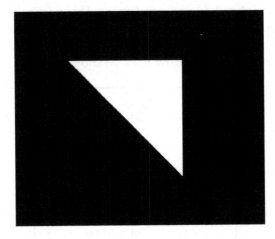

Hooray! After about 20 pages of theory, we have a triangle. This may be a little bit discouraging, but keep in mind that everything from this point on is going to get much, much easier. Congratulations on making it this far!

Using textures

A basic, white triangle is not very exciting to look at. The next obvious improvement to make to our code is making textures available to the fragment shader, so that they can be sampled and applied to our geometry. Unfortunately, OpenGL does not provide a way of actually loading image data, especially since there are so many different formats to keep up with. For that, we are going to use one of our resources listed at the beginning of this chapter, the STB image loader. It is a small, single header C library, used to load image data into a buffer that can later be used by OpenGL, or any other library for that matter.

The texture class

Remember the remark that everything is going to get much easier at this point? It is true. Let us breeze through the texturing process, starting with a class definition for a texture object:

```
class GL_Texture {
public:
  GL_Texture(const std::string& l_fileName);
  ~GL_Texture();

  void Bind(unsigned int l_unit);
private:
  GLuint m_texture;
};
```

Although OpenGL does not actually handle loading texture data, it is still going to be handled within the confines of this class. Because of that, the constructor of our texture class is still going to take a path to the texture file to be loaded. Also, much like the shader class, we are going to need to bind to a specific texture before it can be used when rendering geometry. For now, ignore the argument it takes. It will be explained down the line.

The OpenGL textures, just like shaders or geometry data, have to be stored on the GPU. Because of that, it stands to reason that texture data will be referred to by a `GLuint` identifier, just like shaders or buffers.

Implementing the texture class

Let us take a look at what needs to be done in order to successfully load textures from the hard disk, and push them into the GPU:

```
GL_Texture::GL_Texture(const std::string& l_fileName) {
  int width, height, nComponents;
  unsigned char* imageData = stbi_load(l_fileName.c_str(),
    &width, &height, &nComponents, 4);
  if (!imageData) { return; }

  glGenTextures(1, &m_texture);
  glBindTexture(GL_TEXTURE_2D, m_texture);

  glTexParameteri(GL_TEXTURE_2D, GL_TEXTURE_WRAP_S, GL_REPEAT);
  glTexParameteri(GL_TEXTURE_2D, GL_TEXTURE_WRAP_T, GL_REPEAT);
  glTexParameterf(GL_TEXTURE_2D, GL_TEXTURE_MIN_FILTER, GL_LINEAR);
  glTexParameterf(GL_TEXTURE_2D, GL_TEXTURE_MAG_FILTER, GL_LINEAR);
```

```
glTexImage2D(GL_TEXTURE_2D, 0, GL_RGBA, width, height, 0,
    GL_RGBA, GL_UNSIGNED_BYTE, imageData);

stbi_image_free(imageData);
}
```

First, a few integers are created in order to be filled in with information about the texture that is going to be loaded. We then invoke the `stbi_load()` function, which is part of the STB image loading library, passing in a path to the texture file, pointers to the width, height, and the component count variables that are about to be written to, as well as the number of components the file is expected to have. The data is stored in the form of an *unsigned char*, a pointer to which is returned by the `stbi_load()` function. If `nullptr` was returned, we obviously need to return, as the loading process failed.

The number of components an image has is simply the number of color channels. Passing in a value of 0 would mean the image data is loaded as is, while any other value *forces* the data to contain other color channel information. The component number to channel configuration can be evaluated like so:

Components	Channels
1	Gray
2	Gray, alpha
3	Red, green, blue
4	Red, green, blue, alpha

From this point on, we follow what should be a familiar pattern by now. First, a texture object is generated using `glGenTextures`, to which the number of textures we want is passed as the first argument, and the pointer to the texture identifier or a list of them as the second argument. We then bind to the newly created texture using `glBindTexture`. The first argument of this function simply lets OpenGL know what kind of texture we are dealing with. In this case, `GL_TEXTURE_2D` is used, because it is a basic 2D image.

OpenGL supports a myriad of different types of textures for various tasks, including 3D textures, cube maps, and so on.

Once a texture is bound to, we can manipulate various details it comes with. For textures, the parameter manipulation function is named `glTexParameter()`. There are many different types of this single function, all with different suffixes that give a hint to the programmer of what data type it is expecting. For our purposes, we are going to be using two types: *integer* and *float*, appropriately ended by letters *i* and *f*.

The first two lines deal with defining behavior for cases when texture data is being read outside of the boundaries of its size, that is, how the texture is wrapped. The `GL_TEXTURE_WRAP_S` parameter deals with wrapping on the *X* axis, while the `GL_TEXTURE_WRAP_T` parameter deals with the *Y* axis. Why *S* and *T* you may ask? The answer to that is simple. Positional vectors, color data, and texture coordinates are enumerated differently, but they both mean roughly the same thing. Consider the following table:

	1	2	3	4
Position	X	Y	Z	W
Color	R	G	B	A
Textures	S	T	P	Q

They are all vectors of four values. Accessing the position *X* value is the same as accessing the red channel of a color structure, and so on.

The next two function calls deal with how the texture is interpolated when being sized down or up. Both cases specify the `GL_LINEAR` parameter, which means the pixels will be linearly interpolated.

Finally, we actually submit the loaded pixel information to the GPU by invoking the `glTexImage2D()` method. Its first argument, once again, lets OpenGL know what type of texture we are submitting. The second argument is the texture's level of detail, which will be used for mip-mapping. The value `0` simply means it is the base level texture.

Mip-mapping is an optional technique that can be utilized by OpenGL, in which multiple versions of the same texture, but of different resolutions, are loaded and submitted to the GPU, and later applied to geometry depending on how far it is from the viewer. If it is further away, a lower resolution texture (with a higher mip-mapping level) is used. This can be done for performance reasons, when necessary.

The third argument lets OpenGL know what arrangement the pixel information data is in. This is necessary, because certain formats may store it in varying configurations. The width and height information is passed in next, along with a number of pixels that can be used to add a border to the texture. We are not going to be using that feature, which is why 0 is passed in. The next argument is, once again, a flag for a certain arrangement of pixels. This time it lets OpenGL know which arrangement we want it to store the pixel data in. Finally, a flag for the type that our loaded texture is in is passed, along with a pointer to the actual texture data. We are using the `GL_UNSIGNED_BYTE` parameter, because that is what the STB image loader returns, and the *char* type is exactly one byte long.

After the texture information is submitted to the GPU, we no longer need to keep the image data buffer around. It's destroyed by calling `stbi_image_free`, and passing in the pointer to the buffer.

The data we submitted to the GPU needs to be released once we no longer need the texture:

```
GL_Texture::~GL_Texture() { glDeleteTextures(1, &m_texture); }
```

The `glDeleteTextures` function takes the number of textures we want to dispose of, as well as a pointer to an array of *GLuint* identifiers.

Finally, let's implement the `Bind()` method, which is going to give us the ability to use the texture when rendering:

```
void GL_Texture::Bind(unsigned int l_unit) {
  assert(l_unit >= 0 && l_unit < 32);
  glActiveTexture(GL_TEXTURE0 + l_unit);
  glBindTexture(GL_TEXTURE_2D, m_texture);
}
```

OpenGL actually supports the ability for multiple textures to be bound all at once while rendering, so that complex geometry can be textured more efficiently. The exact number, at least at the time of writing, is 32 units. Most of the time we are not going to need that many, but it is nice to have the option. The identifier of the unit we want to use is passed in as an argument to the `Bind()` method. In order to avoid confusion, we are going to perform an `assert()` method and make sure that the `l_unit` value is in the right range first.

In order to enable a specific unit for a texture, the `glActiveTexture()` method needs to be called. It takes a single argument, which is the enumerated texture unit. It ranges from `GL_TEXTURE0` all the way to `GL_TEXTURE31`. Because those values are sequential, a neat trick is to simply add the `l_unit` to the `GL_TEXTURE0` definition, which will give us the right unit enumeration. After that, we simply bind to the texture as before, using the `glBindTexture()` method and passing in the type of texture we have, along with its identifier.

Model and shader class changes

To add support for textured geometry, we first need to make some changes to the vertex information that gets stored. Let us take a look at the `GL_Vertex` structure to see what needs to be added:

```
enum class VertexAttribute{ Position, TexCoord, COUNT };

struct GL_Vertex {
  GL_Vertex(const glm::vec3& l_pos,
    const glm::vec2& l_texCoord)
    : m_pos(l_pos), m_texCoord(l_texCoord) {}

  glm::vec3 m_pos; // Attribute 1.
  glm::vec2 m_texCoord; // Attribute 2.
  // ...
};
```

As you can see, we need an additional vertex attribute, which is the coordinate of the texture a vertex is associated with. It is a simple two-dimensional vector that represents the texture coordinates, as shown here:

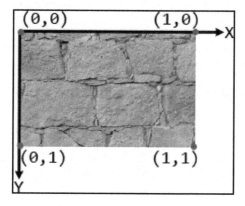

The great thing about representing texture coordinates in this fashion is the fact that it makes the coordinates resolution-independent. A point *(0.5,0.5)* on a smaller texture is going to be the exact same point on its larger counterpart.

Because we now have more information about a single vertex that needs to be stored and accessed, the VAO needs to know exactly how to do so:

```
GL_Model::GL_Model(GL_Vertex* l_vertices,unsigned int l_vertCount)
{
    ...
    auto stride = sizeof(l_vertices[0]);
    auto texCoordOffset = sizeof(l_vertices[0].m_pos);

    glBindBuffer(GL_ARRAY_BUFFER, m_vertexVBO);
    glBufferData(GL_ARRAY_BUFFER,
        l_vertCount * sizeof(l_vertices[0]),
        l_vertices, GL_STATIC_DRAW);
    glEnableVertexAttribArray(
        static_cast<GLuint>(VertexAttribute::Position));
    glVertexAttribPointer(
        static_cast<GLuint>(VertexAttribute::Position), 3, GL_FLOAT,
        GL_FALSE, stride, 0);
    glEnableVertexAttribArray(
        static_cast<GLuint>(VertexAttribute::TexCoord));
    glVertexAttribPointer(
        static_cast<GLuint>(VertexAttribute::TexCoord), 2, GL_FLOAT,
        GL_FALSE, stride, (void*)texCoordOffset);
    ...
}
```

We now get to utilize the stride and offset parameters that were discussed previously! The stride is, of course, the full size of a GL_Vertex structure, while the offset to obtain texture coordinates is the size of the vertex position vector, because that is the amount by which the pointer needs to be offset.

After the data is submitted to the buffer, we enable the vertex position attribute and provide its pointer with the stride. The offset remains 0, because Position is the first attribute.

We also need to enable the TexCoord attribute, because it will be passed to the shaders as well. Its pointer is set up similarly to that of position, except we have 2 floats instead of 3, and the offset now needs to be applied, so that the position data is skipped.

Note the `void*` cast for the last argument. This is because the offset actually takes a pointer, rather than a number of bytes. It is one of the leftover *legacy* details, and only means the number of bytes in newer versions.

The final change to our C++ code pertains to updating the `GL_Shader` class, in order to register the new attribute that is going to be passed in to the vertex shader:

```
GL_Shader::GL_Shader(const std::string& l_fileName) {
  ...
  glBindAttribLocation(m_program,
    static_cast<GLuint>(VertexAttribute::Position), "position");
  glBindAttribLocation(m_program,
    static_cast<GLuint>(VertexAttribute::TexCoord),
    "texCoordVert");
  ...
}
```

It simply establishes a name for our texture coordinate attribute, which is now `"texCoordVert"`.

Updating the shaders

The actual sampling of the texture takes place inside the fragment shader. However, as the data is actually received in the vertex shader first, let us see how it needs to be updated to cater to our needs:

```
#version 450

attribute vec3 position;
attribute vec2 texCoordVert;
varying vec2 texCoord; // Pass to fragment shader.
void main(){
  gl_Position = vec4(position, 1.0);
  texCoord = texCoordVert; // Pass to fragment shader.
}
```

As you can see, the `texCoordVert` attribute is established here, along with a `varying` 2D vector named `texCoord`. A varying type simply means that its data is going to be passed down the rendering pipeline and received by the next shader in line. In our case, `texCoord` is going to be accessible inside the fragment shader. Its value is set to the input attribute of `texCoordVert`. Why? Because varying data received by any shader down the line is **interpolated**. That's right. Take a look at the following diagram:

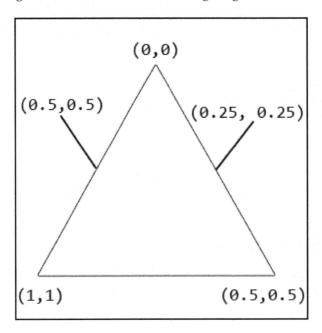

In order to accurately sample color information for each pixel of our geometry, we do not really need to do any math by ourselves. Interpolation, or weighted averaging, takes care of that for us. If one vertex has texture coordinates of, let's say **(1,1)**, and the opposite vertex has the coordinates **(0,0)**, the fragment shader executing on a pixel somewhere in between those vertices will receive the **interpolated** value of **(0.5, 0.5)**. This makes coloring a pixel as easy as this:

```
#version 450
uniform sampler2D texture;
varying vec2 texCoord; // Receiving it from vertex shader.

void main(){
    gl_FragColor = texture2D(texture, texCoord);
}
```

First, note the `uniform` variable of type `sampler2D`, called `texture`. We do not need to manually pass this into our shaders as it is done behind the scenes. It simply provides access to the data of the current texture that it is bound to. Next, we set up the varying variable `texCoord`, which completes the *piping* of data from the vertex shader to the fragment shader. The fragment color is then set to a `vec4`, which gets returned from the `texture2D()` function that takes in the texture received by the fragment shader, as well as the coordinates we want to sample. Since the `vec4` that gets returned represents the color of the pixel, that is all that it takes to texture geometry!

Using a texture

Applying the texture to our geometry is quite simple at this point. First, the `GL_Texture` class needs to be added as a data member to the `Game` object. We can then proceed to set everything else up as follows:

```
Game::Game() ... {
  ...
  GL_Vertex vertices[] = {
    //                |---POSITION----| |TEXTURE|
    //            X     Y     Z       X  Y
    GL_Vertex({ -0.5, -0.5, 0.5 }, { 0, 0 }), // 0
    GL_Vertex({ -0.5, 0.5, 0.5 }, { 0, 1 }), // 1
    GL_Vertex({ 0.5, 0.5, 0.5 }, { 1, 1 }), // 2
  };
  m_texture = std::make_unique<GL_Texture>(
    Utils::GetWorkingDirectory() + "GL/brick.png");
  ...
}

void Game::Render() {
  m_window.BeginDraw();
  // Render here.
  m_texture->Bind(0);
  m_shader->Bind();
  m_model->Draw();
  m_window.EndDraw();
}
```

The `GL_Vertex` objects now take an additional argument, which represents the texture coordinates of the vertex. We also load the brick texture in the constructor, which is then bound to in the `Render()` method, right before the shader. When our model is rendered, it should look as follows:

We now have a motionless model with a texture applied. Still not very exciting, but we are getting there!

Applying transformations

Moving, rotating, and otherwise manipulating vertex data may seem quite straight forward. One may even be tempted to simply update the vertex position information and simply resubmit that data back to the VBO. While things may have been done that way for a while in the past, there are much more efficient, albeit more math-intensive ways of performing this task. Displacing vertices is now done in the vertex shader by simply multiplying the vertex positions by something called a **matrix**.

Matrix basics

Matrices are extremely useful in graphics programming, because they can represent any kind of rotation, scale, or displacement manipulation that can be applied to a vector. There are many different types of matrices, but they are all just blocks of information that look similar to this:

$$
\left\{
\begin{matrix}
1, & 0, & 0, & 0 \\
0, & 1, & 0, & 0 \\
0, & 0, & 1, & 0 \\
0, & 0, & 0, & 1
\end{matrix}
\right\}
$$

This particular matrix is a 4×4 identity matrix, but a variety of differently sized matrices exist, such as 3×3, 2×3, 3×2, and so on. There are rules when it comes to adding, subtracting, multiplying, or dividing them. We are not really going to get into that as it is beyond the scope of this chapter. The nice thing is that the `glm` library abstracts all of this away for us, so it is not absolutely necessary to know much about this for now. A thing to take away from this is that positional vectors can be transformed when added to or multiplied by matrices.

The world space

Up until this point, we have been working with vertex positions that are specified in the normalized device coordinate space. This means that each vertex coordinate is actually relative to the center of the screen. In order to properly deal with transformations; however, we want to treat our geometry as being relative to an origin point that falls within the **model space**, as shown here:

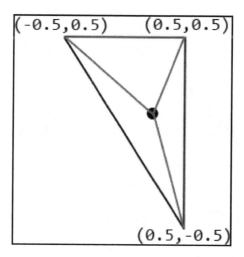

If a model has an origin, it can also have a global position within our world, where its origin is relative to some arbitrary point within the game world we have constructed. This global position, as well as some other attributes, such as the scale and rotation of the object, can be represented by a matrix. Applying these attributes to the vertex coordinates that are in model space, which is exactly what happens when they are multiplied by the **model matrix**, allows us to bring those coordinates into what is known as **world space**, as shown here:

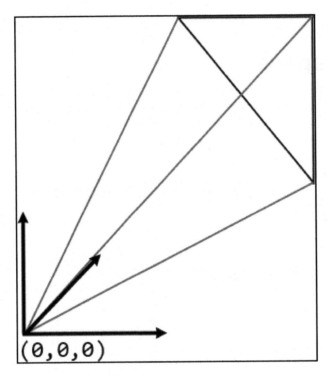

This transformation simply means that the vertices are now relative to the world's origin, rather than the model origin, allowing us to accurately represent models in our own coordinate system before drawing them on screen.

The transform class

Before any transformations can be applied, they should be properly grouped together and represented by a single data structure. The GL_Transform class is going to do exactly that for us:

```cpp
#include <glm.hpp>
#include <gtx/transform.hpp>
class GL_Transform {
public:
  GL_Transform(const glm::vec3& l_pos = { 0.f, 0.f, 0.f },
    const glm::vec3& l_rot = { 0.f, 0.f, 0.f },
    const glm::vec3& l_scale = { 1.f, 1.f, 1.f });

  glm::vec3 GetPosition()const;
  glm::vec3 GetRotation()const;
  glm::vec3 GetScale()const;

  void SetPosition(const glm::vec3& l_pos);
  void SetRotation(const glm::vec3& l_rot);
  void SetScale(const glm::vec3& l_scale);

  glm::mat4 GetModelMatrix();
private:
  void RecalculateMatrix();
  glm::vec3 m_position;
  glm::vec3 m_rotation;
  glm::vec3 m_scale;
};
```

First, note the included headers on top. These are necessary for the data types and transformation functions that are going to be used in this class. Outside of that, we have three vectors that are going to represent the model's position, rotation, and scale, which are going to be used for calculating the model matrix that transforms vertices into world coordinates.

Implementing the transform class

The constructor simply takes in the appropriate arguments and sets up some data members using the initializer list:

```
GL_Transform::GL_Transform(const glm::vec3& l_pos,
    const glm::vec3& l_rot, const glm::vec3& l_scale)
    : m_position(l_pos), m_rotation(l_rot), m_scale(l_scale)
{}
```

The meat of this class is the `GetModelMatrix()` method, as it deals with all the necessary math:

```
glm::mat4 GL_Transform::GetModelMatrix() {
    glm::mat4 matrix_pos = glm::translate(m_position);
    glm::mat4 matrix_scale = glm::scale(m_scale);
    // Represent each stored rotation as a different matrix, because
    // we store angles.
    //          x   y   z
    glm::mat4 matrix_rotX = glm::rotate(m_rotation.x,
        glm::vec3(1, 0, 0));
    glm::mat4 matrix_rotY = glm::rotate(m_rotation.y,
        glm::vec3(0, 1, 0));
    glm::mat4 matrix_rotZ = glm::rotate(m_rotation.z,
        glm::vec3(0, 0, 1));
    // Create a rotation matrix.
    // Multiply in reverse order it needs to be applied.
    glm::mat4 matrix_rotation = matrix_rotZ*matrix_rotY*matrix_rotX;
    // Apply transforms in reverse order they need to be applied in.
    return matrix_pos * matrix_rotation * matrix_scale;
}
```

The model matrix is going to be a result of many other matrices being multiplied together, thus making it contain all of the necessary transformation information. We begin by creating what is known as a **translation matrix**. Calling `glm::translate` creates one for us, with the position information of `m_position`. It is used to bring the positions of our vertices into world space.

We then create a **scale matrix**, which is responsible for representing scaling or shrinking of a model. For example, if a model should be drawn as twice as big as it's stored on the GPU, the scale matrix will be used to adjust the positions of all vertices to make it look that way. Using `glm::scale` and passing in the scale vector as the argument will construct one for us.

The final type of matrix we need is the **rotation matrix**. It obviously represents different rotation values of an object, thus displacing all the vertices around an origin point. This one, however, is not quite so straightforward due to the fact that we are storing rotation information as a vector of **degrees**. Because of that, matrices of each axis need to be created using the `glm::rotate` function, which takes the degree of rotation, as well as a **directional vector**, representing the axis around which the rotation is desired. It simply means setting a value of 1 for the *x*, *y*, or *z* component, depending on which axis we are dealing with. The final rotational matrix is then calculated by multiplying all three previous matrices together. Using a different multiplication order will produce different results. Generally, a rule of thumb is to multiply all matrices in reverse order of application.

Finally, we can calculate the model matrix by multiplying all previous matrices together like so:

$$
\begin{array}{cc}
\text{Translation} & \text{Rotation X} \\
\left\{ \begin{array}{cccc} 1, & 0, & 0, & X \\ 0, & 1, & 0, & Y \\ 0, & 0, & 1, & Z \\ 0, & 0, & 0, & 1 \end{array} \right\} * & \left\{ \begin{array}{cccc} 1, & 0, & 0, & 0 \\ 0, & \cos(\vartheta), & -\sin(\vartheta), & 0 \\ 0, & \sin(\vartheta), & \cos(\vartheta), & 0 \\ 0, & 0, & 0, & 1 \end{array} \right\}
\end{array}
$$

$$ * $$

$$
\text{Rotation Y} \\
\left\{ \begin{array}{cccc} \cos(\vartheta), & 0, & \sin(\vartheta), & 0 \\ 0, & 1, & 0, & 0 \\ -\sin(\vartheta), & 0, & \cos(\vartheta), & 0 \\ 0, & 0, & 0, & 1 \end{array} \right\}
$$

$$ * $$

$$
\text{Rotation Z} \\
\left\{ \begin{array}{cccc} \cos(\vartheta), & -\sin(\vartheta), & 0, & 0 \\ \sin(\vartheta), & \cos(\vartheta), & 0, & 0 \\ 0, & 0, & 1, & 0 \\ 0, & 0, & 0, & 1 \end{array} \right\}
$$

$$ * $$

$$
\text{Scale} \\
\left\{ \begin{array}{cccc} sX, & 0, & 0, & 0 \\ 0, & sY, & 0, & 0 \\ 0, & 0, & sZ, & 0 \\ 0, & 0, & 0, & 1 \end{array} \right\}
$$

The resulting model matrix is then returned.

The rest of this class is fairly straightforward, as there is nothing else except setters and getters left:

```
glm::vec3 GL_Transform::GetPosition() const { return m_position; }
glm::vec3 GL_Transform::GetRotation() const { return m_rotation; }
glm::vec3 GL_Transform::GetScale() const { return m_scale; }

void GL_Transform::SetPosition(const glm::vec3& l_pos)
{ m_position = l_pos; }
void GL_Transform::SetRotation(const glm::vec3& l_rot)
{ m_rotation = l_rot; }
void GL_Transform::SetScale(const glm::vec3& l_scale)
{ m_scale = l_scale; }
```

Updating the shader class

Once again, we are going to be using the shader class to submit the necessary matrix information to the vertex shader, where it will be used. The reason this is done inside the vertex shader is because the GPU is optimized for operations like this. Let us take a look at what we need to change:

```
enum class UniformType{ Transform, COUNT };

class GL_Shader {
public:
   ...
   void Update(GL_Transform& l_transform);
   ...
private:
   ...
   GLuint m_uniform[static_cast<unsigned int>(UniformType::COUNT)];
};
```

First, note a new enumeration that we have established. It enumerates all the uniform variable types that our shaders need, which, for now, consists of only one.

A uniform performs a different task from the usual shader attributes or varying variables. Attributes are *filled in* by OpenGL behind the scenes, using data from the VBO. Varying shader variables are passed between shaders. A uniform variable is actually passed into the shader by our C++ code, which is why we need to treat it differently.

The GL_Shader class now also needs an Update() method, which is going to take in a reference to the GL_Transform class and use it to pass the model matrix to the vertex shader. Lastly, we need to store identifiers that are used to locate uniform variables within shaders, so that they can be used. The m_uniform data member exists for that exact purpose.

Let's see how a uniform variable location can be obtained and stored:

```
GL_Shader::GL_Shader(const std::string& l_fileName) {
  ...
  m_uniform[static_cast<unsigned int>(UniformType::Transform)] =
    glGetUniformLocation(m_program, "transform");
}
```

As you can see, OpenGL provides a nice function for that, called glGetUniformLocation. It takes an identifier of the program we are using, as well as the name of the uniform variable inside the shader, which is "transform".

Setting the value of a uniform variable also comes down to a single function call:

```
void GL_Shader::Update(GL_Transform& l_transform) {
  glm::mat4 modelMatrix = l_transform.GetModelMatrix();
  glUniformMatrix4fv(static_cast<GLint>(
    m_uniform[static_cast<unsigned int>(UniformType::Transform)]),
    1, GL_FALSE, &modelMatrix[0][0]);
}
```

First, we obtain the model matrix from the transform class. The glUniform function is then called. It has a suffix of the exact data type we are submitting, which, in this case, is a 4×4 matrix of floats. The uniform ID we stored earlier is used as the first argument. The amount of data being submitted is the second argument, which in this case is only 1, as one matrix is being submitted. The third argument is a flag that lets us transpose the matrix. We do not need to do that, so GL_FALSE is passed in. Finally, a pointer to the first element of the matrix is passed as the last argument. OpenGL knows exactly how big the matrix is, as we are calling the appropriate function, which allows it to read the entire matrix.

Lastly, we need to modify the vertex shader in order to actually perform the transformation:

```
#version 450

attribute vec3 position;
attribute vec2 texCoordVert;
varying vec2 texCoord; // Pass to fragment shader.

uniform mat4 transform; // Passed in by the shader class.

void main(){
  gl_Position = transform * vec4(position, 1.0);
  texCoord = texCoordVert; // Pass to fragment shader.
}
```

Note the `uniform` of type `mat4` being added. We simply need to multiply it by the position in the main function, which gives us our transformed vertex position.

Manipulating the triangle

Once again, all we have left to do in order to apply the code we have written is add it to the Game class:

```
class Game{
  ...
private:
  ...
  GL_Transform m_transform;
  ...
};
```

It really does not need any more setting up than that. We can jump straight to manipulation of the transform's properties, by editing the `Update()` method:

```
void Game::Update() {
  ...
  auto rotation = m_transform.GetRotation();
  rotation.x += 0.001f;
  rotation.y += 0.0002f;
  rotation.z += 0.002f;
  if (rotation.x >= 360.f) { rotation.x = 0.f; }
  if (rotation.y >= 360.f) { rotation.y = 0.f; }
  if (rotation.z >= 360.f) { rotation.z = 0.f; }
  m_transform.SetRotation(rotation);
  m_shader->Update(m_transform);
}
```

In this case, we are simply playing around with rotations along all axes. After making those modifications, it is important to pass the transform object to the `GL_ShaderUpdate()` method, so that the vertices can be properly transformed, giving us this resulting rotation:

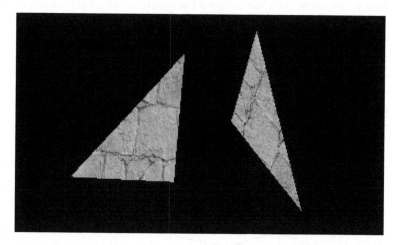

Now we are getting somewhere! Still, we have no interaction with the scene. This whole time we are just sitting still while the geometry just spins around. At best, this is just a very elaborate screensaver. Let's actually implement something that will give us some *mobility*.

Creating a camera

OpenGL, unlike SFML, does not offer any means of actually moving around the view or the camera. While this may seem odd at first, that is mainly because there is no camera or view to move around. Yes, you heard that right. No camera, no views, just vertex data, shaders, and raw math to the rescue. How? Let's take a look!

View projection essentials

All of the rendering and programming trickery that lots of libraries abstract away is exactly that – tricks. When it comes to moving around the game world, there is no real *camera* that conveniently films the right sides of geometry to be rendered. The camera is just an illusion, used to abstract away concepts that are not intuitive. Moving around a game world involves nothing else except additional matrix math that is performed on the **vertices themselves**. The act of rotating the *camera* around the scene simply comes down to the exact opposite of that: rotating the scene around a point in space that is referred to as the camera. Once again, we are going to be transforming our vertices to be relative to yet another point of origin, and this time, it is the camera itself. Consider the following diagram:

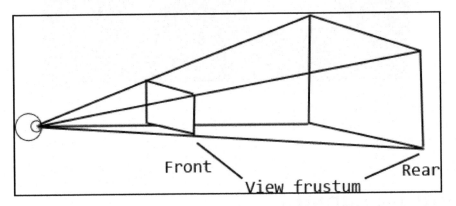

In order to implement the camera class and be able to *move around* the world, we need to know a few basics. First of all, we have to decide how wide the view angle of the camera should be. This affects how much we can actually see. The other important detail is correctly setting up the **view frustum**. Think of it as a pyramid shaped piece of geometry that defines the range of the camera's view. It determines how close certain things can be until they are no longer seen, as well as what's the maximum distance of an object from the camera until it's no longer rendered.

The aspect ratio of our window, as well as the field of view, near/far distances of the view frustum, and the position of the camera all add up to a total of two matrices we are going to calculate: the **view matrix** and **projection matrix**. The former deals with positioning vertices relative to the camera's position, while the latter adjusts and warps them, which depends on how close or far away they are from the view frustum, the field of view, and other attributes.

There are mainly two projection types we can work with: **perspective** and **orthographic**. The perspective projection offers a realistic result where objects can appear to be further away from the camera, while orthographic projection is more of a fixed depth feel, making objects look the same size regardless of their distances. We are going to be using the perspective projection for our purposes.

The camera class

With all of this information covered, we are finally ready for the smoke and mirrors that is the GL_Camera class. Let us see what it takes in order to manoeuvre around our world:

```
class GL_Camera {
public:
    GL_Camera(const glm::vec3& l_pos, float l_fieldOfView,
        float l_aspectRatio, float l_frustumNear, float l_frustumFar);

    glm::mat4 GetViewProjectionMatrix();
private:
    void RecalculatePerspective();

    float m_fov;
    float m_aspect;
    float m_frustumNear;
    float m_frustumFar;

    glm::vec3 m_position;
    glm::vec3 m_forwardDir;
    glm::vec3 m_upDir;

    glm::mat4 m_perspectiveMatrix;
};
```

As you can see, we are storing all of the covered details, as well as a couple of new ones. Along with the field of view angle, the aspect ratio, and the near and far frustum values, we also need to keep around the position, a forward direction vector, and the up direction vector. The `m_forwardDir` is a normalized directional vector that represents which way the camera is looking. The `m_upDir` is also a normalized directional vector, but it simply stores the *up* direction. This will all start to make sense soon.

Implementing the camera class

Let us see what the constructor of this class looks like:

```
GL_Camera::GL_Camera(const glm::vec3& l_pos, float l_fieldOfView,
    float l_aspectRatio, float l_frustumNear, float l_frustumFar)
    : m_position(l_pos), m_fov(l_fieldOfView),
    m_aspect(l_aspectRatio), m_frustumNear(l_frustumNear),
    m_frustumFar(l_frustumFar)
{
    RecalculatePerspective();
    m_forwardDir = glm::vec3(0.f, 0.f, 1.f);
    m_upDir = glm::vec3(0.f, 1.f, 0.f);
}
```

Outside of initializing our data members, the constructor has three tasks. It recalculates the perspective matrix, which only needs to be done once unless the window is resized, and it sets up both the forward direction, and the up direction. The camera starts out looking towards the positive Z axis, which is literally *towards* the screen, if you imagine it in those terms. The *up* direction is the positive Y axis.

Calculating the perspective matrix is quite simple, thanks to the `glm` library:

```
void GL_Camera::RecalculatePerspective() {
    m_perspectiveMatrix = glm::perspective(m_fov, m_aspect,
        m_frustumNear, m_frustumFar);
}
```

Our matrix is constructed by the `glm::perspective` function, which takes in the field of view, the aspect ratio, and both frustum distances.

Finally, we can obtain the **view projection matrix**, which is simply a combination of the view and projection matrix:

```
glm::mat4 GL_Camera::GetViewProjectionMatrix() {
  glm::mat4 viewMatrix = glm::lookAt(m_position,
    m_position + m_forwardDir, m_upDir);
  return m_perspectiveMatrix * viewMatrix;
}
```

We begin by calculating the view matrix, using the `glm::lookAt` function. It takes in the position of the camera, the point the camera is looking at, and the *up* direction. Afterwards, the multiplication of our perspective matrix and the view matrix results in obtaining the view projection matrix, which is returned for later use.

Updating the rest of the code

Because our geometry needs to, once again, be transformed relative to yet another origin, we need to update the `GL_Shader` class:

```
void GL_Shader::Update(GL_Transform& l_transform,
  GL_Camera& l_camera)
{
  glm::mat4 modelMatrix = l_transform.GetModelMatrix();
  glm::mat4 viewProjMatrix = l_camera.GetViewProjectionMatrix();

  glm::mat4 modelViewMatrix = viewProjMatrix * modelMatrix;
  glUniformMatrix4fv(static_cast<GLint>(
    m_uniform[static_cast<unsigned int>(UniformType::Transform)]),
    1, GL_FALSE, &modelViewMatrix[0][0]);
}
```

Because the vertex shader is already multiplying its position by a transform, we can simply change which matrix it uses inside the `Update()` method. After the model matrix is obtained, we also grab the view projection matrix and multiply the two together. The resulting **model view matrix** is then passed down to the vertex shader.

Finally, the camera needs to be created inside the `Game` class:

```
class Game{
    ...
private:
    ...
    std::unique_ptr<GL_Camera> m_camera;
};
```

It also needs to be set up with the appropriate information:

```
Game::Game() ... {
    ...
    float aspectRatio =
        static_cast<float>(m_window.GetWindowSize().x) /
        static_cast<float>(m_window.GetWindowSize().y);
    float frustum_near = 1.f;
    float frustum_far = 100.f;

    m_camera = std::make_unique<GL_Camera>(
        glm::vec3(0.f, 0.f, -5.f), 70.f, aspectRatio,
        frustum_near, frustum_far);
}
```

We begin by calculating the window's aspect ratio, which is its width divided by its height. After the `frustum_near` and `frustum_far` values are set up, they get passed in to the camera's constructor, along with its initial position, the field of view angle, and the aspect ratio of the window.

Finally, we just need to update the shader class with the camera's information:

```
void Game::Update() {
    ...
    m_shader->Update(m_transform, *m_camera);
}
```

Upon successful compilation and execution, we should see our triangle slightly further away from the camera, because its position was set to `-5.f` on the Z axis.

Moving the camera around

Having a programmable camera is nice, but it still does not allow us to freely roam the scene. Let 's actually give our camera class the ability to be manipulated in real time, so that we can have the illusion of floating around the world:

```
enum class GL_Direction{ Up, Down, Left, Right, Forward, Back };

class GL_Camera {
public:
  ...
  void MoveBy(GL_Direction l_dir, float l_amount);
  void OffsetLookBy(float l_speed, float l_x, float l_y);
  ...
};
```

As you can see, we are going to use two methods for that: one for moving the camera, and another for rotating it. We are also defining a helpful enumeration of all six possible directions.

Moving a position vector is fairly simple. Assume we have a scalar value that represents the speed of the camera. If we multiply it by a direction vector, we get a proportional position change based on which direction the vector was pointed at, like so:

With that in mind, let us implement the MoveBy() method:

```
void GL_Camera::MoveBy(GL_Direction l_dir, float l_amount) {
  if (l_dir == GL_Direction::Forward) {
    m_position += m_forwardDir * l_amount;
  } else if (l_dir == GL_Direction::Back) {
    m_position -= m_forwardDir * l_amount;
  } else if (l_dir == GL_Direction::Up) {
    m_position += m_upDir * l_amount;
  } else if (l_dir == GL_Direction::Down) {
    m_position -= m_upDir * l_amount;
  } ...
}
```

If we are moving the camera forwards or backwards, the `l_amount` scalar value is multiplied by the forward direction. Moving the camera up and down is equally as simple, since the up direction can be used for that.

Moving left or right is slightly more complex. We cannot just statically change the position, because the camera's idea of *left* or *right* depends on which way we are looking. This is where the **cross product** comes in:

$$\vec{a} \times \vec{b} = \begin{bmatrix} a.y*b.z - a.z*b.y \\ a.z*b.x - a.x*b.z \\ a.x*b.y - a.y*b.x \end{bmatrix}$$

The cross product of two vectors is a slightly harder formula to memorize, but it is very useful. It gives us a vector that is **orthogonal** to the vectors *a* and *b*. Consider the following diagram:

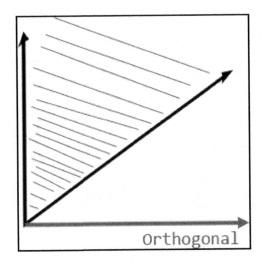

Orthogonal

An orthogonal vector is one way of saying that the direction of that vector is **perpendicular** to the plane the other two vectors form. Knowing that, we can implement left and right strafing with relative ease:

```
    } else if (l_dir == GL_Direction::Left) {
        glm::vec3 cross = glm::cross(m_forwardDir, m_upDir);
        m_position -= cross * l_amount;
    } else if (l_dir == GL_Direction::Right) {
        glm::vec3 cross = glm::cross(m_forwardDir, m_upDir);
        m_position += cross * l_amount;
    } ...
```

After obtaining the cross product of the forward and up vectors, we simply multiply it by the scalar and add the result to the camera's position, creating left and right movement.

Rotating the camera is slightly more involved, but not trivial:

```
    void GL_Camera::OffsetLookBy(float l_speed, float l_x, float l_y)
    {
        glm::vec3 rotVector = glm::cross(m_forwardDir, m_upDir);
        glm::mat4 rot_matrix = glm::rotate(-l_x * l_speed, m_upDir) *
                    glm::rotate(-l_y * l_speed, rotVector);
        m_forwardDir = glm::mat3(rot_matrix) * m_forwardDir;
    }
```

Once again, we use the cross product to obtain the orthogonal vector of the forward direction and up direction vectors plane. A rotation matrix is then calculated, by multiplying two rotation matrices of X and Y axes. For the X axis, we are simply rotating around the up direction vector, as shown here:

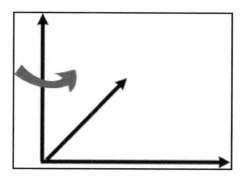

The Y axis rotation is made available by rotating along the orthogonal vector of the view direction and up vector's plane:

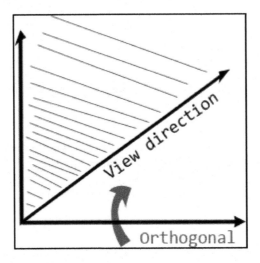

Having this functionality now allows us to program in actual camera movement, like so:

```
void Game::Update() {
...
  m_mouseDifference = sf::Mouse::getPosition(
    *m_window.GetRenderWindow()) - m_mousePosition;
  m_mousePosition = sf::Mouse::getPosition(
    *m_window.GetRenderWindow());

  float moveAmount = 0.005f;
  float rotateSpeed = 0.004f;

  if (sf::Keyboard::isKeyPressed(sf::Keyboard::W)) {
    // Forward.
    m_camera->MoveBy(GL_Direction::Forward, moveAmount);
  } else if (sf::Keyboard::isKeyPressed(sf::Keyboard::S)) {
    // Back.
    m_camera->MoveBy(GL_Direction::Back, moveAmount);
  }
  if (sf::Keyboard::isKeyPressed(sf::Keyboard::A)) {
    // Left.
    m_camera->MoveBy(GL_Direction::Left, moveAmount);
  } else if (sf::Keyboard::isKeyPressed(sf::Keyboard::D)) {
    // Right.
    m_camera->MoveBy(GL_Direction::Right, moveAmount);
  }
  if (sf::Keyboard::isKeyPressed(sf::Keyboard::Q)) {
```

```
    // Up.
    m_camera->MoveBy(GL_Direction::Up, moveAmount);
  } else if (sf::Keyboard::isKeyPressed(sf::Keyboard::Z)) {
    // Down.
    m_camera->MoveBy(GL_Direction::Down, moveAmount);
  }

  if (sf::Mouse::isButtonPressed(sf::Mouse::Left)) {
    m_camera->OffsetLookBy(rotateSpeed,
      static_cast<float>(m_mouseDifference.x),
      static_cast<float>(m_mouseDifference.y));
  }
  ...
}
```

We are using the keyboard keys *W*, *S*, *A*, and *D* to move around the camera, and mouse position changes as scalar values to rotate it, provided the left mouse button is pressed.

Drawing with vertex indices

One last thing that is quite important for us before moving on is covering a more efficient way of rendering shapes. Our current method is fine for rendering a single triangle, but it can get inefficient really quickly when rendering something more complex, like a cube. If we are using vertices only, it would require a grand total of *36* to render *six* cube faces. A much more efficient approach would obviously be submitting *eight* vertices for each corner of the cube and then reusing them to draw each face. Luckily, there is a way to do just that by using an **index array**.

Using indices simply means that for each model we are drawing, we also need to store an array of indices that represent the draw order of vertices. Each vertex in a model is given an index, starting from 0. An array of these indices would then be used to connect the vertices, instead of having to re-submit them. Let's implement this functionality, starting with the GL_Model class:

```
class GL_Model {
  ...
private:
  ...
  GLuint m_indexVBO;
  ...
};
```

As the new data member suggests, we need to store these indices in their own VBO, all of which happens inside the constructor:

```
GL_Model::GL_Model(GL_Vertex* l_vertices,
  unsigned int l_vertCount, unsigned int* l_indices,
  unsigned int l_indexCount)
{
  m_drawCount = l_indexCount;

  glGenVertexArrays(1, &m_VAO);
  glBindVertexArray(m_VAO);
  glGenBuffers(1, &m_vertexVBO);
  glGenBuffers(1, &m_indexVBO);
  ...
  glBindBuffer(GL_ELEMENT_ARRAY_BUFFER, m_indexVBO);
  glBufferData(GL_ELEMENT_ARRAY_BUFFER,
    l_indexCount * (sizeof(l_indices[0])),
    l_indices, GL_STATIC_DRAW);
  ...
}
```

The constructor needs to take two extra arguments: a pointer to an array of indices, and the count of indices in that array. Note that m_drawCount is now being set to l_indexCount. This is because we only need *eight* vertices for a cube model, but there are *36* indices that describe how to draw it.

After a new VBO is generated for the indices, we bind to it and submit the index data pretty much in the same way as before. The main difference here is the GL_ELEMENT_ARRAY_BUFFER flag. We cannot use GL_ARRAY_BUFFER, as the indices actually refer to the vertex data, which is located inside another VBO.

Obviously, this new data needs to be released once the model is no longer needed:

```
GL_Model::~GL_Model() {
  glDeleteBuffers(1, &m_vertexVBO);
  glDeleteBuffers(1, &m_indexVBO);
  glDeleteVertexArrays(1, &m_VAO);
}
```

Drawing our model using indices requires a different `Draw()` call altogether:

```
void GL_Model::Draw() {
  glBindVertexArray(m_VAO);
  glDrawElements(GL_TRIANGLES, m_drawCount, GL_UNSIGNED_INT, 0);
  glBindVertexArray(0);
}
```

The call to the `glDrawElements()` method takes four arguments: the type of primitives we are going to be drawing, the total number of indices, the data type that these indices are represented by, and an offset that can be used to skip them.

That is all there is to drawing geometry using indices! Now let's set up a more exciting model to show it off:

```
Game::Game() ... {
  ...
  GL_Vertex vertices[] = {
    //          |---POSITION----| |TEXTURE|
    //          X    Y    Z       X, Y
    GL_Vertex({ -0.5, -0.5,  0.5 }, { 0, 0 }), // 0
    GL_Vertex({ -0.5,  0.5,  0.5 }, { 0, 1 }), // 1
    GL_Vertex({  0.5,  0.5,  0.5 }, { 1, 1 }), // 2
    GL_Vertex({  0.5, -0.5,  0.5 }, { 1, 0 }), // 3
    GL_Vertex({ -0.5, -0.5, -0.5f }, { 1, 0 }), // 4
    GL_Vertex({ -0.5,  0.5, -0.5f }, { 1, 1 }), // 5
    GL_Vertex({  0.5,  0.5, -0.5f }, { 0, 0 }), // 6
    GL_Vertex({  0.5, -0.5, -0.5f }, { 0, 1 }) // 7
  };

  unsigned int indices[] = {
    2, 1, 0, 0, 3, 2, // Back
    5, 4, 0, 0, 1, 5, // Right
    3, 7, 6, 6, 2, 3, // Left
    6, 7, 4, 4, 5, 6, // Front
    1, 2, 6, 6, 5, 1, // Top
    0, 4, 7, 7, 3, 0 // Bottom
  };

  m_model = std::make_unique<GL_Model>(vertices, 8, indices, 36);
  ...
}
```

As you can see, we've now set up 8 vertices, and we've created another array for indices. Once the model is rendered, we would see something like this:

Note that the bottom face is actually rendered on top for some reason. This is caused by OpenGL not knowing which geometry to render on top, and this will be solved in the next section.

Face culling and depth buffer

One way of solving the draw order issues is by using a **depth buffer**. In the simplest terms, a depth buffer, also commonly known as the **Z-buffer**, is basically a texture managed by OpenGL in the background that contains depth information of each pixel. When a pixel is being rendered, its depth (Z value) is checked against that on the depth buffer. If a pixel being rendered has a lower Z value, the pixel is overwritten, as it is clearly on top.

Enabling the depth buffer only comes down to a single `glEnable()` method call:

```
Game::Game() ... {
  ...
  glEnable(GL_DEPTH_TEST);
  ...
}
```

Keep in mind that the depth buffer is a texture. It is imperative to make sure it gets allocated when the window is created, and it has enough data to work with. We can make sure of that by creating an `sf::ContextSettings` structure and filling out its `depthBits` data member before passing it to the SFML's window `Create()` method:

```
void GL_Window::Create() {
  ...
  sf::ContextSettings settings;
  settings.depthBits = 32; // 32 bits.
  settings.stencilBits = 8;
  settings.antialiasingLevel = 0;
  settings.majorVersion = 4;
  settings.minorVersion = 5;

  m_window.create(sf::VideoMode(m_windowSize.x,
    m_windowSize.y, 32), m_windowTitle, style, settings);
}
```

If we just ran the code as is, the screen would be completely blank. Why? Well, remember that the Z-buffer is a texture. A texture, just like the display, needs to be cleared every cycle. We can accomplish that like so:

```
void GL_Window::BeginDraw() {
  glClearColor(0.f, 0.f, 0.f, 1.f); // BLACK
  glClear(GL_COLOR_BUFFER_BIT | GL_DEPTH_BUFFER_BIT);
}
```

Adding the pipe symbol allows us to perform a bitwise or operation on the `glClear`'s argument, joining in the `GL_DEPTH_BUFFER_BIT` definition. This ensures that the depth buffer is also cleared to black, and we can finally enjoy our cube:

Back face culling

In order to save on performance, it is a good idea to let OpenGL know that we would like to cull faces that are not visible from the current perspective. This feature can be enabled like so:

```
Game::Game() ... {
  ...
  glEnable(GL_DEPTH_TEST);
  glEnable(GL_CULL_FACE);
  glCullFace(GL_BACK);
  ...
}
```

After we `glEnable` face culling, the `glCullFace` function is invoked to let OpenGL know which faces to cull. This will work right out of the box, but we may notice weird artifacts like this if our model data is not set up correctly:

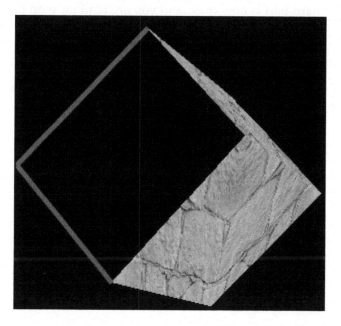

This is because the order our vertices are rendered in actually defines whether a face of a piece of geometry is facing inwards or outwards. For example, if the vertices of a face are rendered in a clockwise sequence, the face, by default, is considered to be facing **inwards** of the model and vice versa. Consider the following diagram:

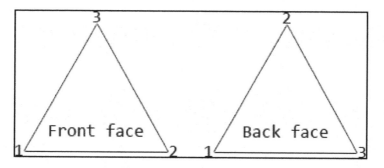

Setting up the model draw order correctly allows us to save on performance by not drawing invisible faces, and having our cube back just the way it was.

Summary

That may have been quite a lot to take in, but if you have made it all the way to the end, congratulations! The hard part is now over, and you are familiar with the modern versions of OpenGL, the programmable pipeline and general-purpose rendering. Even SFML itself was built around basic principles like the ones we have gone over, some of which we have already covered extensively.

In the next chapter, we are going to be covering the basics of lighting to create a more dynamic feel to our world. See you there!

8
Let There Be Light - An Introduction to Advanced Lighting

There is a certain standard expected of a game in this day and age. As technology progresses and the number of transistors in any given computational unit increases, there is more and more power at our disposal to do what was previously unheard of. One thing that definitely makes use of all of this extra horse power is dynamic lighting. Because of its stunning visual results, it has become an integral part of most video games, and is now one of the core technologies that are expected to come with them.

In this chapter, we're going to cover the following topics:

- Using the technique of deferred rendering/shading
- Implementing a multi-pass lighting shader
- Faking geometry complexity using normal maps
- Using specular maps to create shiny surfaces
- Using height maps to make lighting feel more three-dimensional

Let's start shedding some light on this subject!

Using third-party software

None of the material maps used in this chapter are hand-drawn. For the generation of certain material maps, *Crazybump* was used, which can be found at `http://crazybump.com/`.

There are other free alternatives that can be found online.

Deferred rendering

Deferred rendering/shading is a technique that gives us greater control over how certain effects are applied to a scene by not enabling them during the first pass. Instead, the scene can be rendered to an off screen buffer, along with other buffers that hold other material types of the same image, and then drawn on the screen in a later pass, after the effects have been applied, potentially in multiple passes as well. Using this approach allows us to separate and compartmentalize certain logic that would otherwise be entangled with our main rendering code. It also gives us an opportunity to apply as many effects to the final image as we want. Let's see what it takes to implement this technique.

Modifying the renderer

In order to support all the fancy new techniques we're about to utilize, we need to make some changes to our renderer. It should be able to keep a buffer texture and render to it in multiple passes in order to create the lighting we're looking for:

```
class Renderer {
    friend Window;
public:
    ...
    void EnableDeferredRendering();
    void BeginSceneRendering();
    void BeginTextureRendering();
    sf::RenderTexture* GetCurrentTexture();
    sf::RenderTexture* GetFinishedTexture();
    void SwapTextures();
    void ClearCurrentTexture();
    void ClearFinishedTexture();
    void ClearTextures();
    void DrawBufferTexture();
    void DisableDeferredRendering();
    ...
private:
    void CreateTextures();
    ...
    sf::Shader* m_currentShader;
    sf::RenderTexture* m_currentTexture;
    sf::RenderTexture m_texture1;
    sf::RenderTexture m_texture2;
    ...
```

```
    bool m_deferred;
};
```

For convenience, we have a couple of methods for toggling the deferred rendering process. Also, since rendering a scene to a texture is slightly different than rendering a texture to another texture, because of where the camera (view) is positioned, we will use the `BeginSceneRendering()` and `BeginTextureRendering()` methods to properly handle the task.

Note the use of two textures in this class as well as a pointer to point to the texture that is currently in use. The essence of a multi-pass approach is being able to sample the texture holding the information of the previous render pass while drawing to the current render target.

Lastly, we'll discuss three methods for clearing the current texture, the texture of a previous render pass, and both of these. The most recent render pass texture can then be rendered by calling the `DrawBufferTexture()` method.

Implementing changes in the Renderer class

Let's start with something simple. Implement the deferred rendering toggle methods; they will help you keep track of the current rendering state:

```
void Renderer::EnableDeferredRendering() {
  if (!m_useShaders) { return; }
  m_deferred = true;
}
```

```
void Renderer::DisableDeferredRendering() { m_deferred = false; }
```

As you can see, it's as simple as flipping a flag. In the case of enabling deferred rendering, we also need to check whether the use of shaders is allowed.

Also, the textures we're using as buffers clearly need to be created:

```
void Renderer::CreateTextures() {
  if (!m_useShaders) { return; }
  m_texture1.create(m_screenSize.x, m_screenSize.y);
  m_texture2.create(m_screenSize.x, m_screenSize.y);
  ClearTextures();
  m_texture1.display();
  m_texture2.display();
  m_currentTexture = &m_texture1;
}
```

This particular method is invoked inside the constructor of `Renderer`.

Next, we have something equally as simple, yet quite a bit more important:

```
void Renderer::BeginSceneRendering() {
  auto& view = m_window->GetRenderWindow()->getView();
  m_currentTexture->setView(view);
}

void Renderer::BeginTextureRendering() {
  auto& view = m_window->GetRenderWindow()->getDefaultView();
  m_currentTexture->setView(view);
}
```

By using these methods at the appropriate time, we can successfully draw shapes that would have world coordinates for a standalone texture buffer the size of a window. We can also simply draw information from another window-sized texture to the buffer.

Some helpful getter methods are always useful:

```
sf::RenderTexture* Renderer::GetCurrentTexture() {
  if (!m_useShaders) { return nullptr; }
  return m_currentTexture;
}

sf::RenderTexture* Renderer::GetFinishedTexture() {
  if (!m_useShaders) { return nullptr; }
  if (!m_currentTexture) { return nullptr; }
  return (m_currentTexture == &m_texture1 ?
    &m_texture2 : &m_texture1);
}
```

While the first one simply returns a pointer to the current buffer texture being used, the second method does the exact opposite. It determines which texture is *not* the current buffer; once it identifies this, it returns a pointer to that object instead. Why exactly this is useful will become apparent shortly.

Clearing these textures is just as simple as one might think:

```
void Renderer::ClearCurrentTexture() {
  if (!m_useShaders) { return; }
  if (!m_currentTexture) { return; }
  m_currentTexture->clear();
}

void Renderer::ClearFinishedTexture() {
  if (!m_useShaders) { return; }
```

```
    auto texture = GetFinishedTexture();
    if (!texture) { return; }
    texture->clear();
}

void Renderer::ClearTextures() {
    if (!m_useShaders) { return; }
    m_texture1.clear();
    m_texture2.clear();
}
```

In order to prepare for another render pass and display all the changes made to the first buffer, the textures must be swapped like so:

```
void Renderer::SwapTextures() {
    if (!m_useShaders) { return; }
    if (m_currentTexture) { m_currentTexture->display(); }
    if (m_currentTexture != &m_texture1) {
        m_currentTexture = &m_texture1;
    } else {
        m_currentTexture = &m_texture2;
    }
}
```

Note the call to the texture's `display` method. Calling `display` is required because we want all of the changes made to the texture to be reflected. Without calling this method, our progress would not manifest.

Another key alteration to this class is making sure the buffer texture is being used while deferred rendering is enabled:

```
void Renderer::Draw(const sf::Drawable& l_drawable,
    sf::RenderTarget* l_target)
{
    if (!l_target) {
        if (!m_deferred || !m_useShaders) {
            l_target = m_window->GetRenderWindow();
        } else { l_target = m_currentTexture; }
    }
    sf::RenderStates states = sf::RenderStates::Default;
    if (m_addBlend) { states.blendMode = sf::BlendAdd; }
    if (m_useShaders && m_currentShader) {
        states.shader = m_currentShader;
    }
    l_target->draw(l_drawable, states);
    ++m_drawCalls;
}
```

After a couple of checks to make sure we're not overwriting an already provided render target and that the use of shaders is enabled, we select the buffer texture by overwriting the `l_target` pointer with its address.

Finally, the buffer texture that has all of the render pass information can be drawn on the screen like so:

```
void Renderer::DrawBufferTexture() {
   if (!m_useShaders) { return; }
   auto texture = GetFinishedTexture();
   if (!texture) { return; }
   m_sprite.setTexture(texture->getTexture());
   Draw(m_sprite);
}
```

This simple, yet powerful, design provides us with the possibilities of implementing almost any postprocessing effect imaginable.

A minimal example

One of the effects incidentally, the focus of this chapter is dynamic lighting. Before we go further and implement the more advanced features or delve into more complex concepts, let's walk through the process of using the newly implemented renderer features. Let's take one step at a time.

First, the scene should be drawn to the texture buffer as usual:

```
renderer->EnableDeferredRendering();
renderer->UseShader("default");
renderer->BeginSceneRendering();

for (unsigned int i = 0; i < Sheet::Num_Layers; ++i) {
   context->m_gameMap->Draw(i);
   context->m_systemManager->Draw(window, i);
   particles->Draw(window, i);
}
particles->Draw(window, -1);

renderer->SwapTextures();
```

As you can see, once deferred rendering is enabled, the default shader is used and the scene rendering process begins. For each layer, the map, entities, and particles are all drawn as usual. The only difference now is that the buffer texture is being used behind the scenes. Once everything is rendered, the textures are swapped; this allows the current back buffer texture to display all the changes:

```
renderer->BeginTextureRendering();

if(renderer->UseShader("LightPass")) {
  auto shader = renderer->GetCurrentShader();
  auto time = context->m_gameMap->GetTimeNormal();
  shader->setUniform("AmbientLight",
    sf::Glsl::Vec3(time, time, time));
  sf::Vector3f lightPos(700.f, 300.f, 10.f);
  sf::Vector2i screenPos = window->GetRenderWindow()->
    mapCoordsToPixel({ lightPos.x, lightPos.y });
  shader->setUniform("LightPosition",
    sf::Glsl::Vec3(screenPos.x, window->GetWindowSize().y -
    screenPos.y, lightPos.z));
  shader->setUniform("LightColor",
    sf::Glsl::Vec3(0.1f, 0.1f, 0.1f));
  shader->setUniform("LightRadius", 128.f);

  shader->setUniform("texture",
    renderer->GetFinishedTexture()->getTexture());

  auto size = context->m_wind->GetWindowSize();

  sf::VertexArray vertices(sf::TrianglesStrip, 4);
  vertices[0] = sf::Vertex(sf::Vector2f(0, 0),
    sf::Vector2f(0,    1));
  vertices[1] = sf::Vertex(sf::Vector2f(size.x, 0),
    sf::Vector2f(1, 1));
  vertices[2] = sf::Vertex(sf::Vector2f(0, size.y),
    sf::Vector2f(0, 0));
  vertices[3] = sf::Vertex(sf::Vector2f(size),
    sf::Vector2f(1, 0));

  renderer->Draw(vertices);
  renderer->SwapTextures();
}
```

Once the scene is rendered, we enter what from now on is going to be referred to as the light pass. This special pass uses its own shader and is responsible for the illumination of the scene. It sets up what is known as *ambient light* as well as regular omnidirectional light.

Ambient light is a type of light that has no position. It illuminates any part of the scene evenly, regardless of the distance.

As illustrated in the preceding code, the point light first has its world coordinates converted into screen-space coordinates, which are then passed as a uniform to the shader. Then, the light color and radius are passed to the shader along with the texture of the previous pass, which, in this case, is simply the color (diffuse) map of the scene.

Point light is a type of light that emits light in all directions (omnidirectional) from a single point, creating a sphere of illumination.

The screen-space coordinate system has its Y axis inversed from the world coordinate format, meaning the positive Y values go up, not down. This is the reason the light position's Y coordinate has to be adjusted before it is passed to the shader.

The next portion of the code is essentially meant to just trigger a full redraw of the diffuse texture onto the buffer texture. We're making a quad comprised of two triangular strips represented as `sf::VertexArray`. It's made to be the size of the entire window so that all the pixels could surely be redrawn. Once the quad is drawn, the textures are once again swapped to reflect all the changes:

```
renderer->DisableDeferredRendering();
window->GetRenderWindow()->setView(
  window->GetRenderWindow()->getDefaultView());
renderer->DrawBufferTexture();
window->GetRenderWindow()->setView(currentView);
renderer->DisableShader();
```

The last bit of this example simply turns off deferred rendering so that all render operations from now on are done to the window. The window view is then set to its default state, so that the buffer texture can be drawn onscreen easily. Finally, we reset the view back, shortly before whatever shader is still active is disabled.

Shader code

We're almost done! The last, but definitely not the least, important piece of this puzzle is writing the lighting pass shader correctly in order to get proper results. Given what we already know about the light pass procedure in our C++ code, let's see what GLSL has to offer:

```
uniform sampler2D texture;
uniform vec3 AmbientLight;
uniform vec3 LightPosition;
uniform vec3 LightColor;
uniform float LightRadius;

void main()
{
  vec4 pixel = texture2D(texture, gl_TexCoord[0].xy);

  float dist = sqrt(
    pow(LightPosition.x - gl_FragCoord.x, 2) +
    pow(LightPosition.y - gl_FragCoord.y, 2) +
    pow(LightPosition.z - gl_FragCoord.z, 2));
  vec4 finalPixel;
  if(dist <= LightRadius)
    finalPixel = (gl_Color * pixel) +
    (pixel * vec4(LightColor, 1.0));
  else
    finalPixel = (gl_Color * pixel) * vec4(AmbientLight, 1.0);
  gl_FragColor = finalPixel;
}
```

As expected, we need to process the diffuse texture in this pass in order to preserve color information. The other uniform values consist of a 3D vector that represents the ambient color, two 3D vectors for the position and color of a regular source of light, and a floating point value for the radius of the same light.

The texture that was passed to the shader is sampled at the appropriate, interpolated texture coordinates and stored in the `pixel` variable. The distance between the pixel being processed and the light's center is then calculated using the Pythagorean variant distance formula:

$$d = \sqrt{(X_2 - X_1)^2 + (Y_2 - Y_1)^2 \ldots}$$

The `gl_FragCoord` parameter holds the pixel coordinates in the screen space. Its Z component is a depth value, which we're not going to use for the time being.

 The `pow` function simply returns a value that is raised to the power of its second argument.

After the distance is calculated, a check is made to determine whether the distance between the light and the pixel we're working with is within the light's radius. If it is, the color information of our pixel is multiplied by the light color and added to the final pixel that's going to be written. Otherwise, the color information is simply multiplied by the ambient color.

This fairly basic principle gives us, as one should expect, fairly basic and non-realistic lighting:

Although it works, in reality, light is emitted in all directions. It also slowly loses its brightness. Let's see what it takes to make this happen in our game.

Attenuating light

Light attenuation, also known as gradual loss in intensity, is what we're going to use when creating the effect of a light source that is slowly bleeding away. It essentially comes down to using yet another formula inside the light pass shader. There are many variations of attenuating light that work for different purposes. Let's take a look:

```
uniform sampler2D texture;
uniform vec3 AmbientLight;
uniform vec3 LightPosition;
uniform vec3 LightColor;
uniform float LightRadius;
uniform float LightFalloff;

void main()
{
  vec4 pixel = texture2D(texture, gl_TexCoord[0].xy);
  // Nornalized light vector and distance to the light surface.
  vec3 L = LightPosition - gl_FragCoord.xyz;
  float distance = length(L);
  float d = max(distance - LightRadius, 0);
  L /= distance;
  // calculate basic attenuation
  float attenuation = 1 / pow(d/LightRadius + 1, 2);
  attenuation = (attenuation - LightFalloff) / (1 - LightFalloff);
  attenuation = max(attenuation, 0);
  vec4 finalPixel = (gl_Color * pixel);
  finalPixel *= vec4(AmbientLight, 1.0); // IF FIRST PASS ONLY!
  finalPixel += (pixel * vec4(LightColor, 1.0) * attenuation);
  gl_FragColor = finalPixel;
}
```

Once again, we're dealing with the same uniform values being passed in, but with one additional value of `LightFalloff`. It's a factor between *0* and *1* that determines how fast a source of light would lose its brightness.

Inside the `main()` function, the diffused pixel is sampled as usual. This is done before we calculate a vector `L` that represents the position difference between the pixel and the light's center. This vector is then converted into distance using the `length` function. This is the same type of distance that we calculated manually in the first iteration of this shader. The floating number variable `d` is then used to calculate the distance between the fragment and the outside of the light by subtracting the light's radius from it. The `max()` function simply makes sure we don't get a negative value back if the pixel is inside the light's bubble.

The attenuation itself, as mentioned before, can have many variations. This particular variation visually works best for the type of game we're dealing with.

After the calculations are performed, the final output pixel is multiplied by the ambient light (which should only be done during the first pass if there are multiple light passes). Additionally, the light information is multiplied by the diffuse pixel and the attenuation factor is added to it. This last bit of multiplication ensures that, given the pixel is outside the effective light range, no additional light is added to it. The result of this is slightly more appealing to look at:

At this point, a very good question you could ask is 'How on earth is this going to work with multiple light input?' Luckily, this is a bit simpler than one might think.

Multi-pass shading

Much like C/C++ code, GLSL does support the use of data arrays. Using them can seem like an obvious choice to just push information about multiple light streams into the shader and have it all done in one pass. Unlike C++, however, GLSL needs to know the sizes of these arrays at compile time, which is very much like C. At the time of writing, dynamic size arrays aren't supported. While this information can put a damper on a naive plan of handling multiple light sources with ease, there are still options to choose from, obviously.

One approach to combat this may be to have a very large, statically sized array of data. Only some of that data would be filled in and the shader would process it by looping over the array while using a uniform integer that tells it how many lights were actually passed to it. This idea comes with a few obvious bottlenecks. First, there would be a threshold for the maximum number of light streams allowed on the screen. The second issue is performance. Sending data over to the GPU is costly and can quickly become inefficient if we send over too much information all at once.

As flawed as the first idea is, it has one component that comes in handy when considering a better strategy: the maximum number of light streams allowed. Instead of pushing tons and tons of data through to the GPU at once, why not just do it a little bit at a time in different passes. If the right number of light streams is sent each time, both the CPU and GPU performance bottlenecks can be minimized. The results of each pass can then be blended together into a single texture.

Modifying the light pass shader

There are a couple of challenges we need to overcome in order to correctly blend the buffer textures of multiple passes. First, there's loss of information due to ambient lighting. If the light is too dark, every subsequent pass becomes less and less visible. To fix this problem, in addition to the color information of the last render pass, we're going to need access to the actual diffuse map.

The second issue is choosing the right number of light streams per shader pass. This can be benchmarked or simply gotten right through trial and error. For our purposes, we'll go with 3-4 light streams per pass. Let's take a look at how the light shader can be modified to achieve this:

```
uniform sampler2D LastPass;
uniform sampler2D DiffuseMap;
uniform vec3 AmbientLight;
uniform int LightCount;
uniform int PassNumber;

struct LightInfo {
  vec3 position;
  vec3 color;
  float radius;
  float falloff;
};

const int MaxLights = 3;
uniform LightInfo Lights[MaxLights];
```

First, note the new `sampler2D` uniform type being passed in for the diffuse map. This is going to be invaluable in order to avoid light colors from being washed out with additional passes. The other two bits of additional information we're going to need are values that determine the number of light streams that have been sent to the shader for the current pass and the pass we're dealing with at the moment.

The actual light information is now neatly stored away in a `struct` that holds the usual data we expect. Underneath it, we need to declare a constant integer for the number of maximum light streams per shader pass and the uniform array that's going to be filled in by our C++ code for the light information.

Let's see the changes that the body of the shader needs to undergo in order to support this:

```
void main()
{
  vec4 pixel = texture2D(LastPass, gl_TexCoord[0].xy);
  vec4 diffusepixel = texture2D(DiffuseMap, gl_TexCoord[0].xy);
  vec4 finalPixel = gl_Color * pixel;
  if(PassNumber == 1) { finalPixel *= vec4(AmbientLight, 1.0); }
  // IF FIRST PASS ONLY!
  for(int i = 0; i < LightCount; ++i) {
     vec3 L = Lights[i].position - gl_FragCoord.xyz;
     float distance = length(L);
     float d = max(distance - Lights[i].radius, 0);
     L /= distance;
```

```
        float attenuation = 1 / pow(d/Lights[i].radius + 1, 2);
        attenuation = (attenuation - Lights[i].falloff) /
          (1 - Lights[i].falloff);
        attenuation = max(attenuation, 0);
        finalPixel += diffusepixel *
          ((vec4(Lights[i].color, 1.0) * attenuation));
    }
    gl_FragColor = finalPixel;
}
```

First, we need to sample the diffuse pixel as well as the pixel from the previous shader pass. The `finalPixel` variable is established early on and uses the information from the previous shader pass. It is important you note this, because the previous pass would be lost otherwise. Since we have access to the pass number in the shader now, we can selectively apply the ambient light to the pixel only during the first pass.

We can then jump into a `for` loop that uses the `LightCount` uniform passed in from the C++ side. This design gives us control to only use as much data as was sent to the shader and not go overboard if the last shader pass has fewer light streams than the maximum number allowed.

Finally, let's see what needs to change when it comes to the actual shading of the fragment. All our calculations remain the same, except for using light data. The lights uniform is now accessed with the square brackets to fetch the correct information during each iteration of the loop. Note the final pixel calculation at the very bottom of the loop. It now uses the diffuse pixel instead of the pixel of a previous shader pass.

Changes in the C++ code

None of the fanciness in the GLSL we've just finished is complete without appropriate support from our actual code base. First, let's start with something simple and conveniently represent a light stream in a proper `struct`:

```
struct LightBase {
  LightBase(const sf::Vector3f& l_pos,
    const sf::Vector3f& l_color, float l_rad, float l_fall)
    : m_lightPos(l_pos), m_lightColor(l_color), m_radius(l_rad),
    m_falloff(l_fall) {}
  LightBase(const sf::Vector3f& l_color): m_lightColor(l_color) {}
  sf::Vector3f m_lightPos;
  sf::Vector3f m_lightColor;
  float m_radius;
  float m_falloff;
};
```

That's better! Now let's begin passing in all of the additional information to the shader itself:

```
... // Diffuse pass.
renderer->SwapTextures();
auto DiffuseImage = renderer->GetFinishedTexture()->
  getTexture().copyToImage();
DiffuseImage.flipVertically();
auto DiffuseTexture = sf::Texture();
DiffuseTexture.loadFromImage(DiffuseImage);
renderer->BeginTextureRendering();
...
std::vector<LightBase> lights;
// {Position}, {Color}, Radius, Falloff
lights.push_back({ { 700.f, 350.f, 10.f }, { 1.f, 0.f, 0.f },
  128.f, 0.005f });
lights.push_back({ { 600.f, 350.f, 10.f }, { 0.f, 1.f, 0.f },
  128.f, 0.005f });
lights.push_back({ { 500.f, 350.f, 10.f }, { 0.f, 0.f, 1.f },
  128.f, 0.005f });
lights.push_back({ { 400.f, 600.f, 10.f },{ 1.f, 0.f, 0.f },
  128.f, 0.005f });
lights.push_back({ { 300.f, 600.f, 10.f },{ 0.f, 1.f, 0.f },
  128.f, 0.005f });
lights.push_back({ { 200.f, 600.f, 10.f },{ 0.f, 0.f, 1.f },
  128.f, 0.005f });
lights.push_back({ { 600.f, 550.f, 0.f }, { 1.f, 1.f, 1.f },
  128.f, 0.005f });

const int LightsPerPass = 3;
```

Right after we're done with drawing onto the diffuse texture, it's copied over and stored in a separate buffer. It's then flipped along the *Y* axis, as the copying process inverts it.

The copying and flipping of the texture here is a proof of concept. It shouldn't be performed in production code, as it's highly inefficient.

At this point, we're ready to begin the light pass. Just before we start this, ensure that a couple of light streams are added to `std::vector` and are waiting to be passed in. Also, declare a constant at the very bottom that denotes how many light streams are supposed to be passed to a shader every time. This number has to match the constant inside the shader.

Let's begin with the actual light pass and see what it involves:

```
if (renderer->UseShader("LightPass")) {
  renderer->BeginTextureRendering();
  auto shader = renderer->GetCurrentShader();
  shader->setUniform("AmbientLight",
    sf::Glsl::Vec3(0.f, 0.f, 0.2f));
  int i = 0;
  int pass = 0;
  auto lightCount = lights.size();
  for (auto& light : lights) {
    std::string id = "Lights[" + std::to_string(i) + "]";
    sf::Vector2i screenPos = window->GetRenderWindow()->
      mapCoordsToPixel({light.m_lightPos.x, light.m_lightPos.y});
    shader->setUniform(id + ".position", sf::Glsl::Vec3(
      screenPos.x, window->GetWindowSize().y - screenPos.y,
      light.m_lightPos.z));
    shader->setUniform(id + ".color",
      sf::Glsl::Vec3(light.m_lightColor));
    shader->setUniform(id + ".radius", light.m_radius);
    shader->setUniform(id + ".falloff", light.m_falloff);
    ++i;
    if (i < LightsPerPass && (pass * LightsPerPass) + i
      < lightCount)
    { continue; }
    shader->setUniform("LightCount", i);
    i = 0;
    shader->setUniform("PassNumber", pass + 1);
    shader->setUniform("LastPass",
      renderer->GetFinishedTexture()->getTexture());
    shader->setUniform("DiffuseMap", DiffuseTexture);
    renderer->Draw(vertices);
    renderer->SwapTextures();
    renderer->BeginTextureRendering();
    ++pass;
  }
}
...
```

Ambient lighting is first set up, as it's not going to change between the iterations. In this case, we're giving it a slight blue tint. Additionally, a couple of local variables for the iteration and pass are created in order to have this information handy.

As we're iterating over each light stream, a string called `id` is created with the integer of each iteration passed inside. This is meant to represent the array access analysis of the light streams' uniform inside the shader, and it will serve as a helpful way of allowing us to access and overwrite that data. The light information is then passed in using the `id` string with an attached dot operator and the name of the `struct` data member. The light's identifier `i` is incremented shortly after. At this point, we need to decide whether the required number of light streams have been processed in order to invoke the shader. If the last light stream for the pass has been added, or if we're dealing with the last light stream of the scene, the rest of the uniforms are initialized and the fullscreen `sf::VertexArray` quad we talked about earlier is drawn, invoking a shader for each visible pixel. This effectively gives us a result like this:

Now we're getting somewhere! The only downside to this is all of the mess we have to deal with in our C++ code, as none of this data is managed properly. Let's fix this now!

Managing light input

Good data organization is important in every aspect of software design. It's hard to imagine an application that would run quickly and efficiently, yet wants have a strong, powerful, and flexible framework running in the backend. Our situation up until this point has been fairly manageable, but imagine you want to draw additional textures for the map, entities, and all your particles. This would quickly become tiresome to deal with and maintain. It's time to utilize our engineering ingenuity and come up with a better system.

Interface for light users

First and foremost, each class that desires to use our lighting engine would need to implement their own version of drawing certain types of textures to the buffer(s). For diffuse maps, we already have the plain old regular `Draw` calls, but even if they are all lucky enough to have the same signature, that's not good enough. A common interface for these classes is needed in order to make them a successful part of the lighting family:

```
class LightManager;
class Window;

class LightUser {
  friend class LightManager;
  virtual void Draw(MaterialMapContainer& l_materials,
    Window& l_window, int l_layer) = 0;
};
```

The `LightUser` class forces any derivatives to implement a special `Draw` method that uses a material container. It also has access to the `Window` class and knows which layer it's trying to draw to. 'What's a material container?' you may ask? Let's find out by taking this design further.

The light manager class

Before we design a grand class that would take care of all our lighting needs, let's talk about materials. As it so happens, we've already dealt with one type of material: the diffuse map. There are many other possible materials we're going to work with, so let's not beat around the bush any longer and see what they are:

```
enum class MaterialMapType { Diffuse, Height, Normal,
  Specular, COUNT };
using MaterialMapContainer = std::unordered_map<
  MaterialMapType, std::unique_ptr<sf::RenderTexture>>;
```

In addition to diffuse maps, we're going to build *height*, *normal*, and *specular* maps as well. None of these terms will probably make sense right now, but that's alright. Each one will be explained in detail as we cross that bridge.

The material map container type is simply a map that links a type to a `sf::RenderTexture`. This way, we can have a separate texture for each material type.

For the light manager, we're only going to need two type definitions:

```
using LightContainer = std::vector<LightBase>;
using LightUserContainer = std::vector<LightUser*>;
```

As you can see, they're extremely simple. We're going to store the light streams themselves along with pointers to the light user classes in vectors, as nothing fancier is necessary here. With that, let's take a look at the actual definition of the `LightManager` class:

```
class Window;

class LightManager {
public:
  LightManager(Window* l_window);

  void AddLight(const LightBase& l_light);
  void AddLightUser(LightUser* l_user);
  LightBase* GetAmbientLight();

  void RenderMaterials();
  void RenderScene();

  const unsigned int LightsPerPass = 4;
protected:
  MaterialMapContainer m_materialMaps;
private:
  void ClearAll();
  void SetViews();
  void DisplayAll();
  LightBase m_ambientLight;
  LightContainer m_lights;
  LightUserContainer m_users;

  sf::VertexArray m_fullScreenQuad;

  Window* m_window;
};
```

As you can see, this is as basic as it can be. The constructor takes in a pointer to the `Window` class. We have a couple of `add`methods for the light users, as well as the light streams themselves. We also have a few render methods for specific tasks. Note the constant integer that this class defines for the maximum number of light streams allowed per shader pass. Rendering only three light streams like we did before is a bit wasteful, so this can be upped even more, provided it doesn't become detrimental to the performance of the process.

The helper methods of which there are three–deal with clearing the buffer textures, setting their views, and displaying the changes made to them. We also store the `sf::VertexArray` of the quad that we're going to use to perform a light pass operation.

Implementing the light manager

As always, let's begin by seeing what needs to be constructed when the light manager is created:

```
LightManager::LightManager(Window* l_window) : m_window(l_window),
  m_ambientLight({ 0.f, 0.f, 0.f })
{
  auto windowSize = l_window->GetWindowSize();
  for (auto i = 0;
    i < static_cast<int>(MaterialMapType::COUNT); ++i)
  {
    auto pair = m_materialMaps.emplace(
      static_cast<MaterialMapType>(i),
      std::move(std::make_unique<sf::RenderTexture>()));
    auto& texture = pair.first->second;
    texture->create(windowSize.x, windowSize.y);
  }

  m_fullScreenQuad = sf::VertexArray(sf::TriangleStrip, 4);

  m_fullScreenQuad[0] = sf::Vertex(
    sf::Vector2f(0, 0), sf::Vector2f(0, 1));
  m_fullScreenQuad[1] = sf::Vertex(
    sf::Vector2f(windowSize.x, 0), sf::Vector2f(1, 1));
  m_fullScreenQuad[2] = sf::Vertex(
    sf::Vector2f(0, windowSize.y), sf::Vector2f(0, 0));
  m_fullScreenQuad[3] = sf::Vertex(
    sf::Vector2f(windowSize), sf::Vector2f(1, 0));
}
```

The initializer list is useful for storing the `Window` pointer, as well as initializing the ambient lighting to absolute black. Once this is done, the window size is obtained and all the material textures are created. Lastly, the window-sized quad is set up for later use.

The adder and getter methods are quite simple, yet they are necessary:

```
void LightManager::AddLight(const LightBase& l_light) {
  m_lights.push_back(l_light);
}
void LightManager::AddLightUser(LightUser* l_user) {
  m_users.emplace_back(l_user);
}
LightBase* LightManager::GetAmbientLight() {
  return &m_ambientLight;
}
```

Dealing with material maps all at once can be quite wasteful typing-wise, so we need a few methods to help us do this quickly:

```
void LightManager::ClearAll() {
  for (auto& map : m_materialMaps) { map.second->clear(); }
}

void LightManager::SetViews() {
  auto view = m_window->GetRenderWindow()->getView();
  for (auto& map : m_materialMaps) { map.second->setView(view); }
}

void LightManager::DisplayAll() {
  for (auto& map : m_materialMaps) { map.second->display(); }
}
```

Note the view we're using in `SetViews()`. Since these material maps are going to be used instead of the window, they must use the window's view in order to handle the world coordinates of all the visuals being drawn.

Speaking of material maps, every class that wishes to use our light manager should be able to draw to every single one of them. Luckily, we've made it easier on ourselves by making it a requirement that these classes implement a purely virtual `Draw` method:

```
void LightManager::RenderMaterials() {
  ClearAll();
  SetViews();
  // Render each elevation in proper order.
  for (auto i = 0; i < Sheet::Num_Layers; ++i) {
    for (auto& user : m_users) {
      user->Draw(m_materialMaps, *m_window, i);
    }
  }
  // Render everything above allowed height.
  for (auto& user : m_users) {
    user->Draw(m_materialMaps, *m_window, -1);
  }
  DisplayAll();
}
```

After all the textures are cleared and their views are set, each light user needs to draw something for each of the allowed layers our game engine supports. Quite literally, on top of this, any visuals that are above these elevations also need to have a chance to be rendered, which we can achieve by using the second loop. All the material textures are then updated by invoking the `DisplayAll()` method.

Once the materials are drawn, we need to go through the same process of multi-pass shading as we did in our minimal code example:

```
void LightManager::RenderScene() {
  auto renderer = m_window->GetRenderer();
  auto window = m_window->GetRenderWindow();
  auto size = window->getSize();
  auto currentView = window->getView();

  renderer->EnableDeferredRendering();

  if (renderer->UseShader("LightPass")) {
    // Light pass.
    auto shader = renderer->GetCurrentShader();
    shader->setUniform("AmbientLight",
      sf::Glsl::Vec3(m_ambientLight.m_lightColor));
    shader->setUniform("DiffuseMap",
      m_materialMaps[MaterialMapType::Diffuse]->getTexture());
    ...
    int LightID = 0;
    int pass = 0;
```

```
    for (auto& light : m_lights) {
        std::string id = "Lights[" + std::to_string(LightID) + "]";
        sf::Vector2i screenPos = window->mapCoordsToPixel(
            { light.m_lightPos.x, light.m_lightPos.y }, currentView);
        float y = static_cast<float>(
            static_cast<int>(size.y) - screenPos.y);
        shader->setUniform(id + ".position",
            sf::Glsl::Vec3(screenPos.x, y, light.m_lightPos.z));
        shader->setUniform(id + ".color",
            sf::Glsl::Vec3(light.m_lightColor));
        shader->setUniform(id + ".radius", light.m_radius);
        shader->setUniform(id + ".falloff", light.m_falloff);
        ++LightID;
        if (LightID < LightsPerPass && (pass * LightsPerPass)
            + LightID < m_lights.size())
        { continue; }
        renderer->BeginTextureRendering();
        shader->setUniform("LightCount", LightID);
        LightID = 0;
        shader->setUniform("PassNumber", pass + 1);
        if (pass == 0) {
            shader->setUniform("LastPass",
                m_materialMaps[MaterialMapType::Diffuse]->getTexture());
        } else {
            shader->setUniform("LastPass",
                renderer->GetFinishedTexture()->getTexture());
        }
        renderer->Draw(m_fullScreenQuad);
        renderer->SwapTextures();
        ++pass;
    }
}
renderer->DisableDeferredRendering();
renderer->DisableShader();
window->setView(window->getDefaultView());
renderer->DrawBufferTexture();
window->setView(currentView);
}
```

This is very close to the already established model we discussed before. A couple of changes to note here are: the use of an internal data member called m_materialMaps for passing material information to the light pass shader and the check near the bottom where the diffuse texture is passed in as the "LastPass" uniform if it is the very first shader pass. This has to be done otherwise we'd be sampling a completely black texture.

Integrating the light manager class

Once the light manager is implemented, we can add all the classes that use it to its list:

```
State_Game::State_Game(StateManager* l_stateManager)
  : BaseState(l_stateManager),
    m_lightManager(l_stateManager->GetContext()->m_wind)
{
  auto context = m_stateMgr->GetContext();
  m_lightManager.AddLightUser(context->m_gameMap);
  m_lightManager.AddLightUser(context->m_systemManager);
  m_lightManager.AddLightUser(context->m_particles);
}
```

In this case, we're only working with the game map, the system manager, and the particle manager classes as light users.

Setting up our previous light information is equally as easy now as it was before:

```
void State_Game::OnCreate() {
  ...
  m_lightManager.GetAmbientLight()->m_lightColor =
    sf::Vector3f(0.2f, 0.2f, 0.2f);
  m_lightManager.AddLight({ { 700.f, 350.f, 32.f },
    { 1.f, 0.f, 0.f }, 128.f, 0.005f });
  m_lightManager.AddLight({ { 600.f, 350.f, 32.f },
    { 0.f, 1.f, 0.f }, 128.f, 0.005f });
  m_lightManager.AddLight({ { 500.f, 350.f, 32.f },
    { 0.f, 0.f, 1.f }, 128.f, 0.005f });
  m_lightManager.AddLight({ { 400.f, 600.f, 32.f },
    { 1.f, 0.f, 0.f }, 128.f, 0.005f });
  m_lightManager.AddLight({ { 300.f, 600.f, 32.f },
    { 0.f, 1.f, 0.f }, 128.f, 0.005f });
  m_lightManager.AddLight({ { 200.f, 600.f, 32.f },
    { 0.f, 0.f, 1.f }, 128.f, 0.005f });
  m_lightManager.AddLight({ { 600.f, 550.f, 33.f },
    { 1.f, 1.f, 1.f }, 128.f, 0.01f });
}
```

Finally, we just need to make sure the material maps are drawn, just like the scene itself:

```
void State_Game::Draw() {
  m_lightManager.RenderMaterials();
  m_lightManager.RenderScene();
}
```

Now, the only thing left to do is to adapt those pesky classes to the new lighting model we have set up here.

Adapting classes to use lights

Obviously, each and every single class that does any rendering in our game does it differently. Rendering the same graphics to different types of material maps is no exception to this rule. Let's see how every light-supporting class should implement their respective `Draw` methods in order to stay in sync with our lighting system.

The Map class

The first class we need to deal with is the `Map` class. It will be a bit different due to the way it handles the drawing of tiles. So let's take a look at what needs to be added in:

```
class Map : ..., public LightUser {
public:
  ...
  void Draw(MaterialMapContainer& l_materials,
    Window& l_window, int l_layer);
protected:
  ...
  Void CheckTextureSizes(int l_fromZ, int l_toZ);
  std::array<sf::RenderTexture, Sheet::Num_Layers> m_textures;
  ...
};
```

So far, so good! The `Map` class is now using the `LightUser` interface. The `m_textures` data member is an established array that existed before all of this and it simply stores different textures for each supported elevation. One new protected member function is added though, called `CheckTextureSizes`:

```
void Map::CheckTextureSizes(int l_fromZ, int l_toZ) {
  auto realMapSize = m_tileMap.GetMapSize() *
    static_cast<unsigned int>(Sheet::Tile_Size);
  for (auto layer = l_fromZ; layer <= l_toZ; ++layer) {
    if (m_textures[layer].getSize() != realMapSize) {
      ... // Information printed to the console.
      if (!m_textures[layer].create(realMapSize.x, realMapSize.y))
      { ... } // Error message.
    }
    ... // Other textures.
  }
}
```

This is just a handy way of making sure all the future textures, as well as the current diffuse maps, have the appropriate size.

Let's see what the `Redraw` method now needs to do in order to fully support the light manager:

```
void Map::Redraw(sf::Vector3i l_from, sf::Vector3i l_to) {
    ...
    CheckTextureSizes(l_from.z, l_to.z);
    ClearMapTexture(l_from, originalTo);
    auto renderer = m_window->GetRenderer();

    if (renderer->UseShader("default")) {
      // Diffuse pass.
      for (auto x = l_from.x; x <= l_to.x; ++x) {
        for (auto y = l_from.y; y <= l_to.y; ++y) {
          for (auto layer = l_from.z; layer <= l_to.z; ++layer) {
            auto tile = m_tileMap.GetTile(x, y, layer);
            if (!tile) { continue; }
            auto& sprite = tile->m_properties->m_sprite;
            sprite.setPosition(
              static_cast<float>(x * Sheet::Tile_Size),
              static_cast<float>(y * Sheet::Tile_Size));
            renderer->Draw(sprite, &m_textures[layer]);
          }
        }
      }
    }
    ... // Other passes.
    renderer->DisableShader();
    DisplayAllTextures(l_from.z, l_to.z);
}
```

Only a few extra lines add the support here. We just need to make sure the renderer is involved when the drawing is happening because it allows the right shader to be used in the process.

Since we're going to add more material maps quite soon, clearing of these textures also needs to be integrated into the existing code:

```
void Map::ClearMapTexture(sf::Vector3i l_from, sf::Vector3i l_to){
    ...
    if (l_to.x == -1 && l_to.y == -1) {
      // Clearing the entire texture.
      for (auto layer = l_from.z; layer <= toLayer; ++layer) {
        m_textures[layer].clear({ 0,0,0,0 });
        ... // Other textures.
```

```
      }
      return;
    }
    // Portion of the map needs clearing.
    ...
    for (auto layer = l_from.z; layer <= toLayer; ++layer) {
      m_textures[layer].draw(shape, sf::BlendMultiply);
      ... // Other textures.
    }
    DisplayAllTextures(l_from.z, toLayer);
  }
```

The spaces for doing so are marked with comments, which is exactly the same for the helper methods that aid in displaying all the changes made to these buffer textures:

```
void Map::DisplayAllTextures(int l_fromZ, int l_toZ) {
  for (auto layer = l_fromZ; layer <= l_toZ; ++layer) {
    m_textures[layer].display();
    ... // Other textures.
  }
}
```

The actual `Draw` method from the `LightUser` class can be implemented like this:

```
void Map::Draw(MaterialMapContainer& l_materials,
  Window& l_window, int l_layer)
{
  if (l_layer < 0) { return; }
  if (l_layer >= Sheet::Num_Layers) { return; }
  auto rect = sf::IntRect(sf::Vector2i(0, 0),
    sf::Vector2i(m_textures[l_layer].getSize()));
  m_layerSprite.setTextureRect(rect);
  // Diffuse.
  m_layerSprite.setTexture(m_textures[l_layer].getTexture());
  m_window->GetRenderer()->Draw(m_layerSprite,
    l_materials[MaterialMapType::Diffuse].get());
  ... // Other textures.
}
```

Because of the way the `Map` class works, all we have to do is set up the sprite we're working with to use the right texture for the appropriate material type. In this case, all we need is the diffuse texture.

The entity renderer system

If you recall, the `SystemManager` class is the one we added to `LightManager` as `LightUser`. Although there's only one system that does the rendering for now, we still want to keep it this way and simply forward all the arguments passed to `SystemManager`. This keeps our options for additional systems doing the same thing open in the future:

```
void SystemManager::Draw(MaterialMapContainer& l_materials,
   Window& l_window, int l_layer)
{
   ...
   auto system = dynamic_cast<S_Renderer*>(itr->second.get());
   system->Draw(l_materials, l_window, l_layer);
}
```

The forwarded arguments are sent to `S_Renderer` and can be used like so:

```
void S_Renderer::Draw(MaterialMapContainer& l_materials,
   Window& l_window, int l_layer)
{
   ...
   if (renderer->UseShader("default")) {
     // Diffuse pass.
     for (auto &entity : m_entities) {
       auto position = entities->GetComponent<C_Position>(
         entity, Component::Position);
       if (position->GetElevation() < l_layer) { continue; }
       if (position->GetElevation() > l_layer) { break; }
       C_Drawable* drawable = GetDrawableFromType(entity);
       if (!drawable) { continue; }
       drawable->Draw(&l_window,
         l_materials[MaterialMapType::Diffuse].get());
     }
   }
   ... // Other passes.
   renderer->DisableShader();
}
```

It's fairly similar to how the `Map` class handles its redrawing process. All we need to do is make sure the Renderer class is used to do the drawing to the diffuse texture, which is what happens under the hood, as `C_Drawable` simply passes these arguments down the line:

```
class C_Drawable : public C_Base{
   ...
   virtual void Draw(Window* l_wind,
     sf::RenderTarget* l_target = nullptr) = 0;
};
```

```
class C_SpriteSheet : public C_Drawable{
  ...
  void Draw(Window* l_wind, sf::RenderTarget* l_target = nullptr){
    if (!m_spriteSheet) { return; }
    m_spriteSheet->Draw(l_wind, l_target);
  }
  ...
};

void SpriteSheet::Draw(Window* l_wnd, sf::RenderTarget* l_target) {
  l_wnd->GetRenderer()->Draw(m_sprite, l_target);
}
```

The particle system

Drawing particles in this way is not much different from how other `LightUser` do it:

```
void ParticleSystem::Draw(MaterialMapContainer& l_materials,
  Window& l_window, int l_layer)
{
  ...
  if (renderer->UseShader("default")) {
  // Diffuse pass.
    for (size_t i = 0; i < container->m_countAlive; ++i) {
      if (l_layer >= 0) {
        if (positions[i].z < l_layer * Sheet::Tile_Size)
        { continue; }
        if (positions[i].z >= (l_layer + 1) * Sheet::Tile_Size)
        { continue; }
      } else if(positions[i].z<Sheet::Num_Layers*Sheet::Tile_Size)
      { continue; }
      renderer->AdditiveBlend(blendModes[i]);
      renderer->Draw(drawables[i],
        l_materials[MaterialMapType::Diffuse].get());
    }
  }
  renderer->AdditiveBlend(false);
  ... // Other passes.
  renderer->DisableShader();
  }
}
```

Once again, it's all about making sure the materials are passed through `Renderer`.

Preparing for additional materials

Drawing basic light streams is fairly nifty. But let's face it, we want to do more than that! Any additional processing is going to require further material information about the surfaces we're working with. As far as storing those materials goes, the `Map` class needs to allocate additional space for textures that will be used for this purpose:

```
class Map : ..., public LightUser {
public:
  ...
  void Draw(MaterialMapContainer& l_materials,
    Window& l_window, int l_layer);
protected:
  ...
  std::array<sf::RenderTexture, Sheet::Num_Layers> m_textures;
  std::array<sf::RenderTexture, Sheet::Num_Layers> m_normals;
  std::array<sf::RenderTexture, Sheet::Num_Layers> m_speculars;
  std::array<sf::RenderTexture, Sheet::Num_Layers> m_heightMap;
  ...
};
```

These textures will also need to be checked for incorrect sizes and adjusted if it ever comes to that:

```
void Map::CheckTextureSizes(int l_fromZ, int l_toZ) {
  auto realMapSize = m_tileMap.GetMapSize() *
    static_cast<unsigned int>(Sheet::Tile_Size);
  for (auto layer = l_fromZ; layer <= l_toZ; ++layer) {
    ...
    if (m_normals[layer].getSize() != realMapSize) {
      if (!m_normals[layer].create(realMapSize.x, realMapSize.y))
      { ... }
    }
    if (m_speculars[layer].getSize() != realMapSize) {
      if (!m_speculars[layer].create(realMapSize.x,realMapSize.y))
      { ... }
    }
    if (m_heightMap[layer].getSize() != realMapSize) {
      if (!m_heightMap[layer].create(realMapSize.x,realMapSize.y))
      { ... }
    }
  }
}
```

Clearing the material maps is equally as simple; we just need to add a couple of extra lines:

```
void Map::ClearMapTexture(sf::Vector3i l_from, sf::Vector3i l_to)
{
  ...
  if (l_to.x == -1 && l_to.y == -1) {
    for (auto layer = l_from.z; layer <= toLayer; ++layer) {
      ...
      m_normals[layer].clear({ 0,0,0,0 });
      m_speculars[layer].clear({ 0,0,0,0 });
      m_heightMap[layer].clear({ 0,0,0,0 });
    }
    return;
  }
  ...
  for (auto layer = l_from.z; layer <= toLayer; ++layer) {
    ...
    m_normals[layer].draw(shape, sf::BlendMultiply);
    m_speculars[layer].draw(shape, sf::BlendMultiply);
    m_heightMap[layer].draw(shape, sf::BlendMultiply);
  }
  DisplayAllTextures(l_from.z, toLayer);
}
```

Displaying the changes that were made to the buffer textures follows the same easy and manageable approach:

```
void Map::DisplayAllTextures(int l_fromZ, int l_toZ) {
  for (auto layer = l_fromZ; layer <= l_toZ; ++layer) {
    m_textures[layer].display();
    m_normals[layer].display();
    m_speculars[layer].display();
    m_heightMap[layer].display();
  }
}
```

Finally, drawing this information to the internal buffers of `LightManager`, in the case of the `Map` class, can be done like so:

```
void Map::Draw(MaterialMapContainer& l_materials,
  Window& l_window, int l_layer)
{
  ... // Diffuse.
  // Normal.
  m_layerSprite.setTexture(m_normals[l_layer].getTexture());
  m_window->GetRenderer()->Draw(m_layerSprite,
    l_materials[MaterialMapType::Normal].get());
  // Specular.
```

```
m_layerSprite.setTexture(m_speculars[l_layer].getTexture());
m_window->GetRenderer()->Draw(m_layerSprite,
  l_materials[MaterialMapType::Specular].get());
// Height.
m_layerSprite.setTexture(m_heightMap[l_layer].getTexture());
m_window->GetRenderer()->Draw(m_layerSprite,
  l_materials[MaterialMapType::Height].get());
}
```

Easy enough? Good! Let's keep progressing and build shaders that can handle the process of drawing these material maps.

Preparing the texture manager

In order to automatically load the additional material maps when loading diffuse images, we need to make some very quick and painless changes to the `ResourceManager` and `TextureManager` classes:

```
class ResourceManager{
public:
  bool RequireResource(const std::string& l_id,
    bool l_notifyDerived = true)
  {
    ...
    if (l_notifyDerived) { OnRequire(l_id); }
    return true;
  }

  bool ReleaseResource(const std::string& l_id,
    bool l_notifyDerived = true)
  {
    ...
    if (l_notifyDerived) { OnRelease(l_id); }
    return true;
  }
protected:
  ...
  virtual void OnRequire(const std::string& l_id) {}
  virtual void OnRelease(const std::string& l_id) {}
};

class TextureManager : ...{
public:
  ...
  void OnRequire(const std::string& l_id) {
    if (RequireResource(l_id + "_normal", false)) { ... }
```

```
    if (RequireResource(l_id + "_specular", false)) { ... }
  }

  void OnRelease(const std::string& l_id) {
    if (ReleaseResource(l_id + "_normal", false)) { ... }
    if (ReleaseResource(l_id + "_specular", false)) { ... }
  }
};
```

By adding the `OnRequire()` and `OnRelease()` methods and integrating them properly with the `l_notifyDerived` flag to avoid infinite recursion, `TextureManager` can safely load in both the normal and specular material maps when a diffuse texture is loaded, provided they are found. Note that the texture manager actually passes in `false` as the second argument when it needs these maps to avoid infinite recursion.

Material pass shaders

There will be two types of material pass shaders we'll use. One type, simply referred to as *MaterialPass*, will sample the material color from a texture:

```
uniform sampler2D texture;
uniform sampler2D material;
void main()
{
  vec4 pixel = texture2D(texture, gl_TexCoord[0].xy);
  vec4 materialPixel = texture2D(material, gl_TexCoord[0].xy);
  materialPixel.a *= pixel.a;
  gl_FragColor = gl_Color * materialPixel;
}
```

It retrieves the diffuse pixel and the material texture pixel, as well as uses the diffuse alpha value to display the right color. This effectively means that if we're dealing with a transparent pixel on a diffuse map, no material color is going to be rendered for it. Otherwise, the material color is completely independent of the diffuse pixel. This is useful for drawing images that also have material maps located in a different texture.

The second type of material shader, known from here on out as *MaterialValuePass*, will also sample the diffuse pixel. Instead of using a material texture, however, it'll simply use a static color value for all the pixels that aren't transparent:

```
uniform sampler2D texture;
uniform vec3 material;
void main()
{
  vec4 pixel = texture2D(texture, gl_TexCoord[0].xy);
```

```
    float alpha = 0.0;
    if(pixel == vec4(0.0, 0.0, 0.0, 1.0))
        alpha = gl_Color.a;
    else
        alpha = pixel.a;
    gl_FragColor = gl_Color * vec4(material.rgb, alpha);
}
```

Here, we first verify that the sampled pixel isn't completely black. If it is, the alpha value of gl_Color is used instead of that of the pixel. Then, we simply write the static material color value to the fragment. This type of shader is useful for drawable objects that don't have material maps and instead use a static color for every single pixel.

Normal maps

Lighting can be used to create visually complex and breath taking scenes. One of the massive benefits of having a lighting system is the ability it provides to add extra details to your scene, which wouldn't have been possible otherwise. One way of doing so is using **normal maps**.

Mathematically speaking, the word *normal* in the context of a surface is simply a directional vector that is perpendicular to said surface. Consider the following illustration:

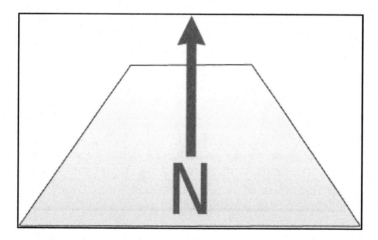

In this case, what's normal is facing up because that's the direction perpendicular to the plane. How is this helpful? Well, imagine you have a really complex model with many vertices; it'd be extremely taxing to render said model because of all the geometry that would need to be processed with each frame. A clever trick to work around this, known as **normal mapping,** is to take the information of all of those vertices and save them on a texture that looks similar to this one:

It probably looks extremely funky, especially if being looked at in a physical release of this book that's in grayscale, but try not to think of this in terms of colors, but directions. The red channel of a normal map encodes the -x and +x values. The green channel does the same for -y and +y values, and the blue channel is used for -z to +z. Looking back at the previous image now, it's easier to confirm which direction each individual pixel is facing. Using this information on geometry that's completely flat would still allow us to light it in such a way that it would make it look like it has all of the detail in there; yet, it would still remain flat and light on performance:

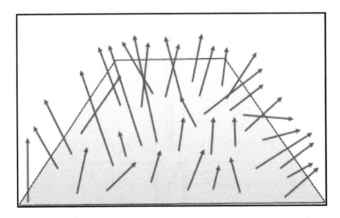

These normal maps can be hand-drawn or simply generated using software such as *Crazybump*. Let's see how all of this can be done in our game engine.

Implementing normal map rendering

In the case of maps, implementing normal map rendering is extremely simple. We already have all the material maps integrated and ready to go, so at this time, it's simply a matter of sampling the texture of the tile sheet normals:

```
void Map::Redraw(sf::Vector3i l_from, sf::Vector3i l_to) {
  ...
  if (renderer->UseShader("MaterialPass")) {
    // Material pass.
    auto shader = renderer->GetCurrentShader();
    auto textureName = m_tileMap.GetTileSet().GetTextureName();
    auto normalMaterial = m_textureManager->
      GetResource(textureName + "_normal");
    for (auto x = l_from.x; x <= l_to.x; ++x) {
      for (auto y = l_from.y; y <= l_to.y; ++y) {
        for (auto layer = l_from.z; layer <= l_to.z; ++layer) {
          auto tile = m_tileMap.GetTile(x, y, layer);
          if (!tile) { continue; }
          auto& sprite = tile->m_properties->m_sprite;
          sprite.setPosition(
            static_cast<float>(x * Sheet::Tile_Size),
            static_cast<float>(y * Sheet::Tile_Size));
          // Normal pass.
          if (normalMaterial) {
            shader->setUniform("material", *normalMaterial);
            renderer->Draw(sprite, &m_normals[layer]);
          }
        }
      }
    }
  }
  ...
}
```

The process is exactly the same as drawing a normal tile to a diffuse map, except that here we have to provide the material shader with the texture of the tile-sheet normal map. Also note that we're now drawing to a normal buffer texture.

The same is true for drawing entities as well:

```
void S_Renderer::Draw(MaterialMapContainer& l_materials,
  Window& l_window, int l_layer)
{
  ...
  if (renderer->UseShader("MaterialPass")) {
    // Material pass.
```

```
          auto shader = renderer->GetCurrentShader();
          auto textures = m_systemManager->
            GetEntityManager()->GetTextureManager();
          for (auto &entity : m_entities) {
            auto position = entities->GetComponent<C_Position>(
              entity, Component::Position);
            if (position->GetElevation() < l_layer) { continue; }
            if (position->GetElevation() > l_layer) { break; }
            C_Drawable* drawable = GetDrawableFromType(entity);
            if (!drawable) { continue; }
            if (drawable->GetType() != Component::SpriteSheet)
            { continue; }
            auto sheet = static_cast<C_SpriteSheet*>(drawable);
            auto name = sheet->GetSpriteSheet()->GetTextureName();
            auto normals = textures->GetResource(name + "_normal");
            // Normal pass.
            if (normals) {
              shader->setUniform("material", *normals);
              drawable->Draw(&l_window,
                l_materials[MaterialMapType::Normal].get());
            }
          }
        }
      }
      ...
    }
```

You can try obtaining a normal texture through the texture manager. If you find one, you can draw it to the normal map material buffer.

Dealing with particles isn't much different from what we've seen already, except for one small detail:

```
void ParticleSystem::Draw(MaterialMapContainer& l_materials,
  Window& l_window, int l_layer)
{
  ...
  if (renderer->UseShader("MaterialValuePass")) {
    // Material pass.
    auto shader = renderer->GetCurrentShader();
    for (size_t i = 0; i < container->m_countAlive; ++i) {
      if (l_layer >= 0) {
        if (positions[i].z < l_layer * Sheet::Tile_Size)
        { continue; }
        if (positions[i].z >= (l_layer + 1) * Sheet::Tile_Size)
        { continue; }
      } else if (positions[i].z <
        Sheet::Num_Layers * Sheet::Tile_Size)
      { continue; }
```

```
// Normal pass.
shader->setUniform("material",
  sf::Glsl::Vec3(0.5f, 0.5f, 1.f));
renderer->Draw(drawables[i],
  l_materials[MaterialMapType::Normal].get());
    }
  }
  ...
}
```

As you can see, we're actually using the material value shader in order to give particles static normals, which are always sort of pointing to the camera. A normal map buffer should look something like this after you render all the normal maps to it:

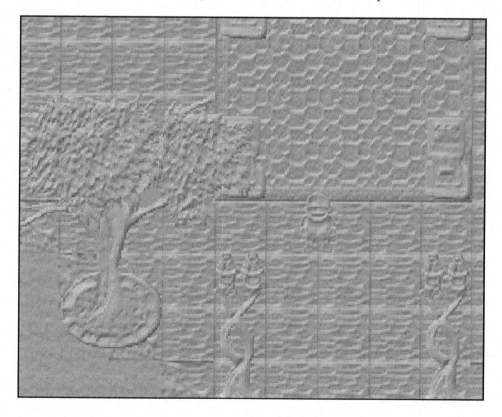

Changing the lighting shader

Now that we have all of this information, let's actually use it when calculating the illumination of the pixels inside the light pass shader:

```
uniform sampler2D LastPass;
uniform sampler2D DiffuseMap;
uniform sampler2D NormalMap;
uniform vec3 AmbientLight;
uniform int LightCount;
uniform int PassNumber;

struct LightInfo {
  vec3 position;
  vec3 color;
  float radius;
  float falloff;
};

const int MaxLights = 4;
uniform LightInfo Lights[MaxLights];

void main()
{
  vec4 pixel = texture2D(LastPass, gl_TexCoord[0].xy);
  vec4 diffusepixel = texture2D(DiffuseMap, gl_TexCoord[0].xy);
  vec4 normalpixel = texture2D(NormalMap, gl_TexCoord[0].xy);
  vec3 PixelCoordinates =
    vec3(gl_FragCoord.x, gl_FragCoord.y, gl_FragCoord.z);
  vec4 finalPixel = gl_Color * pixel;
  vec3 viewDirection = vec3(0, 0, 1);
  if(PassNumber == 1) { finalPixel *= vec4(AmbientLight, 1.0); }
  // IF FIRST PASS ONLY!
  vec3 N = normalize(normalpixel.rgb * 2.0 - 1.0);
  for(int i = 0; i < LightCount; ++i) {

    vec3 L = Lights[i].position - PixelCoordinates;
    float distance = length(L);
    float d = max(distance - Lights[i].radius, 0);
    L /= distance;
    float attenuation = 1 / pow(d/Lights[i].radius + 1, 2);
    attenuation = (attenuation - Lights[i].falloff) /
      (1 - Lights[i].falloff);
    attenuation = max(attenuation, 0);
    float normalDot = max(dot(N, L), 0.0);
    finalPixel += (diffusepixel *
      ((vec4(Lights[i].color, 1.0) * attenuation))) * normalDot;
  }
```

```
gl_FragColor = finalPixel;
}
```

First, the normal map texture needs to be passed to it, as well as sampled, which is where the first two highlighted lines of code come in. Once this is done, for each light we're drawing on the screen, the normal directional vector is calculated. This is done by first making sure that it can go into the negative range and then normalizing it. A normalized vector only represents a direction.

Since the color values range from *0* to *255*, negative values cannot be directly represented. This is why we first bring them into the right range by multiplying them by *2.0* and subtracting by *1.0*.

A **dot product** is then calculated between the normal vector and the normalized L vector, which now represents the direction from the light to the pixel. How much a pixel is lit up from a specific light is directly contingent upon the dot product, which is a value from *1.0* to *0.0* and represents magnitude.

A **dot product** is an algebraic operation that takes in *two vectors*, as well as the *cosine* of the angle between them, and produces a scalar value between *0.0* and *1.0* that essentially represents how "orthogonal" they are. We use this property to light pixels less and less, given greater and greater angles between their normals and the light.

Finally, the dot product is used again when calculating the final pixel value. The entire influence of the light is multiplied by it, which allows every pixel to be drawn differently as if it had some underlying geometry that was pointing in a different direction.

The last thing left to do now is to pass the normal map buffer to the shader in our C++ code:

```
void LightManager::RenderScene() {
  ...
  if (renderer->UseShader("LightPass")) {
    // Light pass.
    ...
    shader->setUniform("NormalMap",
      m_materialMaps[MaterialMapType::Normal]->getTexture());
    ...
  }
  ...
}
```

This effectively enables normal mapping and gives us beautiful results such as this:

The leaves, the character, and pretty much everything in this image, now look like they have a definition, ridges, and crevices; it is lit as if it had geometry, although it's paper-thin. Note the lines around each tile in this particular instance. This is one of the main reasons why normal maps for pixel art, such as tile sheets, shouldn't be automatically generated; it can sample the tiles adjacent to it and incorrectly add bevelled edges.

Specular maps

While normal maps provide us with the possibility of faking how bumpy a surface is, specular maps allow us to do the same with the shininess of a surface. This is what the same segment of the tile sheet we used as an example for a normal map looks like in a specular map:

It's not as complex as a normal map, since it only needs to store one value: the shininess factor. We can leave it up to each light to decide how much *shine* it will cast upon the scenery by letting it have its own values:

```
struct LightBase {
  ...
  float m_specularExponent = 10.f;
  float m_specularStrength = 1.f;
};
```

Adding support for specularity

Similar to normal maps, we need to use the material pass shader to render to a specularity buffer texture:

```
void Map::Redraw(sf::Vector3i l_from, sf::Vector3i l_to) {
  ...
  if (renderer->UseShader("MaterialPass")) {
    // Material pass.
    ...
    auto specMaterial = m_textureManager->GetResource(
      textureName + "_specular");
    for (auto x = l_from.x; x <= l_to.x; ++x) {
      for (auto y = l_from.y; y <= l_to.y; ++y) {
        for (auto layer = l_from.z; layer <= l_to.z; ++layer) {
          ... // Normal pass.
          // Specular pass.
          if (specMaterial) {
            shader->setUniform("material", *specMaterial);
            renderer->Draw(sprite, &m_speculars[layer]);
          }
        }
      }
    }
  }
  ...
}
```

The texture for specularity is once again attempted to be obtained; it is passed down to the material pass shader if found. The same is true when you render entities:

```
void S_Renderer::Draw(MaterialMapContainer& l_materials,
  Window& l_window, int l_layer)
{
  ...
  if (renderer->UseShader("MaterialPass")) {
    // Material pass.
    ...
    for (auto &entity : m_entities) {
      ... // Normal pass.
      // Specular pass.
      if (specular) {
        shader->setUniform("material", *specular);
        drawable->Draw(&l_window,
          l_materials[MaterialMapType::Specular].get());
      }
    }
  }
  ...
}
```

Particles, on the other hand, also use the material value pass shader:

```
void ParticleSystem::Draw(MaterialMapContainer& l_materials,
  Window& l_window, int l_layer)
{
  ...
  if (renderer->UseShader("MaterialValuePass")) {
    // Material pass.
    auto shader = renderer->GetCurrentShader();
    for (size_t i = 0; i < container->m_countAlive; ++i) {
      ... // Normal pass.
      // Specular pass.
      shader->setUniform("material",
        sf::Glsl::Vec3(0.f, 0.f, 0.f));
      renderer->Draw(drawables[i],
        l_materials[MaterialMapType::Specular].get());
    }
  }
}
```

For now, we don't want any of them to be specular at all. This can obviously be tweaked later on, but the important thing is that we have that functionality available and yielding results, such as the following:

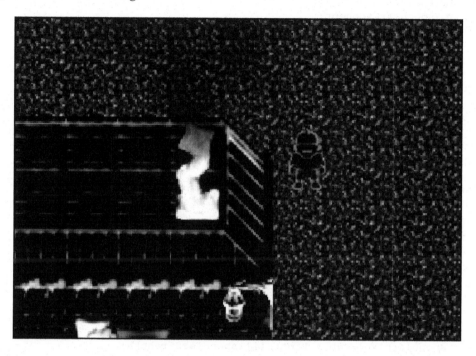

This specularity texture needs to be sampled inside a light pass, just like a normal texture. Let's see what this involves.

Changing the lighting shader

Just as before, a uniform `sampler2D` needs to be added to sample the specularity of a particular fragment:

```
uniform sampler2D LastPass;
uniform sampler2D DiffuseMap;
uniform sampler2D NormalMap;
uniform sampler2D SpecularMap;
uniform vec3 AmbientLight;
uniform int LightCount;
uniform int PassNumber;

struct LightInfo {
```

```
    vec3 position;
    vec3 color;
    float radius;
    float falloff;
    float specularExponent;
    float specularStrength;
};

const int MaxLights = 4;
uniform LightInfo Lights[MaxLights];

const float SpecularConstant = 0.4;

void main()
{
    ...
    vec4 specularpixel = texture2D(SpecularMap, gl_TexCoord[0].xy);
    vec3 viewDirection = vec3(0, 0, 1); // Looking at positive Z.
    ...
    for(int i = 0; i < LightCount; ++i){
        ...
        float specularLevel = 0.0;
        specularLevel =
            pow(max(0.0, dot(reflect(-L, N), viewDirection)),
            Lights[i].specularExponent * specularpixel.a)
            * SpecularConstant;
        vec3 specularReflection = Lights[i].color * specularLevel *
            specularpixel.rgb * Lights[i].specularStrength;
        finalPixel +=
            (diffusepixel * ((vec4(Lights[i].color, 1.0) * attenuation))
            + vec4(specularReflection, 1.0)) * normalDot;
    }
    gl_FragColor = finalPixel;
}
```

We also need to add in the specular exponent and strength to each light's struct, as it's now part of it. Once the specular pixel is sampled, we need to set up the direction of the camera as well. Since that's static, we can leave it as is in the shader.

The specularity of the pixel is then calculated by taking into account the dot product between the pixel's normal and the light, the color of the specular pixel itself, and the specular strength of the light. Note the use of a specular constant in the calculation. This is a value that can, and should, be tweaked in order to obtain the best results, as 100% specularity rarely looks good.

Then, all that's left is to make sure the specularity texture is also sent to the light pass shader, in addition to the light's specular exponent and strength values:

```
void LightManager::RenderScene() {
  ...
  if (renderer->UseShader("LightPass")) {
    // Light pass.
    ...
    shader->setUniform("SpecularMap",
      m_materialMaps[MaterialMapType::Specular]->getTexture());
    ...
    for (auto& light : m_lights) {
      ...
      shader->setUniform(id + ".specularExponent",
        light.m_specularExponent);
      shader->setUniform(id + ".specularStrength",
        light.m_specularStrength);
      ...
    }
  }
}
```

The result may not be visible right away, but upon closer inspection of moving a light stream, we can see that correctly mapped surfaces will have a glint that will move around with the light:

While this is nearly perfect, there's still some room for improvement.

Height maps

The main point of illuminating the world is to make all the visual details pop up in a realistic manner. We have already added artificial dynamic lighting, fake 3D geometry, and shininess, so what's left? Well, there's nothing that shows the proper height of the scene yet. Until this very moment, we've been dealing with the scene as if it's completely flat when calculating the lighting distances. Instead of this, we need to work on something referred to as the height map that will store the heights of the pixels.

Adapting the existing code

Drawing heights properly can be quite tricky, especially in the case of tile maps. We need to know which way a tile is facing when drawing realistic heights. Consider the following illustration:

The tiles right next to point **A** have no normals associated with them, while the tiles next to point **B** are all facing the camera. We can store normal data inside our map files by making these few simple alterations:

```
struct Tile {
  ...
  sf::Vector3f m_normal;
};

void TileMap::ReadInTile(std::stringstream& l_stream) {
  ...
  sf::Vector3f normals(0.f, 1.f, 0.f);
  l_stream >> normals.x >> normals.y >> normals.z;
  tile->m_normal = normals;
  ...
}


TILE 57 15 3 1 1 // Tile entry without a normal.
TILE 144 15 8 1 1 0 0 1 // Tile entry with a normal 0,0,1
```

The `Tile` structure itself holds on to a normal value now, which will be used later on. When tiles are being read in from a file, additional information is loaded at the very end. The last two lines here show the actual entries from a map file.

Drawing the heights of these tiles based on their normals is all done in the appropriate shader, so let's pass all of the information it needs:

```
void Map::Redraw(sf::Vector3i l_from, sf::Vector3i l_to) {
  ...
  if (renderer->UseShader("HeightPass")) {
    // Height pass.
    auto shader = renderer->GetCurrentShader();
    for (auto x = l_from.x; x <= l_to.x; ++x) {
      for (auto y = l_from.y; y <= l_to.y; ++y) {
        for (auto layer = l_from.z; layer <= l_to.z; ++layer) {
          auto tile = m_tileMap.GetTile(x, y, layer);
          if (!tile) { continue; }
          auto& sprite = tile->m_properties->m_sprite;
          sprite.setPosition(
            static_cast<float>(x * Sheet::Tile_Size),
            static_cast<float>(y * Sheet::Tile_Size));
          shader->setUniform("BaseHeight",
            static_cast<float>(layer * Sheet::Tile_Size));
          shader->setUniform("YPosition", sprite.getPosition().y);
          shader->setUniform("SurfaceNormal",
            sf::Glsl::Vec3(tile->m_normal));
          renderer->Draw(sprite, &m_heightMap[layer]);
```

```
          }
        }
      }
    }
    ...
  }
```

The height pass shader uses a value for the base height of the drawable, which, in this case, is just elevation in world coordinates. It also uses the *Y* world coordinate of the `Drawable` class and takes in the surface normal. The same values need to be set up for the entities as well:

```
void S_Renderer::Draw(MaterialMapContainer& l_materials,
  Window& l_window, int l_layer)
{
  ...
  if (renderer->UseShader("HeightPass")) {
    // Height pass.
    auto shader = renderer->GetCurrentShader();
    shader->setUniform("BaseHeight",
      static_cast<float>(l_layer * Sheet::Tile_Size));
    shader->setUniform("SurfaceNormal",
      sf::Glsl::Vec3(0.f, 0.f, 1.f));
    for (auto &entity : m_entities) {
      auto position = entities->GetComponent<C_Position>(
        entity, Component::Position);
      if (position->GetElevation() < l_layer) { continue; }
      if (position->GetElevation() > l_layer) { break; }
      C_Drawable* drawable = GetDrawableFromType(entity);
      if (!drawable) { continue; }
      if (drawable->GetType() != Component::SpriteSheet)
      { continue; }
      auto sheet = static_cast<C_SpriteSheet*>(drawable);
      shader->setUniform("YPosition", position->GetPosition().y);
      drawable->Draw(&l_window,
        l_materials[MaterialMapType::Height].get());
    }
  }
  ...
}
```

In this case, however, we're using the same normal for all the entities. This is because we want them to face the camera and be illuminated as if they're standing perpendicular to the ground. Particles, on the other hand, are not facing the camera, but instead have normals pointing up toward the positive *Y* axis:

```cpp
void ParticleSystem::Draw(MaterialMapContainer& l_materials,
    Window& l_window, int l_layer)
{
    ...
    if (renderer->UseShader("HeightPass")) {
        // Height pass.
        auto shader = renderer->GetCurrentShader();
        shader->setUniform("SurfaceNormal",
            sf::Glsl::Vec3(0.f, 1.f, 0.f));
        for (size_t i = 0; i < container->m_countAlive; ++i) {
            if (l_layer >= 0) {
                if (positions[i].z < l_layer * Sheet::Tile_Size)
                { continue; }
                if (positions[i].z >= (l_layer + 1) * Sheet::Tile_Size)
                { continue; }
            } else if (positions[i].z <
                Sheet::Num_Layers * Sheet::Tile_Size)
            { continue; }
            shader->setUniform("BaseHeight", positions[i].z);
            shader->setUniform("YPosition", positions[i].y);
            renderer->Draw(drawables[i],
                l_materials[MaterialMapType::Height].get());
        }
    }
    ...
}
```

Writing the height pass shader

The height pass is the only program we've written so far that uses both the vertex and the fragment shaders.

Let's take a look at what needs to happen in the vertex shader:

```
uniform float YPosition;
out float Height;
void main()
{
  gl_Position = gl_ModelViewProjectionMatrix * gl_Vertex;
  gl_TexCoord[0] = gl_TextureMatrix[0] * gl_MultiTexCoord0;
  gl_FrontColor = gl_Color;
  Height = gl_Vertex.y - YPosition;
}
```

There's only one line here that isn't standard from what is traditionally known as a vertex shader, outside of the uniform variable and the out variable, of course. The vertex shader outputs a floating point value called Height to the fragment shader. It's simply the height between the Y component of the vertex of a shape in world coordinates and the base Y position of that same shape. The height is then interpolated between all the fragments, giving a nice, gradient distribution.

> The gl_Vertex information is stored in world coordinates. The bottom Y coordinates always start at the same height as the drawable, which makes the top Y coordinates equal to the sum of its position and height.

Finally, we can take a look at the fragment shader and actually do some filling up of fragments:

```
uniform sampler2D texture;
uniform vec3 SurfaceNormal;
uniform float BaseHeight;
in float Height;
void main()
{
  vec4 pixel = texture2D(texture, gl_TexCoord[0].xy);
  float value = (BaseHeight - (Height * SurfaceNormal.z)) / 255.0;
  gl_FragColor = vec4(value, value, value, pixel.a);
}
```

As shown previously, it takes in the diffuse texture, the surface normal, the base height of the drawable, and the interpolated `Height` value from the vertex shader. The diffuse pixel is then sampled in order to use its alpha value for transparency. The height value itself is calculated by subtracting the result of the pixel height being multiplied by the surface normal's Z component from the base height of the drawable. The whole thing is finally divided by *255* because we want to store color information in a normalized format.

Changing the lighting shader

Finally, the light pass shader can be changed as well by sampling the height map:

```
...
uniform sampler2D HeightMap;
...
void main()
{
  ...
  float pixelheight = texture2D(HeightMap, gl_TexCoord[0].xy).r
    * 255;
  vec3 PixelCoordinates =
    vec3(gl_FragCoord.x, gl_FragCoord.y, pixelheight);
  ...
  gl_FragColor = finalPixel;
}
```

Once the pixel height is sampled and multiplied by *255* to bring it back to world coordinates, all we need to do is replace the `gl_FragCoord.z` value with `pixelHeight` when calculating the distance between a pixel and a fragment. Yes, that's really all it takes!

The `HeightMap` can then be actually passed to the shader for sampling, like so:

```
void LightManager::RenderScene() {
  ...
  if (renderer->UseShader("LightPass")) {
    // Light pass.
    ...
    shader->setUniform("HeightMap",
      m_materialMaps[MaterialMapType::Height]->getTexture());
    ...
  }
  ...
}
```

This gives us a very nice effect that can actually show off the height of a particular structure, given it has elevated properly and has the right normals:

The light post on the left has no normals, while the post on the right has normals that face the +Z direction. The light position is exactly the same in both these images.

Summary

If you are still here, congratulations! That was quite a bit of information to take in, but just as our world is finally beginning to take shape visually, we're about to embark on an even more stunning feature that will be discussed in the next chapter. See you there!

9
The Speed of Dark - Lighting and Shadows

Contrasting differences are the very essence of existence, as the *yin-yang* symbol properly illustrates. Light and darkness are opposites, yet complementary, as they offset one another and give meaning through variety. Without darkness there can be no light, as they are never truly separate. By breathing light into our world, we are inevitably forced to add back the darkness that it creates. Let's follow the previous chapter and truly complete to our lighting engine by reintroducing the concept of darkness to it.

In this chapter, we will be covering the following topics:

- Using OpenGL to render to and sample from cubemap textures
- Advanced shadow mapping for omni-directional point lights
- The use of Percentage Closer Filtering to smooth out shadow edges
- Combating common and frustrating issues with shadow mapping

There's quite a bit of theory to get out of the way, so let's get to it!

Use of third-party software

Before diving into such a difficult subject to debug, it's always nice to have proper tools that will ease the headaches and reduce the number of questions one might ask oneself during development. While normal code executed on the *CPU* can just be stepped through and analyzed during runtime, shader code and OpenGL resources, such as textures are a bit more difficult to handle. Most, if not all, C++ compilers don't have native support for dealing with *GPU-bound* problems. Luckily, there is software out there that makes it easier to deal with that very predicament.

Among the few tools that exist out there to alleviate such headaches, *CodeXL* by *AMD Developer Tools Team* stands out. It's a free piece of software that can be used as a standalone application for Windows and Linux or even as a plugin for Visual Studio. Its most prominent features include being able to view OpenGL resources (including textures) while the program is running, profile the code and find bottlenecks, and even step through the shader code as it's being executed (given the right hardware). The tool can be found and downloaded here: `http://gpuopen.com/compute-product/codexl/`.

Theory behind shadowing techniques

There are a couple of different techniques that can be used when implementing realistic looking shadows in games. Choosing the right one can not only impact the kind of performance your application is going to exhibit, but can also heavily influence how good the effect is going to look in the end.

An approach that isn't at all uncommon for 2D is referred to as **ray tracing**. Depending on the type of light, a number of rays are cast in an appropriate direction. Shadows are then implemented depending on which solids these rays actually intersect with. Some simpler games tend to create an overlay mask and fill in geometrically the parts of it that are "in the shadow". This mask is later overlaid on top of the usual scene and blended in order to create the aesthetic of darkened areas meant to represent shadows. More advanced 3D games tend to allow rays to bounce around the scene, carrying different information about the particular fragments that they intersect with. By the time a ray reaches the camera, it will have enough information to do more than create simple shadows. Scenes that require extremely advanced lighting tend to use this technique, and rightly so, as it imitates the way light bounces off objects and hits the observer's eye in real life.

An older, but still widely used approach for specifically creating shadows is called **shadow mapping**. The essence of this technique comes down to simply rendering the scene to an off screen buffer from the point of view of the light. All the solids' depth information, as opposed to color information, is written to this buffer as pixel data. When the real scene is rendered, some matrix math is then used to sample the right pixels of the shadow map to figure out whether they can be directly seen by the light, thus being illuminated, or whether they're being obstructed by something, and therefore sitting in the shadow.

Shadow mapping

The main idea behind creating a shadow map is rendering the scene from the point of view of the light, and effectively encoding the depth of a particular piece of geometry being rendered as a color value that can later be sampled. The depth value itself is nothing more than the distance between the position of the light and the position of the vertex. Consider the following diagram:

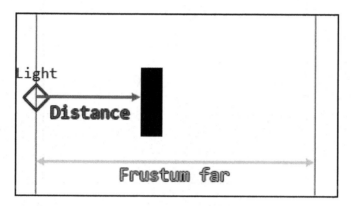

The distance between the light and a given vertex will be converted to a color value by simply dividing it by the frustum far distance, yielding a result in a range *[0;1]*. The frustum far value is simply the distance of how far the light/camera can see.

Omni-directional point lights

In the previous chapter, we managed to create lights that emit in all directions from a center point. These types of lights have a very fitting name: omni-directional point lights. Dealing with shadow mapping for these lights comes with a certain layer of complexity, as the scene now needs to be drawn in all six directions, rather than just one if we were dealing with a directional light. This means we need a good way of storing the results of this process that can be accessed with relative ease. Luckily, OpenGL provides a new type of texture we can use, the **cubemap**.

Cubemap textures

A cubemap is pretty much exactly what it sounds like. It's a special texture that really holds six textures for each face of the cube. These textures are internally stored in an *unfolded* manner, as shown here:

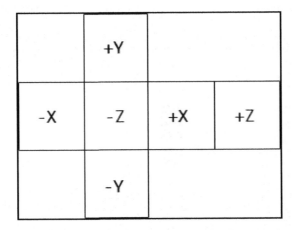

Because of this property, rendering shadow maps for omni-directional lights can be as simple as rendering the scene once for each direction of a cubemap. Sampling them is also quite easy. The shape of a cube lends itself to some useful properties we can exploit. If all of the cube's vertices are in relation to its absolute center, then the coordinates of these vertices can also be thought of as directional vectors:

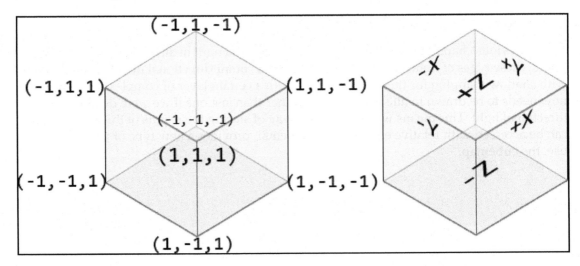

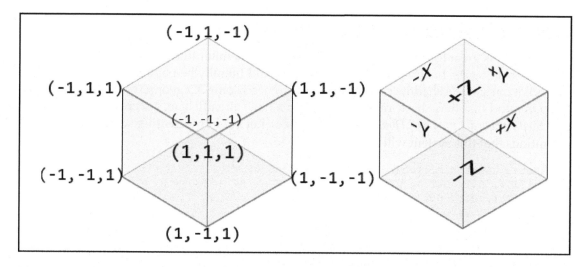

The direction (0, 1, 0) from the center of the cube would be pointing directly in the middle of the +Y face, for example. Since each face of a cubemap texture also holds a texture of its own that represents the view of the scene, it can easily be sampled using these coordinates. For a 2D texture, our shaders had to use the `sampler2D` type and provide 2D coordinates of the sampling location. Cubemaps have their own sampler type, `samplerCube`, and use a 3D vector for sampling. The consequence of this is that the largest member of the 3D vector is used to determine which face is to be sampled, and the other two members become the UV texture coordinates for that particular 2D texture/face.

 Cube textures can be used for much more than shadow mapping. 3D environments can take advantage of them when implementing skyboxes and reflective/refractive materials, to name just a few techniques.

Preparations for rendering

It's safe to say that all of this functionality is a bit beyond the scope of SFML, as it seeks to deal with simple two-dimensional concepts. While we're still going to be using SFML to render our sprites, the lighting and shadowing of the scene will have to fall back on raw OpenGL. This includes setting up and sampling cubemap textures, as well as creating, uploading, and drawing 3D primitives used to represent objects that cast shadows.

Representing shadow casters

While SFML is great for rendering sprites, we must remember that these are two-dimensional objects. In 3D space, our character would literally be paper thin. This means that all of our game's shadow casters are going to need some 3D geometry behind them. Keep in mind that these basic rendering concepts have already been covered in Chapter 7, *One Step Forward, One Level Down – OpenGL Basics*. Let's start by creating some common definitions that this system will use:

```
static const glm::vec3 CubeMapDirections[6] = {
  { 1.f, 0.f, 0.f },  // 0 = Positive X
  { -1.f, 0.f, 0.f }, // 1 = Negative X
  { 0.f, 1.f, 0.f },  // 2 = Positive Y
  { 0.f, -1.f, 0.f }, // 3 = Negative Y
  { 0.f, 0.f, 1.f },  // 4 = Positive Z
  { 0.f, 0.f, -1.f }  // 5 = Negative Z
};
```

This is going to be a common lookup array for us, and it's important that the directional vectors here are defined correctly. It represents a direction towards each face of the cubemap texture.

Another common data structure we will be using is a list of indices used to draw the cubes/3D rectangles that represent our shadow casters:

```
static const int ShadowMeshIndices = 36;
static const GLuint CubeIndices[ShadowMeshIndices] = {
  0, 4, 7, 7, 3, 0,  // Front
  0, 1, 5, 5, 4, 0,  // Left
  3, 7, 6, 6, 2, 3,  // Right
  1, 2, 6, 6, 5, 1,  // Back
  7, 4, 5, 5, 6, 7,  // Up
  1, 0, 3, 3, 2, 1   // Down
};
```

Since the cubes have 6 faces and each face uses 6 indices to enumerate the two triangles that make them up, we have a total of 36 indices.

Finally, we need an up vector for each direction of a cubemap texture:

```
static const glm::vec3 CubeMapUpDirections[6] = {
    { 0.f, -1.f, 0.f },  // 0 = Positive X
    { 0.f, -1.f, 0.f }, // 1 = Negative X
    { 0.f, 0.f, -1.f },  // 2 = Positive Y
    { 0.f, 0.f, -1.f }, // 3 = Negative Y
    { 0.f, -1.f, 0.f },  // 4 = Positive Z
    { 0.f, -1.f, 0.f }  // 5 = Negative Z
};
```

In order to get correct shadow mapping for the geometry, we're going to need to use these up directions when rendering to a shadow cubemap. Note that, unless we're rendering to *Y* faces of the cubemap, the *Y* direction is always used as up. This allows the geometry being rendered to be seen correctly by the camera.

Implementing the shadow caster structure

Representing the literally shapeless entities of our game is the task we're going to be tackling next. In order to minimize the memory usage of this approach, it will be broken down into two parts:

- **Prototype**: This is a structure that holds handles to uploaded geometry used by OpenGL. This kind of object represents a unique, one of a kind model.
- **Caster**: This is a structure that holds a pointer to a prototype it's using, along with its own transform, to position, rotate, and scale it correctly.

The prototype structure needs to hold on to the resources it allocates, as follows:

```
struct ShadowCasterPrototype {
    ...
    glm::vec3 m_vertices[ShadowMeshVertices];
    GLuint m_VAO;
    GLuint m_VBO;
    GLuint m_indexVBO;
};
```

The constructor and destructor of this structure will take care of allocation/de-allocation of these resources:

```
ShadowCasterPrototype() : m_VAO(0), m_VBO(0), m_indexVBO(0) {}
~ShadowCasterPrototype() {
    if (m_VBO) { glDeleteBuffers(1, &m_VBO); }
    if (m_indexVBO) { glDeleteBuffers(1, &m_indexVBO); }
    if (m_VAO) { glDeleteVertexArrays(1, &m_VAO); }
}
```

Once the internal `m_vertices` data member is properly filled out, the geometry can be submitted to the GPU as follows:

```
void UploadVertices() {
    if (!m_VAO) { glGenVertexArrays(1, &m_VAO); }
    glBindVertexArray(m_VAO);
    if (!m_VBO) { glGenBuffers(1, &m_VBO); }
    if (!m_indexVBO) { glGenBuffers(1, &m_indexVBO); }

    glBindBuffer(GL_ARRAY_BUFFER, m_VBO);
    glBufferData(GL_ARRAY_BUFFER,
        ShadowMeshVertices * sizeof(m_vertices[0]), m_vertices,
        GL_STATIC_DRAW);
    // Position vertex attribute.
    glEnableVertexAttribArray(0);
    glVertexAttribPointer(0, 3, GL_FLOAT, GL_FALSE,
        sizeof(glm::vec3), 0);

    glBindBuffer(GL_ELEMENT_ARRAY_BUFFER, m_indexVBO);
    glBufferData(GL_ELEMENT_ARRAY_BUFFER,
        ShadowMeshIndices * sizeof(CubeIndices[0]), CubeIndices,
        GL_STATIC_DRAW);
    glBindBuffer(GL_ARRAY_BUFFER, 0);
    glBindBuffer(GL_ELEMENT_ARRAY_BUFFER, 0);

    glBindVertexArray(0);
}
```

Once the vertex array object and two buffers for vertices and indices are properly created, they're all bound and used to push the data to. Note the highlighted portion of the code that deals with the vertex attributes. Since this geometry is only going to be used to generate shadows, we really don't need anything else except the vertex position. The necessary math of converting all of that information into color values that represent distance from the light source is going to be done inside the shaders.

Also, note the usage of indices to render this geometry here. Doing it this way allows us to save some space by not having to upload twice as many vertices to the GPU as we would have to otherwise.

The drawing of the shadow primitives is just as simple as one would imagine:

```
void Draw() {
  glBindVertexArray(m_VAO);
  glBindBuffer(GL_ARRAY_BUFFER, m_VBO);
  glBindBuffer(GL_ELEMENT_ARRAY_BUFFER, m_indexVBO);
  glDrawElements(GL_TRIANGLES, ShadowMeshIndices,
    GL_UNSIGNED_INT, 0); // 0 = offset.
  glBindBuffer(GL_ELEMENT_ARRAY_BUFFER, 0);
  glBindBuffer(GL_ARRAY_BUFFER, 0);
  glBindVertexArray(0);
}
```

Once all of the buffers are bound, we invoke `glDrawElements`. Let it know we're drawing triangles, give the method the count of indices to use, specify their data type, and provide the proper offset for those indices, which in this case is *0*.

Finally, because we're using prototypes to store unique pieces of geometry, it's definitely useful to overload the == operator for easy checking of matching shapes:

```
bool operator == (const ShadowCasterPrototype& l_rhs) const {
  for (unsigned short i = 0; i < ShadowMeshVertices; ++i) {
    if (m_vertices[i] != l_rhs.m_vertices[i]) { return false; }
  }
  return true;
}
```

Each vertex of the shadow primitive is iterated over and compared to the equivalent vertex of the provided argument. So far, nothing out of the ordinary!

The prototypes are going to need to be identified in some way when they're being stored. Using string identifiers can be quite intuitive in this case, so let's define a proper storage container type for this structure:

```
using ShadowCasterPrototypes = std::unordered_map<std::string,
  std::unique_ptr<ShadowCasterPrototype>>;
```

With that out of the way, we can implement our simple `ShadowCaster` structure that's going to hold all of the variable information about the prototype:

```
struct ShadowCaster {
  ShadowCaster() : m_prototype(nullptr) { }
  ShadowCasterPrototype* m_prototype;
  GL_Transform m_transform;
};
```

As you can see, it's a very simple data structure that holds a pointer to a prototype it uses, as well as its own `GL_Transform` member, which is going to store the displacement information of an object.

The shadow casters are also going to need a proper storage data type:

```
using ShadowCasters = std::vector<std::unique_ptr<ShadowCaster>>;
```

This effectively leaves us with the means to create and manipulate different types of shadow-casting primitives in a memory-conservative manner.

Creating the transform class

The transform class that we're using is exactly the same as the one in Chapter 7, *One Step Forward, One Level Down – OpenGL Basics*. For a quick refresher, let's take a look at the most important part of it that we're going to need for this process–the generation of a model matrix:

```
glm::mat4 GL_Transform::GetModelMatrix() {
  glm::mat4 matrix_pos = glm::translate(m_position);
  glm::mat4 matrix_scale = glm::scale(m_scale);
  // Represent each stored rotation as a different matrix,
  // because we store angles.
  //                  Directional vector  x, y, z
  glm::mat4 matrix_rotX =
    glm::rotate(m_rotation.x, glm::vec3(1, 0, 0));
  glm::mat4 matrix_rotY =
    glm::rotate(m_rotation.y, glm::vec3(0, 1, 0));
  glm::mat4 matrix_rotZ =
    glm::rotate(m_rotation.z, glm::vec3(0, 0, 1));
  // Create a rotation matrix. Multiply in reverse order it
  // needs to be applied.
  glm::mat4 matrix_rotation = matrix_rotZ*matrix_rotY*matrix_rotX;
  // Apply transforms in reverse order they need to be applied in.
  return matrix_pos * matrix_rotation * matrix_scale;
}
```

All of this should be familiar by now, and if it isn't, a quick zip through Chapter 7, *One Step Forward, One Level Down – OpenGL Basics* is definitely in order. The main idea, however, is combining the translation, scale, and rotation matrices in the right order to retrieve a single matrix that contains all of the information about the primitive required to bring its vertices from object space to world space.

Creating a camera class

Similar to the GL_Transform class, we're also going to incorporate the GL_Camera class from Chapter 7, *One Step Forward, One Level Down – OpenGL Basics*. When we're rendering shadow maps, the projection and view matrices for all six directions will need to be submitted to the respective shaders. This makes the GL_Camera class perfect for representing a light in a scene that needs to draw what it sees into a cubemap texture. Once again, this has been covered already, so we're just going to breeze through it:

```
GL_Camera::GL_Camera(const glm::vec3& l_pos, float l_fieldOfView,
    float l_aspectRatio, float l_frustumNear, float l_frustumFar)
    :m_position(l_pos),m_fov(l_fieldOfView),m_aspect(l_aspectRatio),
    m_frustumNear(l_frustumNear), m_frustumFar(l_frustumFar)
{
    RecalculatePerspective();
    m_forwardDir = glm::vec3(0.f, 0.f, 1.f);
    m_upDir = glm::vec3(0.f, 1.f, 0.f);
}
```

Appropriately enough, shadow maps are going to be drawn using a perspective projection. After all the necessary information about view frustum is collected, we can begin constructing the matrices necessary to transform those vertices from world space to the light's view space, as well as to clip space:

```
glm::mat4 GL_Camera::GetViewMatrix() {
    return glm::lookAt(m_position, m_position + m_forwardDir,
        m_upDir);
}
glm::mat4& GL_Camera::GetProjectionMatrix() {
    return m_perspectiveMatrix;
}

void GL_Camera::RecalculatePerspective() {
    m_perspectiveMatrix = glm::perspective(glm::radians(m_fov),
        m_aspect, m_frustumNear, m_frustumFar);
}
```

We're using `glm::lookAt` to construct a view matrix for the light's camera. Then, `glm::perspective` is used in another method to create the perspective projection matrix for the camera.

 It's very important to remember that `glm::perspective` takes the field of view angle of the view frustum as the first argument. It expects this parameter to be in **radians**, not degrees! Because we're storing it in degrees, `glm::radians` is used to convert that value. This is a very easy mistake to make and many people end up having problems with their shadow maps not mapping correctly.

Defining a cube texture class

Now that we have the storage of geometry and representation of the light's view frustum figured out, it's time to create the cube texture we're going to use to actually render the scene to.

Let's start by creating a simple class definition for it:

```
class CubeTexture {
public:
  CubeTexture();
  ~CubeTexture();

  void RenderingBind();
  void RenderingUnbind();
  void SamplingBind(unsigned int l_unit);
  void SamplingUnbind(unsigned int l_unit);

  GLuint GetTextureHandle()const;

  void RenderToFace(unsigned int l_face);
  void Clear();

  static const unsigned int TextureWidth = 1024;
  static const unsigned int TextureHeight = 1024;
private:
  void Create();
  void CreateBuffers();
  void CreateFaces();
  GLuint m_textureID; // Texture handle.
  GLuint m_fbo; // Frame-buffer handle.
  GLuint m_rbo; // Render-buffer handle.
};
```

The texture is going to be used for two distinctive actions: being rendered to and being sampled. Both of these processes have a method for binding and unbinding the texture, with the notable difference that the sampling step also requires a texture unit as an argument. We're going to cover that soon. This class also needs to have a separate method that needs to be called for each of the six faces when they're being rendered.

Although cube textures can be used for many things, in this particular instance, we're simply going to be using them for shadow mapping. The texture dimensions, therefore, are defined as constants of *1024px*.

> The size of a cubemap texture matters greatly, and can cause artifacting if left too small. Smaller textures will lead to sampling inaccuracies and will cause jagged shadow edges.

Lastly, alongside the helper methods used when creating the texture and all of the necessary buffers, we store the handles to the texture itself, the frame buffer object, and render buffer object. The last two objects haven't been covered until this point, so let's dive right in and see what they're for!

Implementing the cube texture class

Let's start, as always, by covering the construction and destruction of this particular OpenGL asset:

```
CubeTexture::CubeTexture() : m_textureID(0), m_fbo(0), m_rbo(0)
  { Create(); }
CubeTexture::~CubeTexture() {
  if (m_fbo) { glDeleteFramebuffers(1, &m_fbo); }
  if (m_rbo) { glDeleteRenderbuffers(1, &m_rbo); }
  if (m_textureID) { glDeleteTextures(1, &m_textureID); }
}
```

Similar to geometry classes, the handles are initialized to values of *0* to indicate their state of not being set up. The destructor checks those values and invokes the appropriate `glDelete` methods for the buffers/textures used.

Creating the cubemap is quite similar to a regular 2D texture, so let's take a look:

```
void CubeTexture::Create() {
  if (m_textureID) { return; }
  glGenTextures(1, &m_textureID);
  CreateFaces();
  glTexParameteri(GL_TEXTURE_CUBE_MAP,
```

```
        GL_TEXTURE_MAG_FILTER, GL_NEAREST);
    glTexParameteri(GL_TEXTURE_CUBE_MAP,
        GL_TEXTURE_MIN_FILTER, GL_NEAREST);
    glTexParameteri(GL_TEXTURE_CUBE_MAP,
        GL_TEXTURE_WRAP_R, GL_CLAMP_TO_EDGE);
    glTexParameteri(GL_TEXTURE_CUBE_MAP,
        GL_TEXTURE_WRAP_S, GL_CLAMP_TO_EDGE);
    glTexParameteri(GL_TEXTURE_CUBE_MAP,
        GL_TEXTURE_WRAP_T, GL_CLAMP_TO_EDGE);

    CreateBuffers();
    glBindTexture(GL_TEXTURE_CUBE_MAP, 0);
}
```

First, a check is made to make sure we haven't already allocated this object. Provided that isn't the case, `glGenTextures` is used, just like for 2D textures, to create space for one texture object. Our first private helper method is then invoked to create all six faces of the cubemap, which brings us to the parameter setup. The *Min/Mag* filters are set up to use the nearest-neighbor interpolation, but can later be converted to `GL_LINEAR` for smoother results, if necessary. The texture wrapping parameters are then set up so that they're clamped to the edge, giving us a seamless transition between faces.

 Note that there are three parameters for texture wrapping: R, S, and T. That's because we're dealing with a three-dimensional texture type now, so each axis must be accounted for.

Lastly, another helper method is invoked for the creation of the buffers, just before we unbind the texture as we're done with it.

The creation of the cubemap faces, once again, is similar to how we set up its 2D counterpart back in Chapter 7, *One Step Forward, One Level Down – OpenGL Basics*, but the trick is to do it once for each face:

```
void CubeTexture::CreateFaces() {
    glBindTexture(GL_TEXTURE_CUBE_MAP, m_textureID);
    for (auto face = 0; face < 6; ++face) {
        glTexImage2D(GL_TEXTURE_CUBE_MAP_POSITIVE_X + face, 0, GL_RGBA,
            TextureWidth, TextureHeight, 0, GL_RGBA,
            GL_UNSIGNED_BYTE, nullptr);
    }
}
```

Once the texture is bound, we iterate over each face and use `glTexImage2D` to set the face up. Each face is treated as a 2D texture, so this should really be nothing new to look at. Note, however, the use of the `GL_TEXTURE_CUBE_MAP_POSITIVE_X` definition usage is the first argument. 2D textures would take in a `GL_TEXTURE_2D` definition, but because cubemaps are stored in an unfolded manner, getting this part right is important.

 There are six definitions of `GL_TEXTURE_CUBE_MAP_*`. They're all defined in a row of +X, -X, +Y, -Y, +Z, and -Z, which is why we can use some basic arithmetic to pass in the correct face to the function by simply adding an integer to the definition.

Clearing the cubemap texture is relatively easy:

```
void CubeTexture::Clear() {
  glClearColor(1.f, 1.f, 1.f, 1.f);
  glClear(GL_COLOR_BUFFER_BIT | GL_DEPTH_BUFFER_BIT);
}
```

Note that we're specifying the clear color as white, because that represents *infinite distance from the light* in a shadow map.

Finally, sampling the cubemap is actually not any different from sampling a regular 2D texture:

```
void CubeTexture::SamplingBind(unsigned int l_unit) {
  assert(l_unit >= 0 && l_unit <= 31);
  glActiveTexture(GL_TEXTURE0 + l_unit);
  glEnable(GL_TEXTURE_CUBE_MAP);
  glBindTexture(GL_TEXTURE_CUBE_MAP, m_textureID);
}
void CubeTexture::SamplingUnbind(unsigned int l_unit) {
  assert(l_unit >= 0 && l_unit <= 31);
  glActiveTexture(GL_TEXTURE0 + l_unit);
  glBindTexture(GL_TEXTURE_CUBE_MAP, 0);
  glDisable(GL_TEXTURE_CUBE_MAP);
}
```

Both binding and unbinding for sampling requires us to pass in the texture unit we want to use. Once the unit is active, we should enable the use of cubemaps and then bind the cubemap texture handle. The reverse of this procedure should be followed when unbinding the texture.

Keep in mind that the respective `sampler2D`/`samplerCube` uniforms inside fragment shaders are set to hold the unit ID of the texture they're sampling. When a texture is bound, the specific ID of that unit will be used to access it in a shader from then on, not the actual texture handle.

Rendering to an off-screen buffer

Something we didn't cover in Chapter 7, *One Step Forward, One Level Down – OpenGL Basics* is rendering a scene to a buffer image, rather than drawing directly onscreen. Luckily, because OpenGL operates as a giant state machine, it's just a matter of invoking the right functions at the right time, and doesn't involve us having to redesign the rendering procedures in any way.

In order to render to a texture object, we must use what is called a **framebuffer**. It's a very basic object that directs draw calls to a texture the FBO is bound to. While FBOs are useful for color information, they don't carry the depth components with them. A **renderbuffer** object is used for that very purpose of attaching additional components to the FBO.

The first step to drawing something offscreen is creating a FRAMEBUFFER object and a RENDERBUFFER object:

```
void CubeTexture::CreateBuffers() {
  glGenFramebuffers(1, &m_fbo);
  glBindFramebuffer(GL_FRAMEBUFFER, m_fbo);
  glGenRenderbuffers(1, &m_rbo);
  glBindRenderbuffer(GL_RENDERBUFFER, m_rbo);

  glRenderbufferStorage(GL_RENDERBUFFER, GL_DEPTH_COMPONENT24,
    TextureWidth, TextureHeight);
  glFramebufferRenderbuffer(GL_FRAMEBUFFER, GL_DEPTH_ATTACHMENT,
    GL_RENDERBUFFER, m_rbo);
  auto status = glCheckFramebufferStatus(GL_FRAMEBUFFER);
  if (status != GL_FRAMEBUFFER_COMPLETE) { ... } // Print status.
  glBindFramebuffer(GL_FRAMEBUFFER, 0);
}
```

After the buffers have been generated, the render buffer needs to have some storage allocated for any additional components it will provide. In this case, we're simply dealing with the depth component.

The GL_DEPTH_COMPONENT24 simply indicates that each depth pixel has a size of 24 bits. This definition can be replaced with a basic GL_DEPTH_COMPONENT, which will allow the application to choose the pixel size.

The depth render buffer is then attached to the FBO as a depth attachment. Finally, if there were any errors during this procedure, glCheckFramebufferStatus is used to catch them. The next line simply prints out the status variable using std::cout.

 Frame buffers should always be unbound when no longer used, using glBindFramebuffer(GL_FRAMEBUFFER, 0)! That's the only way we're ever going to go back to rendering subsequent geometry to the screen, rather than the buffer texture.

Now that we have the buffers set up, let's use them! When drawing to a buffer texture is desired, it's first necessary to bind the frame buffer:

```
void CubeTexture::RenderingBind() {
  glBindFramebuffer(GL_FRAMEBUFFER, m_fbo);
}
void CubeTexture::RenderingUnbind() {
  glBindFramebuffer(GL_FRAMEBUFFER, 0); // Render to screen.
}
```

Unbinding the FBO is necessary after we're done with it. Using RenderingUnbind() means that any subsequent geometry will be drawn onscreen.

Of course, just because the FBO is bound, doesn't mean we're going to magically start drawing to the cubemap. In order to do that, we must draw to one face at a time by binding the frame buffer to the desired face of the cubemap:

```
void CubeTexture::RenderToFace(unsigned int l_face) {
  glFramebufferTexture2D(GL_FRAMEBUFFER, GL_COLOR_ATTACHMENT0,
    GL_TEXTURE_CUBE_MAP_POSITIVE_X + l_face, m_textureID, 0);
  Clear();
}
```

The first argument to glFramebufferTexture2D simply indicates we're dealing with an FBO. We then specify that we want to use GL_COLOR_ATTACHMENT0. Frame buffers can have multiple attachments and use shaders to output different data to each one of them. For our purposes, we're only going to need to use one attachment.

Because we're rendering to one face of the cubemap at a time, basic definition arithmetic is, once again, used to pick the correct face of the cube to render to. Finally, the texture handle and mipmapping level are passed in at the very end, just before Clear() is invoked to clear the face we currently bound to complete white.

Rendering the shadow maps

We now have everything we need in order to start rendering shadow maps of our scene. Some rather significant changes are going to have to be made to the `LightManager` class in order to support this functionality, not to mention properly store and use these shadow map textures during later passes. Let's see what changes we need to make in order to make this happen.

Modifying the light manager

First, let's make some adjustments to the light manager class definition. We're going to need a couple of methods to add shadow caster prototypes, add actual shadow casting objects, and render the shadow maps:

```
class LightManager {
public:
    ...
    const std::string& AddCasterPrototype(const std::string& l_name,
        std::unique_ptr<ShadowCasterPrototype> l_caster);
    ShadowCaster* AddShadowCaster(const std::string& l_prototypeName);
    ShadowCasterPrototype* GetPrototype(const std::string& l_name);
    ...
private:
    ...
    void DrawShadowMap(GLuint l_shadowShader, LightBase& l_light,
        unsigned int l_texture);
    ...
    ShadowCasterPrototypes m_casterPrototypes;
    ShadowCasters m_shadowCasters;
    GL_Camera m_perspectiveCamera;
    std::unique_ptr<CubeTexture> m_cubeTextures[LightsPerPass];
    ...
};
```

In addition to the aforementioned methods, the `LightManager` class is also going to need to store extra information to support these changes. A list of both shadow primitive prototypes and the primitives themselves will need to be used to manage the entities that have to cast shadows. Additionally, we need to have the camera class that will be used as the point of view of the light.

Lastly, an array of cubemap textures is required, since each light onscreen will be potentially seeing the scene from a completely different point of view, of course. The size of this array is simply the number of lights we're dealing with per shader pass, because these cubemap textures only need to exist for as long as they're being sampled. Once the lighting pass for those particular lights is over, the textures can be re-used for the next batch.

Implementing the light manager changes

The adjustments to the constructor of the `LightManager` class are fairly simple to make this work:

```
LightManager::LightManager(...) : ...,
  m_perspectiveCamera({0.f, 0.f, 0.f}, 90.f,
    CubeTexture::TextureWidth / CubeTexture::TextureHeight,
    1.f, 200.f)
{
  ...
  for (auto i = 0; i < LightsPerPass; ++i) {
    m_cubeTextures[i] = std::make_unique<CubeTexture>();
  }
}
```

The first thing we need to worry about is setting up the perspective camera correctly. It's initialized to be positioned at absolute zero coordinates in the world, and has its field of view angle set to **90 degrees**. The aspect ratio of the perspective camera is obviously going to be *1*, because the width and height of the textures we're using for rendering shadow casters to are identical. The view frustum minimum value is set to *1.f*, which ensures that the geometry won't be rendered if the light is intersecting with a face. The maximum value, however, will change for each light, depending on its radius. This default value isn't really important.

 Setting the field of view angle of **90** degrees for rendering a scene to a cubemap texture is important, as that's the only way the scene is going to be captured completely for each direction the camera looks at. Going too low on this value means there are going to be blind spots, and going too high will cause overlapping.

The last thing we need to do in the constructor is make sure that all cubemap textures are allocated properly.

Next, let's worry about adding shadow caster prototypes to the light manager:

```cpp
const std::string& LightManager::AddCasterPrototype(
  const std::string& l_name,
  std::unique_ptr<ShadowCasterPrototype> l_caster)
{
  auto itr = m_casterPrototypes.find(l_name);
  if (itr != m_casterPrototypes.end()) {
    l_caster.release(); return l_name;
  }
  for (auto& prototype : m_casterPrototypes) {
    if (*prototype.second == *l_caster) {
      l_caster.release(); return prototype.first;
    }
  }
  m_window->GetRenderWindow()->setActive(true);
  l_caster->UploadVertices();
  m_casterPrototypes.emplace(l_name, std::move(l_caster));
  return l_name;
}
```

When adding a prototype, the caller of this particular method will provide a string identifier for it, as well as move its established and allocated smart pointer to the second argument after the vertices have been properly loaded. First, we make sure the name provided as an argument isn't already taken. If it is, that same string is returned back just after the memory for the prototype provided as an argument is released.

The second test makes sure that a prototype with the exact arrangement of vertices doesn't already exist under a different name, by iterating over every stored prototype and using the == operator we implemented earlier to compare the two. If something is found, the name of that prototype is returned instead, just after the l_caster is released.

Finally, since we can be sure that the prototype we're adding is completely unique, the render window is set to active. UploadVertices on the object is invoked to send the data to the GPU and the prototype is placed inside the designated container.

Using sf::RenderWindow::setActive(true) ensures that the main context is used while the vertices are uploaded. OpenGL **does not** share its states among different contexts, and since SFML likes to keep a number of different contexts alive internally, it's imperative to make sure the main context is selected during all operations.

Adding shadow casters themselves is relatively easy as well:

```
ShadowCaster* LightManager::AddShadowCaster(
  const std::string& l_prototypeName)
{
  auto prototype = GetPrototype(l_prototypeName);
  if (!prototype) { return nullptr; }
  m_shadowCasters.emplace_back();
  auto& caster = m_shadowCasters.back();
  caster = std::make_unique<ShadowCaster>();
  caster->m_prototype = prototype;
  return caster.get();
}
```

This method only takes a string identifier for the prototype to be used, and allocates space for a new shadow caster object, provided the prototype with said name exists. Note the line just before the `return` statement. It ensures that the located prototype is passed to the shadow caster, so that it can use the prototype later.

Obtaining the prototypes is incredibly simple, and only requires a lookup into an `unordered_map` container:

```
ShadowCasterPrototype* LightManager::GetPrototype(
  const std::string& l_name)
{
  auto itr = m_casterPrototypes.find(l_name);
  if (itr == m_casterPrototypes.end()) { return nullptr; }
  return itr->second.get();
}
```

We now only have one task at hand drawing the shadow maps!

Drawing the actual shadow maps

In order to keep this manageable and compartmentalized, we're going to break down the `DrawShadowMap` method into smaller parts that we can discuss independently of the rest of the code. Let's start by looking at the actual blueprint of the method:

```
void LightManager::DrawShadowMap(GLuint l_shadowShader,
  LightBase& l_light, unsigned int l_texture)
{
  ...
}
```

First, it takes in a handle for the shadow pass shader. This is about as raw as it gets, since the handle is a simple unsigned integer we're going to bind to before drawing. The second argument is a reference to a light that we're currently drawing the shadow map for. Lastly, we have an *unsigned integer* that serves as the ID for the light that's being rendered in the current pass. In the case of having 4 lights per shader pass, this value will range from 0 to 3, and then get reset in the next pass. It is going to be used as an index for the cubemap texture lookup.

Now, it's time to really get into the actual rendering of the shadow maps, starting with enabling necessary OpenGL features:

```
glEnable(GL_DEPTH_TEST);
glEnable(GL_CULL_FACE);
glCullFace(GL_FRONT);
```

The first and most obvious feature we're going to be using here is the depth test. This ensures that different shadow caster geometry isn't rendered in the wrong order, overlapping each other. Then, we're going to be performing some face culling. Unlike normal geometry, however, we're going to be culling the front faces only. Drawing the back faces of shadow geometry will ensure that the front faces of sprites we're using will be lit, since the depth stored in the shadow map is the depth of the very back of the shadow-casting primitives.

```
glUseProgram(l_shadowShader);
auto u_model = glGetUniformLocation(l_shadowShader, "m_model");
auto u_view = glGetUniformLocation(l_shadowShader, "m_view");
auto u_proj = glGetUniformLocation(l_shadowShader, "m_proj");
auto u_lightPos = glGetUniformLocation(l_shadowShader,"lightPos");
auto u_frustumFar = glGetUniformLocation(l_shadowShader,
   "frustumFar");
```

The next part here deals with actually binding the shadow pass shader and fetching locations of different shader uniform variables. We have a model matrix uniform, a view matrix uniform, a projection matrix uniform, a light position uniform, and the frustum far uniform to update.

```
auto& texture = m_cubeTextures[l_texture];
auto l_pos = l_light.m_lightPos;
m_perspectiveCamera.SetPosition({ l_pos.x, l_pos.z, l_pos.y });
glViewport(
   0, 0, CubeTexture::TextureWidth, CubeTexture::TextureHeight);
texture->RenderingBind();
glUniform3f(u_lightPos, l_pos.x, l_pos.z, l_pos.y);
```

This next part of the code obtains a reference to the appropriate cubemap texture for the particular light, storing the light position, and positioning the perspective camera at that exact position.

 Note the swapped *Z* and *Y* coordinates. By default, OpenGL deals with the right-hand coordinate system. It also deals with the default *up* direction being the +*Y* axis. Our lights store coordinates using the +*Z* axis as the *up* direction.

After the camera is set up, `glViewport` is invoked to resize the render target to the size of the cubemap texture. The cubemap is then bound to for rendering and we submit the light position uniform to the shaders. Just as before, the *Z* and *Y* directions here are swapped.

With the setup out of the way, we can actually begin rendering the scene for each face of the cubemap:

```
for (auto face = 0; face < 6; ++face) {
  texture->RenderToFace(face);
  m_perspectiveCamera.SetForwardDir(CubeMapDirections[face]);
  m_perspectiveCamera.SetUpDir(CubeMapUpDirections[face]);
  m_perspectiveCamera.SetFrustumFar(l_light.m_radius);
  m_perspectiveCamera.RecalculatePerspective();
  auto viewMat = m_perspectiveCamera.GetViewMatrix();
  auto& projMat = m_perspectiveCamera.GetProjectionMatrix();
  glUniformMatrix4fv(u_view, 1, GL_FALSE, &viewMat[0][0]);
  glUniformMatrix4fv(u_proj, 1, GL_FALSE, &projMat[0][0]);
  glUniform1f(u_frustumFar, m_perspectiveCamera.GetFrustumFar());
  for (auto& caster : m_shadowCasters) {
    auto modelMat = caster->m_transform.GetModelMatrix();
    glUniformMatrix4fv(u_model, 1, GL_FALSE, &modelMat[0][0]);
    caster->m_prototype->Draw();
  }
}
```

The cubemap texture is first told which face we wish to render to in order to set up the FBO correctly. The forward and up directions for that particular face are then passed to the light's camera, along with the frustum far value, being the radius of the light. The perspective projection matrix is then recalculated, and both the view and projection matrices are retrieved from `GL_Camera` to pass to the shader, along with the frustum far value.

Lastly, for each of the 6 faces of the cubemap, we iterate over all of the shadow caster objects, retrieve their model matrices, pass them into the shader, and invoke the prototype's `Draw()` method, which takes care of the rendering.

After all of the texture's faces have been drawn to, we need to set the state back to what it was before rendering shadow maps:

```
texture->RenderingUnbind();
glViewport(
    0, 0, m_window->GetWindowSize().x, m_window->GetWindowSize().y);
glDisable(GL_DEPTH_TEST);
glDisable(GL_CULL_FACE);
glCullFace(GL_BACK);
```

The texture is first unbound for rendering, which sets the FBO to 0 and allows us to draw to the screen again. The viewport is then resized back to the original size our window had, and the depth test, along with face culling, are both disabled.

The shadow pass shaders

The C++ side of shadow mapping is finished, but we still have some logic to cover. The shaders here play an important role of actually translating the vertex information into depth. Let's take a look at the vertex shader first:

```
in vec3 position;
uniform mat4 m_model;
uniform mat4 m_view;
uniform mat4 m_proj;
uniform vec3 lightPos;
uniform float frustumFar;
out float distance;

void main() {
  vec4 worldCoords = m_model * vec4(position, 1.0);
  float d = length(worldCoords.xyz - lightPos);
  d /= frustumFar;
  gl_Position = m_proj * m_view * worldCoords;
  distance = d;
}
```

The `vec3` input coordinates of a vertex position we receive on the GPU are in local space, which means they have to be passed through a number of matrices to be brought to world, view, and clip spaces in that order. The world coordinates are calculated first and stored separately, because they're used to determine the distance between the vertex and the light. That distance is stored in the local variable d, which is divided by the frustum far value to convert it to a range of *[0;1]*. The position of the vertex is then converted to clip space by using the world, view, and projection matrices, and the distance value is passed on to the fragment shader, where it's stored as a color for a particular pixel:

```
in float distance;

void main() {
   gl_FragColor = vec4(distance, distance, distance, 1.0);
}
```

Remember that the output variables from the vertex shader are interpolated between the vertices, so each fragment in between those vertices will be shaded in a gradient-like manner.

Results

While we still don't have any actual geometry in the project to see the results of this, once we're done, it will look like the following screenshot:

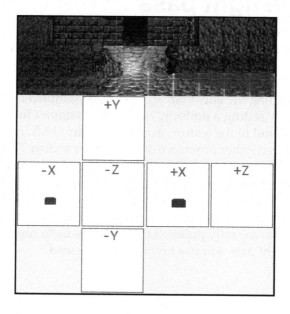

In this particular case, the primitives were extremely close to the light, so they're shaded really dark. Given greater distances, a particular face of a shadow map would look a little something like this, where *#1* is a primitive close to the camera, *#2* is further away, and *#3* is near the far end of the view frustum:

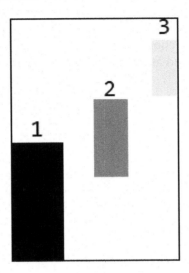

Adapting the light pass

With the shadow maps rendered, it may be extremely tempting to try and sample them in our existing code, since the hard part is over, right? Well, not entirely. While we were extremely close with our previous approach, sadly, sampling of cubemap textures is the only thing that we couldn't do because of SFML. The sampling itself isn't really the problem, as much as binding the cubemap textures to be sampled is. Remember that sampling is performed by setting a uniform value of the sampler inside the shader to the **texture unit ID** that's bound to the texture in our C++ code. SFML resets these units each time something is rendered either onscreen, or to a render texture. The reason we haven't had this problem before is because we can set the uniforms of the shaders through SFML's `sf::Shader` class, which keeps track of references to textures and binds them to appropriate units when a shader is used for rendering. That's all fine and good, except for when the time comes to sample other types of textures that SFML doesn't support, which includes cubemaps. This is the only problem that requires us to completely cut SFML out of the picture during the light pass and use raw OpenGL instead.

Replacing the m_fullScreenQuad

First things first, replacing the `sf::VertexArray` object inside the `LightManager` class that's used to redraw an entire buffer texture, which we were utilizing for multipass rendering. Since SFML has to be completely cut out of the picture here, we can't use its built-in vertex array class and render a quad that covers the entire screen. Otherwise, SFML will force its own state on before rendering, which isn't going to work with our system properly as it re-assigns its own texture units each time.

Defining a generic frame buffer object

Just like before, we need to create a frame buffer object in order to render to a texture, rather than the screen. Since we've already done this once before for a cubemap, let's breeze through the implementation of a generic FBO class for 2D textures:

```
class GenericFBO {
public:
    GenericFBO(const sf::Vector2u& l_size);
    ~GenericFBO();

    void Create();

    void RenderingBind(GLuint l_texture);
    void RenderingUnbind();
private:
    sf::Vector2u m_size;
    GLuint m_FBO;
    GLuint m_RBO;
};
```

The main difference here is the fact that we're using variable sizes for textures now. They may vary at some point, so it's a good idea to store the size internally, rather than using constant values.

Implementing a generic frame buffer object

The constructor and destructor of this class, once again, deals with resource management:

```
GenericFBO::GenericFBO(const sf::Vector2u& l_size) :
  m_size(l_size), m_FBO(0), m_RBO(0) {}

GenericFBO::~GenericFBO() {
  if (m_FBO) { glDeleteFramebuffers(1, &m_FBO); }
  if (m_RBO) { glDeleteRenderbuffers(1, &m_RBO); }
}
```

We're not storing a texture handle, because that too will vary depending on circumstances.

Creating the buffers for this class is pretty similar to what we've done before:

```
void GenericFBO::Create() {
  if (!m_FBO) { glCreateFramebuffers(1, &m_FBO); }
  glBindFramebuffer(GL_FRAMEBUFFER, m_FBO);
  if (!m_RBO) { glCreateRenderbuffers(1, &m_RBO); }
  glBindRenderbuffer(GL_RENDERBUFFER, m_RBO);

  glRenderbufferStorage(GL_RENDERBUFFER, GL_DEPTH_COMPONENT24,
    m_size.x, m_size.y);
  glFramebufferRenderbuffer(GL_FRAMEBUFFER, GL_DEPTH_ATTACHMENT,
    GL_RENDERBUFFER, m_RBO);
  auto status = glCheckFramebufferStatus(GL_FRAMEBUFFER);
  if (status != GL_FRAMEBUFFER_COMPLETE) { ... } // Print status.
  glBindFramebuffer(GL_FRAMEBUFFER, 0);
  glBindRenderbuffer(GL_RENDERBUFFER, 0);
}
```

Just like the cubemap textures, we need to attach a depth render buffer to the FBO. After allocation and binding, the FBO is checked for errors and both buffers are unbound.

Rendering FBO points to a 2D texture is much easier. Binding for rendering needs to take a handle to a texture, because one is not stored internally, since this is a generic class that will be used with many different textures:

```
void GenericFBO::RenderingBind(GLuint l_texture) {
  glBindFramebuffer(GL_FRAMEBUFFER, m_FBO);
  glFramebufferTexture2D(GL_FRAMEBUFFER, GL_COLOR_ATTACHMENT0,
    GL_TEXTURE_2D, l_texture, 0);
}

void GenericFBO::RenderingUnbind() {
  glBindFramebuffer(GL_FRAMEBUFFER, 0);
}
```

Once the FBO is bound, we again invoke `glFramebufferTexture2D`. This time, however, we use `GL_TEXTURE_2D` as the type of the texture, and pass in the `l_texture` argument into the function instead.

Rendering from a buffer to another buffer in OpenGL

During our potentially numerous light passes, we're going to need a way of redrawing every pixel onscreen to the buffer texture just like we did before, except without using SFML this time. For this purpose, we're going to construct a quad that has four vertices, all positioned in screen coordinates, and covers the screen entirely. These vertices are also going to have texture coordinates that will be used to sample the buffer texture. A basic structure of such vertex, similar to the one we created in `Chapter 7`, *One Step Forward, One Level Down – OpenGL Basics* looks like this:

```
struct BasicVertex {
  glm::vec3 m_pos;
  glm::vec2 m_tex;
};
```

This small structure will be used by the quad primitive that will cover the entire screen.

Creating a basic quad primitive

The quad primitive, just like any other piece of geometry, must be pushed to the GPU for later use. Let's construct a very basic class that will break down this functionality into manageable methods we can easily call from other classes:

```
class BasicQuadPrimitive {
public:
  BasicQuadPrimitive();
  ~BasicQuadPrimitive();

  void Create();
  void Bind();
  void Render();
  void Unbind();
private:
  GLuint m_VAO;
  GLuint m_VBO;
  GLuint m_indices;
};
```

Once again, we have methods for creating, rendering, binding, and unbinding the primitive. The class stores the m_VAO, m_VBO, and m_indices of this primitive, which all need to be filled out.

Implementing the quad primitive class

Construction and destruction of this class, once again, all take care of the resource allocation/de-allocation:

```
BasicQuadPrimitive::BasicQuadPrimitive() : m_VAO(0),
  m_VBO(0), m_indices(0) {}

BasicQuadPrimitive::~BasicQuadPrimitive() {
  if (m_VAO) { glDeleteVertexArrays(1, &m_VAO); }
  if (m_VBO) { glDeleteBuffers(1, &m_VBO); }
  if (m_indices) { glDeleteBuffers(1, &m_indices); }
}
```

Creating and uploading the primitive to the GPU is exactly the same as before:

```
void BasicQuadPrimitive::Create() {
  glGenVertexArrays(1, &m_VAO);
  glBindVertexArray(m_VAO);
  glGenBuffers(1, &m_VBO);
  glGenBuffers(1, &m_indices);

  glBindBuffer(GL_ARRAY_BUFFER, m_VBO);

  BasicVertex vertices[4] = {
    //    x     y     z        u     v
    { { -1.f, 1.f, 0.f }, { 0.f, 1.f } }, // Top-left.
    { { 1.f, 1.f, 0.f }, { 1.f, 1.f } },  // Top-right.
    { { 1.f, -1.f, 0.f }, { 1.f, 0.f } }, // Bottom-right.
    { { -1.f, -1.f, 0.f }, { 0.f, 0.f } } // Bottom-left.
  };

  auto stride = sizeof(vertices[0]);
  auto texCoordOffset = sizeof(vertices[0].m_pos);
  glBufferData(GL_ARRAY_BUFFER, 4 * sizeof(vertices[0]),
    &vertices[0], GL_STATIC_DRAW);
  glEnableVertexAttribArray(0);
  glVertexAttribPointer(0, 3, GL_FLOAT, GL_FALSE, stride, 0);
  glEnableVertexAttribArray(1);
  glVertexAttribPointer(1, 2, GL_FLOAT, GL_FALSE, stride,
    (void*)texCoordOffset);

  glBindBuffer(GL_ELEMENT_ARRAY_BUFFER, m_indices);
```

```
unsigned int indices[6] = { 0, 1, 2, 2, 3, 0 }; // CW!
glBufferData(GL_ELEMENT_ARRAY_BUFFER, 6 * sizeof(unsigned int),
    &indices[0], GL_STATIC_DRAW);
Unbind();
}
```

The main difference here is that we're defining the vertices inside the method, since they're never going to change. The vertex attribute pointers are set up after the data is pushed onto the GPU; indices get defined in a clockwise manner (default for SFML), and pushed to the GPU.

Binding and unbinding the buffers for rendering is, once again, exactly the same as with all of the other geometry for OpenGL:

```
void BasicQuadPrimitive::Bind() {
  if (!m_VAO) { return; }
  glBindVertexArray(m_VAO);
  glBindBuffer(GL_ARRAY_BUFFER, m_VBO);
  glBindBuffer(GL_ELEMENT_ARRAY_BUFFER, m_indices);
}

void BasicQuadPrimitive::Unbind() {
  if (!m_VAO) { return; }
  glBindBuffer(GL_ELEMENT_ARRAY_BUFFER, 0);
  glBindBuffer(GL_ARRAY_BUFFER, 0);
  glBindVertexArray(0);
}
```

Since we're using indices, rendering the quad is achieved by calling `glDrawElements`, just like before:

```
void BasicQuadPrimitive::Render() {
  glDrawElements(GL_TRIANGLES, 6, GL_UNSIGNED_INT, 0);
}
```

This concludes the necessary preparations for rendering from an offscreen buffer to the screen.

Making the changes to the light manager

Given the complete re-architecture of our rendering process for shadows, it's obvious some things are going to have to change within the `LightManager` class. First, let's start with some new data we're going to need to store:

```
using MaterialHandles = std::unordered_map<
```

```
  MaterialMapType, unsigned int>;
using MaterialUniformNames = std::unordered_map<
  MaterialMapType, std::string>;
```

The `MaterialHandles` and `MaterialUniformNames` containers will be used to store the names and locations of uniforms in our light pass shader. This is an effort made entirely to make the mapping of new material map types and uniforms much easier by automating it.

With that out of the way, let's take a look at the `LightManager` class definition and the changes we need to make to it:

```
class LightManager {
  ...
private:
  void GenerateMaterials();
  void Bind2DTextures(GLuint l_program, int l_pass);
  void Unbind2DTextures();
  void SubmitLightUniforms(GLuint l_program,
    unsigned int l_lightID, const LightBase& l_light);
  ...
  MaterialHandles m_materialHandles;
  MaterialUniformNames m_materialNames;
  //sf::VertexArray m_fullScreenQuad;
  GenericFBO m_rendererFBO;
  BasicQuadPrimitive m_fullScreenQuad;
  ...
};
```

In addition to creating some new helper methods for generating material names, binding and unbinding all of the necessary 2D textures for the light pass sampling, and submitting the uniforms of a given light to the light pass shader, we're also storing the material names and handles. The `m_fullScreenQuad` class is replaced by our own class, and to accompany it, we have the `GenericFBO` object that will help us render to an offscreen buffer.

Implementing light manager changes

The constructor of our `LightManager` class now has additional work to do in setting up all of the new data members we added:

```
LightManager::LightManager(...) : ...,
  m_rendererFBO(l_window->GetWindowSize()), ...
{
  m_window->GetRenderWindow()->setActive(true);
  GenerateMaterials();
  m_materialNames[MaterialMapType::Diffuse] = "DiffuseMap";
```

```
m_materialNames[MaterialMapType::Normal] = "NormalMap";
m_materialNames[MaterialMapType::Specular] = "SpecularMap";
m_materialNames[MaterialMapType::Height] = "HeightMap";
m_window->GetRenderWindow()->setActive(true);
m_rendererFBO.Create();
m_window->GetRenderWindow()->setActive(true);
m_fullScreenQuad.Create();
    ...
}
```

First, the FBO we'll be using is set up in the initializer list to hold the size of our window. We then ensure that the main OpenGL context is active by activating our window, and invoke the `GenerateMaterials` method that will take care of material texture allocation and storage of the texture handles for the same.

The uniform sampler2D names for all material types are then stored in the appropriate container. These names have to match the ones inside the light pass shader!

Finally, the main OpenGL context is selected again and the FBO is created. We do this one more time for the `m_fullScreenQuad` class as well.

The `GenerateMaterials()` method can be implemented like this:

```
void LightManager::GenerateMaterials() {
  auto windowSize = m_window->GetWindowSize();
  for (auto i = 0; i <
    static_cast<int>(MaterialMapType::COUNT); ++i)
  {
    auto type = static_cast<MaterialMapType>(i);
    auto pair = m_materialMaps.emplace(type,
      std::move(std::make_unique<sf::RenderTexture>()));
    auto& texture = pair.first->second;
    texture->create(windowSize.x, windowSize.y);
    m_materialHandles[type] = texture->
      getTexture().getNativeHandle();
  }
}
```

It iterates over each material type and creates a new texture for it, just like we did before. The only difference here is that we also store the handle of the newly created texture in `m_materialHandles`, in an effort to tie a specific `MaterialMapType` to an existing texture. We're still using SFML's render textures, because they did a fine job at managing 2D resources.

Binding all of the necessary textures to be sampled in the light pass shader would look like this:

```
void LightManager::Bind2DTextures(GLuint l_program, int l_pass) {
  auto finishedTexture = m_window->GetRenderer()->
    GetFinishedTexture()->getTexture().getNativeHandle();
  auto lastPassHandle = (l_pass == 0 ?
    m_materialHandles[MaterialMapType::Diffuse] :
    finishedTexture);
  m_window->GetRenderWindow()->setActive(true);
  glActiveTexture(GL_TEXTURE0);
  glBindTexture(GL_TEXTURE_2D, lastPassHandle);
  glUniform1i(glGetUniformLocation(l_program, "LastPass"), 0);

  for (int i = 0;i<static_cast<int>(MaterialMapType::COUNT);++i) {
    auto type = static_cast<MaterialMapType>(i);
    glActiveTexture(GL_TEXTURE1 + i);
    glBindTexture(GL_TEXTURE_2D, m_materialMaps[type]->
      getTexture().getNativeHandle());
    auto uniform = glGetUniformLocation(l_program,
      m_materialNames[type].c_str());
    glUniform1i(uniform, i + 1);
  }
}
```

This particular method will be used inside the `RenderScene` method for rendering lights. It takes two arguments: a handler for the light pass shader, and the ID of the current pass taking place.

The finished texture handle is then obtained from the `Renderer` class. Just like before, we must pass the right texture as the `"LastPass"` uniform in the light pass shader. If we're still on the very first pass, a diffuse texture is used instead.

 Passing textures to a shader for sampling simply means we're sending one integer to the shader. That integer represents the texture unit we want to sample.

The render window is then set to active once again to make sure the main OpenGL context is active. We then bind to the texture unit 0 and use it for the `"LastPass"` uniform. All of the other materials are taken care of inside a `for` loop that runs once for each material type. The texture unit `GL_TEXTURE1 + i` is activated, which ensures that we start from unit 1 and go up, since unit 0 is already being used. The appropriate texture is then bound to, and the uniform of the correct sampler for that material type is located. The uniform is then set to the texture unit we've just activated.

Unbinding these textures is easier still:

```
void LightManager::Unbind2DTextures() {
  for (int i = 0; i <=
    static_cast<int>(MaterialMapType::COUNT); ++i)
  {
    glActiveTexture(GL_TEXTURE0 + i);
    glBindTexture(GL_TEXTURE_2D, 0);
  }
}
```

Note that we're now iterating from 0 up and including the material type count. This ensures that even texture unit 0 is unbound, since we're activating `GL_TEXTURE0 + i`.

Re-working the light pass

Finally, we'll take a look at the `RenderScene()` method. For clarity, we're going to break it down into smaller chunks, just like before:

```
void LightManager::RenderScene() {
  ...
}
```

First, let's start at the top of the method and set up some variables that are going to be used throughout:

```
... // Inside the RenderScene() method.
auto renderer = m_window->GetRenderer();
auto passes = static_cast<int>(
  std::ceil(static_cast<float>(m_lights.size()) / LightsPerPass));
auto& beginning = m_lights.begin();
auto LightPassShaderHandle = renderer->
  GetShader("LightPass")->getNativeHandle();
auto ShadowPassShaderHandle = renderer->
  GetShader("ShadowPass")->getNativeHandle();
auto CurrentShaderHandle = (renderer->GetCurrentShader() ?
  renderer->GetCurrentShader()->getNativeHandle() : 0);

auto window = m_window->GetRenderWindow();
```

The `passes` variable works out how many passes we're going to need with the given number of lights. We then obtain a reference to the beginning of the light container, the light pass shader handle, the shadow pass shader handle, and the shader handle of the currently used shader that's set up inside the `Renderer` object, if there is one. Lastly, the `window` pointer is obtained for easy access.

Still inside the `RenderScene` method, we enter into a `for` loop that's going to iterate for each pass:

```
... // Inside the RenderScene() method.
for (int pass = 0; pass < passes; ++pass) {
  auto& first = beginning + (pass * LightsPerPass);
  auto LightCount = 0;
  ...
}
```

Another reference to a light container iterator is obtained. This time, it points to the first light for this current pass. Also, a `LightCount` variable is set up to keep track of the number of lights rendered for the current pass so far.

Before we go on to do any actual light rendering, we need to draw the shadow maps for the lights we're going to be using in this pass:

```
... // Inside the pass loop.
for (int lightID = 0; lightID < LightsPerPass; ++lightID) {
  // Drawing shadow maps.
  auto& light = first + lightID;
  if (light == m_lights.end()) { break; }
  window->setActive(true);
  DrawShadowMap(ShadowPassShaderHandle, *light, lightID);
  ++LightCount;
}
```

Here, we iterate over each light that belongs to this pass. A check needs to be made to make sure we haven't reached the end of the container, however. Provided that's not the case, the main OpenGL context is enabled by calling `setActive(true)`, and the shadow map for the current light is drawn to the cubemap buffer texture. The `LightCount` is then incremented to let the rest of the code know how many lights we're dealing with during this pass.

After shadow maps have been rendered, it's time to actually bind the light pass shader and begin passing information to it:

```
... // Inside the pass loop.
glUseProgram(LightPassShaderHandle);
Bind2DTextures(LightPassShaderHandle, pass);
glUniform3f(glGetUniformLocation(LightPassShaderHandle,
    "AmbientLight"),
  m_ambientLight.m_lightColor.x,
  m_ambientLight.m_lightColor.y,
  m_ambientLight.m_lightColor.z);
glUniform1i(glGetUniformLocation(LightPassShaderHandle,
```

```
    "LightCount"), LightCount);
  glUniform1i(glGetUniformLocation(LightPassShaderHandle,
    "PassNumber"), pass);
```

After the light pass shader has been bound, we must also bind all of the 2D textures of necessary material maps. This is followed by submission of the ambient light uniform, along with the light count, and current pass uniforms.

All of this is great, but we still haven't addressed the main concept that caused a necessity for this massive redesign to begin with the cubemap textures:

```
... // Inside the pass loop.
auto BaseCubeMapUnit = static_cast<int>(MaterialMapType::COUNT)+1;
for (int lightID = 0; lightID < LightCount; ++lightID) {
  auto& light = first + lightID; // Verified by previous loop.
  SubmitLightUniforms(LightPassShaderHandle, lightID, *light);
  // Bind the CUBE texture of the light.
  m_cubeTextures[lightID]->SamplingBind(BaseCubeMapUnit +lightID);
  auto ShadowMapName = "ShadowMap["+std::to_string(lightID)+"]";
  glUniform1i(glGetUniformLocation(LightPassShaderHandle,
    ShadowMapName.c_str()), BaseCubeMapUnit + lightID);
}
```

The texture unit for binding the very first cubemap texture is defined by simply adding *1* to the count of material map types. We have four types at this moment, and with unit *0* dedicated to the `LastPass` texture, it means units 1-4 will be used for material map textures. This leaves units 5 and up free for other samplers.

Another `for` loop is entered, this time using the `LightCount` variable for maximum value. We've already determined how many lights we're dealing with during the shadow pass, so we don't need to make that check again here.

A reference to a light is fetched and passed into the `SubmitLightUniforms()` method, along with the light pass shader handle and the light number currently being used. The cubemap texture for that specific light is then bound for sampling. Note the use of `BaseCubeMapUnit + lightID`. This ensures that each light gets its own texture unit.

Inside the light pass shader, the shadow map samplers are going to be stored inside an array. Because of this, a string name for each element of the array is constructed based on the current light ID we're working with, and the uniform for the texture unit is sent to the shader.

Finally, because all of the uniforms and textures are properly bound and updated, we can actually invoke the light-pass shader by rendering `m_fullScreenQuad`:

```
... // Inside the pass loop.
m_rendererFBO.RenderingBind(renderer->GetCurrentTexture()->
  getTexture().getNativeHandle());
m_fullScreenQuad.Bind();
m_fullScreenQuad.Render(); // This is where the magic happens!
m_fullScreenQuad.Unbind();
m_rendererFBO.RenderingUnbind();
Unbind2DTextures();
```

First, the FBO is bound to the handle of the current texture being used as a buffer. The quad itself is then bound, rendered, and unbound again. This is all we need to redraw the entire finished buffer texture to the current buffer texture, so the FBO is unbound. The 2D textures are also unbound at this point, since the light pass shader has just commenced executing.

Speaking of unbinding, all of these cubemap textures need to be unbound as well:

```
... // Inside the pass loop.
for (int lightID = 0; lightID < LightCount; ++lightID) {
  m_cubeTextures[lightID]->SamplingUnbind(
    BaseCubeMapUnit + lightID);
}
```

At this point, the very last thing left to do inside the lighting pass loop is to swap the buffer textures inside the `Renderer` class:

```
... // Inside the pass loop.
renderer->SwapTextures();
```

This makes sure the most recent buffer is always stored as the finished texture.

Finally, once the light passes have, commenced, we must clean up the state of everything and actually render the finished buffer texture:

```
... // Right after the pass loop, inside RenderScene().
glUseProgram(CurrentShaderHandle);
window->resetGLStates();
auto currentView = window->getView();
window->setView(window->getDefaultView());
renderer->DrawBufferTexture();
window->setView(currentView);
```

The shader program is first reset to whatever it was before the light pass was executed. The SFML window itself has its OpenGL states reset, because our use of OpenGL functions most likely altered them. Afterwards, we obtain the current window view, reset the window to its default view, draw the buffer texture, and swap the previous view back, just as in Chapter 8, *Let There Be Light! – An Introduction to Advanced Lighting*.

Submitting light uniforms to the shader

One more little piece of code we still haven't covered is the actual light uniform submission to the light pass shader:

```
void LightManager::SubmitLightUniforms(GLuint l_program,
  unsigned int l_lightID, const LightBase& l_light)
{
  auto window = m_window->GetRenderWindow();
  auto id = "Lights[" + std::to_string(l_lightID) + "].";

  sf::Vector2i screenPos = window->mapCoordsToPixel(
    { l_light.m_lightPos.x, l_light.m_lightPos.y },
    window->getView());
  float y = static_cast<float>(
    static_cast<int>(window->getSize().y) - screenPos.y);

  glUniform3f(glGetUniformLocation(l_program,
      (id + "position").c_str()),
    screenPos.x, y, l_light.m_lightPos.z);
  glUniform3f(glGetUniformLocation(l_program,
      (id + "color").c_str()),
    l_light.m_lightColor.x,
    l_light.m_lightColor.y,
    l_light.m_lightColor.z);
  glUniform1f(glGetUniformLocation(l_program,
    (id + "radius").c_str()), l_light.m_radius);
  glUniform1f(glGetUniformLocation(l_program,
    (id + "falloff").c_str()), l_light.m_falloff);
  glUniform1f(glGetUniformLocation(l_program,
      (id + "specularExponent").c_str()),
    l_light.m_specularExponent);
  glUniform1f(glGetUniformLocation(l_program,
      (id + "specularStrength").c_str()),
    l_light.m_specularStrength);
}
```

This chunk of code is pretty much exactly the same as in Chapter 8, *Let There Be Light! – An Introduction to Advanced Lighting,* except it uses raw OpenGL functions to submit the uniforms.

The new and improved light pass shaders

Since the light pass had to be completely rewritten to use raw modern OpenGL, the shaders need to reflect those changes too. To begin with, the vertex shader is much simpler now, because it no longer uses outdated and deprecated ways of obtaining and transforming vertex information, texture coordinates, and so on:

```
in vec3 position;
in vec2 texCoordIn;
out vec2 texCoords;
void main()
{
  texCoords = texCoordIn;
  gl_Position = vec4(position, 1.0);
}
```

The position being passed to this shader is that of m_fullScreenQuad, so it's already in clip space. There's no reason to transform it. The texture coordinates are simply passed along to the fragment shader, where they get interpolated between vertices, ensuring sampling of every pixel:

```
const int MaxLights = 4;
const float LightHeightOffset = 16.0;
in vec2 texCoords;
uniform sampler2D LastPass;
uniform sampler2D DiffuseMap;
uniform sampler2D NormalMap;
uniform sampler2D SpecularMap;
uniform sampler2D HeightMap;
uniform samplerCube ShadowMap[MaxLights];
uniform vec3 AmbientLight;
uniform int LightCount;
uniform int PassNumber;
```

The fragment shader of the light pass has a couple of new values at the very top. We have a constant that's going to be used to offset the light's height, which we're going to cover very shortly. There's also the input value from the vertex shader of the texture coordinates we're going to need to sample. Lastly, we're using an array of samplerCube uniforms to access the shadow map information.

Let's take a look at the main body of the light pass fragment shader:

```
void main()
{
  vec4 pixel = texture2D(LastPass, texCoords);
  vec4 diffusepixel = texture2D(DiffuseMap, texCoords);
  vec4 normalpixel = texture2D(NormalMap, texCoords);
  vec4 specularpixel = texture2D(SpecularMap, texCoords);
  float pixelheight = texture2D(HeightMap, texCoords).r * 255.0;
  vec3 PixelCoordinates =
    vec3(gl_FragCoord.x, gl_FragCoord.y, pixelheight);
  vec4 finalPixel = pixel;
  ...
  if(PassNumber == 0) { finalPixel *= vec4(AmbientLight, 1.0); }
  for(int i = 0; i < LightCount; ++i){
    ...
    float ShadowValue = CalculateShadow(
      PixelCoordinates, Lights[i].position, i);
    finalPixel += (diffusepixel *
                  (vec4(Lights[i].color, 1.0) * attenuation) +
                  vec4(specularReflection, 1.0))
      * normalDot * ShadowValue;
  }
  gl_FragColor = finalPixel;
}
```

Things have changed, yet oddly enough stayed the same. We're sampling all of the values from different textures just like before, only now we're using the texCoords variable passed down from the vertex shader.

Another small change is the pass number that gets checked for ambient lighting. It used to be *1* for clarity in the previous chapter. It's now changed to *0*.

Finally, the very reason we're here today the shadow calculations. A floating point value is obtained from the CalculateShadow function, that takes in coordinates of the current fragment, the position of the current light, and the number identifier of the current light as well. This value is later used when calculating the final pixel color. The pixel is simply multiplied by ShadowValue at the end, which determines how much in the shadow it is.

This function is for calculating the shadow value of a fragment that is implemented at the top of the shader as follows:

```
float CalculateShadow(vec3 fragment, vec3 light, int lightID) {
    light.z += LightHeightOffset;
    vec3 difference = fragment - light;
    float currentDepth = length(difference);
    difference.y *= -1.0;
    float nearestDepth = texture(ShadowMap[lightID],
        difference.xzy).r;
    return (currentDepth > nearestDepth * Lights[lightID].radius
        ? nearestDepth : 1.0);
}
```

Looks simple enough, right? Well, it is. First, the light's height is offset by the height offset constant we defined at the top of the shader. This is just a detail of further tweaking that ensures lighting looks as good as it can, and could be completely changed. The current value simply looks better than the default 0.

The difference between the fragment's position and the light's position is then calculated by subtracting one from the other. The order matters here because this is going to be used as a directional vector to determine which face of the cubemap texture should be sampled.

 Keep in mind that our fragment and light positions use the Z component as the height. This effectively makes Y the depth axis, which can be visualized as the direction to and from the screen, as opposed to left/right for X, and up/down for Z.

The `currentDepth` variable is the distance from the light to the fragment being sampled. The Y component of the difference vector is then inverted, because in the right-hand coordinate system OpenGL uses, pointing towards the screen means going into the negatives.

Now it's time to actually sample the shadow map texture and obtain the nearest depth at that particular fragment. This is done by passing the difference vector as a directional vector. Don't worry about it not being normalized, because it doesn't have to be. Also note the Z and Y components swapped. Again, we use Z for height, while OpenGL uses Y. Finally, we check whether the depth between the fragment and the light is greater than the depth sampled from the current shadow map, and if it is, it means the fragment is in the shadow. 0 could be returned, but in order to create shadows that slowly fade out with distance, `nearestDepth` is returned instead. This is the value that the final pixel gets multiplied by, and because it's in the range [0;1], we get the linear fade with distance.

Note `nearestDepth` being multiplied by the light radius, which represents the frustum far value, when it's being checked. This transforms it from the range *[0;1]*, to the actual distance at which the shadow primitive is away from the light.

Consider the following diagram to help get the point across:

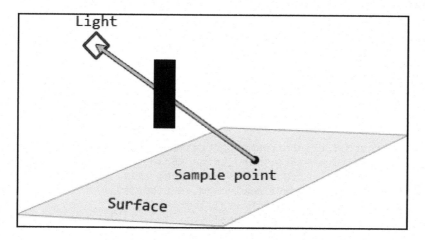

Here, the main arrow from the sample point to the light is `currentDepth`, and the `nearestDepth` after being multiplied by the light's radius is the arrow from the black box in the middle to the light.

Adding shadow casters to entities

Now that we have all of the rendering resolved, we still need to make sure entities can cast shadows. This will be achieved by actually attaching special components to entities that will hold pointers to 3D geometry used during shadow pass. This geometry will obviously need to be updated to match the position of the entities it represents, which is why the component data is going to be accompanied by a separate system, used to actually keep everything synced up.

Adding the shadow caster component

First, because our entities exist within the ECS paradigm, we need to add a component that represents the shadow volume of an entity:

```
class C_ShadowCaster : public C_Base {
public:
  C_ShadowCaster() : C_Base(Component::ShadowCaster),
    m_shadowCaster(nullptr) {}

  void SetShadowCaster(ShadowCaster* l_caster) {
    m_shadowCaster = l_caster;
  }
  void UpdateCaster(const glm::vec3& l_pos) {
    m_shadowCaster->m_transform.SetPosition(l_pos);
  }

  void ReadIn(std::stringstream& l_stream) {
    m_shadowPrimitive = std::make_unique<ShadowCasterPrototype>();
    for (auto i = 0; i < ShadowMeshVertices; ++i) {
      l_stream >> m_shadowPrimitive->m_vertices[i].x >>
      m_shadowPrimitive->m_vertices[i].y >>
      m_shadowPrimitive->m_vertices[i].z;
    }
  }

  std::unique_ptr<ShadowCasterPrototype> m_shadowPrimitive;
private:
  ShadowCaster* m_shadowCaster;
};
```

This component will be used to load entity shadow caster primitives from the entity file, as well as update their respective `ShadowCaster` instances. The player entity file, for example, would look like this with the new component added:

```
Name Player
Attributes 511
|Component|ID|Individual attributes|
...
Component 8 -0.5 0.0 0.5 -0.5 0.0 -0.5 0.5 0.0 -0.5 ...
```

Creating the shadow system

Updating these components should be done in a separate, designated system for this very purpose. Because we've done this so many times before, let's just take a look at the relevant parts of the code:

```
S_Shadow::S_Shadow(SystemManager* l_systemMgr)
  : S_Base(System::Shadow, l_systemMgr),
  m_lightManager(nullptr)
{
  Bitmask req;
  req.TurnOnBit((unsigned int)Component::Position);
  req.TurnOnBit((unsigned int)Component::ShadowCaster);
  m_requiredComponents.push_back(req);
  req.Clear();
}
```

The constructor of this system simply sets up the entity requirements to belong here. It requires the position and shadow caster components, obviously.

Updating these components is equally as easy:

```
void S_Shadow::Update(float l_dT) {
  if (!m_lightManager) { return; }
  EntityManager* entities = m_systemManager->GetEntityManager();
  for (auto &entity : m_entities) {
    auto position = entities->GetComponent<C_Position>(
      entity, Component::Position);
    auto caster = entities->GetComponent<C_ShadowCaster>(
      entity, Component::ShadowCaster);
    float height = static_cast<float>(
      (position->GetElevation() * Sheet::Tile_Size) -
        Sheet::Tile_Size);
    caster->UpdateCaster({
      position->GetPosition().x,
      height,
      position->GetPosition().y - 8.f });
  }
}
```

For each entity that belongs to this system, the position and shadow caster components are obtained. The shadow caster's `UpdateCaster` method is then invoked, with the 2D position and height being passed in. The constant value of `8.f` is simply used to offset the shadow primitive in order to center it properly.

 Note that the *Y* and *Z* values are, once again, swapped around.

Finally, because we want to properly emplace and manage unique shadow caster prototypes in the light manager, the shadow system must implement a method that will be called when the entity has finished loading and is about to be added, in order to set everything up properly:

```
void S_Shadow::OnEntityAdd(const EntityId& l_entity) {
    auto component = m_systemManager->GetEntityManager()->
     GetComponent<C_ShadowCaster>(l_entity,Component::ShadowCaster);
    if (!component) { return; }
    std::string entityType;
    if (!m_systemManager->GetEntityManager()->
      GetEntityType(l_entity, entityType))
    {
      ... // Error
      return;
    }

    auto name = m_lightManager->AddCasterPrototype("Entity_" +
      entityType, std::move(component->m_shadowPrimitive));
    auto caster = m_lightManager->AddShadowCaster(name);
    if (!caster) { return; } // Error
    component->SetShadowCaster(caster);
    caster->m_transform.SetScale({ 16.f, 16.f, 16.f });
}
```

Once the shadow caster component is retrieved, the entity type name is obtained from the entity manager. This is simply the name of the entity prototype, such as player, skeleton, and so on. The primitive prototype with the appropriate name is then attempted to be added, and should there be an exact same shadow caster prototype already in `LightManager`, that name is returned instead. The shadow caster itself is then created, passed on to the `C_ShadowCaster` component, and scaled to a decent size. For the time being, this is a constant value, but it can obviously be made to change depending on the entity type, if it's stored inside the entity file along with the rest of the component data.

Integrating the changes made

Finally, all we have left to do in order to make this work is add the newly created component and system types to the ECS:

```
void Game::SetUpECS() {
  ...
  m_entityManager->AddComponentType<C_ShadowCaster>
    (Component::ShadowCaster);
  ...
  m_systemManager->AddSystem<S_Shadow>(System::Shadow);
  ...
  m_systemManager->GetSystem<S_Shadow>(System::Shadow)->
    SetLightManager(m_lightManager.get());
}
```

The shadow system itself also needs a pointer to the light manager for obvious reasons. Running the game now, with all of the lights properly set up and shadow casters correctly loaded, we should have three-dimensional shadows!

Because the entities can hop elevations, the lights can be made to change their heights, and the actual light pass of the scene incorporates different heights of tile layers. Moving the lights around actually creates results in three-dimensional space, allowing the shadows to flow across walls, if at a right angle. After all of that hard work, the effect is absolutely astonishing!

Potential issues and how to address them

Although we aren't facing any of these issues at this very point, most 3D games will have to deal with them as soon as basic shadows are established using this method.

Shadow acne is a graphical artefact that can be summarized as horrible *tearing*, where lit areas are horribly defaced with dark and white lines closely nested together. This happens because shadow maps are of finite size and pixels that are right next to each other will end up spanning a small distance on actual, *real* geometry being shaded. It can be fixed by simply adding or subtracting a simple *bias* floating point value to or from the shadow map's depth sample inside the light pass shader. This floating point value would, ideally, not be a constant and instead depend on the slope between the point on the geometry and the light.

Peter panning can be described as shadows that appear to be *floating* away from the geometry that casts them. Adding the floating point bias to fix shadow acne will usually make this problem worse, especially when dealing with incredibly thin geometry. A common and easy fix for this problem is simply avoiding thin geometry and using front face culling during the shadow pass, as we did.

Percentage closer filtering

You may have noticed that the shadows produced by our geometry are rather hard and don't exactly smooth out around the edges. As always, there is a solution that will resolve this, and it involves sampling the shadow map a couple more times per pixel.

By sampling not only the calculated pixel of the shadow map, but also the surrounding ones, we can easily take an average value of all of them and use it to *smooth* out the edge. If, for example, our sampled pixel is in the shadow but *50%* of all other sampled pixels around it are lit up, the center pixel itself should only be *50%* opaque. By eliminating this binary rule of a pixel either being completely lit or completely dark, we can successfully implement soft shadows using this technique. Higher numbers of surrounding pixels will obviously yield smoother results, but will also bog down performance.

Summary

Congratulations on making it to the end of this chapter! Although it took quite a while to re-architect our lighting engine, the results cannot be dismissed as miniscule. The shadows created by this method add a lot of graphical diversity to our world. In the next chapter, we're going to be discussing optimizations that can be applied to make the game run as fast as it possibly can after all of the fancy, clock cycle sucking techniques used throughout this book. See you there!

10
A Chapter You Shouldn't Skip - Final Optimizations

What's the most important aspect of any game? According to a very famous e-celebrity, it's being able to play it. Fancy graphics and advanced techniques definitely add a necessary touch of polish to a medium as visual and interactive as video games, but if that gets in the way of enjoying the most fundamental experience of smooth gameplay, the whole thing might as well just be a fancy screensaver. Optimizing code, even when the application runs fine on higher-end machines, is extremely important, since every iteration excludes potential machines that are older but could still be used to expand the fan base of a game.

In this chapter, we will be covering the following topics:

- The basics of profiling and reading code metrics
- Analyzing and repairing inefficiencies in our code
- The basics of light culling

Let's not waste any more clock cycles and get to cleaning up some of those inefficiencies!

Use of third-party software

As expected, we can't do all of this work with no additional tools. Profiling applications is a subject that requires a backend of established software, used to neatly organize and present us with the data of performance subtleties. *CodeXL* is an application we have already covered in `Chapter 9`, *The Speed of Dark – Lighting and Shadows* and although we used it to view runtime OpenGL states, it also has quite a suite of options used to profile both CPU and GPU code. It can be found and downloaded here: `http://gpuopen.com/compute-product/codexl/`.

Of course, if we don't have AMD hardware, only a very limited set of tools for profiling are available. Although we can get by with the limited CPU profiling options, GPU profiling on an Nvidia card, for example, would require a different tool. There are some choices out there, but one notable option is *Nvidia Nsight*: `http://www.nvidia.com/object/nsight.html`.

It's worth mentioning, however, that the newest versions of Nsight don't support some of the legacy functions SFML invokes, so the functionalities are, once again, rather limited.

The devil's in the details

They say that a master craftsman knows not only how, but also when to use their tools. Many programmers often enough arrive at the false conclusion that they must constantly write beautiful, efficient, and overall perfect code that will never fail. In practice, this couldn't be farther from the truth. Many find this out the hard way. As *Donald Knuth* said:

> *"Programmers waste enormous amounts of time thinking about, or worrying about, the speed of noncritical parts of their programs, and these attempts at efficiency actually have a strong negative impact when debugging and maintenance are considered. We should forget about small efficiencies, say about 97% of the time: premature optimization is the root of all evil."*

This doesn't mean that one shouldn't take performance into consideration. Things such as designing a class with later features in mind, or even picking the right algorithm for the job both fall under that remaining 3%. Rather, it simply means that, unless the application is noticeably slow, tackling performance issues in code should be one of the final tasks at all times.

Another common mistake programmers often make is relying on intuition when it comes to evaluating performance. It's easy to forget that a program has tons of underlying complexity and moving parts, which is why it's incredibly hard to always know exactly how a specific chunk of code is going to behave unless properly tested. That's the key here always profile! Is the game running slow? Break out the profiler and take it for a spin. Feeling like enemy path-finding code is really weighing down on performance? Don't feel, just profile! The same thing can be said about the state of your code after optimizations have been made. Don't just replace a ton of code and assume it runs faster. Take a base measurement, make the appropriate changes, and profile the final result to make sure the new code runs faster. Starting to see the picture? Good. With that out of the way, let's jump straight into the basics of profiling!

Profiling basics

There's a variety of different ways an application can be profiled. Anything from branching and individual instructions, to usage of caches and patterns of data access can be tracked in a project. Since our game isn't exactly overflowing with complexity, however, we really only need to worry about time-based profiling.

There are three basic ways a profiler can gather information about an application:

- **Sampling**: This is a periodic application stack capture that yields relatively inaccurate results, yet has very little overhead.
- **Event collection**: This involves tapping into the compilation process and configuring it in such a way that allows certain information to be sent to the profiling DLLs. A higher amount of overhead with a higher precision.
- **Instrumentation**: This involves direct code injection into the application during run time that allows for the most precise results and has the highest level of overhead.

Any of these techniques can be utilized, depending on what software is being used and the data it needs to collect. Because we don't really need incredibly precise results to locate the hotspots of our code, it's best to go with a sampling approach.

 As we have already established, profiling is not a free task. In some instances, it can slow down an application to a crawl, which, depending on the task, can be absolutely normal.

Time-based sampling

Using the time-based sampling technique will create a rough estimate of all of the application's function/method calls, initializations/destructions, virtually anything that can be created or invoked, and assign a sample value to them. This even includes underlying libraries, such as STL, SFML, OpenGL, and so on. If your code uses it, it will be on the list.

This sample value represents how much time is spent executing a certain line of code. There are two types of time samples:

- **Inclusive**: This involves all of the time spent inside a specific line/chunk of code, including all of the time it took to execute other functions that may have been called.
- **Exclusive**: This involves only the amount of time that a specific line/chunk of code took to execute on its own.

We are not necessarily going to be dealing with exclusive sample counts, but it's important to understand these terms nonetheless.

Lastly, it's important to understand that samples are relative. If a program is running slowly, fewer samples will be captured across the board. This particular benchmark shouldn't be interpreted based on quantity, but rather in comparison to the rest of the code.

 Sampling should always be done with all of the relevant project's optimizations enabled, because it strips away unnecessary code that's used for debugging, which would interfere with the results. In the case of Visual Studio, the release mode should be used when sampling.

Sampling our application

Now that we have the fundamentals covered, let's actually fire up a profile and get started! The first important aspect of this process is actually spending enough time sampling the state of the desired application. In our case, sampling should be done in the Game state, and for at least 20 seconds, to capture enough information. It isn't going to help us understand the time complexities of the entity component system, for example, if the majority of the application sampling time is spent inside the menu state.

Secondly, we should probably test our application in a stressful state, just to make sure it holds up well under nonideal conditions. For our purposes, we will simply add a bunch more entities, particle emitters, and lights to the scene until a **stress test** that looks like the following is constructed:

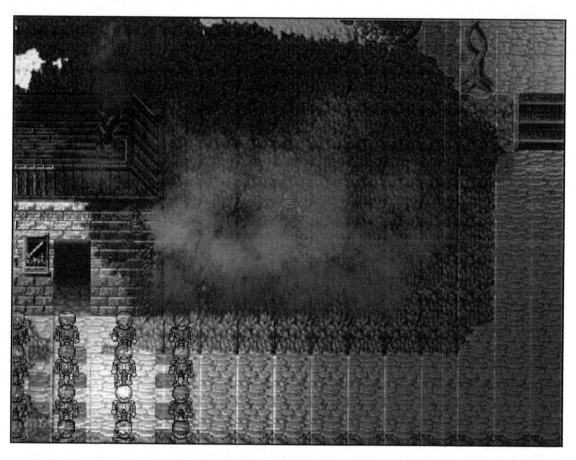

It isn't pretty, but then again, neither are performance issues.

Once the application has been sampled enough and is terminated, most profilers will show a *profile overview* of all the processes that have been running during the sampling process. It's important to select only our game by clicking on it, because that's what we're interested in.

After navigating to the **Function** tab, we should be left with something similar to this:

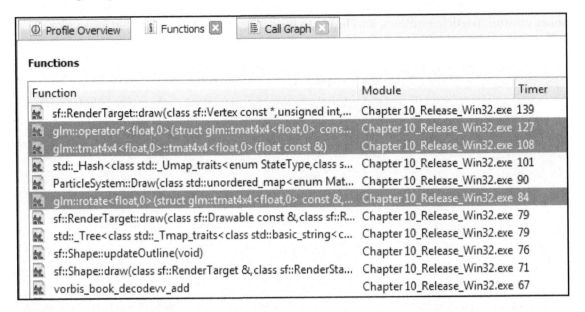

By clicking on the **Timer** tab and sorting entries in a descending order, we can view the functions that have the highest amount of samples, thus taking the most time to run. This is where you will find the trade-off between using a general purpose library such as *SFML* and sacrificing some performance. While it's true that writing case-specific code would probably be more optimal in terms of performance, it's still a worthy price to pay when considering how versatile SFML is for small to medium-sized projects.

While it's obvious our own SFML rendering code could probably use some work and utilize vertex arrays when rendering sprites and tiles to reduce this bottleneck, we're not going to concern ourselves with SFML-specific optimizations this time. Instead, let's analyze the highlighted entries on the list first. As the `glm::` namespace seems to suggest, the OpenGL math library we're using for various calculations is the culprit. Upon closer inspection, it seems that all three of these hotspots have to do with matrix operations; the most expensive of which is the `glm::operator*`. By right-clicking on the entry, we can view it in a call graph.

A **call graph** is a tool that helps locate all points in our code that use a specific function.

By simply analyzing the information onscreen, we're now able to see what code uses the GLM matrices in such a way that causes performance problems:

Function (5599 functions, 549 shown)	Self Samples
Functions	
glm::operator*<float,0>(struct glm::tmat4x4<float,0> const &,struct glm::tmat4x4<float,0>...	127
sf::priv::MutexImpl::unlock(void)	9
glm::rotate<float,0>(struct glm::tmat4x4<float,0> const &,float,struct glm::tvec3<float,0> ...	84
alcCloseDevice	93
glm::tmat4x4<float,0>::tmat4x4<float,0>(float const &)	108
std::_Hash<class std::_Umap_traits<enum StateType,class std::function<class BaseState * >,...	101
Chapter 10_Release_Win32.exe!0x014808b4	

Immediate Parents and Children of Function: **glm::operator*(struct glm::tmat4x4 const &,struct glm::tmat4x4 co**

Parents	Samples	% of samples	Module
GL_Transform::GetModelMatrix(void)	126	99.21%	Chapter 10_Release_Win32.exe
LightManager::DrawShadowMap(unsig...	1	0.79%	Chapter 10_Release_Win32.exe

As the **Parents** section indicates, the majority of time samples regarding this particular bottleneck are located inside the `GL_Transform::GetModelMatrix()` method. Double-clicking on the function allows us to also view the code and specific hotspots of each individual line:

Line	Address	Source Code	Hotspot Samples	% of Hotspot Samples	Timer
14	0x13aec20	glm::mat4 GL_Transform::GetModelMatrix() {			
15	0x13aec38	glm::mat4 matrix_pos = glm::translate(m_position);	2	16.67%	2
16	0x13aec6b	glm::mat4 matrix_scale = glm::scale(m_scale);	3	25.00%	3
17		// Represent each stored rotation as a different matrix, because we store angles.			
18		// Directional vector x, y, z			
19	0x13aec99	glm::mat4 matrix_rotX = glm::rotate(m_rotation.x, glm::vec3(1, 0, 0));	2	16.67%	2
20	0x13aecf0	glm::mat4 matrix_rotY = glm::rotate(m_rotation.y, glm::vec3(0, 1, 0));	2	16.67%	2
21	0x13aed47	glm::mat4 matrix_rotZ = glm::rotate(m_rotation.z, glm::vec3(0, 0, 1));	2	16.67%	2
22		// Create a rotation matrix. Multiply in reverse order it needs to be applied.			
23	0x13aeda1	glm::mat4 matrix_rotation = matrix_rotZ * matrix_rotY * matrix_rotX;			
24		// Apply transforms in reverse order they need to be applied in.			
25	0x13aedce	return matrix_pos * matrix_rotation * matrix_scale;	1	8.33%	1
26	0x13aedf6	}			

This should all start to add up by now. The two most sampled lines in relation to matrices were `glm::tmat4x4<float,0>::tmat4x4<float,0>(float const&)`, which is the matrix constructor, and `glm::rotate`, which we're calling three times. Every time we want to obtain a model matrix from this class (which is once for each shadow caster every frame), a bunch of new matrices are constructed and filled out using quite expensive GLM function calls, not to mention being multiplied later as well.

Finding GPU bottlenecks

Finding GPU bottlenecks is fairly similar to what we did with the CPU. It also utilizes time sampling and will generate similar looking reports that list OpenGL code based on how long it took to execute, as follows:

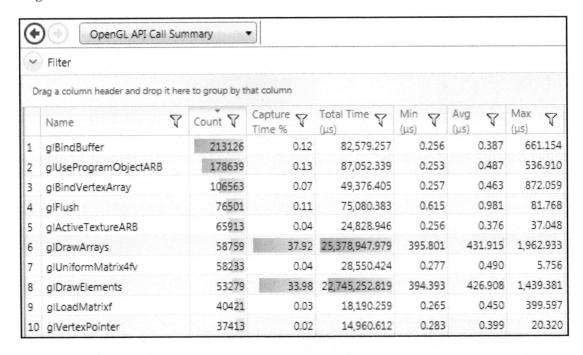

We're not going to be covering GPU optimizations heavily here, but the idea is exactly the same: finding bottlenecks, re-implementing code in a more efficient manner, and testing again.

Some GPU profiling tools, such as Nvidia Nsight, don't support legacy OpenGL API calls made by SFML.

Improving CPU code performance

After establishing a baseline reading, we can begin making changes to our code. Some of these changes involve simply understanding the libraries we're using and being more cautious about the way they're deployed, while others revolve around making better design choices, applying faster and more appropriate algorithms, designing data structures better, and using the newest features of the C++ standard. Let's begin by taking a look at some easy changes that can be made to our code.

Optimizing the three most obvious bottlenecks

Judging by the profiler's results, there is quite a bit of room for improvement of the code we've written so far. In this section, we're going to be addressing three of the most inefficient implementations and how they can be fixed.

GL_Transform optimizations

The very first example we used to illustrate how time sampling works is a perfect candidate for improvement. There really is nothing subtle about it. First, the recalculation of all matrices involved in obtaining a model matrix every time one is requested is incredibly inefficient. To add insult to injury, all 7 of those matrices has to be created all over again. That's a lot of clock cycles wasted for no reason. Let's see how that can be quickly improved:

```
class GL_Transform {
public:
  ...
  const glm::mat4& GetModelMatrix();
private:
  ...
  bool m_needsUpdate;
  glm::mat4 m_matPos;
  glm::mat4 m_matScale;
  glm::mat4 m_matRotX;
  glm::mat4 m_matRotY;
  glm::mat4 m_matRotZ;
  glm::mat4 m_matRotCombined;
```

```
    glm::mat4 m_modelMatrix; // Final matrix.
};
```

Firstly, notice the change of the return parameter of `GetModelMatrix` to a *const reference*. This ensures that we're not returning a newly constructed matrix each time. Additionally, we have added a Boolean flag that will help us keep track of whether the position, scale, or rotation of the object has changed and whether the model matrix needs to be updated to reflect that. Lastly, we're storing all 7 matrices inside the transform object now, so that they are created only once. This is important, because we don't want to recalculate three rotational matrices along with its combined matrix, for example, just because the position of the object was changed.

Next, let's actually implement these changes, starting with the setters of this class:

```
void GL_Transform::SetPosition(const glm::vec3& l_pos) {
  if (l_pos == m_position) { return; }
  m_position = l_pos;
  m_matPos = glm::translate(m_position);
  m_needsUpdate = true;
}
```

The general idea here is to first check whether the argument provided to the setter method isn't already the current value of whatever parameter it's supposed to override. If it isn't, the position is changed and the position matrix is updated, along with the `m_needsUpdate` flag being set to `true`. This will ensure that the model matrix is updated later on.

Rotation follows the exact same principle:

```
void GL_Transform::SetRotation(const glm::vec3& l_rot) {
  if (l_rot == m_rotation) { return; }
  if (l_rot.x != m_rotation.x) {
    m_matRotX = glm::rotate(m_rotation.x, glm::vec3(1, 0, 0));
  }
  if (l_rot.y != m_rotation.y) {
    m_matRotY = glm::rotate(m_rotation.y, glm::vec3(0, 1, 0));
  }
  if (l_rot.z != m_rotation.z) {
    m_matRotZ = glm::rotate(m_rotation.z, glm::vec3(0, 0, 1));
  }
  m_matRotCombined = m_matRotZ * m_matRotY * m_matRotX;
  m_rotation = l_rot;
  m_needsUpdate = true;
}
```

Before the assignment is committed to, however, we must check each individual member of the vector class, because each one of them has their own matrix. The point, as it's becoming clearer and clearer now, is to only calculate what we absolutely have to.

Scale, once again, follows this idea exactly:

```
void GL_Transform::SetScale(const glm::vec3& l_scale) {
    if (l_scale == m_scale) { return; }
    m_scale = l_scale;
    m_matScale = glm::scale(m_scale);
    m_needsUpdate = true;
}
```

The GetModelMatrix method should now be implemented this way:

```
const glm::mat4& GL_Transform::GetModelMatrix() {
    if (m_needsUpdate) {
        m_modelMatrix = m_matPos * m_matRotCombined * m_matScale;
        m_needsUpdate = false;
    }
    return m_modelMatrix;
}
```

First, the update flag is checked to determine whether the matrix needs to be updated. If it does, all three relevant matrices are multiplied and the flag is reset back to false. We then return the const reference to the m_modelMatrix data member, ensuring one isn't created just to be thrown away later.

Let's follow our own advice and profile the application again to make sure our changes worked:

Functions

Function	Module	Timer
ForceUpdater::Update(float, class ParticleContainer *)	Chapter 10_Release_Win32.exe	2
GL_Transform::GetModelMatrix(void)	Chapter 10_Release_Win32.exe	3
glBindTexture	Chapter 10_Release_Win32.exe	1
glColorPointer	Chapter 10_Release_Win32.exe	8
glLoadMatrixf	Chapter 10_Release_Win32.exe	2
glm::tmat4x4<float,0>::tmat4x4<float,0>(float const &)	Chapter 10_Release_Win32.exe	2
glVertexPointer	Chapter 10_Release_Win32.exe	4

All three of the previously highlighted lines to do with `glm::` have now completely disappeared from the top of the list! The highlighted exception in this illustration was taken during the sampling of `GL_Transform::GetModelMatrix()` that **did not** return by const reference, just to show that our approach does indeed work. When the method does return a const reference, even the highlighted function completely vanishes. This perfectly illustrates how avoiding useless copies of data can vastly improve overall performance.

Particle system optimizations

Another massive bottleneck that's right at the top of the sample list is the `ParticleSystem::Draw` method. In fact, it's the highest sampled piece of code that we have actually written. It's understandable that rendering so many particles would be taxing, but in this case, the unoptimized version of this method knocks the frame rate of our game down to 10 FPS:

Fraps is a free piece of screen capture software that can record video, take screenshots, and most importantly for our purposes, show the frame rate! Although it's Windows specific, there are other tools like it for Linux and OSX. The frame rate counter can also be easily implemented by simply counting the frames in our code and displaying the result using SFML.

That is absolutely unforgivable, so let's break out the profiler and dissect the `Draw` method:

Source Code	Code Hotspot Samples	% of Hotspot Sample	Timer
if (renderer->UseShader("MaterialValuePass")) {			
// Material pass.			
auto shader = renderer->GetCurrentShader();			
for (size_t i = 0; i < container->m_countAlive; ++i) {	14	14.14%	14
if (l_layer >= 0) {	1	1.01%	1
if (positions[i].z < l_layer * Sheet::Tile_Size) { continue; }	6	6.06%	6
if (positions[i].z >= (l_layer + 1) * Sheet::Tile_Size) { continue; }	6	6.06%	6
} else if (positions[i].z < Sheet::Num_Layers * Sheet::Tile_Size) { continue; }	3	3.03%	3
// Normal pass.			
shader->setUniform("material", sf::Glsl::Vec3(0.5f, 0.5f, 1.f));	1	1.01%	1
renderer->Draw(drawables[i], l_materials[MaterialMapType::Normal].get());	4	4.04%	4
// Specular pass.			
shader->setUniform("material", sf::Glsl::Vec3(0.f, 0.f, 0.f));	13	13.13%	13
renderer->Draw(drawables[i], l_materials[MaterialMapType::Specular].get());	20	20.20%	20
}			
}			

(Arrows labeled A point to the Normal pass rows; arrows labeled B point to the Specular pass rows.)

Judging by the sample count, the main inefficiency lies somewhere inside the material value shader pass, where each particle is rendered for the normal and specular passes. There is something slightly weird going on, though, and that's the fact that the normal pass samples seem to be really low, but when the time comes to render for the specular pass, they suddenly jump much higher. This may look especially weird considering all we're doing is setting a `vec3` uniform and drawing to a render texture. This is where further digging through the function stack and understanding of how SFML needs to handle things behind the scenes comes in:

Functions		
Function	Module	Timer
ParticleSystem::Draw(class std::unordered_map<enum Mat...	Chapter 10_Release_Win32.exe	99
• • •		
sf::RenderTexture::activate(bool)	Chapter 10_Release_Win32.exe	47
sf::ThreadLocal::setValue(void *)	Chapter 10_Release_Win32.exe	47
sf::Lock::~Lock(void)	Chapter 10_Release_Win32.exe	40
Renderer::Draw(class sf::Shape const &,class sf::RenderTarg...	Chapter 10_Release_Win32.exe	36
sf::Context::setActive(bool)	Chapter 10_Release_Win32.exe	32
sf::GlResource::TransientContextLock::~TransientContextLo...	Chapter 10_Release_Win32.exe	32
sf::Shader::bind(class sf::Shader const *)	Chapter 10_Release_Win32.exe	32
sf::Transformable::getTransform(void)	Chapter 10_Release_Win32.exe	32
sf::priv::GlContext::setActive(bool)	Chapter 10_Release_Win32.exe	31

Because of context switching and the way render textures work behind the scenes, it's extremely inefficient to render two different types of material maps as we did. Switching textures too many times during runtime can cause serious performance bottlenecks, which is why sprite and tile sheets are used by games, rather than individual images.

Let's try and split up these two different types into two separate loops, making sure only one texture is being rendered two at a time:

```
void ParticleSystem::Draw(MaterialMapContainer& l_materials, ...) {
  ...
  if (renderer->UseShader("MaterialValuePass")) {
    auto shader = renderer->GetCurrentShader();
    // Normal pass.
    auto texture = l_materials[MaterialMapType::Normal].get();
    shader->setUniform("material",
      sf::Glsl::Vec3(0.5f, 0.5f, 1.f));
    for (size_t i = 0; i < container->m_countAlive; ++i) {
      ...
```

```
        renderer->Draw(drawables[i], texture);
    }

    // Specular pass.
    texture = l_materials[MaterialMapType::Specular].get();
    shader->setUniform("material", sf::Glsl::Vec3(0.f, 0.f, 0.f));
    for (size_t i = 0; i < container->m_countAlive; ++i) {
        ...
        renderer->Draw(drawables[i], texture);
    }
}
...
}
```

Note that the material uniform is also moved outside of the loop to prevent unnecessary copies from being constructed and sent to the shader every time. By just running the application now, a very obvious jump in performance will quickly become apparent. Let's see how much faster it got by simply splitting up the little bit of code we had into two pieces:

We just jumped from 10 FPS to 65 FPS by simply separating the normal and specular material passes! That's more like it! You will notice that this sudden jump in performance will increase the sample count drastically:

Functions		
Function	Module	Timer
ParticleSystem::Draw(class std::unordered_map<enum Mat...	Chapter 10_Release_Win32.exe	331
sf::Shape::updateOutline(void)	Chapter 10_Release_Win32.exe	281
sf::RenderTarget::draw(class sf::Vertex const *,unsigned int,...	Chapter 10_Release_Win32.exe	255
std::_Hash<class std::_Umap_traits<enum StateType,class s...	Chapter 10_Release_Win32.exe	225
sf::Transform::combine(class sf::Transform const &)	Chapter 10_Release_Win32.exe	217

This is because the game is running much faster now and doesn't indicate that the function is taking more time to execute. Remember, the samples are relative. Upon looking through the list, the two previously highlighted bits of code are found much lower now, with sample counts in the 20s. That's only slightly lower than before, but because the samples are relative and they all jumped up to about 6 times higher, it indicates a huge performance gain.

Light culling

The last main inefficiency we have to fix has to do with the lighting system implemented in Chapter 8, *Let There Be Light! – An Introduction to Advanced Lighting*, and Chapter 9, *The Speed of Dark – Lighting and Shadows*.

Dealing with multiple lights in a scene by using multipass shading/rendering is a great technique, but it can quickly become inefficient when those passes start to add up. The first obvious step to fixing that issue is not rendering lights that will not affect anything in the final image. The technique of reducing the number of objects being rendered by eliminating those that cannot be directly observed by the scene's view frustum, also known as **culling**, is going to help out with that.

Since we're only dealing with omni-directional point lights at this moment, culling lights can be achieved by simply checking for circle on rectangle collisions.

Let's set up some helper functions to help us do that:

```
inline float GetDistance(const sf::Vector2f& l_1,
  const sf::Vector2f& l_2)
{
  return std::sqrt(std::pow(l_1.x - l_2.x, 2) +
    std::pow(l_1.y - l_2.y, 2));
}

inline bool CircleInView(const sf::View& l_view,
  const sf::Vector2f& l_circleCenter, float l_circleRad)
{
  auto HalfSize = l_view.getSize() / 2.f;
  float OuterRadius = std::sqrt((HalfSize.x * HalfSize.x) +
    (HalfSize.y * HalfSize.y));
  float AbsoluteDistance = GetDistance(l_view.getCenter(),
    l_circleCenter);
  if (AbsoluteDistance > OuterRadius + l_circleRad) {
    return false;
  }
  float InnerRadius = std::min(l_view.getSize().x,
    l_view.getSize().y) / 2.f;
  if (AbsoluteDistance < InnerRadius + l_circleRad){return true;}
  glm::vec2 dir = {
    l_circleCenter.x - l_view.getCenter().x,
    l_circleCenter.y - l_view.getCenter().y
  };
  dir = glm::normalize(dir);
  sf::Vector2f point = l_circleCenter +
    sf::Vector2f(l_circleRad * dir.x, l_circleRad * dir.y);
  auto rect = sf::FloatRect(
    l_view.getCenter() - HalfSize,
    l_view.getSize());
  return rect.contains(point);
}
```

The function works by first creating an outer radius around the view's rectangle, so that we can default to a circle-on-circle collision checking for the majority of cases where the light is nowhere near the view frustum. The distance between the view's centre and circle's centre is obtained and checked for exceeding the sum of the view's outer bounding circle's radius summed with the circle's radius. This is the easiest way to check whether the light circle is anywhere close to the view's rectangle.

If the light is closer to the view, another circle radius for the view's rectangle is constructed. This time, the circle is inside the view and only has the radius of the smaller dimension of the rectangle's size. If the distance between the light and the view's center is lower than the sum of the inner radius and the circle's radius, we know for sure that we have a collision. That's another common case that we can scratch off the list, before defaulting to a more complicated algorithm.

Finally, if we know the light may be intersecting with one of the corners, its direction towards the view is normalized and used to obtain the closest point that is then checked for intersecting a constructed `sf::FloatRect` that represents our view.

Actual changes to the `RenderScene()` method of the light manager class simply involve storing a new list of lights that are definitely affecting something on screen, so that they can be passed to the shader:

```
void LightManager::RenderScene() {
  ...
  std::vector<LightBase*> unculled;
  for (auto& light : m_lights) {
    if (!Utils::CircleInView(currentView,
      { light.m_lightPos.x, light.m_lightPos.y },
      light.m_radius))
    { continue; }
    unculled.emplace_back(&light);
  }
  auto& beginning = unculled.begin();
  auto passes = static_cast<int>(std::ceil(
    static_cast<float>(unculled.size()) / LightsPerPass));
  if (passes == 0) { passes = 1; }
  for (int pass = 0; pass < passes; ++pass) {
    ...
    for (int lightID = 0; lightID < LightsPerPass; ++lightID) {
      ...
      DrawShadowMap(ShadowPassShaderHandle, **light, lightID);
      ...
    }
    ...
    for (int lightID = 0; lightID < LightCount; ++lightID) {
      ...
```

```
        SubmitLightUniforms(LightPassShaderHandle,lightID, **light);
        ...
    }
    ...
    renderer->SwapTextures();
  }
  ...
}
```

Note that we're not taking into account the light's falloff or how it's attenuated in the shader to determine whether it should be culled or not.

After all the unnecessary lights have been culled, only the very busy areas will experience some performance loss. At this point, it's the area of level design that should show concern and improve the architecture of the map.

Summary

Congratulations on making it all the way to the end! It has been quite a journey, and we can certainly say that a lot of things have been covered here that should inspire confidence in advanced game development in anyone. Even so, as always, there's still a ton of features, optimizations, techniques, and topics that we either just briefly touched upon, or haven't even acknowledged yet. Use that as inspiration to seek greatness, because, as we have already established, master craftsmen know not only how, but when to use their tools. While we have covered the basics, there are still many more tools to add to your tool belt. Use them, abuse them, break them and replace them. Do whatever it takes, but always remember to take something out of it and make it better next time.

With that, may your next project exhibit that extra level of polish, and run just a little bit faster! Thanks for reading!